Jacksonian Jew

Jacksonian Jew

THE TWO WORLDS OF MORDECAI NOAH

JONATHAN D. SARNA

HOLMES & MEIER PUBLISHERS, INC.

NEW YORK • LONDON

First published in the United States of America 1981 by
Holmes & Meier Publishers, Inc.
30 Irving Place
New York, N.Y. 10003

Great Britain:
Holmes & Meier Publishers, Ltd.
131 Trafalgar Road
Greenwich, London SE10 9TX

Library of Congress Cataloging in Publication Data

Sarna, Jonathan D.
    Jacksonian Jew.

    Bibliography: p.
    Includes index.
    1. Noah, Mordecai Manuel, 1785–1851. 2. Jews in
the United States—Biography.   3. United States—
Biography.   4. New York (City)—Politics and government—
To 1898. I. Title.
E184.J5S324   1980   973'.04'924 [B]   79-24329

ISBN 0-8419-0567-3

Manufactured in the United States of America

To my parents

"Three combine in the making of a man:
God, Father and Mother."

Kiddushin 30b

Contents

Preface

On the very last page of his *Major Noah* (1938), Isaac Goldberg sought to discourage scholars from consulting contemporary newspapers about the subject of his work. "There will be very little use in such consultation," he solemnly advised. In a sense, his words are my point of departure.

I discovered a new and different Mordecai Noah in contemporary letters and newspapers. He was not the trivial "Major" of Goldberg's book, the impractical dreamer of so many other accounts, or the "curious, pompous, likeable combination of contradictions" described by Lee Friedman. Instead, the Mordecai Noah of this book is a highly significant figure on the American scene, a leader of the American Jewish community, and most important, the first man in history to confront and grapple boldly with the tensions between these two distinct roles.

My interest in Noah stems from the belief that, through his life, much can be learned about the American Jewish experience in general. The tensions which he sought to resolve are tensions which are rooted in American Jewish history. More broadly, they are the tensions faced by all minority groups which seek to preserve a measure of their identity while integrating into a larger, and at times hostile, mass society. Thus, Noah's "search for synthesis" should not be seen as an obscure or purely personal search. It is the same search conducted, in other forms, by millions of people in all corners of the world.

Yet, to view Noah only in a Jewish or a minority group context is not to see the man as he lived or as he saw himself. He was, by birth and temperament, quintessentially American. His contributions to American diplomacy, journalism, politics, and drama; his views on immigration, slavery, and other vital issues of the day; and his relations with the major figures of the Jacksonian period must all be understood in their American context. Otherwise, they can scarcely be understood at all.

The life of Mordecai Noah is part of a larger story, one which might be titled, "The Making of the American Jew." Somehow, in their 325 years in America, American Jews have become a unique community—different from other Americans, different from other Jews. The forces that shaped these American Jews were, I think, many of the same forces that shaped Mordecai Noah. To understand Noah is to begin to understand the process which transformed radically dissimilar Jews, from very different backgrounds, into the vibrant and creative American Jewish community of today.

I am pleased to acknowledge the many people—teachers, relatives, and friends—who influenced my life from a very young age. Their effect on this book has been incalculably great. Unfortunately, a list of these people would be prohibitively long; but their influence is no less real for their being unnamed here. I thank them all heartily—and silently.

I also received invaluable assistance from those who more directly aided me in my work on Mordecai Noah. Professors David Brion Davis and Sydney E. Ahlstrom guided my studies at Yale, and left me chastened, wiser, and still awe-struck four years later. My debt to them, and to my other Yale professors, is incalculable. Professor Jacob Rader Marcus took me under his protective wing at an early stage of my research. Since then, he has spent innumerable hours advising me. Every chapter of this book has fallen under his scrutiny— all have been thereby improved. Professor Jerome Mushkat put his encyclopedic knowledge of New York politics completely at my disposal, and commented extensively on my chapters. A spirited and highly enlightening correspondence ensued, one from which many useful ideas ultimately took form. Finally, my friend Robert Weisbrot took time from his own dissertation to read mine, saving it from many infelicities and pitfalls. His conversation and cooperation during the year in which this was written have enriched the manuscript and deepened our friendship.

The Yale University libraries were my "laboratories" during the time that I researched this book. Their agreeably long hours, thoughtfully courteous staff, magnificently helpful inter-library loan office, and of course, their abundantly rich collection of books and microfilms made even the most tenacious questions yield to my probings. My friends at the American Jewish Historical Society and the American Jewish Archives also performed valiant service, catering to even my most unreasonable demands with supreme graciousness. I owe debts, in addition, to institutions which I visited on brief research trips: the American Antiquarian Society, Boston Public Library, Federal Archives and Records Center (Waltham), Harvard University, Library of Congress, National Archives, New York Historical Society, and New York Public Library. Staff members in all these organizations rendered invaluable assistance, for which I am most grateful.

The following institutions, not previously mentioned, were kind enough to provide me with information by mail, and I deeply thank them for taking so much of their time to save me a great deal of trouble: Brandeis University Library, Brown University Library, Buffalo and Erie County Historical Society, Buffalo and Erie County Public Library, Charleston Library Society, Chicago Historical Society, Clemson University Library, Columbia University Library, Cornell University Library, Dartmouth College Library, Federal Archives and Records Center (Bayonne), General Society of Mechanics and Tradesmen, Haverford College Library, Hebrew Union College Library, Hebrew University Library, Historical Society of Pennsylvania, Huntington Library, Leo Baeck Institute, Maryland Historical Society, New York State Library, New York Society Library, Patten Free Library (Bath, Maine),

Princeton University Library, University of Rochester Library, University of South Carolina Library, and University of Virginia Library.

Friends, acquaintances, and people I have never met, took time from their own work on my behalf. Each deserves a more personal acknowledgment than I can offer here. Each, I hope, will understand my dilemma and accept my brief thanks as a token of the enormous gratitude that I feel: Selig Adler, Terry Alford, Marc D. Angel, Audrey Arellanes, Israel Bartal, Nehemiah Ben-Zev, Jay Berkowitz, Julius Bisno, Solomon Breibart, Carl Brown, William Cullen Bryant II, Esther Cember, Arthur A. Chiel, Stanley S. Chyet, Thomas J. Curran, William Cutter, Ross Fuerman, Richard M. Goldberg, Israel Goldstein, Elliot Gorn, Victor Greene, Samuel Gross, W. Edwin Hemphill, Leo Hershkowitz, Samuel H. Jacobs, Leon A. Jick, Nathan M. Kaganoff, Abraham J. Karp, Martha Katz-Hyman, Morton Keller, Shmuel Klatzkin, Marion E. Klinge, Bertram W. Korn, Hillel Levine, Evelyn Miller, Ruth Necheles, Abraham J. Peck, Jonathan V. Plaut, W. Gunther Plaut, Hans G. Reissner, Samuel Rezneck, C. Duncan Rice, J. Albert Robbins, Ira Robinson, Robert D. Rutland, Morris U. Schappes, Robert Seager II, Maxine Seller, Joyce Seltzer, Robert Shapiro, Robert Singerman, Marshall Sklare, Haym Soloveitchik, Malcolm Stern, Norton B. Stern, Norman Stillman, Ronald Swerczek, Florence Thomas, Seth Ward, Bernard Wax, Georges Weill, Maxwell Whiteman, Stephen J. Whitfield, and Fannie Zelcer.

My research and writing have been greatly facilitated by a series of generous grants. Yale University's scholarship, stipend, and travel allowance freed me to devote much more time to this work than would otherwise have been possible. The American Jewish Archives, through the generosity of Mr. and Mrs. Allen A. Berkman, awarded me the Loewenstein-Weiner Fellowship, an award which permitted me to spend a blissful month working at the Archives and the Klau Library of Hebrew Union College in Cincinnati. The Archives also paid many of my subsequent photocopying costs. The National Foundation for Jewish Culture, by awarding me both a summer and an academic-year grant, allowed me to work full time on Mordecai Noah during 1978-9. Preparation of this work was supported in an important way, too, by the Memorial Foundation for Jewish Culture. Of course, neither these institutions, nor any of the other people who helped me, bear any responsibility whatsoever for my errors or misjudgments.

I thank my family last, only because I have no words to thank them adequately. My brother and sister-in-law, David and Rachel Sarna, provided me with hospitality and encouragement during every one of my all-too-frequent research trips to New York. They also made many practical suggestions which redounded to my benefit. My parents have had so profound, vivid, and enduring an effect on my entire life that they simply cannot be thanked with the usual words. My feelings of love and indebtedness are far too intense to be reduced to writing. The fact that I dedicate this work to them will somehow have to speak for itself.

Chapter I

Formative Years

It was hard to be a Jew in early America—one seemed altogether different from everybody else. Ninety percent of Americans lived in towns or rural farms; most Jews lived in cities. Americans largely went to church; Jews went to synagogue. Americans generally engaged in manual labor; Jews overwhelmingly engaged in non-manual labor. As a small minority in a sea of Christians, American Jews had to maintain contacts and help one another in order to survive as a group. By accident or design, their children met, fell in love, and married. The small community became one big, interrelated family.

The roots of this family went back to 1654 when twenty-three Jews arrived in New Amsterdam aboard the *Ste. Catherine*. Gradually, over the next century-and-a-half, more Jews arrived: some from Holland, England, Portugal, and Italy, others from Jewish settlements in the New World, and still others from Central Europe, Eastern Europe, and North Africa. They came individually or in small groups. Generally, they settled in the developing port cities: New York, Philadelphia, Newport, Charleston, and Savannah. They sought economic opportunity, civic equality, and freedom of worship.[1]

By 1790, the Jewish community had swelled to a population of 1,500 to 2,500 in a national population about two thousand times larger—3,929,000.[2] But most Jews were not lost in the crowd. Although some intermarried, and others assimilated, the majority maintained their religious identities. They courageously determined to be Americans and Jews at the same time, and hoped that their children would follow in their footsteps. Many children, among them Mordecai Noah, did just that.

Mordecai Manuel Noah[3] was born "on a hot July day" (probably July 19) in 1785. His parents, Manuel Mordecai (1755–1822) and Zipporah Phillips (1764–1792), lived on Water Street in Philadelphia in "a yellow house up two pair of stairs facing the water." A native of Mannheim, Germany, Manuel Noah immigrated to the United States and served in the Pennsylvania militia during the Revolutionary War. He then entered the business world, but "lacking both ability and responsibility," he went bankrupt a year after his marriage in 1784. Sometime between 1791 and 1792, deeply in debt, Manuel Noah left home, going first to Charleston, South Carolina, and then to Europe. His abandoned wife, Zipporah, nine years his junior, did not long survive this strain. She died in Charleston, where her relatives lived, on November 18, 1792, at the age of twenty-eight. Mordecai and his sister Judith (1789–1868),[4] now orphans, fell under the care of their grandparents, Jonas and Rebecca (Machado) Phillips.[5]

Noah's grandparents were remarkable people. Over a thirty-year period, they brought into the world no fewer than twenty-one children. Most of them survived, prospered, and formed families of their own. Jonas Phillips himself was a German immigrant who in 1756 had arrived in Charleston, South Carolina, as an indentured servant. By 1790, he was already a successful Philadelphia merchant with a large plot of land. While working his way up the ladder to this prosperity, Phillips had also made a name for himself as a defender of Jewish rights. Under Pennsylvania law, he could not hold public office until he was willing to acknowledge the divinity of the New Testament. To ensure that the same restrictions would not exist under American law, he petitioned the Constitutional Convention to create a government "where all religious societies are on an equal footing." Unbeknown to Phillips, the Constitutional Convention had secretly voted to guarantee religious liberty eighteen days earlier. But this didn't end his troubles on the local scene. As late as 1793, a court required him to pay a fine because he refused to violate Jewish law by testifying on Saturday, his Sabbath.[6]

Mordecai Noah was heavily influenced by his grandfather. From him, he learned about the potentials and pitfalls which lay before Jews in American society. More than likely, he also learned much about the place of Ashkenazim (German Jews) in American Jewish society. Sephardic (Spanish and Portuguese) Jews generally looked down on German Jews; they considered them ill-bred and uncouth. Other American observers agreed. As Hannah Adams wrote in her *History of the Jews* (1812): "The manners of the Portuguese Jews differ from the rest of the [Jewish] nation and are more polished." As for Ashkenazic Jews, whatever they privately thought of the Sephardim, they conceded that the Sephardim had more status and more money. They also knew that generous contributions from new and old world Sephardic congregations helped to keep American synagogues afloat financially. To protect this source of income, and to improve their self-image, Ashkenazic Jews like Jonas Phillips "Sephardized" themselves. Some married Sephardic women and changed their names; others merely adapted themselves to the prevailing Sephardic rite. In both cases, Ashkenazim played down their heritage. Under these conditions, Sephardic traditions prevailed for a full century, even though the majority of American Jews were Ashkenazim.[7]

Mordecai Noah became a typical "Sephardized" Jew. Although three of his four grandparents came from Germany, Noah spoke only of his Sephardic ancestors—the family of his maternal grandmother. He often repeated the exciting escape story of his great-grandfather, Dr. Samuel Nuñez, "physician of the grand inquisitor." He cherished his ancestor, Reverend David Mendes Machado, who administered to Shearith Israel from 1736–47. He even wrote long articles about Spain. Regarding his Ashkenazic roots, however, he remained silent—at least until B'nai Jeshurun, the Ashkenazi congregation, was formed in 1825.[8]

Noah carefully selected his ancestors. He displayed only those who enhanced his own status; the rest he ignored. When it came to his relatives, he assumed a more tolerant stance. Noah knew that relatives were basic to survival: goods and information passed along family lines; kinsmen demanded and performed mutual favors. Therefore, it was important to maintain close ties with as many of them as possible.

Mordecai Noah was born into a family endowed with a particularly impressive coterie of relations. His mother's sister-in-law was a granddaughter of both the revolutionary broker Haym Solomon and the wealthy merchant Jacob Hart. His father's sister had married Ephraim Hart, one of the wealthiest Jews in New York. He had as great uncles the merchants Philip Moses and Jacob I. Cohen. Then there were familial connections with the multitudinous offspring of Jonas and Rebecca Phillips. Numbered among these uncles and aunts were (or would be) several famous Phillipses, as well as members of such distinguished Jewish families as Moses, Cardozo, Seixas, and Levy (the family of Commodore Uriah Phillips Levy). Noah thus was related to many of the most important Jews in North America. He had kinsmen in all the principal Jewish settlements, from Montreal in the north to Charleston in the south. In his youth, these relations assisted him. They lodged him, advised him, and helped him to find work. Later, the situation changed. Noah attained a position through which he could perform favors for others, and he did so gladly. He knew from experience how valuable such favors could be.[9]

Mordecai Noah's childhood was as unstable as his later political career. Although his early days are difficult to chart clearly, he apparently moved from place to place, held down a variety of jobs, and educated himself in between. As a very young boy in New York, he attended Latham's School in Garden Street, where he played with boys who grew up to be his political opponents: "We all rode the old white goat, Billy Warner, belonging to the stables in New Street and went down in shoals to Coffee House Slip to eat molasses with a straw from the hogsheads."

For a while, he also attended New York's only—and sparsely attended—Jewish school, the Sunday and afternoon school of Shearith Israel, where Gershom Seixas taught Hebrew. He left, along with his cousin(?), Uriah Noah, in October 1794. He next studied in Lityle's School in Southwark, Philadelphia, where he may have sat in class with Stephen Decatur, later a naval hero. For a time, Noah may also have attended the old Philadelphia College, and he is reputed to have studied on his own in the Franklin library.

But he didn't spend all of his time studying, or in Philadelphia. "Somewhere about the year 1796," Noah later recalled, he lived in New York and was "one among a crowd of boys which hovered near the doors of the John Street theatre," hoping for a free seat. He would return to the theater again and again. To get in, he needed money. And if he wanted money, he had to work for it.[10]

According to Noah's later recollections, he first found employment as a messenger "in the auditor's office in Philadelphia under Joseph Nourse." He "carried many official papers to Mr. Gallatin" (Albert Gallatin was then a member of Congress), and he called on Robert Morris, then in debtors' prison, to inquire "what notes of his afloat in the market were genuine or forged." Perhaps it was this early experience which attracted him to politics. Politics, however, was not what Jonas Phillips had in mind for his grandson. Influenced as ·he probably was by the Enlightenment's stress on manual labor, he apprenticed the boy to a carver and gilder, so that he might learn a "productive" trade. But Noah's "taste and ambition did not harmonize with his employment." He was often beaten and flogged—a discipline he retrospectively termed "wholesome"—and he never learned to carve and gild.[11]

Whether or not Noah's discipline actually proved "wholesome," his overall apprenticeship experience may well have been. His master soon set him to a more typical Jewish profession. He became a salesman, a peddler of his master's wares. Noah used this opportunity to see the country. Though his actual labors must have been degrading—"One Who Knows Him" later mocked Noah for having "earned his livelihood by carrying [carved] images round the streets of Albany"—he made many valuable friends in lower Canada and upstate New York. In 1810, these proved useful: "citizens of the United States residing within the Province of Lower Canada and in the State of New York" cited Noah's "frequent intercourse" with the province of Quebec when they recommended him for the post of consul to Lower Canada.[12] Noah was to use this upstate New York experience again in the 1820s when he proposed that Jews set up a colony, Ararat, near the mouth of the proposed Erie Canal.[13]

Not much more can be said about Noah's late teenage years. We have no record of where he lived, or how he reacted to the death of his grandfather in 1803. All that can be said with assurance is that by 1807 the twenty-two-year-old Noah's *wanderjahre* were over. He was back in Philadelphia, poised to begin his career.

It was perhaps inevitable that Noah would turn his sights to politics. His grandfather had been acutely aware of political happenings, and had not hesitated to initiate and sign political manifestoes. His uncle, Naphtali Phillips, with whom he was very close, had entered Democratic politics in the state of New York. As for Noah himself, he had already tasted of political fruits when he worked in the Pennsylvania auditor's office. He had clearly enjoyed that job more than carving and gilding.

Unsurprisingly, Noah joined forces with the Democratic-Republicans. Philadelphia Federalists had made some unpleasant attacks on Jews. They held old-fashioned ideas about aristocracy, church–state relations, and limited franchise—ideas which did not endear them to the Jewish community. The Democratic-Republicans, on the other hand, welcomed Jews, and allowed several of them to rise to high positions within the party. A few rich and influential Jews, notably the Gratzes, did identify as Federalists. Most Jews, however, probably leaned more toward the view of Philadelphia merchant and former Congregation Mikve Israel president, Benjamin Nones: "I am a Jew, and if for no other, for that reason am I a republican."[14]

In 1808, there was a more specific reason to be a Democratic-Republican: Simon Snyder. A German immigrant, the ambitious Snyder held high hopes of becoming the first nonaristocrat and the first German to be elected governor of the state of Pennsylvania. He had already served as Speaker of the Assembly and had met defeat in an 1805 gubernatorial quest. But, in 1808, Snyder ran on a Republican ticket against the unpopular Governor Thomas McKean. His chances seemed better than in 1805. Snyder had close personal ties with Aaron Levy, a prominent Jewish land agent whom he knew from his hometown of Lancaster. Eight other Jews, among them two sons of Jonas Phillips (Zalegman and Manuel) also knew Snyder and actively supported his candidacy. No Jew, however, more actively supported the gubernatorial hopeful than Mordecai Noah. Noah was a member of the Democratic Young Men, and in September 1808, he was elected to its board of managers. Reputedly, he also served as an assistant to John Binns, editor of the newly established pro-Snyder *Democratic Press*. He may have been Binns' Harrisburg correspondent, perhaps serving as a Snyder speechwriter on the side. Whatever the case—and Noah quite possibly later exaggerated his role in the campaign—the Democratic young man certainly performed well enough to earn a patronage reward once the victorious Snyder assumed office. Through the new governor's influence, he won election to the post of major in the Pennsylvania militia. Forever after, he was known as "Major Noah."[15]

Noah's choice of journalism as a profession may have reflected nothing more than the influence of his uncle, Naphtali Phillips, who had become the publisher of the *Public Advertiser* in New York. But it is curious that so many Jews, even without having relatives in journalism, nevertheless chose to enter this profession. When one considers the insignificant number of Jews in early America, it is remarkable that Naphtali Phillips, Mordecai Noah and his sons Manuel and Jacob, the brothers Isaac and Samuel Harby, Jacob N. Cardozo, Lewis C. Levin, Abraham G. Levy, Jacob De Cordova, Edwin De Leon, Levi Laurens, Jacob I. Cohen, Jr., and doubtless others, all worked on antebellum newspapers. In post-Civil War America, Jews continued their deep involvement in journalism. European Jews actively participated in journalism as well. Of course, Jews never monopolized the media, either in Europe or in America. But the question remains: what especially attracted Jews to the press?[16]

In part, Jewish interest in journalism stemmed from the nature of the enterprise. The press grew very rapidly in the nineteenth century as wars and political divisions generated wider public interest in news, while technological developments permitted the lower prices which allowed for greatly improved and far more widely circulated newspapers. Since the demand for journalists far outpaced the supply, Jews had no problem entering the industry; once they entered, they could also rise quickly. A lowly assistant could become an influential, powerful, and respected force in his community. Journalism thus permitted the kind of independence and mobility that Jews have often looked for in their occupations. A later generation would enter the clothing trade, filled with small-time operators and the hope of big-time profits, partly for the same reason. A further lure of journalism was that Jews had a rudimentary knowledge of the business before they started. Commerce on a large or small scale depends on information. Jewish merchants, travelers, peddlers and, of course, relatives served as "reporters" long before the public press had any interest in printing their news. What is more, Jews had the kind of cosmopolitan outlook which journalism demands. America's insular, xenophobic, small-town ruralites had little interest in news from abroad; news of local events contented them. Those who wanted to stay in touch with the world were primarily the Jews, city dwellers, and immigrants.

This same triangular coalition joined forces to support an American theater. They vigorously opposed native Protestants who deemed drama sinful, acting immoral, secular plays degenerate, and all theaters worthy of being banned. They fought for years to remove the shackles of colonial restriction, insisting that dramatists and dramatic productions could only enhance the overall quality of American life.

American Jews were in the forefront of this struggle. In 1791, Moses M. Hays led the fight against Boston's theater ban. Two years later, seven Jews contributed to the construction of New York's controversial Park Theater. In the nineteenth century, Isaac Harby wrote a stirring "Defense of the Drama" (1828)—one of the most memorable pieces of pro-theater propaganda to emerge from the entire century-long debate. But American Jews did not confine themselves merely to polemics. They also achieved substantial status among early American playwrights and actors. Perhaps these Jews (Noah, Samuel and Emanuel Judah, Isaac and Washington Harby, Aaron, Jonah and Jonas B. Phillips, and others) felt that they were continuing a long-standing European Jewish tradition of drama. Perhaps by acting, or masking their identity, they merely performed on stage actions which came naturally to them in the diaspora. Whatever the case, American Jews firmly sided with those who fought the evangelical establishment. They felt secure enough to dissent from orthodox norms.[17]

Mordecai Noah wholeheartedly identified with these views. From a young age, he considered himself "the firm friend of the drama." He made "great efforts" to scrape together the eighteen dollars necessary for a season's ticket to Philadelphia's theater, and by his own admission, he "seldom missed a night." He also wrote, produced, and reviewed plays, though not very successfully. His productions were apparently performed by a little theater company which he had himself helped to found. Most of his reviews appeared in a magazine which he helped to edit, *The Trangram or Fashionable Trifler* (1809). Still, some of his reviews did win publication in the Philadelphia press, and one of his plays was actually published. That play, a thin melodrama entitled *The Fortress of Sorrento* (1809), never reached the New York stage, and years later Noah quite understandably felt "almost ashamed to own it." He must have realized that his well-worn motif—a wife who dressed up as a man to save her husband from the hands of his enemies who had unjustly imprisoned him—had received better treatment in more competent hands. But if *Fortress of Sorrento* did not win Noah dramatic immortality, it at least brought him a fine library of published plays. Instead of giving him cash for his work, publisher David Longworth paid Noah in books. Another benefit also accrued to the rather vain fledgling dramatist. At the age of twenty-three, he could already boast that one of his own literary productions had appeared in print.[18]

Noah was motivated to write *The Fortress of Sorrento* by the same feelings which motivated all of America's early dramatists: love of the theater and patriotism. He wished to prove that the theater was not merely a "receptacle of vice and immorality." He insisted that, in proper hands, it was "capable of inculcating lessons of morality and patriotism." He sought to demonstrate by his own example, that Americans had the skills to produce plays on a level with those produced in Europe.[19]

Noah lamented Shakespeare's domination of the American stage. He feared that excessive praise for the great bard would "retard the improvement of dramatic composition." He knew that original American plays would only find small audiences so long as timeless English ones, which could be performed without paying author's royalties, remained so popular. He therefore published *Shakspeare [sic] Illustrated*, a book based on a work by Charlotte Lennox, which sought to discredit Shakespeare by calling him a plagiarist and a purveyor of "indelicate and offensive" material. In a fit of sophomoric iconoclasm, Noah belittled Shakespeare's accomplishment, and tried to carve out a niche for himself and his countrymen. He attacked the English-speaking world's standard of excellence in order to stimulate creative innovation.[20]

Noah produced but one volume of *Shakspeare Illustrated*, and he dedicated it "To the Rev. James Abercrombie D.D.," in honor of the latter's scientific pursuits. A projected second volume never appeared, although thirty-three years later Noah still "cherished a wish to complete the work." Had it been published, the second volume might have been of somewhat greater interest than the first. Noah had promised on his original title page that, in volume two, he would go beyond Mrs. Lennox's work and give "the story on which Shakespeare founded his Merchant of Venice from the Gesta Romanorum." The version of the story which Noah had in mind was most likely the then-unpublished medieval work in which the "pound of flesh" motif occurs in a totally non-Jewish setting. Where Noah obtained a copy of this work is unknown. It is, however, easy to imagine his apologetic motives. The same concerns lay behind Isaac Gomez's 1820 critique of *The Merchant of Venice*, Isaac Harby's vastly more important critique of 1827, and a long list of subsequent Jewish critiques stretching down to our own day.[21]

Despite his youth—he was still in his early twenties—Mordecai Noah had already involved himself in the theater, the press, and the world of politics. He loved company, enjoyed writing, and craved publicity and prestige. He lacked only one thing: money. Neither his occupations nor his avocations proved particularly lucrative. Nor did he have a rich father able to support him in times of need. Having failed as a gilder and carver, and apparently unsuited to the business world, he looked to a different means of attaining wealth. He sought appointment to a diplomatic post. Noah understood that as a diplomat he could tacitly earn money on the side, quite apart from any government salary or expense account. He also knew that he could use a diplomatic position to develop various kinds of connections. Finally, he surely realized that a diplomatic post held the promise of assorted fringe benefits. Besides the status attached to the position, the job offered him the chance to see the world.[22]

Noah's initial hope in 1810 was nevertheless for a job close to home. He applied for a minor post: American agent assigned to protect the interests of citizens trading with Lower Canada. Perhaps he felt that his experience and political connections entitled him to no better appointment. Still, the job he sought would have allowed him to be among old friends and relatives. For this reason, and to help his own commercial ventures, Uncle Ephraim Hart signed and likely helped to engineer a petition to President Madison on Noah's behalf. Although Hart possessed considerable influence, the petition failed. No American agent of any sort was assigned to Lower Canada. Instead, Secretary of State Robert Smith urged Noah "to apply for a consulate in Europe."[23]

Noah quickly realized that he had to justify his application in terms that would appeal to the Executive Branch, and to Congress. He therefore assured the Secretary of State that his personal interests were of no consequence: "I am not induced by motives of gain nor a desire for personal aggrandisement." Rather, he appealed to higher national interests, which as a Jew he felt uniquely qualified to promote:

> I wish to prove to foreign Powers that our Government is not regulated in the appointment of their officers by religious distinction, and on the score of policy I know of no measure which can so promptly lead members of the Hebrew Nation to emigrate to this country with their capitals, than to see one of their persuasion appointed to an honourable office attended with the confidence of the people.

He then went further. Not only would his appointment display American tolerance and stimulate the immigration of wealthy Jewish capitalists, but,

Noah hinted as he extolled Jewish loyalty, it might help President Madison politically as well:

> The friendly disposition you have manifested towards our nation in the conversation I had the honour to have with you, I have made known to them by letter. Ever grateful for any testimony of the good opinion of their Government, they estimate your exertions on their behalf with the warmest gratitude, and trust that no action of any one of their people will deprive them of the confidence of the administration or lessen the esteem with which you are disposed to regard them. I am proud to say that a very large majority of them express a sincere attachment towards the administration and in all the modifications of Government, I believe it will be admitted they have comported themselves like good Citizens and have always venerated the constituted authorities of the Union.[24]

Noah acted somewhat like a professional court Jew. He appealed on behalf of his people; he promised Jewish loyalty; he hinted at rewards for services rendered; and he kept silent about potential personal gains. To back up his claims, he displayed letters of recommendation from "the principal members of our persuasion," among them: Reuben Etting of Baltimore, Cherry Moise and Solomon Hyams of Charleston, Jacob S. Cohen of Philadelphia, and Israel B. Kursheedt of New York. He also showed off recommendations from several non-Jews, most notably that of the poet and diplomat, Joel Barlow. After several interviews and a delay of six months, he received his wish. On June 4, 1811, the President appointed him to be the first United States consul to Riga. President Madison, according to Noah, had wanted him to wait for one of the more difficult Barbary Power consular posts to open up. That, however, would have required a further delay of a year, and Noah's finances did not permit him any such leisure. Consequently, on July 2, 1811, he accepted the Riga appointment and prepared to depart. Privately, he made plans for just the kind of "personal aggrandisement" that he had earlier foresworn: "...In the article of Looking Glass Plates I can make advantageous purchases. From all that I can gather every appearance is manifest that I shall do considerable business. Peace between England and Russia will secure our property in the Baltic and immense quantities of Goods will be shipped from Russia to the U.S."[25]

Like so many of Noah's schemes, this one, too, was built on air. As war loomed between Russia and France, as well as between the United States and Great Britain, the recently appointed consul delayed his departure. Soon after his Senate confirmation, on November 27, 1811, he asked to be transferred to a consulate in the Barbary states as his "services in that quarter would be of more importance to the government." Meanwhile, unspecified "business of importance" had taken Noah to Charleston. After receiving orders, he promised to leave for Riga on or before March 6, 1812. But events overtook him. When war with England broke out, he still had not left Charleston. As it turned out, no American consul settled in Riga until 1834.[26]

The "business of importance" that sent Noah scurrying toward Charleston remains a mystery. One contemporary claimed that the consul received a teaching post which he later declined to accept. Perhaps the offer came from schoolmaster Isaac Harby. Noah also studied law in Charleston, but it is doubtful that he removed there for this purpose. Still another version had him going to Charleston "as a missionary of De Witt Clinton [Governor of New York]," armed with orders to offer a $25,000 subsidy to E.S. Thomas of the *Charleston City Gazette* to induce him to support Clinton for President. Anti-Clinton forces in Tammany Hall had not yet coalesced in 1811, and many Americans felt dissatisfied with the performance in office of President James Madison. Perhaps Clinton exploited this dissatisfaction and recruited the impecunious Noah for his campaign. If so, he had recruited the wrong man.[27]

Within a few months of his arrival in Charleston, Noah began to make a name for himself. He published a series of articles in the *Charleston Times* entitled "Oriental Correspondence" (April–June 1812). Written under the pseudonym "Muly Malak" (note the initials—M. M.), "Oriental Correspondence" described the manners and customs of Charlestonians as they might have been viewed by a Turkish visitor writing home. Mildly satiric, gently irreverent, and charmingly naive, the "letters" were bountifully spiced with glowing praise and stern condemnation. Even a brief example reveals why, in an age of dry political journalism, Muly Malak proved exceedingly popular:

> Among the most singular and incomprehensible efforts of the reigning taste, is a strange mode adopted by the ladies, to display their figures to advantage, by bracing their delicate bosoms with certain ligatures into various forms, convex and concave, octagon and diagonal, and which has no very distant resemblance to the complex angles in the Dardanelles. At a loss to conceive the origin and growth of this extraordinary custom, I referred to a dashing buck, who was sailing about with his hands crammed in his coat pocket, and required a solution of the enigma—he was loquacious and satisfactory. You must know, my dear Mr. Turk, said he, as I perceive you are a Turk, because you wear a turban—these ornaments are sanctioned and approved by the most celebrated and fashionable belles, and have now become general; they are composed of various materials; iron, silver, steel and whalebone; just as whim or caprice directs... Sacred Mahomet can it be possible that such monstrous absurdities should be practiced in the name and under the sanction and protection of fashion? Can it be, that the aspirations of beauty should be fettered by these ignoble bars? That the ivory bosom should be encircled and bound by cold and metallic substances, when Nature meant only to confine it in silken bands? Yet it is so, Caled, and persisted in with a determined and invincible spirit.[28]

Noah continued in this manner until his "letter" of June 2. Then, suddenly, Muly Malak shifted tone. He began talking about "rights and privileges," and he described in his column a meeting of citizens called to support the government in the crisis with Britain. In fact, such a meeting had been held, and Mordecai Noah had distinguished himself with a fine, extemporaneous, pro-war speech which "was heard with the most profound attention." A far less generous reception had been accorded another young politician, Joshua Toomer. Most inappropriately, he had spoken against the government's handling of the crisis. Outraged, Muly Malak subjected the dissident to ridicule. Allegedly to preserve his honor, Toomer challenged Noah (whose pseudonymous identity was common knowledge) to a duel. Much to Noah's relief, however, E.S. Thomas mediated the dispute, and the duel did not take place. Thomas assured Toomer that Noah's attack was aimed only at his public, not his private conduct. Toomer was satisfied; unfortunately, the crowds who had gathered for the duel were not. Duels were the public sport of Charleston. The city's best young men displayed their masculinity by battling over honor. By not dueling, Noah called into question his own courage. The public's doubts received seeming confirmation when a second challenge, this one from a man identified only as Crafts (probably William Crafts, an irascible young Federalist lawyer in Charleston), also concluded honorably without battle. In the end, however, Noah was forced to fight. A Charleston Jew, apparently the artist John Canter, sent Noah a challenge for some unknown (Noah termed it "trifling") cause, and warned "that he would neither accept explanation nor apology." Armed with a good pistol, and accompanied by his friend Hyam Cohen, Noah accepted the challenge and shot Canter before "a large party of gentlemen." Canter received a serious, but not fatal wound; as for Noah, his conduct "was pronounced superfine throughout." All doubts as to his courage having been removed, Noah entered Charleston's high society. He had completed the rite of passage; never again was he challenged.[29]

The onset of war and the journalistic debut of one of Noah's new political opponents ("Caled the Elder") brought the Muly Malak series to an end in June 1812. But Noah had by no means finished with either politics or War Hawk propaganda. He simply shifted his focus. In New York, Governor Clinton had violated party discipline, allied himself with Federalists, and had cast doubt on the wisdom of "Mr. Madison's war." The Martling faction of Tammany Hall, several among whom were Noah's relatives and friends, formally split with Clinton over these actions, and raised powerful opposition to his presidential bid. After consultation with Uncle Naphtali Phillips, editor of the Martling faction's newspaper, Noah became the anti-Clintonians' southern representative. On October 1, 1812, he published (under the name of Diodorus Siculus) *"A Letter Addressed to the Members of the Legislature of South Carolina Examining the Claims and Qualifications of Dewitt Clinton to the Presidency of the United States."*[30]

In this letter, which was really a thirty-three page pamphlet, Noah vigorously defended President Madison against all of De Witt Clinton's supposedly base charges. He declared the President a man of "superior claims and merits." He defended the congressional caucus system, whereby party congressmen rather than party conventions, nominated presidential candidates. Most important, he condemned Clinton's presidential bid as wrong and divisive. On the basis of "actual observation...personal knowledge and assured conviction," the twenty-seven-year-old Noah charged the forty-three-year-old Clinton with youth and inexperience. He alleged that the New York governor was "consolidating within himself powers as vast as those of a Roman Dictator," and accused Clinton of having displayed dangerous political misjudgment and "an overweening desire to make peace with Britain" at all costs. He therefore offered precautionary advice: "Principle, as well as policy dictates us, never to abandon a worthy, useful and experienced officer to substitute one of doubtful or precarious standing."[31]

Noah's *Letter* displayed many of the features which characterized his political writings for the next forty years. It contained good propaganda; no doubts or qualifications marred the argument. On the other hand, the argument rested on half-truths. Noah laced his pages with evocative words like "Federalist" and "aristocratic hopes" in referring to Clinton as against "the immortal Washington" and "national honour," in reference to Madison. Needless to say, the author made no mention of any former connections that he himself might have had with Clinton. He also failed to reveal his own ties to the opposition party.

Noah's candidate, James Madison, captured South Carolina's presidential electors and went on to win the presidency. But Noah was to deal with De Witt Clinton again, many times.

With the excitement of the 1812 election past, Noah turned to the third of his three occupations (after politician and journalist): he wrote a play. The melodrama, *Paul and Alexis, or the Orphans of the Rhine*, was commissioned by Charles Young for his actress wife, a woman Noah remembered as "remarkable for her personal beauty and amiable deportment." Mrs. Young apparently wanted to play a male role; Noah obligingly fashioned her one from a popular French drama: R.C. Guilbert-Pixerécourt's *Le Pèlerin Blanc*. To his credit, Noah did not merely translate from the French as did so many of his contemporaries. He added a new character, and he adapted many parts of the play for an English-speaking audience. But the basic plot of the play still dealt with the efforts of Paul and Justin ("the wandering boys") to regain their rights to an estate which a cousin had usurped. Surviving a variety of obstacles, including a near poisoning, the boys ultimately triumphed over adversity and achieved their objective.

To a modern critic, *Paul and Alexis* is "a poor thing" with "dropsical prose." But it ranked among the best of its genre; Noah was one of but six early American playwrights to borrow anything at all from the French stage. His play was innovative, and it enjoyed wide popularity. It later appeared on the London stage, only the second American play ever to be so honored. After being adapted by John Kerr, who renamed the play *The Wandering Boys*, the drama returned to the United States where it played successfully for many years.[32]

The sum Noah received for his work on *Paul and Alexis* did little to alleviate his perilous financial condition. By March 1813 he again found himself "reduced to a low ebb"; so low, in fact, that he was forced to borrow twenty dollars from Naphtali Phillips. Understandably, he soon made renewed efforts to obtain a consulship—this time in Barbary. As before, he desperately wanted "liberty to draw on the treasury" to pay off his debts. But he knew that his appointment depended primarily on his politics. His support of Governor Snyder, his opposition to De Witt Clinton, his anti-British stance, his many Democratic-Republican friends, and his Jewish connections all counted as political assets. He doubtless pointed to these assets when he traveled to Washington in order to personally present his case to the President. The President apparently understood. Noah came away from the meeting very encouraged (he would later also be very boastful), and forthwith he assured his uncle that "the President has made up his mind to appoint me Charge des affaires [sic] at Tunis.... It will put me in possession of handsome funds."[33]

Unfortunately for Noah, the President had more important things on his mind than Tunis, and he kept his twenty-seven-year-old petitioner waiting. Noah could do nothing but return to Charleston, and hope that his documents would follow. But he did not sit idle; he no sooner arrived home than he became involved in a fierce political controversy involving Governor Joseph Alston, several members of his administration, and five "war hawk" congressmen: John Calhoun, Langdon Cheves, William Loundes, Elias Earle, and David Evans. Alston tried to oust the congressmen by claiming that they never officially informed him of their intentions to accept the Washington posts to which they were elected. The congressmen claimed that, with Congress starting early, they assumed that their commissions would automatically be sent to them at the capital. The entire issue was exposed by E.S. Thomas of the *Charleston City Gazette* who cast the governor in a very bad light. He received strong support from a correspondent named "Argus"—none other than Thomas's "confidential friend," Mordecai Noah. Noah hammered away at Alston, and quoted South Carolina's secretary of state to back up his charges, that the governor wanted to hold a new election. He charged the governor with promoting "discord and disunion in the republican party" and called on Alston "instantly to resign." For his part, Alston employed John Mackey's *Charleston Investigator* to defend his actions and attack Noah. Mackey fought valiantly and was not above using anti-Jewish innuendo—"Your Red Whiskers and Hooked Nose tell me too plainly who you are"—but to no avail. Public clamor forced Alston to send the five congressmen their commissions.[34]

Meanwhile, on March 29, 1813, the *Charleston Gazette* had announced "the appointment, by the President of the United States, of Major M. M. Noah, of this city, to be Consul at Tunis." "Nestor" in the *Charleston Investigator* violently protested, but on May 28, Noah departed, leaving several lawsuits behind him. In the sequel, E. S. Thomas paid a fine for printing slander about the governor (truth was no defense); John Mackey received a similar sentence for his attacks on Noah.[35]

Noah's departure marked the end of his formative period. He had, in a remarkably short time, secured for himself an enviable reputation in politics, journalism, and drama; he had established for himself a significant place in the more radical ranks of the Democratic-Republican Party; and, he had demonstrated his masterly skills in propaganda and political intrigue. He had even faced personal, political, and religious challenges—all of which left him unfazed. The "stout young gentleman, with sandy hair, a large Roman nose, and large red whiskers,"[36] imagined that his formative years would be followed by an extended diplomatic career. He was wrong. In fact, his basic path in life was set.

Chapter II

Consul Noah

Mordecai Noah's appointment as consul to Tunis continued a long tradition in the history of diplomacy: the appointment of Jews as intermediaries between Christian and Moslem countries. Because of their minority status, Jewish diplomats could claim to be religiously "neutral." More important, their Jewish communal ties provided them with independent channels of communication and influence. They held advantages that non-Jewish diplomats, restricted to normal diplomatic channels, simply could not match. As Mordecai Noah discovered, however, these advantages also had their darker side. Once invoked, religion could not be restricted solely to the domain of appointments; a Jew who was appointed on the basis of religion could be dismissed on precisely the same grounds.[1]

Early in his correspondence with the Department of State in 1811, Mordecai Noah had spelled out his special qualification for the consular post in Barbary: "It would be a favourable circumstance in sending a member of the Hebrew nation to the Barbary Powers...supported as I should be with the wealth and influence of forty thousand residents." While his figures were exaggerated, his point was well taken. Jews certainly did hold highly influential positions in North Africa. Major Jewish families like the Bacris maintained intimate connections with Moslem rulers; they controlled most commerce; they directed from afar considerable numbers of pirates. Under these conditions, it certainly seemed plausible to send Jewish consuls to North Africa. The idea that they might exert extra leverage over their coreligionists made obvious sense—so much sense, in fact, that the Dutch and the British had frequently sent Jewish diplomats to North Africa. Since America's relations with the Barbary States had become particularly delicate in 1813, it is not surprising that President Madison agreed to try the same tactic.[2]

Previously, America had handled the Barbary States (Morocco, Algiers, Tunis, and Tripoli) with a modified carrot-and-stick approach. On the one hand, it strove to prevent piracy and the enslavement of sailors through generous tributes—a policy strongly advocated by Consul Tobias Lear during his stint in Algiers. On the other hand, it punished the Barbary Powers through the use of brute force—a policy just as strongly advocated by Consul William Eaton during his term of service in Tunis. With the onset of the War of 1812, however, the carrot-and-stick policy became ineffectual. British propaganda, backed by impressive naval victories, convinced North Africans that America's days as a naval power were numbered.[3]

The first to test America's mettle was the Dey, the ruling governor of Algiers. First, he demanded increased tribute, arguing that money should be paid based on the lunar (Moslem) rather than on the longer solar calendar. He then complained about the allegedly poor quality of America's annual present. Finally, he ousted Consul Tobias Lear and again permitted naval piracy. On August 25, 1812, Algerian forces surrounded and seized the merchant brig, *Edwin*. They doomed its captain, George Smith, and his ten-man crew to wretched enslavement.[4]

The enslavement of white Americans stirred up patriotic passions throughout the United States. Graphic captivity stories detailed the brutal treatment accorded past American captives in Barbary. Meanwhile, eyewitness reports from the scene made clear that Algerian treatment of the *Edwin's* seamen was no better. Public clamor impelled the government to act. Consequently, Secretary of State Monroe instructed Consul Noah to devise and execute a secret, low-budget mission of rescue:

> On your way to Tunis, perhaps at Malaga or Marseilles, you may probably devise means for the liberation of our unfortunate countrymen at Algiers, whose situation has excited the warmest sympathy of their friends, and indeed of the people generally of this country—Should you find a suitable channel, through which you can negotiate their immediate release, you are authorised to go as far as three thousand dollars a man; but a less sum may probably effect the object. Whatever may be the result of the attempt, you will, for obvious reasons, not let it be understood to proceed from this government, but rather from the friends of the parties themselves. As yet, we have information only of eleven persons; the crew of the Brig Edwin, of Salem, being confined at Algiers, and it is to be hoped that no addition has been made to that number. If success should attend your efforts, you will draw upon this department for the necessary funds for paying their ransom, and providing for their comfortable return to their country and friends.

Monroe's orders were clear and precise: Noah was to pay no more than three thousand dollars per man to free the American captives, and he was to work in the strictest secrecy. To disclose the source of the money would be to decrease the chances for success and to increase the ransom price prohibitively. The embattled government really wanted a bargain-rate, morale-building victory. Had Noah delivered one, he might have returned home to a hero's welcome.[5]

Noah set sail from Charleston on May 28, 1813. By coincidence, his schooner, the *Joel Barlow*, was named for the diplomat who years before had recommended him for a consular post. By a further coincidence, his scheduled voyage ended just the way his mission would end—abruptly. On July 31, the British frigate *Sir Thomas Staines* captured the *Joel Barlow* and took it in tow. While Noah received respectful treatment at the hands of his captors, he was not permitted to continue on to his destination. Instead, the British frigate landed him at Plymouth, England. Dutifully, he first sent a secret letter to Secretary of State Monroe reporting where he was and what intelligence he had gleaned from his British captors. He then spent the next nine weeks enthusiastically touring England.[6]

By October, Noah had received a passport and had traveled to Cadiz, Spain, where he lodged with Consul Richard Hackley. At last, he began work on his secret mission. Unfortunately, he worked harder at arranging his mission than on keeping his secret. Eager for status, he promiscuously discussed his various options with other tenants in Richard Hackley's compound. One tenant, Richard Raynal Keene, seemed particularly interested. He soon volunteered to act as Noah's Algerian agent.[7]

Keene was a native of Maryland who had studied at Princeton and read law under Maryland's attorney general, Luther Martin. From a very young age, he had displayed an unstable and mysterious character. Enemies and scandals continued to pursue him throughout his career. According to one rumor, he married his wife, Eleonora Martin, only after seducing her. Certainly her father, Luther Martin, opposed the match. Others charged Keene with violations of the Embargo Act and with complicity in the Burr Conspiracy. But even if all of these charges were false, there can be no doubt that he actively took part in a plan to form an Irish Catholic colony in Mexico. To this end, he covered up his American ancestry, and in 1814 began to correspond with the King of Spain. Many people, especially Jeffersonians (Keene was a Federalist), feared the ramifications of a Catholic border state. They labeled Keene a traitor to his country.[8]

Noah, of course, knew nothing about any of these allegations. As he later admitted, he viewed Keene as a Maryland resident who had become a Spanish citizen presumably "to cover some commercial views." Overall, Keene seemed to him to be "a man of talents." He was impressed that the émigré "was on terms of very general intimacy with the American merchants at Cadiz." Keene also displayed other qualifications: he promised to obtain letters of support from both the Spanish and British ambassadors; he agreed to undertake the Algiers mission at a very reasonable cost (one thousand dollars in advance, two thousand dollars more, plus any unspent ransom money, if he succeeded); and he received the highest recommendation from Consul Hackley. Without hesitation, Noah hired him. By early 1814, Keene was on his way.[9]

Noah accompanied Keene as far as Gibraltar where, with the help of merchant Aaron Cardoza, the richest and most powerful Jew on the island, and Horatio Sprague, a Boston merchant, he received permission both to land and to establish credit for his "secret" mission. According to Swedish consul, John Norderling—no friend of the Jews—Noah also made the most of his local Jewish connections:

> If any credit can be given to reports from several quarters, the jews in Gibraltar,
> bursting with pride in seeing one of their brethren in such an exalted situation
> called him the Major of such and such a Regiment, and the Ambassador of the
> United States to the Kingdom of Tunis, and gave him the place of honor in their
> synagogue, proclaiming their triumph with ridiculous extravagance. Further I
> am told, that, being charged with a certain delicate commission respecting your
> twelve countrymen here, he applied for information and advice to his tribe and to
> an Algerine Reis [traveller] he met in Gibraltar.

Even if Norderling's account is embellished, there can be no doubt as to the
advice which Noah received from members of his "tribe" in Gibraltar: he was
told to work through the Bacri family. Armed with "very special letters of
recommendation" from "King of the Jews" Aaron Cardoza, Keene went
directly to Algiers. But word of his mission had leaked out. By the time he
arrived, the Dey himself suspected the "Spaniard" was representing a
United States consul, not merely American merchants in Cadiz. Accordingly,
he refused to soften his stance. Within twenty-four hours of Keene's arrival in
Algiers, he received the Dey's curtly worded rejection of all ransom offers:
"my policy and my views are to increase not to diminish the number of my
American slaves...not for a million of dollars would I release them." All
subsequent efforts by Keene and the various foreign consuls in Algiers proved
unavailing. The Dey's mind seemed unalterably made up.[10]

Keene was about to return to Cadiz in despair when, quite unexpectedly, his
luck changed. Charles Walker, an American seaman impressed on an English
frigate, deserted ship at Algiers and converted to Islam—probably to save his
life. This precipitated an international incident, as the Dey compassionately
permitted Walker to flee inland, in spite of British demands for his return.
Insulted, the British vice-consul sternly threatened dire revenge. But for
reasons which are not totally clear (quite possibly a bribe) he meekly agreed to
accept as compensation Algiers' release of two American seamen. Forthwith,
the Dey released the two whose ancestry seemed most in doubt; to save face,
he dubbed them both "British subjects." The lucky seamen soon reverted to
American citizenship, but not before Keene had ransomed them, probably
from the British ambassador, for a consideration of four thousand dollars.
Joining the seamen were four alleged Louisianans, brought to the Algerian port
by the English frigate *Franchise*. Keene ransomed them, also probably from
the consul, for a consideration of an additional six thousand dollars. All told,
he had released two of the twelve hostages whom he was charged with
releasing. For these, he claimed from Noah a full six thousand dollars. He also
released four "hostages" whose very existence had been unknown up to that
time. He claimed for them only half-reward: another six thousand dollars.[11]

Satisfied with his accomplishments, Keene left Algiers for Algeciras, Spain.
There, he composed a long letter to Consul Noah (May 22, 1814) in which he
detailed his achievements, analyzed American–Algerian relations, and described in detail the fortifications with which an American force invading
Algiers would have to contend. Noah, who was greatly relieved to hear from

his agent after four long months, pronounced himself well satisfied. Borrowing money from George Butler, a merchant in Gibraltar, Noah paid Keene his $15,852 ($12,000 plus expenses), arranged to ship the ransomed seamen home, and billed the government for his total costs including expenses and interest: $25,910. He then dispatched a cover letter and documents to Secretary Monroe and left for Paris. From Paris, he planned to travel directly to Tunis.[12]

From Noah's point of view, his first diplomatic mission was over; it was neither a glorious success nor a total failure. But in Washington, discussion had only begun. In 1814, the capital had been too concerned with a British invasion to worry much about the Barbary Coast. The State Department only turned its attention back to the impressed sailors in Barbary after the Peace of Ghent. Even from the relatively few documents which remain, it is quite clear that the department was unhappy with Noah's performance.[13]

The first problem was Richard Raynal Keene. Secretary Monroe had never told Noah to hire an agent, and had certainly not instructed him to pay a thousand dollars in advance to someone who might accomplish nothing. He probably envisaged a quiet effort—what Attorney General Rush later termed "interference on a footing private and unostentatious." The attorney general admitted that Monroe's orders were open to misinterpretation; still, he remained convinced that the "true meaning" of Monroe's instruction "was lost sight of by the employment of Mr. Keene." As for Noah's promise of one thousand dollars regardless of results, Rush, like the State Department, found the act one in which Noah "was not justified." These two conclusions, of course, would have applied to the employment of any agent. The fact that Noah chose Keene, a man who lay under grave suspicion in Washington, did nothing to enhance the State Department's faith in its consul's good judgement. Monroe doubtless had trouble understanding that, in far-off Cadiz, Keene really could have posed as a successful and intelligent merchant, and nothing more.[14]

Keene may have been good at concealing his identity. Noah was not. Consequently, the most persuasive charges against his consular activities were those which attacked the widespread publicity in which they were so carelessly engulfed. Secretary Monroe had sternly warned Noah to keep the government's name out of all negotiations on behalf of the *Edwin* crew. Yet, Keene learned the secret, Norderling learned the secret, financier George Butler learned the secret, and in all probability, the Algerian Dey learned the secret as well. Richard Rush's appraisal of the mission was thus basically accurate: "Instead of secrecy and silence, éclat rather mark[ed] its movements." No doubt Keene was partly to blame for this publicity; he, after all, let the Spanish and British consuls in on the secret. But the basic flaws lay in Noah's character: he was both vaingloriously boastful and extravagantly theatrical. These unfortunate traits could be overlooked—indeed, they could occasionally be advantageous—in journalists, politicians, and playwrights. But they fatally compromised the character of diplomats and statesmen. These same traits continued to plague Noah in later years.[15]

Had Noah's secret mission proved a smashing success, his loose tongue, as well as his appointment of Richard Keene, might well have been excused. But it didn't succeed; consequently, his critics gained a sympathetic hearing in government circles. The first evaluation came from Consul John Norderling in Algiers. Even before any hostages had been released, he charged in a letter to his friend, Tobias Lear, that Noah and Keene had squandered their chances for success, for they had failed to write "to a confidential consul on the spot (he doubtless had himself in mind), in order to feel the pulse." Keene, according to Norderling, had then insured himself a negative reception by his indiscreet attempts to deal with the ruling Dey directly. Had the agent followed procedure, the Swedish consul reminded his former colleague, he would have prepared everything well in advance with the Dey's assistants. He also would have avoided the "fuss and parade" which attended his mission from the start. Quiet diplomacy, Norderling averred, would far more likely have achieved success. Lear, who surely agreed, passed the Swedish consul's letter on to the Department of State.[16]

A second letter of criticism also arrived at the State Department from Algiers. This one was dated October 19, 1814, and was written by Captain George Smith of the *Edwin*. Norderling had earlier arranged to have Smith freed from slavery, and placed under conditions of house arrest in the consul's own home. The grateful captain's views undoubtedly reflected those of his diplomatic host. Smith's criticisms of Noah were barbed, blunt, and acrid. He blamed Noah's "want of experience" for the failure of the Keene mission. He scorned the way Keene "delivered his business into the hands of our enemies—the English and Spanish consuls." Finally, he deeply regretted "that Mr. Norderling has been treated with neglect by the American agent." Smith urged Washington to send to Algiers "people who have some knowledge and experience of Oriental Governments." Barring this, he hoped that the State Department would "authorize some person on the spot" to handle negotiations. Permanent residents, he pointed out, "can work in secret [and] take their time…"[17]

In the second part of his letter, Captain Smith made a more specific charge against Keene: he claimed that the two *Edwin* seamen that the agent rescued were, in truth, "British subjects." The native Americans, Smith alleged, still languished in captivity. The State Department believed this charge, notarized affidavits to the contrary notwithstanding. Still, Noah had been ordered to obtain the release of the *Edwin's* entire crew; Monroe had never made special provisions about foreign sailors. All generally agreed, therefore, that Noah's ransom payments were in order. The same could not be said of the payments made to rescue the French-speaking Louisianans. Despite lengthy arguments by Keene and Noah, and despite signed affidavits, Americans found it hard to believe that Frenchmen, on a French vessel, who had not seen American land for eight years, were worth six thousand dollars—especially since the four

Frenchmen were never officially taken hostage and were not covered under Noah's original set of instructions. Characteristically, Noah felt genuine sympathy for the unfortunate French captives. As he later admitted, he would, if necessary, have paid Keene double the amount he had paid for their release. But the government faced a financial crisis, and suspected that the British vice-consul in Algiers had imposed on Keene for his own personal aggrandizement. Noah's compassion notwithstanding, Attorney General Rush sided with the State Department's view of this deal: "it can never, I think, meet the sanction of the Government...no part of the charge for them should be allowed." Convinced in early 1815 that the design, execution, and results of Noah's Algerian mission were thoroughly unsatisfactory, the State Department refused to honor his financial claims. This was tantamount to a government vote of no confidence in its consul. Recall and dismissal followed automatically.[18]

While Washington diplomats carefully reviewed his secret mission, Noah himself assumed his duties in Tunis. He had earlier left Cadiz, after dispatching the rescued hostages to the United States, and had proceeded to Marseilles. There, he intended both to collect his two-thousand dollar personal salary and to procure the four-thousand-dollar official gift which he had been ordered to present to the ruling Bey and his family. (The Bey was the ruler of Tunis; the Dey ruled Algiers.) But, once again, Noah faced unexpected delays. He could not obtain credit in France—the results of the war being still in doubt—and without money, he dared not leave for Tunis. Instead, he spent his time merrily traveling. He befriended consul David Bailie Warden[19]; he met the venerable defender of Jewish rights, Abbé Grégoire (according to Noah, Grégoire "felt sincere pleasure at my appointment, because it was practical evidence of the liberality of our institutions"); and he saw all the usual tourist sites. Family tradition maintains that he also found his father in France, meeting him by chance in a Paris restaurant. The story cannot be confirmed, but it must contain a kernel of truth, for the hitherto missing Manuel Noah accompanied his son to Tunis—a fact that Noah never publicized. Noah finally left France, owing to the "great efforts" of "Mr. Belknap of Boston" (probably Andrew Belknap) who obtained for him the funds which he had been seeking. Forthwith, he took passage on the Swedish brig of war *Forsöken* and set off for Tunis, heavily laden with gifts for "his highness the Bey."[20]

Noah's arrival in Tunis (December 16, 1814) came at a moment of great instability. Hamouda Pacha, a long-reigning and benevolent monarch, had died suddenly in the summer, and his brother Ottoman succeeded to the throne. This angered Mahmoud, the legitimate heir, and he staged a bloody coup which the newly settled Noah observed first-hand. Seventy-two hours later, Mahmoud cooly pronounced himself ready to receive Noah's official credentials and consular present. The new consul arrived at the palace bedecked in "a coat covered from collar to skirts in gold." He was accompanied by both former consul, Charles Coxe, and chancery officer,

Ambrosio Allegro. All obeyed strict North African protocol. They feigned humility, bowed low, and kissed the Bey's hand. This procedure repelled Noah, both as an American and as a Jew. Yet, he refused to rebel against it. He determined from the start to be on good terms with the Bey. Unlike later consuls, he agreed to sacrifice his pride in order to conform to local "laws, habits and customs."[21]

His ceremonial duties completed, Noah settled back to what he hoped would be an aristocratic life. He resided in a magnificent house—by his own admission "one of the best and largest in Tunis." He used china, stemware, and silver of equally fine quality. He even wore a coat tailored in the latest Parisian fashion. All he lacked was money. Like most consuls, he constantly complained of penury, and even threatened to resign unless his salary rose. He pitifully lamented his exorbitant expenses, angrily blamed the Bey for denying him permission to move to cheaper quarters, and resolutely insisted that much of his money went for indispensable staff. No evidence suggests, however, that Noah ever tried to save money through domestic economies. Apparently, he just assumed that his bills would be paid.[22]

Noah, unlike most consuls, expected to work hard for his salary. He carried on an extensive correspondence with the State Department, fellow consuls, and friends, and he strove to secure accurate and detailed information about Tunisian life. As his volume of travels reveals, he was a perceptive observer with a broad curiosity, especially about women. His special area of interest, however, was Tunisian Jewry. Soon after he arrived, he investigated the community at first hand and transmitted his impressions to David Bailie Warden:

> Tunis contains upwards of 100,000 inhabitants—twenty thousand of which are Jews—this unfortunate race live under the greatest oppression and humiliation possibly to be imagined.—On this subject deeply interesting to me I consider it prudent and politic to be *secret and circumspect* for fear that a knowledge of circumstances may effect the interest of the U States. When peace takes place and our squadron appears in these waters I may possibly pursue a contrary policy.[23]

Noah never got the chance to "pursue a contrary policy." Yet, during his six-month stay in Tunis, he was able to gather considerable new information on the Jewish community—information which led him to view its conditions more positively. He became particularly impressed at the community's power, estimating that nearly one hundred thousand Jewish males in the Barbary States were capable of bearing arms. He also found that Jews controlled the principal professions:

> They are in Barbary the principal mechanics, they are at the head of the custom-house, they farm the revenues, the exportation of various articles, and the monopoly of various merchandise, are secured to them by purchase, they control the mint and regulate the coinage of money, they keep the Bey's jewels and valuable articles, and are his treasurers, secretaries, and interpreters; the little

known of arts, science, and medicine, is confined to the Jews, there are many who are possessed of immense wealth, many who are poor.

As to the alleged oppression of the Jews, Noah, in his later writings, claimed "that this oppression [was] in a great measure imaginary." By complaining to the Bey, Jews could receive equal justice. Indeed, he found that Jews possessed "a very controlling influence" at court. Their friendship was prized, their enmity dreaded.[24]

Noah used harsher words to describe Tunis's internal Jewish communal life. He denounced unscrupulous Jewish businessmen, deplored the class and ethnic divisions which fragmented the community, lamented the poverty of the Jewish educational system, and remonstrated against the inferior status of Jewish women. Still, he expressed sympathy for his people, and displayed only antagonism toward their critics. Even when Jewish merchants in Tunis flagrantly cheated him, he remained understanding. He only grieved that Tunisian Jews could not yet know of his personal interest in their advancement. Meanwhile, he expressed every confidence that something would be done for his people at the Congress of Vienna. "The period of reform," he optimistically predicted, "will not be far distant."[25]

Noah's voluminous correspondence, and his concern with the Jews of Tunis did not lead him to neglect more typical consular duties. It must, indeed, have been a relief to turn from Jewish affairs to those of America; for while he could at this juncture do little to improve the image of the Jew in the world, he did have the power in a small way to improve the image of the United States. In Tunis, he found this image ingloriously tarnished. At times the Bey acted as if America did not exist at all.

The Curadi affair changed all this. Curadi was an Italian Christian merchant who, when hounded by Moslem creditors, escaped to the American consulate and received Noah's sympathetic grant of protection. He promised to leave as soon as he could sell his property and pay his debts honorably. No ties of citizenship bound Curadi to the United States, but he was on the country's soil, and according to Noah's understanding of diplomatic principle, "no person was ever [to be] given up who had taken sanctuary in the American Consulate." The Bey, who supported Curadi's pursuers, threatened to "cut the Christian to pieces." Noah held firm and prepared his weapons. Seeing this, the Bey relented and agreed to grant Curadi sixty additional days of grace, so long as the American consul pledged himself for the merchant's safekeeping. Noah gratefully agreed. A few days after Curadi went free, however, the Bey lured the merchant to the palace and threw him into prison. Outraged, Noah rushed to the scene and demanded Curadi's immediate release. He angrily threatened to strike the flag and terminate pacific relations unless his demand was instantly met. The threat worked: the Bey issued an order to his servants to free Curadi, and Noah's self-confidence soared.

Years later, Noah boasted that he had "triumphed over the iniquity and bad faith of these wretches, and once more preserved inviolate the rights of the

American flag." It is strange, however, that he did not boast of his great triumph when it happened. Neither in his letters to Monroe, nor in his letters to Warden is this incident mentioned. While it is possible that correspondence might be missing, it seems more likely that Noah had overstepped his bounds in threatening to break relations with an important Barbary nation over a debt-ridden Italian merchant. He may thus have kept his exploit quiet for a very good reason.[26]

The Curadi incident reveals a great deal about Noah's character. On the one hand, it demonstrates his aggressive patriotism, his natural charity, and his unflinching courage. These virtues Noah would carry with him throughout his life. On the other hand, the incident points up less lovely aspects of his personality. He acted with rash impulsiveness, he took unnecessarily large risks, and he often ignored the possibly fatal consequences of his actions. This time, Noah's gamble worked; in later years, he would often prove far less lucky.

Noah always remembered the Curadi affair as his greatest diplomatic victory. In absolute terms, however, the *Abaellino* controversy was vastly more significant. The effect it had upon Noah's career proved more far-reaching. The *Abaellino* was a privately owned, American armed-brig, captained by William F. Wyer, that sailed from Boston to North Africa in order to privateer. Despite the overwhelming British naval superiority around North Africa, the vessel succeeded in capturing the *Nancy*, an English boat heavily laden with dry goods. Proudly, she escorted her captive into Tunis Bay and advertised her cargo for sale. Mordecai Noah, whom the captain employed as his commercial agent, convinced the Bey that the sale was legal, notwithstanding British objections. Before he could savor his diplomatic triumph, however, Jewish merchants allied with the Bey's son (Sidi Mustapha) offered to buy the *Nancy's* cargo very cheaply. Since nobody dared to compete with the crown prince, the offer was tantamount to an order. Much to his disgust, Noah had to sell the *Nancy's* merchandise at a price far below what the shipment was worth. Lacking redress, an understandably angry Captain Wyer secretly transshipped some of his most valuable goods to another vessel. Tunisian merchants, however, easily discovered the fraud, and the Bey demanded strict indemnification. He also barred the sale of any additional ships which the *Abaellino* might capture.[27]

Before Noah could remonstrate, a far more serious provocation took place. The *Abaellino* captured two more English vessels, the schooner *Dutch Castle* and the brig *Charlotte*, and placed them both under the Bey's protection in the port of Tunis. On February 21, 1815, in broad daylight, the British brig *Lyra*, commanded by Dowell O'Reily, forcibly repossessed the two English vessels and sent them back to Malta where they were restored to their original owners. This was a gross violation of Tunisian sovereignty, and an insult to American prestige. Noah, who watched the proceedings from the terrace of his house, furiously demanded forty-six thousand dollars in compensation. On legal and moral grounds, he held the Bey responsible for insuring the security of vessels in his port. Privately, he may have hoped that the Bey would claim the money from Britain. The Bey, however, demurred. The British naturally disclaimed all responsibility. Consequently, Noah responded with a military threat. He assumed, as he had in the Curadi case, that force was the only language the North Africans would understand. To back up his threat, he urged the United States government to send him a squadron equipped to offer the Bey "serious and determined resistance."[28]

Other consuls attempted to achieve their goals through tributes and bribes. They were cheaper than military expeditions and safer, too. Noah, however, believed in powerful American responses. He sided with those who assumed that force made an indelible impression on primitive minds. He feared that America was viewed as a weak power, and treated accordingly. One show of might, he assured Secretary of State Monroe, and the nations of the area would "forever after respect us."[29]

As a Jew, Noah may have been particularly sensitive to the plight of the powerless. He knew well from the fate of his own people what lay in store for the weak and the defenseless. Perhaps for this reason, power fascinated him throughout his life. He always wanted his country to be powerful. He always wanted the Jewish people to be powerful. He always wanted to be powerful himself.

Unbeknown to Noah, James Monroe had independently decided to show America's military muscle. His reasons, however, differed from those of his consul. He was not just interested in commanding the respect of others for the United States. In the wake of the unpopular Treaty of Ghent, he wanted a victory to "raise us in our own estimation." The obvious place for such a morale-building victory was North Africa. Based in part on the intelligence Keene had gathered in Algiers, two squadrons prepared for duty. The President ordered them to obtain the release of the *Edwin*'s crew, and then to exhibit American power around the North African coast.

The first squadron to depart for Barbary sailed under the command of the renowned naval hero (and Noah's reputed formed classmate), Stephen Decatur. Arriving in the waters off Algiers in June 1815, it quickly defeated the overly touted Algerian navy. Decatur then aimed his guns at Algiers, and secured from the Dey a peace treaty. Under its terms, the system of tribute and piracy ended. America collected a large indemnity for past wrongs. Most important, the remaining American prisoners were freed from slavery. (Unfortunately, they all perished at sea on the way home from Algiers.) Decatur then sailed for Tunis.[30]

Mordecai Noah rode out to meet Decatur as his squadron anchored offshore. He was eager to apprise the Commodore of the *Abaellino* affair and of the deteriorating relations between the United States and the Bey. Before the two men began to talk, however, Decatur presented Noah with a sealed official letter from Washington.[31] Noah, to his "great surprise," read as follows:

Department of State, April 25, 1815

Sir,

At the time of your appointment, as Consul at Tunis, it was not known that the religion which you profess would form any obstacle to the exercise of your Consular functions. Recent information, however, on which entire reliance may be placed, proves that it would produce a very unfavorable effect. In consequence of which, the President has deemed it expedient to revoke your commission. On the receipt of this letter, therefore, you will consider yourself no longer in the public service. There are some circumstances, too, connected with your accounts, which require a more particular explanation, which with that already given, are not approved by the President.

I am, very respectfully, Sir,
Your obedient servant,
(signed) James Monroe

Mordecai M. Noah, esquire, &c. &c.

Noah satisfied himself that Decatur knew nothing of the contents of Monroe's letter. He resolved not to enlighten him. Had Decatur learned of his guest's powerless condition, he might have taken control of the consulate and left him to fight his creditors alone; it was a chance Noah preferred not to take. Displaying remarkable inner strength, Noah folded Monroe's letter and proceeded to acquaint Decatur with the *Abaellino* affair. He pressed the Commodore to demand full compensation (forty-six thousand dollars) from the Bey and urged him to remain on board his ship until this demand was met. As it turned out, this was more than mere disinterested advice.[32] It was, rather, part of a well-thought-out strategy which Noah had probably been planning since mid-June, when he first learned that his bills of exchange had been protested and left unpaid by the State Department. Knowing that he would eventually have to return to the United States—but probably never dreaming of recall—the consul strove to pay off his debts in advance. With the compensation from the Bey, which he would receive as agent of the *Abaellino*, he knew that he could satisfy his foreign creditors. He would handle the *Abaellino's* owners—the rightful recipients of the $46,000—when he returned home.[33]

Noah's strategy worked: Decatur and his squadron intimidated the Bey, and Noah received his money. He also received a promise of additional compensation for the amount he lost through the forced sale of cargo from the *Nancy* to the Bey's son. Noah ultimately, however, received only a third of this promised compensation, largely because by the time payment came due, the commodore and his squadron had departed, leaving the consul powerless.

Still, the money he had already received sufficed to pay both the protested bills and his departure expenses. He then sent the remaining portion of the forty-six thousand dollars in compensation to Marseilles to purchase cargo for the *Abaellino*'s owners. Having put his affairs in order, Noah, on September 21, departed from Tunis for France, where he briefed his successor, Thomas Anderson. After a short delay, which he used to compose a strong letter to the Secretary of State, he returned to the United States, arriving in early 1816. Almost three years had passed since he last had seen his native land.[34]

There is no mystery as to why the President recalled Noah. The government was highly dissatisfied with his handling of the Algerian rescue effort—it knew nothing, as yet, about events in Tunis—and it accused him of, among other things, "going beyond orders, employing a most obnoxious character [and] expending the public money unnecessarily." From the government's perspective, Noah's actions mandated his recall. The ex-consul himself privately admitted in 1820 that "the real cause of disapprobation was probably a just one." The mystery, then, is not why the government recalled Noah, but why it hid the "real cause" of his recall. Why did it falsely claim that it recalled Noah because his religion formed an obstacle to the exercise of his consular functions?[35]

State Department prejudice against Jews is not a sufficient reason. Madison and Monroe appointed Noah with full knowledge of his religion. They also appointed other Jews to consulships: Joel Hart won appointment as consul to Scotland (1816–17) and Nathan Levy served as consul to St. Thomas (1818). Furthermore, Monroe's letter of recall made clear that the State Department expected the North Africans' negative view of Jews to cause problems. Monroe never claimed that Jews in general were unfit for foreign service. And, according to existing evidence, the Bey of Tunis neither complained about Noah nor demanded his recall, although he probably knew of his religion.[36] The record suggests, in fact, that he got along comparatively well with Noah— certainly better than with his disrespectful Christian successor who lasted but a short time in office. Perhaps this is not surprising. The Bey, after all, had many Jewish advisors. Nevertheless, the State Department did have good reason to believe that Noah's religion might in the future cause problems. The experienced John Norderling felt that a Jew "was not a fit subject to send to Barbary," while Commodore David Porter warned "that the Turks and other people on the Barbary coast believe that every Jew who dies turns into a jack ass, and that the Christians mount and ride them instantly and devoutly to the devil." But neither of these comments caused Noah's recall. After hearing from Porter, Monroe felt that "the reason for removing him [Noah] is stronger." In other words, the basic decision had already been made.[37]

The government injected the religious issue into Noah's recall notice precisely because the real reasons—those dealing with the secret Algerian mission—could not be put in writing. Monroe told Noah initially that his rescue attempt should "not...be understood to proceed from this government." He could hardly recall Noah for an action in which the government officially took no part. Furthermore, the government did not wish to reveal what it knew about Richard Raynal Keene. Details of his alleged conspiracy were still being gathered. The religious issue formed, therefore, the perfect cover. It was real in the sense that the government really had information to the effect that Noah's religion would hinder his functions. It was also valid since Noah had promised that his Judaism would be an asset ("it constituted one of the prominent causes why I was sent to Barbary"), and, judging from the Algiers mission, it clearly was not. If anything, it had proved to be a liability. The very reason for appointing Noah could thus be used to dismiss him. On April 24, 1815, President Madison himself gave the order: "In recalling Noah it might be well to rest the reason pretty much on the ascertained prejudice of the Turks against his Religion, and it having become public that he was a Jew."[38]

Noah devoted more than a year to the twin tasks of straightening his accounts and clearing his name. He personally remonstrated before public officials; he asked his friends to write letters of support; and he published a pamphlet and a book to justify his claims. Setting a pattern for later Jews, especially his much maligned cousin, Uriah P. Levy, he stressed the broader implications of his insult, and mobilized Jewish notables on his own behalf. In the end his efforts proved largely successful. But, much to his regret, no President ever again invited him to undertake a diplomatic mission.[39]

Noah quite properly first carried his case to the secretary of state. He received a disappointing reception. Monroe, according to Noah, acted curtly and ungraciously. He spread out a bill of particulars and invited his caller to clear up the affair if he could. Noah responded with no better grace: "I had not presented myself to him with that submissive tone, with that 'bondsman key and bated breath,' that he probably expected," Noah later recalled. Instead, he threatened the President and secretary "with a public exposure of their conduct"—a further indication that the government wanted things kept secret—and he promised to take his case to Congress. Noah's threat was not an idle one. He prepared a 128-page pamphlet, *Correspondence and Documents Relative to the Attempt to Negotiate for the Release of the American Captives at Algiers Including Remarks on our Relations with that Regency*, and sent copies to the secretary of state and selected friends, including Isaac Harby, then editor of the *Southern Patriot*. The pamphlet contained relevant documents, a commentary which portrayed the administration and Tobias Lear in a very bad light, and an apologetic conclusion defending the patriotism of American Jews. It might well have hurt the administration politically—precisely the reason that Noah threatened to publicize his pamphlet still further. Defiantly, the State Department professed itself unconcerned with its ex-consul, and briefly opened *Correspondence and Documents* to public inspection. But Noah's friends, both in and out of Congress, feared for "the character and credit of the United States," and urged Noah to suppress his pamphlet. He complied, pending a review of his case, and *Correspondence and Documents* dropped from sight. Letters from Noah's supporters, meanwhile, continued to arrive at the State Department.[40]

Noah's letters of support came from three different groups: foreign diplomats, domestic politicians, and Jews. Diplomats in North Africa had provided Noah with letters to take back home with him. All genuinely lamented his departure, attested to his good character, and praised his valuable service in Tunis. The politicians became familiar with his case only later. Based on the evidence that they saw, however, they freely declared their strong support for his position. John Gaillard, the distinguished South Carolina senator, sent the State Department a particularly important letter in which he declared Noah "incapable of conducting himself improperly on any occassion." Gaillard tried to shift blame for the appointment of Richard Keene ("the charge apparently most relied on") from Noah's shoulders to those of Consul Hackley, the man who had so warmly recommended him. Finally, the State Department received letters from Jewish notables, including Naphtali Phillips and Isaac Harby. They reacted mainly to the first sentence in Noah's letter of recall and strongly attacked the notion (in the words of Isaac Harby) "that Religion disqualifies a man from the exercise of his political functions."[41]

Since Secretary Monroe was running for President, and no doubt did not wish to risk losing potential supporters, he moved in late 1816 to set Jewish minds at ease. He assured Naphtali Phillips "that the religion of Mr. Noah, so far as related to this government, formed no part of the motive to his recall." What had motivated the government, Monroe claimed, were the alleged feelings of the Moslems and Moors against Jews (Monroe was probably referring to the information supplied by Norderling and Porter) and, "a difficulty... in the settlement of Mr. Noah's accounts." Monroe wanted other Jews, especially those in the South, to understand the State Department's reasons for the dismissal. He therefore arranged that they should be approached by a sympathetic Jewish intermediary, Abraham A. Massias. Armed with an explanatory letter—perhaps the Monroe letter to Phillips—Massias endeavored to explain the true meaning of the first sentence in Noah's letter of recall. In the case of Isaac Harby, Massias claimed success: "he is perfectly satisfied with the interpretation...[and] is astonished that N[oah] could have given it any other."[42]

Harby may have been "perfectly satisfied" with the administration's explanation. Most Jews, however, continued to believe that anti-Jewish prejudice lay behind Noah's recall, and nothing more. Noah encouraged this belief. All of his published writings on Tunis pointed to such an explanation, and even when he alluded to other factors, as he did in his book of travels, he devoted to the Jewish aspects of his recall an overwhelmingly disproportionate share of attention. His motives, in retrospect, are obvious. He knew that if people generally believed that the administration recalled him on account of his religion, then he would seem blameless and worthy of sympathy as an innocent victim of persecution. If, on the other hand, the real factors behind his recall became known, he knew that he would not have appeared quite so saintly. In short, both the administration and Noah exploited anti-Jewish prejudice for their own purposes: the former to cover a secret, the latter to mask a failure. Each for a different reason wanted to see the truth hidden.[43]

To the outside world, Noah could mask the reasons for his recall. Noah's creditors, however, knew the truth and did not hesitate to demand payment from the government. First in line stood George Butler, who in 1814 had loaned Noah the money for the Algerian rescue mission. After several angry letters, and some stern threats against the country's already weak credit, Secretary Monroe, in February 1816, agreed to pay Butler's claims and to recover the money from Noah later. Noah, however, had long before sent Butler his money, paying him from funds which Decatur secured from the Bey. Had Butler only known that his money was en route, he might have remained patient and saved Noah considerable grief. As it was, vituperative correspondence flowed until July 1816, when the confusion was finally sorted out, and Butler pronounced himself satisfied.[44]

The satisfaction of Butler's claims did not put an end to Noah's financial problems. Butler, after all, had been paid with money which Noah held as agent for the owners of the *Abaellino*, Winslow and Henry Lewis. They now came forward and demanded from Noah $21,613.06 in compensation. Noah referred them to the State Department; the State Department told them to settle their problems with Noah on their own. Meanwhile, the government froze Noah's salary. Since all sides now felt dissatisfied, Secretary Monroe submitted the entire question to Attorney General Richard Rush for his opinion. Rush responded with a detailed report highly critical of Noah's actions. The Lewises, however, had no reason to cheer. Although Rush called the creditors "meritorious," he told them to pursue their case in court. He carefully distinguished between Noah the "prize agent of the *Abaellino*," who acted—with dubious legality—as a private citizen, and Noah the "ex-consul" who represented the United States. The ex-consul, Rush ruled, deserved his salary. As Noah soon discovered, the salary hardly compensated him for his trouble. After suspending several of his claims, the State Department awarded him a total of but $5,216.57 for three years' work. His potential liabilities remained far higher. Luckily, they also remained safely potential, for the Lewises pressed their demands before Congress rather than before the courts. The new Secretary of State, John Quincy Adams, supported their claims and Congress went along. On January 22, 1818, President Monroe signed the act of relief awarding Winslow and Henry Lewis $16,396.49. The Lewises received about three-quarters of the amount they had originally requested, and pronounced themselves satisfied.[45]

With the settlement of the Lewis case, Noah had every reason to believe that his long agony was over and his debtors mollified. He reacted, therefore, with "extreme surprise" when, in February 1818, he received a letter from Secretary of State Adams demanding "speedy reimbursement" of one thousand dollars for "two years rent stated to have been left in arrear" for the consular house in Tunis. No "speedy reimbursement" was forthcoming; Noah claimed that he had left fifteen hundred dollars with his chargé d'affaires in Tunis, enough to cover all of his debts. Furthermore, he reminded the Secretary that the Bey was "not fastidious in exacting twice payment for the same object." For these reasons, and because he still blamed the administration for not giving him sufficient time to set his affairs in Tunis in order, he insisted that he not "be made answerable for this sum." Secretary Adams did not press the point. Perhaps he felt that the time had arrived to consign Noah's consulship to history.[46]

Mordecai Noah was not quite ready to forget his stint in the diplomatic service. He still sought vindication, and to that end, in 1819, he published what became his most important book: *Travels in England, France, Spain and the Barbary States in the Years 1813–14 and 15*. Noah had been contemplating a volume of travels even before his recall. As he told David Bailie Warden: "I am taking notes for writing a Book which I fear from my limited information and talent will scarcely be worth perusing. I make the attempt, however (?) boldly and with the best views. I wish to add my poor mite to the store of American literature...." Later, he decided that his book should also deal with the "progress and termination" of his consulship. He therefore artfully merged his travel notes with his consulship documents. A curious, fairly well written, and quite entertaining mixture of travel stories, history, and apologetics resulted. The travelogue included all the standard motifs of the genre: injury on the road, a near robbery, and an embarrassing incident (Noah found himself bathing, presumably nude, in a crowded Spanish beach only to discover "that the large party bathing were women." He relates that "they enjoyed the mistake much better than I did"). Noah also rendered judgment on each country he visited. England, he felt, should be considered a "permanent enemy," ever eager "to check our progress or mar our national prosperity." France, on the other hand, left not a single unfavorable impression: "no circumstance...served to lower the respect which is generally entertained towards this country and its inhabitants." As for Spain, he was very critical of its "indolence" and "prejudices." He urged the country to "tolerate all religions; [to] call back the Moors and Jews;" and to free her South American colonies. These were regular Jeffersonian sentiments, and probably evoked no surprise from his readers. Noah's opinion of Islam showed more originality. Perhaps because he himself was a member of a minority religion he proved surprisingly tolerant of Islam, and he went out of his way to praise its virtues. Critical he was, but not scornful. He certainly saw no need to Christianize the Moslems.[47]

When he turned to Jews, Noah was equally original. *Travels* is still the best primary source on early nineteenth-century Tunisian Jewry. It demonstrates critical powers of observation, laudable objectivity, and keen insight. Noah described different sections of the Jewish community, with praise for some of his Jewish brethren, harsh words for others. He blamed Moslem intolerance for many Jewish vices. He pointed out that Jews hungered after money in North Africa because it purchased "protection and toleration." Finally, he suggested that emancipation and mild treatment might make Jews more useful and beneficial. In later years, he would try to test this theory on American soil.

Noah's objectivity disappeared when he began to discuss his own consulship. In these sections of *Travels*, he demonstrated his vast polemical skills. He shaped the narrative to support his own construction of events; only the reader who laboriously waded through his long section of documents could arrive independently at a different conclusion from the one Noah put forth. Still, by focusing attention on the Jewish aspects of his consulship and recall, Noah probably did the Jewish community a favor. The State Department never again openly cited religion as a factor in the selection of diplomats. In later years, it relegated religion to back-room discussions.[48]

The critical reaction to Noah's *Travels* was generally positive. *The American Monthly and Critical Review, Niles' Weekly Register,* the *Evening Post*, and even Noah's nemesis, the *New York Columbian*, praised the volume and reprinted section for the enjoyment of their readers. Several months later, after the book had sold out, the *Columbian* changed its mind. It commenced a month-long vendetta against *Travels* (a particularly assiduous critic counted sixty-seven grammatical errors), one sufficiently vehement to provoke Noah to write a private note of rebuke ot the editor.[49]

Prominent individuals who commented on *Travels* rarely took any interest in the book as a whole. Many, like John Adams and the Irish novelist, Maria Edgeworth, seemed more excited about Noah's religion than about what he had to say. They viewed his book as a sign of Jewish enlightenment. Bey Hassein of Tunis, on the other hand, cared only about *Travels'* characterization of himself and his brother as "base and depraved" men; presumably, he learned of the epithet from an unfriendly consul. Other critics ignored everything in *Travels* save its harsh attacks on President (former Secretary of State) James Monroe. They thought that allegations such as those which Noah leveled smacked of political disloyalty, and they reminded the author that he still belonged to the Democratic Party. Noah, of course, protested his political devotion and professed to harbor no ill will at all toward his President. But, for good reason, nobody believed him. Nor did anybody offer to return him to diplomatic service, despite his many applications. While he continued to correspond with friends in Tunis, and he maintained his interest in the Islamic and Ottoman Empires throughout his life, it was his readers, rather than the government, who chiefly benefited from his expertise.[50]

What was the effect of the Tunis recall on Noah's life? Some argue that the recall heightened Noah's Jewish identity and transformed him from a passive to an active member of the Jewish community.[51] To some extent, this may be true; perceived anti-Semitism has often led to Jewish revitalization. In the case of Noah, however, a strong sense of Jewish identity existed long before Tunis. He had originally applied for the consulate post on the basis of his religious ties. Even while in Tunis, he cherished hopes that in some way he could aid the Jewish community. Thus, the recall did not essentially change Noah, but rather intensified the basic features of his character, and focused all his resources on the effort to clear his name. The recall became a challenge to Noah. He responded by embarking on the most creative and energetic decade of his life. Marriage, money, and sleep became of secondary concern. Noah spent his fourth decade in pursuit of power, prestige, and fame.

Chapter III

National Advocate Years

In his thirty-second year, Mordecai Noah had reached a low point in his life. His hopes for a secure, lucrative, and prestigious diplomatic career had evaporated. He experienced, as many experience in their early thirties, a rock-bottom feeling of worthlessness. He sought to "bust out," to vindicate himself, to prove himself able. In 1817, full of determination, he took up residence in New York. Immediately, he resumed the meteoric rise which his consulship had interrupted.[1]

Sometime in the middle of 1817, readers of New York's *National Advocate* began to notice subtle changes in their newspaper's style. The Democratic-sponsored Tammany Hall journal had become livelier; its columns were more vituperative; and the quality of its writing had improved markedly. By mid-June, the secret of these changes was out: the *National Advocate* had a new editor. The previous editor of the *Advocate*, Andrew Caldwell Mitchell, left no mark on New York journalism. Intellectually, he was an unworthy successor to the founder of the *National Advocate*, the lawyer (later, diplomat and scholar) Henry Wheaton. Unable to attract the kind of attention and circulation which the publisher, Naphtali Phillips, and the sponsor, Tammany Hall, desired, Mitchell soon departed, unnoticed and unmourned. His successor would never suffer from similar anonymity. The new editor of the *National Advocate* was Naphtali Phillips' nephew, Mordecai M. Noah.[2]

Noah quickly succeeded at his new job. Copying a technique he had used in Charleston, he introduced humor and lighthearted articles into his newspaper. He appealed to women with articles on domestic economy[3] and feminine virtues. He spiced political articles with bons mots, caricatures, and satires, including even the elite among his targets. And, he delighted in fierce controversy and scandalous revelations about his opponents.[4]

Competing editors became Noah's favorite targets. Soon after he assumed his editor's chair, he gleefully published a private letter, which he claimed to have found on his desk, in which the editors of the *Poughkeepsie Observer* promised to revile him in return for some patronage considerations from Alden Spooner, editor of the New York *Columbian*. Noah stood trial for breaking open and publishing the letter—it had been addressed to Spooner—and a jury found him guilty. But the court set aside the verdict on grounds of insufficient evidence, and in the public's eye, Noah emerged triumphant. His self-righteous political enemies, on the other hand, appeared hypocritical and vindictive, and ridiculous as well. Meanwhile, Noah benefited from all the publicity.[5]

In his later tactics, Noah similarly tried to woo readers and ridicule opponents. He often, for example, pointed up glaring contradictions between past and present editorial positions of his fellow editors. Once, William Coleman of the *Evening Post* offered him one hundred dollars if he could produce an original copy of an alleged *Post* editorial attacking Coleman's friend, former United States Senator, Dr. Samuel L. Mitchill. To the editor's astonishment, Noah produced the thirteen-year-old editorial and demanded his money. Coleman refused to pay, claiming that the *National Advocate* had not quoted him word for word. But Noah had proved his point; a shamefaced Coleman apologized in print to Mitchill, and explained the incident away. Noah also liked to poke fun at his competitors' general ignorance. In ridiculing a competitor's historical error, he once set off an intricate controversy among several New York newspapers over settled facts of English history. Unfortunately for him, the facts as finally established did not tally with what he had written. Competitors found him wrong, even wrongheaded, at other times as well, and never hesitated to tell him so. But Noah displayed characteristic good humor on these occasions, and often printed their criticisms as corrections. He felt pleased that other journalists read his *Advocate* so carefully.[6]

Noah did not originate his journalistic gimmicks; some had already been employed by Benjamin Franklin. Nor was Noah the only journalist to deviate from a steady diet of dry news. But if he was not unique, he was certainly influential. Day after day, he demonstrated to his fellow editors that a newspaper could broaden its appeal by printing interesting, lively, and entertaining features. Of course, by catering to the "masses," Noah left himself open to charges that he was "indecent" and "profligate." But at least he had the satisfaction of knowing that others rated his paper "more interest[ing] than any other paper in the city." Not even his circulation figures, which had increased, reflected the breadth of his journal's new popularity. As a traveler to New York observed: "everybody reads the *Advocate*—but everybody does not subscribe."[7]

One reason why "everybody" did not subscribe to the *National Advocate* was the *Advocate's* politics. Journalistic tradition, and the high cost of printing required the newspaper to obtain support and patronage from a party or faction. No American newspaper had sufficient resources to declare independence. The *Advocate's* patronage came from Tammany Hall; specifically, the Democratic-Republican Party's Bucktail faction (the bucktail was the symbol of Tammany Hall), which was allied with ex-Governor Daniel Tompkins (Vice-President under James Monroe), and increasingly dominated by Martin Van Buren. In return for patronage, the Bucktails expected editor Noah—whose $1,500 salary they guaranteed—to represent faithfully the views of party leaders. But the ambitious Noah served as more than an ordinary mouthpiece; he also played an important role, both in the Tammany Society and in Tammany Hall.[8]

The Tammany Society had evolved primarily into a social organization by Noah's time, and he could easily avoid divisive partisan politics when in its midst. When, for example, he addressed the society on July 4, 1817, he filled his speech with patriotic platitudes ("America shall rise in all the majesty of freedom and defy the world") and at least one remarkable metaphor ("we have been lifted like a gold column, standing firmly erect, and surrounded by the crumbling fragments of other republics"). But his message was distinctly apolitical—his few polite references to the Irish notwithstanding. He refrained from partisan politics even when he presided over the Tammany Society as Grand Sachem (1824); he did not want the Society to compete with Tammany Hall. In Tammany Hall, however, Noah did express political views. He also took an active role in formulating policy. As John C. Calhoun knew, the editor's "standing with the party in the city [was] such as to make it critical for him to make a bold stand" on issues of importance. But when the majority at Tammany Hall disagreed with him, Noah, as editor, had a problem. He had to struggle between the demands of patrons who wanted him to espouse views with which he disagreed, and the demands of conscience, which urged him to write what he felt. Survival compelled subservience; self-respect demanded independence.[9]

Unfortunately for Noah, his was not a simple battle for freedom of the press; it was, rather, a battle between freedom of the press and subordination to party discipline. The Bucktails and their state leadership (the Albany Regency) placed a premium on party discipline. As the semi-official *Albany Argus* explained, the principle was nothing less than the basis of politics: "the minority yield to the majority—and the result is announced as the will of the whole." Practically speaking, as Mordecai Noah once admitted, the leadership insisted that "private views and wishes must be surrendered." There was an obvious value to party discipline. It prevented fragmentation, and permitted small factions to exercise maximum power. In unity there is strength. On the other hand, absolute discipline seemed antithetical to freedom. Why agree to what one did not believe? In an era which worried about "tyranny of the majority," and in which doctrines of free will gained increasing support even in religion, it is hardly surprising that political organizations had trouble compelling such a high degree of subservience. Only equally strong fears of factionalism and anarchy prevented the political landscape from being further complicated by minority slates and shifting alliances. Politicians foundered on the horns of the same dilemma which confronted journalists: they saw value in party discipline, yet they valued their individual freedom, as well.[10]

Mordecai Noah's effort to grapple with the tension between party discipline and independence can be seen throughout his years at the *National Advocate*. On the one hand, he received orders, or at least strong advice, from Martin Van Buren, Jesse Hoyt, Edward Livingston, and other Tammany stalwarts. He expressed gratitude for the confidence which his party reposed in him, and he called himself "a faithful and zealous servant," "the organ... and not the oracle" of party will. He also asked for patronage. Yet, at other times, Noah lamented the little control he had over the press and he condemned efforts to shackle him. He spoke several times of resigning his post, though not always for reasons of journalistic freedom, and he once expressed interest in editing a commercial paper so that he would not be troubled by politicians.[11]

Noah actually did quit his editorial position in September 1824, and discipline was one reason why. Henry Eckford, one of the wealthiest men in New York, had obtained a financial interest in the *National Advocate*, and demanded "that he should have the right of deciding, whenever he thought proper to exercise it, on the character of the editorial matter." Noah demurred and resigned; he only agreed to return temporarily with the stipulation that "no editor... can submit to have his independence shackled, or his pen paralyzed by politicians of a day, by designing speculators, or intriguing censors of the press." The words sounded pious, and Noah may actually have secured an important guarantee against prior censorship. But his newspaper never became totally free; nor were other New York papers, though each editor proclaimed his own freedom and condemned his competitors as hirelings. Indeed, even after the growth of advertising and circulation permitted newspapers to emancipate themselves from political control, total freedom did not result. The press remained bound by the demands of businessmen, subscribers, and patrons. Journalists stretched permissible bounds, but flouted them only at their peril.[12]

As a political organ, the *National Advocate* functioned much like a modern-day party whip. It flayed opponents, lay down and defended party policy, and prodded straying politicians into line—at times antagonizing them in the process. Noah did not always agree with party policy, and occasionally he breached discipline with oblique references to his own views. But most of the time, Noah, the Bucktails, and the *National Advocate* adhered to a common platform. Certainly, they all fought against the same political enemies.

Enemy number one, as far as the Bucktails were concerned, was De Witt Clinton. Clinton (1769–1828) had been a force in New York politics since the 1790s, when he entered the public arena under the wing of his uncle, George Clinton. The younger Clinton was an intelligent man and a master organizer. He was also, in the words of a recent critic, "snobbish, spiteful and supercilious... forbiddingly aristocratic." He possessed alluring talents, and at various times in his career he attracted great support. But his haughty and vindictive personality, as well as his repeated flirtations with discredited Federalists, repelled many of those whom his talents attracted. In New York City, Clinton met opposition from Aaron Burr and his followers, as well as from an unstable group of disaffected politicians (including Naphtali Phillips and Mordecai Noah), many of whose requests for patronage he had denied. By 1817, these opponents had coalesced into a faction. They found an unofficial leader in Martin Van Buren.[13]

Martin Van Buren (1782–1862) was younger than Clinton, and lacked his polish and status. But he had great personal charm, a remarkable organizational ability, and an incomparable mastery of politics. It was he who organized New York State's Democratic machine, and it was largely through his efforts that party discipline was promulgated and enforced. During the course of his long career, Van Buren was at various times both friend and foe of Mordecai Noah. Never, however, were the two so friendly as when Noah edited the *National Advocate* and followed Van Buren's directions. Noah printed his mentor's speeches, praised his legislative actions, and offered to perform "any service" Van Buren might require. When, as editor, he criticized Clinton, he expressed Van Buren's views as well as his own.[14]

The *National Advocate*'s attack on Clinton was multipronged. First, as he had in 1812, Noah associated Clinton with despised organizations and symbols. He called Clinton a Federalist, a dictator, and an aristocrat, and he attempted to stigmatize him with the obloquy heaped upon politicians associated with the "traitorous" Hartford Convention. As far as Noah was concerned, Clinton belonged in another party; he was not a Democratic-Republican of the Bucktail mold.[15]

In attacking Clinton in this way, and in provoking counterattacks, Noah was consciously or unconsciously helping to define Bucktail identity. The Bucktail faction was still small in 1817; Clintonians were popular, and despite several setbacks, they continued to command considerable support. Noah's roaring charges helped bring the Bucktails to public notice. Equally important, Noah used his attacks on Clinton as a foil, a negative reference point around which Clinton's opponents could rally.

Personal differences, more than policy, divided Bucktails and Clintonians. Clinton's faction inclined more to Hamiltonian notions of government activism; the Bucktails pledged strict allegiance to Jeffersonian views of a limited government. But each group freely borrowed from the other whatever rhetoric and platforms proved popular. Each faction regularly accused the other of deviance and betrayal, and claimed for itself the mantle of true democratic principles.[16]

In addition to his attacks on Clinton's personal and political history, Noah attacked Clinton's gubernatorial record. He devoted special attention to two issues—the grand [Erie] canal and constitutional reform—and in both cases, he unwittingly demonstrated that expediency and opportunism were the rules of New York's political game. Noah had actually once proclaimed, "all's fair in politics." Sanctimonious politicians often reminded him of these words, and he always maintained that he had been quoted out of context. But he had spoken the truth. His four words could have been the credo of all major New York politicians.[17]

The grand canal was De Witt Clinton's pet project.He did not originate the idea; in late 1815, however, he adopted it, nurtured it, and after much debate, maneuvered it through the legislature. By the time he died, just ten years later, everyone realized that the canal was his greatest achievement, a turning point in the history of both New York and the nation. Mordecai Noah, in 1817, could not have known this. As an opponent of Clinton, he began with a prejudice against the canal. As a fiscal conservative, his suspicions were only heightened. Of course, he was not alone in his suspicions; Thomas Jefferson and James Madison both viewed the canal as impractical and visionary. In New York, however, Clinton's project found widespread approval. New York City Bucktails were almost the only dissenters. From the beginning of Noah's editorship, by which time the canal had been approved by the legislature, until early 1818, scarcely a week went by in which the *National Advocate* did not learnedly "prove" that the canal would take many years to build, would cost far more than planned, and would yield disappointing revenues. By alerting the public beforehand, Noah may have helped to prevent some of the very evils which these predictions of doom foresaw. In the end, however, every one of his gloomy prophecies proved wrong. Clinton's rosy predictions, on the other hand, were more than borne out.[18]

Tammany Hall began to realize its mistakes as early as 1818. In August, Noah admitted to his readers that he "had not written anything about the canal for many months," and assured them that "we have our reasons for it." Eight months later, he finally conceded that "we have been in error." He would repeat the mea culpa for many years to come. Although he admitted his error, Noah was not prepared at this point to give Clinton his due. Politics was the art of the possible, and the Bucktails thought it just possible that they could take credit for the success of the Erie Canal and reap the resulting rewards at the polls. Consequently, Martin Van Buren maneuvered the legislature into appointing a Bucktail majority to the canal commission. Meanwhile, Noah printed stories (actually, fairytales) alleging that Governor Clinton never believed that the canal project would succeed, and that only Bucktail vigilance prevented him from halting the canal project altogether. In 1820, Noah even went so far as to suggest that Clinton should be thrown off the canal board as "punishment." Happily for Noah, this rash advice was ignored. Unhappily for Tammany, the same advice, from a different source, was heeded four years later, although Clinton was by then out of politics, and was serving on the canal commission at no salary.[19]

In 1824, Noah realized the folly of removing Clinton. He was bold enough to hint at his opposition to such a measure, party discipline notwithstanding. He trod carefully, saying only that the proposition "seems to be better understood in other parts of the state than it is here." But he clearly realized that the public would sympathize with Clinton and would vent its anger at the faction that persecuted him. He was not surprised when the voters called Clinton back to politics and returned him to the governor's chair by a wide margin of votes. Still, Tammany had succeeded in securing for itself partial credit for the canal project. When the canal was dedicated in 1825, the ceremony involved all New Yorkers, even the canal's former opponents.[20]

Clinton's triumphant return as governor occurred just three years after Tammany had exuberantly proclaimed him politically dead. Well attuned to public opinion, and a strong advocate of progress while he was fighting for the canal, Clinton had taken a narrow and conservative position on the question of changing New York's outmoded constitution. In a move that had cost him dearly, he had opposed popular calls for a state constitutional convention.

The 1819 depression and burgeoning democratization had heightened demands to amend New York's constitution, written in 1777. Mordecai Noah, who had been agitating this issue on his own for two years, became a leader of the new movement, and he called on the Clintonians to join the Bucktails in strengthening the executive by abolishing the inefficient Councils of Appointment and Revision.[21] He also called for universal white male suffrage (he opposed black suffrage) via the abolition of all property qualifications in voting. Clinton, realizing that broader suffrage would aid the Bucktails, pronounced the constitutional convention a Tammany trick. He proceeded to play into Bucktail hands by thwarting popular will and vetoing the legislature's convention call. A year later, the convention took place anyway, but so strong was the backlash against Clinton that of 126 elected delegates, only three were Clintonians. The result was predictable. Tammany-sponsored reforms were instituted, and a more democratic constitution was created. Clinton wisely decided to retire at the end of his term.[22]

Mordecai Noah had good reason to be pleased at these results. Reforms he advocated had passed, and his party had reached the peak of its power. He also had one reason to be terribly displeased: among the offices which were transferred from the Council of Appointment to the electorate was the office of sheriff. Since he held that post, Noah would have felt more secure knowing that it was a patronage position controlled by the governor. During the convention, he had vigorously editorialized, much to the amusement of his critics, that his position was "too delicate, difficult and responsible... to be dependent on the popular voice." But Tammany was afraid of alienating the public if it arrogated to itself too many patronage positions, and it required Noah to submit. He would later suffer the consequences.[23]

In dealing with the convention, the canal, and other, more minor issues of the day, the *National Advocate* assumed that New York had "but two parties": the Bucktails and the Clintonians. To be sure, this was an oversimplification: the Bucktails and Clintonians were factions which pledged allegiance to the Democratic-Republican Party; the Federalist Party still clung tenuously to life, numerous small factions simmered below the surface. For propaganda purposes, however, Noah found it easier to talk of a two-party system composed only of friends and foes. Such a two-party party system, he believed, was, anyway, in the process of being born. He predicted that "Federalism, Clintonianism and Burrism will be united against the democracy of this state," and he expressed confidence that "the democracy"—by which he meant the Bucktails—would emerge victorious. He was wrong. With the demise of the Federalist Party, American politics entered the "Era of Good Feeling"—a complete misnomer—and all politicians affiliated themselves with the Democratic (or Democratic-Republican) Party. Since politicians continued to disagree, and since there was no competing party to absorb opposing sentiments, fragmentation became inevitable. Both in New York and in the nation, the Democratic Party degenerated into a collection of competing factions, each demanding Democratic patronage (and receiving it, much to Noah's and the Bucktails' disgust), and each supporting different personalities, principles, and presidential candidates.[24]

The first new faction to enter the Democratic ranks was a group known as the King Federalists, a faction of the Federalist party led by New York State Senator Rufus King and his sons. Under terms of a deal struck with Martin Van Buren in Albany, the Kingites agreed to support a Van Buren man (Horatio Seymour) for the canal commission, and Van Buren agreed to arrange for King's reelection to the Senate. Naturally, Van Buren expected his followers to toe the line, but New York City Bucktails remained suspicious. They could not forget the many battles valiantly fought against King Federalists, battles against strong central government and Negro rights, and they wondered how the public would view their sudden about-face. Mordecai Noah was torn between his patrons in Albany and his patrons in New York City. The *National Advocate* floundered, much to the amusement of its critics, and in an enormously revealing letter, Noah described to Martin Van Buren the fierce pressures weighing upon him:

> You know the temper & feeling of our members...they do not appear to be disposed to use their influence to oppose the election of Mr. King [,] they seem to think it adviseable to act without concert leaving to each individual the responsibility of acting as he pleases—they fear the charge of inconsistency & coalition & what may grow out of this step in the state & throughout the Union [.] They all unite in advising me not to advocate in an open and direct manner the choice of Mr. King although it will be necessary to defend & even applaud the measure if adopted—I am in a dilemma.[25]

Noah's dilemma was not eased by the Kingite decision to publish a newspaper, the *American*, and to demand patronage from Tammany Hall. The *National Advocate*'s financial picture looked sufficiently bleak without a competing newspaper siphoning off circulation. Nor was he pleased by King's strong antislavery stance in the Missouri Compromise debate. Despite Van Buren's positive assurance that King's stance reflected "no [anti-slavery] plot," Noah remained convinced that the Senator secretly planned for "the erection of a northern party, the triumph of federalism, or the separation of the nation." Still, the suspicious editor recognized the benefits of the King alliance, and for three years he laid himself open to the charge of inconsistency by vainly attempting to cater to all sides. In early 1823, the Kingites solved his dilemma by breaking with Van Buren and nominating their own candidates. Freed from restraints, Noah began to attack these ex-Federalists with all his might.[26]

The King faction broke with Martin Van Buren partly because it wanted to take an independent stance in the presidential election of 1824. The field was wide open to contenders. James Monroe, despite urgent pleas from Noah and others, had studiously avoided naming his heir apparent. Van Buren and his followers decided to support William Crawford, the Secretary of the Treasury. Crawford maintained that he deserved the nomination, since he had been promised it in 1816 by Monroe supporters. But Monroe had many enemies in 1824, and he made no effort to back his treasury secretary, promise or not. Consequently, Rufus King's candidate, John Quincy Adams, as well as John Calhoun, Henry Clay, and Andrew Jackson, also found supporters in New York, and many of their supporters were Bucktails. Soon, each candidate headed a faction represented by its own newspaper. Every faction but Crawford's eventually met strong criticism from the pen of Noah. Noah called Adams a sectional candidate with friends who "avow principles fatal to the safety of our country." Calhoun, he believed, was not "old enough, prudent enough, republican enough," or popular enough to be elected. He thought Clay might be "a very prominent member of the next administration," but he doubted that he had the popularity or the qualities to head the ticket. As for Andrew Jackson, Noah, using words he would later rue, called him "the most likely [both] to involve the country in war by an impetuous and unrestrained temper, and to establish a MILITARY DESPOTISM."[27]

In response to the plethora of candidates, Noah satirically suggested himself for President: "I have a great notion to offer as a candidate for President myself; it is time that there should be a Jew President; it would be unanswerable proof of the perfect freedom of our political institutions... I should make a good President." On another occasion, he spelled out in the *National Advocate* just what his "creed in national affairs" would be:

> Democratic Republicans in power; no taxes in time of peace; no loans; no sinecures; moderate salaries; no extensive army; a limited and respectable naval force; all unnecessary offices abolished; accountability of public agents; no extravagant appropriations; the national expenditures to be limited to the national income; simplicity of habits, manners and customs among the public men; no court etiquette; people to be the sovereigns; the constitution the supreme law of the land.

Needless to say, he was joking. Ambitious as he was, he did not delude himself into believing that a Jew could be elected President of the United States. Even in his day, Jews exercised more power through appointive offices than through elective ones. But both Jews and non-Jews invoked, in seeming wonder, the myth of a Jewish President. Only in America, they proudly proclaimed, did a Jew have the right even to suggest himself for the nation's highest office. By raising the possibility, albeit in a jocular vein, that a Jew might exercise this right, Noah pointed up the gap separating myth and reality in Americans' view of the Jew. Many of the rights offered Jews in theory, seemed shocking indeed when discussed in a practical way.[28]

In satirically advocating a Jewish President, Noah conveyed the message that political currents were changing, and that "anything" was possible. But he did not himself support these new currents. He condemned the breakdown in party discipline, and called for a return to the rule of Martin Van Buren. Interestingly, he himself was not immune from the same spirit of independence which he so criticized in others. In 1821, he tacitly supported efforts to build a new bank in the upper wards of the city, although members of his own party opposed the move. He publicly claimed that the issue was not political, and that no breach of discipline was involved in his action. He then proceeded to work behind the scenes for the election defeat of his Bucktail opponents, including state assemblymen Michael Ulshoeffer and Samuel B. Romaine. Noah evinced particular hostility toward New York Assembly Speaker Peter Sharpe, whose congressional bid he not-so-privately opposed, and when Sharpe lost his election, he blamed Noah, and helped to organize an unofficial anti-Noah clique. The clique accurately charged Noah with wishing "to dictate the whole policy of [the] party," and with confusing party discipline and self-interest. But the clique could as easily have declared itself guilty on the same charges. Like Noah, it wanted to be independent itself, and wanted to invoke party discipline against others. The anti-Noah coalition proved a formidable force. It was to demonstrate its power when Noah ran for sheriff in 1822.[29]

Noah's interest in the sheriff's post went back to 1820. He was impelled by the same motives that had impelled him to seek the consulship at Tunis: he needed money, he lusted for power, and he craved status. Because of his poverty, Noah had been named official city printer in 1818.[30] But as he discovered, that post entitled him to no special monopoly. A year later, he lost the job altogether. Since Tammany won control of the Council of Appointment in 1820, he quickly began to lobby for the far more lucrative shrievalty. According to his own claims, "many rich merchants and old republicans" supported his application. Yet, he was concerned enough by reports of opposition to write to Martin Van Buren. The Clintonians, of course, opposed Noah. Their press, the *Columbian*, wondered out loud whether "Shylock," if appointed, would "exact the penalty of the law." Bucktails finally won the day, however, and on February 13, 1821, the Council of Appointment voted Noah into office.[31]

As sheriff, Noah spent much of his time collecting debts and watching over debtors. He had for years opposed New York's harsh laws on debts, but the abuses he saw as sheriff ("the whole female troupe of prisoners, confined in a single room, with poor accommodations, and at a cold season of the year, had altogether contracted debts amounting to less than four hundred dollars") shocked him, and inspired him to undertake new efforts to abolish debt imprisonment and to extend the 150-acre limit, beyond which unimprisoned debtors could not travel. He later claimed to have played an instrumental role in securing laws to protect female debtors, and in organizing an association aimed at helping those whose debts were small. (One debtor languished in prison for want of eighteen dollars.) Yet, Noah's most impressive action as sheriff undoubtedly occurred during the yellow fever epidemic. As citizens scurried to escape from the city, he bravely searched out creditors, beseeching them to allow their debtors to flee to safer terrain. Eventually, he threw open the jail doors and, on his own responsibility, allowed debtors to run away. Apparently, many of them never came back. By law, Sheriff Noah had to make good these losses to creditors. His benevolence cost him several thousand dollars.[32]

Noah's benevolence was lost on Peter Sharpe, Benjamin Romaine, and their anti-Noah clique. They had tried to oust Noah from his sheriff's post before the yellow fever epidemic, but without success. Knowing that under the new constitution the shrievalty would be elective, they planned more carefully. First, they tried to prevent Noah's nomination. When that failed, they flouted party discipline and took the unprecedented step of nominating an opponent to Noah (the "regular candidate") from within the faction, after someone extinguished the candles at the Tammany Hall nomination meeting. To forestall criticism, Noah's opponents declared the original nomination for sheriff null and void. They then put forward their own nominee, Peter H. Wendover, as the official Tammany candidate. The ensuing election was as bitter as any known in New York, and is probably unequaled in its gross and public display of anti-Jewish prejudice. Just before the election, the *Evening Post* reminded readers that Wendover was "an old member of the church." It ruminated on the "venomous satisfaction" with which Noah would "give the last pull" on the legs of "any Christian ever to be brought to the gallows." "Pretty Christians to require hanging at all," Noah reputedly replied.[33] As the three-day election progressed, and Noah's support in the Jewish community became evident, the *Commercial Advertiser* cried with alarm that, on the second day, "the Jews prevailed against the Gentiles." Everyone realized that the last day of the election would be the crucial one.[34]

With the election in doubt, all normal restraints vanished. Other candidates at such times found themselves reminded of old scandals. Thomas Jefferson, before election day, used to be reminded of his connections with slave Sally Hemings. Noah was attacked as a reviler of Christianity. On the night before the third day of the election, the *Evening Post* printed excerpts from *Israel Vindicated*, an anonymous pamphlet issued in 1820 to oppose the then newly formed missionary society, the American Society for Meliorating the Condition of the Jews. Editor William Coleman of the *Post* probably did not know that *Israel Vindicated* was principally authored by a non-Jewish freethinker named George Houston. He certainly had no evidence that Mordecai Noah had a hand in the polemically anti-Christian pamphlet (although the possibility cannot be ruled out).[35] What Coleman as a publicist did know was that the pamphlet contained politically explosive material. It mocked believers in the resurrection, called parts of the New Testament "forged," and questioned the very existence of Jesus. The book also attacked directors of the American Society for Meliorating the Condition of the Jews, among them Peter Sharpe and Peter Wendover. Editor Coleman blamed all Jews for *Israel Vindicated* and warned against "abuse" of their "privileges" by "open and outrageous attacks upon the religious faith" of the community. Christians heeded the call. As Noah described it: "Churchmen, Sextons, Bell-ringers [and] Deacons...of the Church Militant scoured the wards to oppose what they called the unbeliever."[36]

Noah was not silent in the face of this anti-Jewish campaign. He protested against "religious prejudices" and "illiberal distinctions," and assured readers that he had "not been wanting in what are called Christian principles." As the election progressed, Noah lamented that "the war has become a religious one...the words now are, Jew and Christian." He warned against this "foolish crusade" and reminded New Yorkers that prejudice could be directed at many groups: "persecute a Jew today and the next day, you will commence with a Catholic and the third with a Quaker." But his warning fell on deaf ears. Noah lost the election, receiving only about 41 percent of the vote. The defeat, as the *New Jersey Eagle* observed, was "produced by a violent, covetous and persecuting spirit of religious intolerance."[37]

Noah pardoned his enemies ("in the spirit of good Christian frankness"), and hoped that all would "forget and forgive." He had learned, or perhaps relearned, that beneath the veneer of American tolerance lay a considerable layer of anti-Jewish prejudice. In theory, a Jew could be President; in practice, he faced grave difficulties in attaining any office at all. Jewish "control" over Christians was more than many Christians could accept. Of course, antipathy to Jews did not motivate everyone who voted against Noah. Certainly some opposed him for personal or political reasons, and others felt that journalists should not run for public office. But religion probably made the difference in the campaign. It surely was the public issue most relied upon by opposition candidates. By "forget and forgive," the disappointed Noah hoped to return New Yorkers to earlier conditions of tolerance, unstable and uncertain as he knew them to be.[38]

Before forgetting the election, Reverend Pascal Strong, the recording secretary of the American Society for Meliorating the Condition of the Jews, wanted to draw a final lesson. In a sermon on the causes of the 1822 yellow fever epidemic, delivered after the election, he declared that "a spirit of political feeling at war with the authority of God" was one of the public sins that provoked God's "judgement." An example of the evil spirit, as he saw it, was the sight of "men of high consideration and influence, maintaining, and publically abetting the election [another source heard "nomination"] of an infidel in preference to a Christian." Rightly or wrongly, Noah and many other New Yorkers believed that they knew the identity of the alleged infidel. "We are no infidels," Noah thundered at Strong, thinking, no doubt, of the many he had saved and the aunt he had lost in the epidemic. He then suggested, among other things, that Strong learn "to comprehend the benign principles of religion generally." The *New York Statesman*, with less reserve, termed Strong's comments "monstrous absurdities." Strong said nothing more on the subject, and, temporarily, the veneer of tolerance reasserted itself.[39]

Noah's election defeat forced him to turn elsewhere in search of funds. He had grown, he claimed, "much poorer," and he worried that his debts might end him up in the "good keeping" of Sheriff Wendover. When Moses I. Cantine, state printer and co-editor of the *Albany Argus*, died suddenly, Noah thought that he had found a way out of his problems. Within a few days of the funeral, in late January 1823, he began lobbying for Cantine's job. Had Noah been prepared to share the position with Isaac Q. Leake, as Cantine had done, he might have had his way. But Noah forced a showdown between himself and Leake, threatened to "exhibit the system of peddling away the patronage of the State" if he lost, and alienated many with what others viewed as arrogant demands. Michael Ulshoeffer lobbied against Noah, and Martin Van Buren apparently opposed him as well. Consequently, he suffered renewed defeat, and he found himself left "without office or patronage." The *National Advocate*'s financial straits, to say nothing of Noah's, became worse. "An effort must be made to assist us," he wrote to Azariah Flagg in Albany; otherwise, he warned, "we shall not be able to sustain ourselves."[40]

One way Mordecai Noah struggled to make ends meet during this period was by writing. He wrote a book, he wrote plays, and he wrote articles. His literary productivity is staggering, and much of his anonymous writing has probably still not been discovered. Unfortunately, his writing brought him limited financial reward. Americans in his day accorded their writers considerable status, but miserably inconsiderable remuneration. Only an occasional commissioned work brought to an author the compensation he deserved.

Noah had long been interested in helping to create a native American literature. After the War of 1812, his desire for cultural independence was strengthened, as it was in America generally. Freed from England militarily, Americans felt that they should be culturally independent as well. The best way to encourage native writing was with a journal, and Noah helped to found one: *The New York Literary Journal and Belles Lettres Repository* (1819–21). His role in this magazine is not known, but a letter reveals that he solicited articles for the first issue ("on any subject except Politics and Religion"), and was interested in contributions from those attached "to the Literature of our Country." *The New York Literary Journal* received good reviews. It lasted two years and then expired for lack of money.[41]

Noah also produced his own contributions to native American literature. Of greatest importance was his *Travels in England, France, Spain and the Barbary States in the Years 1813–14 and 15* (1819). That work of description and apologetics completed, Noah returned to his first love: the drama. In the next four years, he produced four full-length plays. Unlike his earlier plays, which were slightly altered versions of European dramas, he now wrote only on American themes: the American Revolution, the war with the Barbary States, the War of 1812, and the American effort to aid the Greek struggle for liberty. Each of his plays was highly patriotic, each employed a standard motif, often from a French drama (Noah's favorite was the woman who disguised herself as a man in order to achieve her own ends[42]), and in keeping with the fashion of the day, each play closed with a melodramatic ending. Interestingly, not one of his plays contained a Jewish character. Jews did appear in early American drama, but with one minor exception, only in the plays of non-Jews. Fearing charges of parochialism, Jews tended to prefer nationalistic themes. By demonstrating their patriotism, they felt perhaps they could better serve their people's long-term interests.[43]

Noah's feature plays proved uniformly popular. Stilted and trite by today's standards, they nevertheless drew large crowds for many decades. They rank among the most important native dramatic productions of the antebellum era. Under the influence of Noah and his fellow playwrights, Americans broadened their dramatic horizons. They learned that their countrymen could offer them serious drama. They discovered, to their surprise, that episodes in American history were as suitable for the stage as events in the history of Greece, Rome, and England.

Noah wrote the first of his four major plays, *She Would Be a Soldier, or the Plains of Chippewa*, in June 1819, for the benefit of actress Catherine Lee Sugg. The play dealt with a famous land battle in the War of 1812—he was the first to dramatize an 1812 land battle—and employed his favorite "woman in breeches" motif. In the spirit of the day, Noah concluded his piece by telling Americans to "feel toward Britain as freemen should feel towards all the world: *'Enemies in war—in peace, friends.'*" He also introduced onto the stage a remarkably benevolent Indian, one brave enough to criticize the white man's encroachments, and educated enough to speak perfectly standard English. The play won critical acclaim.[44]

The success of *She Would Be a Soldier* may have inspired Noah to return to the stage a year later with a play based on the war against Barbary. *Yusef Caramalli, or the Siege of Tripoli* combined the former consul's personal knowledge of Barbary with standard patriotic fare, an expensive and original set of props, and his most complicated plot. The result was a play which some considered his best—a judgment which cannot be affirmed, since, unfortunately, the text has not been preserved.

Reviewers particularly noted the last scene in *Yusef Caramalli*, the grand ballet. Unfortunately, on the second performance of the play, the grand ballet gave way several hours later to a grand inferno. Nobody was hurt in the fire, but the Park Theater was utterly destroyed. Such tragedies invariably brought out the best in Noah. He immediately returned the $405.72 which he earned from his benefit performance (the only benefit Noah ever was tendered), and asked that it be distributed among the actors and actresses, "corresponding with their losses and wants." Noah's action brought him abundant, well-deserved praise. But his own losses and needs only increased.[45]

From the Barbary wars, Noah, in 1821, turned his playwright's talents to the American Revolution. He agreed to produce a play for New York's Evacuation Day (November 25), and wrote *Marion, or the Hero of Lake George,* perhaps his most enduring drama. Unlike most Revolution plays, this one ignored battle scenes and dealt with an insignificant war hero. The basic theme was not freedom from tyranny, but the domestic struggle between conflicting allegiances—the family internally divided between patriots and tories.

Marion redirected attention to an important but neglected aspect of the Revolutionary War. Advance publicity, and the human appeal of the story, drew an opening night audience of over two thousand. A long and successful run seemed assured. Delighted, the munificent theater managers presented Noah with a pair of handsome pitchers. Only William Coleman of the *Evening Post* complained. He called *Marion* "wretched stuff" and claimed that most of the audience came only because they had received free tickets. Coleman, who had not seen the play himself, was wrong. With delicious irony, Noah dedicated the printed version of *Marion* to him, "without permission!"[46]

Noah had reason to know about ironic dedications. Two years earlier, an anonymous playwright had dedicated the second edition of *Wall Street, or Ten Minutes Before Three* to him ("the stern Solon of dramatic productions") in recognition of the pan he had given to the first edition of this work. Noah was unimpressed and panned the second edition as well.[47]

Noah's last major play, and the last of his plays to be published, was *The Grecian Captive, or the Fall of Athens.* Noah wrote the piece as a benefit for his uncle, the actor Aaron Phillips, and he based his play on the French drama *Mahomet II.* As with his other adaptations, he made liberal changes from the original version. Instead of captured Venetians in Constantinople of 1470, he wrote about captured Athenians in Turkish-held Athens of 1820. The tyrant Mahomet he transformed without any difficulty into the tyrant Ali Pacha. He also inserted two new characters: Alexander Ypsilanti, in the play as in real life the heroic leader of the Greek forces, and Burrows, an American officer. Along with a great many other Americans, Noah saw the continuing Greek struggle for independence as a "just and holy" cause. In his play, the first play to deal with this theme, Noah made the frigate *United States* a vital contributor to the Greek victory.[48]

Noah tried two experiments in *The Grecian Captive*, and both failed ignominiously. First, he distributed printed copies of the play to all members of the audience, an action which embarrassed and angered the actors who hadn't had time to learn the words. Then, he made use of live animals. Unfortunately, the elephant, perhaps as a fitting commentary on the play and its errant actors, introduced what one of the performers later called "an unexpected hydraulic experiment." The play closed amid great confusion, and Noah blamed himself for imprudence.[49]

After the *Grecian Captive* fiasco, Noah added nothing more of importance to American drama. He did write a few short interludes—among them, *Oh Yes! or, the New Constitution*, *The Siege of Yorktown*, and *The Grand*

Canal—but these were one-time presentations commissioned and paid for by impresarios to commemorate specific events. *Oh Yes* feted New York's constitution (on May 4, 1822); *The Siege of Yorktown* honored Lafayette's visit to the city (September 8, 1824); and *The Great Canal*, perhaps Noah's atonement for past folly, celebrated the waterway's dramatic completion (October 18, 1825). Many years later, aided by his cousin Jonas B. Phillips, Noah wrote *Natalie or the Frontier Maid* (1840), a piece composed expressly for the French ballet star Celeste. According to a playbill (the play was not published) the plot dealt with "two prominent events in the history of the American Revolution."[50]

None of these later dramatic writings revealed even the limited creativity which Noah had demonstrated in his major plays. He attempted no more innovations in themes and props, and no more adaptations of French dramas. He left to others the task of creating a national literature. Meanwhile, he turned his attention to other things.

Noah abandoned creative drama mainly because of his perilous financial situation. His plays, as he wrote, added "a trifle to my reputation and nothing at all to my fortune." He promised his public better plays when he found a publisher who "will give us one thousand guineas for a work". No publisher ever offered him anything near that amount. The American theater became less fashionable in the late 1820s, as "lower classes" began to visit playhouses more often. At the same time, a new form of escape, the novel, rose in popularity. Novelists faced fewer literary constraints than dramatists; they worried neither about staging nor acting. Furthermore, novels could be read at home, in private. Both writers and readers, therefore, preferred them. Imports, which were then unprotected by copyright, discouraged all forms of literary creativity in America, even novels. Nobody would pay Mordecai Noah a thousand guineas for a work when English works could be produced free, without paying any royalties whatsoever.[51]

If Noah gave up writing serious drama, he did not give up reviewing it. Indeed, he was later remembered as "the finest theatrical critic of the day in America." In his early years, he spent a considerable amount of time puffing his actor uncle, Aaron Phillips—without, of course, mentioning the family connection. He later became one of the great supporters of British actor Edmund Kean. Unlike many Americans, he was able to praise the actor's genius even while condemning less lovely aspects of his character. Noah's most important critical discovery came in 1825. Visiting Charles Gilfert's Pearl Street Theater in Albany, he saw a performance by a young actor named Edwin Forrest. He was impressed, and advised Charles Gilfert "to make a long engagement with him, and by all means increase his salary." Gilfert promptly complied, and shortly thereafter, Noah, Gilfert and other theater enthusiasts made Forrest a star at New York's Bowery Theater. In later years, Noah actively encouraged new actors and playwrights, led the drive to build New York's Metropolitan Theater, helped arrange innumerable benefit performances[52] and continued to visit the Park Theater "as regularly as the actors themselves." He also delved into other arts, writing occasional, usually unilluminating criticisms of music (especially Italian opera), dance, and literature. Somehow, he even found time to encourage fledgling authors like John Holt Ingraham, John Townsend Trowbridge, and a host of lesser knowns. Perhaps he could help so many because he kept his critical principles so simple. He strove to encourage anything which made people "happier, fuller of pleasure and so better and wiser."[53]

Noah's efforts to increase popular happiness and wisdom extended beyond the realm of criticism. In his early years, particularly, he publicised new inventions, championed a variety of municipal reforms, and advocated social improvements. He originated very little. His expertise lay rather in propaganda and political pressure.

Noah's interest in new inventions is hardly surprising; a newspaperman is perhaps the most likely person to be interested in things that are new. As for his readers, they were probably attracted to anything which revealed the "native genius" at work, even if the work merely involved the importing of a British innovation. Noah therefore reported on new types of pumps, mechanical chimney sweeps, and machines for street cleaning. He often described advances in printing and communications. He urged the spread of gàs lighting, and later, gas cooking. In short, he reported with delight that there was "no pause, or stop to the inventive genius of our countrymen."[54]

Noah took particular interest in inventions and ideas designed to improve the health of New York City. Like other American cities, New York was a center of disease and pestilence. It fell prey every few years to plagues of yellow fever and cholera. Many debated loudly, uselessly, and at excessively great length, whether epidemics came in from outside the city, or originated in the city's crowded slums. Noah wisely concluded that both sides in the argument had merit; "Let both avenues," he urged, "be guarded." One way of guarding the city internally was to ensure that the city had a fresh supply of water. In the early years, Noah advocated canals and cisterns as a solution to the water problem. In 1824, he brought to the attention of the mayor and the Common Council "a new invention for boring the earth for pure water [which] has been in successful operation in England for the last three years." He had procured drawings, "made several improvements upon them," and hoped that the city would suspend other projects while it hunted for water with the aid of the new machine. Apparently, the machine failed in its task. By 1835, he fully supported a measure to bring water to New York via aqueduct (the Croton Aqueduct System). He also supported other public health measures: the proposal to pave the streets, the proposal to pay street sweepers, and the proposal—opposed by the churches—to ban burials within the city limits. Despite his conservatism on fiscal and religious matters, and despite his fears of government activism, Noah advocated change when "public necessity requires it."[55]

Public necessity also lay behind Noah's support of non-health-related municipal reforms. He recognized that New York was growing, and so were its problems. Solutions that had worked in colonial days proved no longer serviceable. As a well-traveled outsider, armed with knowledge of different cities in different parts of the world, Noah had an unusually wide perspective on urban ills. For this reason, he often advocated policies that ran ahead of their times. In 1816, for example, he called for a reform of the watch system. He urged the city to divide watchmen into precincts, to organize "specific beats so no area would be unwatched," and to professionalize the force with hierarchies, badges, and salaries. In effect, he proposed a modern police force. Unfortunately, New York retained its more primitive system until 1845. Strangely, Noah had little new to say about a more serious urban ill, fires. On the other hand, he was ahead of his time in opposing the peculiar New York custom of ending all tenement leases on May first—a custom which wreaked great hardship on the poor. He was even further ahead of his time in advocating widespread insurance coverage to protect city residents.[56]

Noah did not believe that every one of New York's problems required some new solution. Many city ills, he thought, could be solved if people only enforced existing laws. As a good citizen, he did his part when he served as foreman of the New York Grand Jury in 1820. His report to the city advocated a few reforms—a paid police force, a juvenile workhouse, and less easily counterfeited money—but he basically urged greater vigilance and harsher punishments. At the same time, in his newspaper, he demanded more humanitarian treatment of prisoners. He suggested improvements in prison conditions, and he condemned corporal punishment, debt imprisonment, excessive jail terms, and even capital punishment. Like his countrymen, Noah was unsure how to balance the deterrent and reformatory aspects of the penal system. But he wanted as many criminals caught as possible.[57]

Noah did not believe that criminals were innately vicious. Along with many Americans, he held a benevolent view of man; even criminals, he thought, could be redeemed. One way to prevent a great deal of crime, he realized, was through employment. He therefore urged the able-bodied to work with their hands in small "manufactories." He feared that large industrial monopolies might do more harm than good. Noah also noted that New York suffered from a great shortage of mechanics and servants. He suggested that young men and the unemployed look to these fields; too many, he thought, hoped to enter the legal profession and were disappointed.[58] Still, Noah knew that manual labor alone could not prevent crime. He therefore urged New Yorkers to improve their social climate by refraining from smoking, cursing, and excessive drinking. He encouraged everyone to give charity to the unemployable. Even the rich, he exhorted, should practice parsimony, abstain from ostentatious funerals, and avoid indebtedness. Debt was of special concern to Noah, perhaps because he was personally so familiar with it. On one occasion, he even suggested that New York City sell a park as an example of its resolve to live within its means.[59]

If Noah could not appreciate the contribution of parks to a social environment, he at least understood the vital role of education. He therefore urged greater support for free public schooling, in spite of the burden it placed on the city's budget. He also lent considerable assistance to the library set up by the Society of Mechanics and Tradesmen for the benefit of its apprentices. When the society dedicated its library in 1822, and again when it rededicated its enlarged library in 1850, it invited Noah to speak. On both occasions, he reiterated that manual labor, education, and good habits were "a sure investment... against idleness and want."[60]

Noah must have served as an excellent role model for the apprentices of the Society of Mechanics and Tradesmen. Like them, he had begun life as a lowly apprentice. Through hard work and will power, he had quickly risen to formidable heights in New York society. Contemporaries saw him as the "most conspicuous among the editorial brotherhood of New York," and as "a man of considerable talents and great responsibility." All praised his wit, and those who knew him intimately praised his "open handed benevolence" as well. Yet, Noah never quite escaped his lowly origins. "A Tammany Man" attacked his lack of "delicate polish." Samuel Jencks of the *Nantucket Inquirer* sneered at the "slovenly sort of pungency" which edged his humor. Others noted his lack of modesty, his love of money, and his unbridled ambition. The *Columbian* once even attacked him for having "no ties of family or property." Noah, in short, was middle-class. He strove to enter the upper class, but he lacked the money and the demeanor. Despite his formidable array of civic achievements, he failed to gain full acceptance among the urban elite. In a sense, he was a marginal man. He felt ties to workers and laborers, yet he lectured them with the air of one who had succeeded. He attended the theater with the social elite, yet he depended for his livelihood on the good graces of Tammany Hall. Professionals, highly skilled workers, and small businessmen, many of them members of the Society of Mechanics and Tradesmen, understood Noah's position. Together with him they formed a middle class unsure of its identity. In one respect, however, Noah differed even from most of his middle-class peers. He boldly, proudly, and publicly proclaimed himself a Jew.[61]

Mordecai Noah's contemporaries, especially those who opposed him, thought that his religion was newsworthy in itself. Journalists wrote about his Judaism even when he was only a fledgling in Charleston. Following his own example, they then played up the religious aspects of his recall from Tunis. Once he became an editor, they magnified his Judaism into a national matter. From 1816 on, competitors and political enemies ensured that "Noah" and "Jew" were connected in the public mind. Noah could have denied his religion, married a non-Jew, and even converted. Instead, he capitalized on his ascribed status and strove to be recognized as the leading Jew in the United States.

Noah was not the first journalist to be attacked by his enemies for being Jewish. A Pittsburgh journalist, John Israel, who was at most of Jewish extraction, suffered from anti-Jewish slurs in the election of 1800. Similar slurs plagued Naphtali Phillips even before Noah took over as the *National Advocate*'s editor. Neither man, however, faced more than occasional attacks. Noah found his religion maliciously attached to his name throughout his editorial career. Often he was merely "Noah the Jew"—"the Jew," for short. Others reviled him as "Shylock" and taunted him about his "pound of flesh." Still others actually wrote his religion into his proper name by calling him "Moses Manassah." To outsiders, his religion became an inseparable part of his identity. Many editorial writers, in fits of anger, overstepped the bounds of name-calling. One parody had him saying "go to the synagogue and hear me address the people." Another employed a supposedly Jewish dialect to have him beg for "de monish." An even more sinister New York *American* election poem "quoted" him as admitting "I do loathe with holy hate the Christian dogs." After the fact, newspapers occasionally apologized for anti-Jewish slurs. The *American* once asked its readers to excuse "the manner in which we have been compelled to conduct the discussion for some days past." But even this kind of oblique statement was very rare. More often, newspapers denied that they had ever printed anything offensive at all.[62]

Mordecai Noah nevertheless took offense. Soon after he assumed control over the *Advocate*, he struck back at a slur in the pro-Clinton *Columbian* by reminding its editors that many Jews supported Governor Clinton, and that anti-Jewish attacks could prove "bad policy." He went on to suggest that the Clintonians attacked Tammany on the score of religion because they could not "put them down by facts and reason." A few months later, he began referring to William L. Stone, then editor of the *Albany Gazette*, as "Mr. Moses Manassah Stone." He pointed out correctly that "the name belongs to him as much as it does to me." But Noah soon changed his tactics. Although he continued to defend American Jews, he stopped worrying about most of the anti-Jewish attacks directed against him personally—except, as in election campaigns, when the attacks became unusually vehement. Instead, he used the publicity given his religion to propel himself to a leading role in the American Jewish community. He left it to his enemies to make him the most famous Jew in the United States. He then transformed this fame into communal leadership by employing the same energy, ambition, and drive which had made him a leader in journalism, drama, and politics.[63]

Congregation Shearith Israel provided Noah with a platform from which to launch his quest for Jewish leadership. It invited him to give a discourse at the consecration of its new synagogue building (the "Second Mill Street Synagogue") on April 17, 1818. In his oration, Noah cast himself in the role of a knowledgeable and experienced leader, enlightening and gently prodding his people—whom he addressed as "we"—all the while looking over his shoulder to gauge the reaction of the outside world. He instructed his people as to their own history and condition, traced Jewish rights in every country, and concluded, patriotically, that "OUR COUNTRY [is] the bright example of universal tolerance, of liberality, true religion, and good faith." America, he told his audience, was the Jewish people's "chosen country"—at least until Jews could "recover their ancient rights and dominions, and take their rank among the governments of the earth." In passing, Noah mentioned hatred of Jews, which he blamed on ignorance and jealousy. But he expressed more interest in Jewish survival and the future of the Jewish people. For Jewish survival, he credited a divine miracle. The ultimate destiny of Jews— "restoration of the Jewish nation to their ancient rights and dominion"—he similarly left in God's hands. Jews' immediate future, however, he willingly accepted as his own personal concern.

Noah's advice to his people was similar to the advice he gave to all Americans. First, he told them to undertake "useful" manual labor, preferably agriculture. Next, he advocated education. Finally, he admonished his people to the need for "constant attendance and strict adherence to the forms and ceremonies of our religion." Noah was by no means the appointed minister of Shearith Israel. With the death of Gershom Seixas, a layman, Moses Levi Maduro Peixotto filled that role. Still, the aspiring leader had pretensions. He did not fail to remind his audience that his great-grandfather, David Mendes Machado, had officiated as their pastor seventy years earlier.[64]

Shearith Israel promptly printed Noah's address, and had it widely disseminated. Noah himself sent copies to American dignitaries, and at least three of them, John Adams, Thomas Jefferson, and James Madison, sent him warm letters of reply filled with liberal statements about Jewish rights.[65] Noah, by this action, set a precedent, and it is safe to assume that the publicity he received heightened his status in both Jewish and secular circles. The publicity may also have prompted Jacob de la Motta, a highly cultured Jewish doctor, to send his consecration address (for Congregation Mikve Israel in Savannah, Georgia) to Jefferson and Madison two years later.[66]

Noah's consecration address, and the response to it, helped convince America's non-Jews that Noah spoke for the Jewish people at large. Judah Zuntz, a prominent New York Jew, lamented the fact that "Mr. N. is desirous to be at once constituted sole representative of the Jews in the U.S." He knew that American Jews would never have elected him to such a post. But non-Jews believed what they saw, and Noah did nothing to dissuade them. From 1819 to 1826, he lobbied strenuously in his paper for passage of the Maryland Jew bill, the bill to repeal the test oath that barred Jews from public office and legal practice in Maryland. He also defended David G. Seixas, the son of Rev. Gershom Seixas, when he was dismissed from his teaching post at the Pennsylvania School for the Deaf and Dumb. The *National Advocate* claimed that religious reasons played a part in his dismissal. Other battles which Noah fought on behalf of his people included the battle to eliminate explicit identification of Jews from articles on local criminals (no newspaper ever mentioned the religion of Christian criminals), and the battle to make Thanksgiving a day for all religions, not just "all denominations of Christians."

Noah, however, was not limited to the role of apologist. He also answered questions about Judaism, and once even ventured an opinion about an "ancient Hebrew medal discovered in Cork."[67]

As the self-appointed voice of the Jewish people, Mordecai Noah had to be careful. His, after all, was a political paper, not a religious one, and he could not risk alienating his Christian readers. The plight of German Jews, Maryland Jews, or oppressed individual Jews aroused New Yorkers' sympathies. Even if other newspapers did not join him on these issues, they did not disagree with him. All major New York journals claimed to favor religious liberty. When it came to discussing missionaries, however, the Jewish editor found himself on much more treacherous ground. Many distinguished New Yorkers supported the American Society for Meliorating the Condition of the Jews, and in the early 1820s, the society was extremely popular. Consequently, Noah trod carefully.

In 1817, while missionary efforts were being discussed, and before an official society had been chartered, Noah devoted a long article to an attack on missionary efforts in Russia. He told British and Russian missionaries that they would "gain nothing" by "encouraging apostacy and seducing the poor man by promise of reward." Only the "hypocrite and unprincipled" would convert, he maintained, and he claimed that such a person would still "be at heart the same devotee to the religion in which he was born and educated." Noah may have been writing about Russia, but it seems likely that he was writing for people much closer to home. He employed a very similar tactic when he gleefully reported on Sir Manasseh Lopez, a British M.P. who converted to Christianity, and later faced conviction on charges of bribing electors. Noah became slightly more bold in 1823, when reports surfaced that Joseph S.C.F. Frey, the chief missionary to the Jews, had applied very little of the money he collected to charitable purposes. Reprinting an article on this subject from the *Richmond Enquirer*, Noah introduced it with a paragraph in which he carefully attacked Frey rather than the society which employed him. Further emboldened, he later reported on the Jews' Society's annual meeting in 1823. "No disposition was made of the money," he wrote ominously; he then wondered out loud how Unitarian John Quincy Adams (whose presidential bid Noah opposed) could in good conscience serve as first vice president of a society dedicated to missionizing.[68]

Noah did not feel free to express his feelings about missionaries openly until 1826. In that year, the American Society for Meliorating the Condition of the Jews, now greatly reduced in popularity, began to squabble internally. A year later, it would suspend most of its operations. Noah attended the fateful 1826 annual meeting of the missionaries, and he laced his account of the event with caustic sarcastic comments about misappropriation of funds, lack of converts, false piety, and immoral tactics. He also revealed some important details about the origin of the American Society for Meliorating the Condition of the Jews back in 1820:

When the bill to incorporate this society was before the Legislature, the title was the *Society for Evangelizing the Jews*. I was at Albany during the session, and my friend, Mr. Ulshoeffer [later a political rival], wished the title altered, from delicacy towards me. He probably thought that while the party had a Jew for their political editor, it would be rather ungracious, under his very nose, to pass an act converting him to Christianity. If he was an efficient politician, as a Jew, it was a moot point whether that political acumen would be sharpened by his con-version—and actually to save my feelings, the title of the bill was altered to an act for "*Ameliorating the Condition of the Jews*." A very indefinite title indeed. I protested against it, and urged the honest and candid avowal of the real object, namely the *Society for Evangelizing the Jews*; but they overruled me.[69]

The fact that the legislature overruled Noah demonstrates that it attached vastly more significance to Noah, the symbolic Jew, than to Noah, the Tammany editor. In the eyes of legislators, the Jewish editor represented the Jews generally. With him watching, they could not bring themselves to sanction a society dedicated to the chosen people's evangelization. Whatever he said, Noah perfectly well understood his own symbolic importance. He knew that he served as a living demonstration of Jewish "potential," health and well-being. For this reason, he made a point of attending annual meetings of the missionary society. Merely by his presence, without saying a word, he challenged much of what the missionaries stood for. But Noah, who had refused to be the passive voice of Tammany Hall, certainly did not content himself with being the living symbol of the American Jewish community. He actually had great plans of his own for "meliorating the condition of the Jews." Before he could launch these plans, however, he faced urgent political battles. His party was in turmoil.

Noah's defeat in the 1822 election for sheriff taught New York politicians an important lesson. They could challenge the regular candidate of Tammany Hall and defeat him. With most New Yorkers now allowed to vote, factions discovered that they could more easily than before win elections by propa-ganda and chicanery. Like the Bucktails in the previous decade, new factions renounced party discipline and struck out on their own. All the while, they piously claimed that they aimed only to return to pristine democratic values. Fortunately for regulars like Mordecai Noah, the minority factions in Tammany Hall disagreed with one another, followed different leaders, and supported different presidential candidates. Unfortunately for the regulars, by 1823 the factions had a common enemy. They united in their hostility to presidential candidate William Crawford and to the old caucus system of nominations which, they feared, would make him the official Democratic standard bearer. The anti-Crawford factions proposed a new selection system. Instead of having the New York State legislature choose electors, and a national caucus of Democratic congressional delegations choose a party nominee, they called for conventions where popularly elected delegates would make all choices. The convention idea had popular allure: it seemed more democratic. It thus proved the perfect issue around which to rally Tammany insurgents. They made the most of the opportunity by calling themselves The People's Party.[70]

Noah's reaction to the convention issue and the People's Party demonstrates anew the conflict between party discipline and self-determination. Noah had long favored democratic reforms such as those embodied in the New York State constitution. He hated to antagonize public opinion. On the other hand, he had committed himself to William Crawford. He recognized, with Martin Van Buren, how valuable the caucus system was both to his candidate and to his party. He also, of course, received money from Bucktail supporters. As a result, for the most part, he toed the line. He strove valiantly to convince his readers that Federalists plotted the convention scheme to "break up the republican party." He promised that even if someone other than Crawford received the caucus nomination, "it will be our duty to support him." He engaged in lengthy polemics against all those who violated party discipline—especially Charles Gardner's pro-Calhoun *New York Patriot* and Charles King's pro-Adams *New York American*.[71] He even once argued that as a "real friend of the people," he did not "think it would be safe to give them all they ask."[72]

Yet, as the 1823 election approached, Noah for a while agreed to "follow public opinion," and he supported changes in the caucus system. According to contemporary rumors, his private support for the "people's issue" was even greater. The Bucktails lost the election in spite of these efforts. The so-called "dictation of Moses Manassah Noah" played a role in their defeat. The next year saw no improvements in the fortunes either of the Bucktails or of Noah. On the state level, the caucus–convention dispute continued to dominate politics, much to the disadvantage of caucus supporters. The ouster of De Witt Clinton from the canal board only further eroded Bucktail strength. To make matters worse, the Bucktails were divided over their choice for a gubernatorial candidate. Not all the losers proved as ready as Noah to submit "for good of party." On the national scene, prospects looked equally bleak. William Crawford's presidential chances plummeted as fast as reports spread of his ill health. In the summer of 1823, he had suffered a paralytic stroke which his supporters successfully kept quiet for months. But by 1824, with his recovery in doubt, many Bucktails began the search for a new candidate.[73]

The declining fortunes of the Bucktails and William Crawford had their effects on Mordecai Noah. Like his party and his presidential candidate, he too plunged from a former position of power and influence. By 1824, he had lost his source of outside income, and had forfeited considerable political influence. Faced with competition, rising costs, and declining patronage, he seemed about to lose his *National Advocate*, as well.

What temporarily saved Noah from bankruptcy was the Bucktails' reluctance to suffer change. Just as they continued to support the old caucus system, and, after too little soul searching, they continued to support the presidential ambitions of the ailing William Crawford, so the Bucktails continued to support the *National Advocate*. Shipping magnate Henry Eckford and a coalition of other wealthy New Yorkers[74] undertook to finance and manage the paper. Meanwhile, bankrupted publisher Naphtali Phillips was prematurely retired to a sinecure in the Custom House.

Noah and Henry Eckford soon quarrelled. Noah claimed that Eckford wanted to take over the *National Advocate*, and that he therefore treated him coarsely and censored his writing. Eckford claimed that Noah leaned toward De Witt Clinton (a Jackson supporter) and the People's Party, and that he therefore had to be restrained from altering the political course of the *National Advocate*. Eckford had money and owned title to the *National Advocate*. Noah resigned and promised to set up a competing journal. The Bucktails' enemies enjoyed the spectacle.[75]

Although each side in this dispute fought bitterly, both agreed to subordinate their differences to the higher needs of party. For his part, Eckford transferred the *National Advocate* to party regulars. Noah responded by agreeing quietly to resume his editorial chair—at least until after the election. The Bucktails had again forestalled any change, but by maintaining the status quo, they merely ensured their own defeat. Clinton and the People's Party—the latter somewhat weakened by a schism—won the day, and took over the state. In the New York legislature's subsequent presidential caucus, John' Quincy Adams won a large majority. These dismal results spelled the end for Mordecai Noah. On December 8, 1824, the *National Advocate* was sold. The new owner, Thomas Snowden, disliked editor Noah and did not renew his contract beyond the end of the volume (December 14). Two days later, Noah, along with his assistant, E. J. Roberts, set up an independent and competing journal, the *New York National Advocate*.[76]

Noah switched to the *New York National Advocate* at a time when both he and his party were on the wane politically and financially. Both found themselves out of office and out of favor. This reversal should not obscure Noah's progress during his seven-year stint on the *National Advocate*. His pen and his audacity had made him famous. But he had not come nearly so far as he had hoped. Nor did his immediate prospects appear encouraging. Consequently, he declared his independence from the Bucktails. He freed himself to bargain with all factions, and hoped to return to the limelight in an improved political and financial position. He also cherished another means of returning to center stage. He had a plan which he thought would prove lucrative, would bring status, power, and publicity his way, and would benefit multitudes of people in New York, America, and the world. He called the plan "Ararat."

Chapter IV

An Asylum for the Jews

Throughout modern history, proposed Jewish colonies have aroused both excitement and rage. Proponents—Jews and Christians alike—have advocated self-governing Jewish communities as solutions to the "Jewish problem," and as harbingers of the millennium. Opponents have viewed the same colonies as impractical dreams and as barriers to emancipation and integration. Mordecai Noah strove, characteristically, to reconcile these positions. Visions of a meliorated Jewish condition and dreams of a coming millennium did not blind him to the patriotic duty owed his native land. His was rather a grand effort to save the world, promote America, develop New York State, improve the Jewish condition, and aggrandize himself—at one and the same time. Noah saw no contradiction between efforts to promote simultaneously both Jewish self-government and subservience to American law. He never understood why Ararat, like all colonies torn between the Scylla of separatism and the Charybdis of assimilation, was doomed to fail.[1]

From early on, advocates of Jewish colonization had directed their attention toward America. The leaders of London's Bevis Marks synagogue made an unsuccessful effort to set up a Jewish frontier colony as far back as 1734. In 1750, an impoverished Scottish nobleman named Alexander Cuming had a more ambitious plan: he proposed settling three hundred thousand Jewish families in "the Cherokee Mountains." Unsurprisingly, these eighteenth-century schemes, as well as innumerable others, never got beyond the talking stage. Only in the nineteenth century did colonization efforts receive new impetus. In 1807, the first Jewish agricultural colonies in southern Russia were formed. A decade later, Lewis Way, the distinguished English churchman, also actively involved himself in efforts to colonize Jews in Russia. Outside the Jewish community, Catholics, Irish, Germans, and various utopians planned colonies for themselves in North America. At the same time, the American Colonization Society began to advocate colonies for

American Negroes in Africa. In short, all over the western world, reformers came to view colonies—especially, but not exclusively, American frontier colonies—as the best solution to the problems posed by minority, deviant, and oppressed groups. Rather than attempting to create an equitable pluralistic state, they proposed to create insulated communities where each individual group could flourish on its own. Many Jews found the idea alluring.[2]

In America, a myriad of proposals for Jewish colonies emerged in the buoyant, self-confident years which followed the end of the War of 1812. The country's underdeveloped areas seemed like the ideal place for Jews to settle. Moses E. Levy tried to induce Jews to migrate to Florida, where he owned vast tracts of land. Samuel Myers of Norfolk, Virginia, privately advocated a broader immigration–colonization plan, one which involved the frontier areas west of the Mississippi. William D. Robinson, a Christian, later publicly advocated a very similar project in his *Memoir Addressed to Persons of the Jewish Religion in Europe on the Subject of Emigration* (1819). Even The American Society for Meliorating the Condition of the Jews put forward a colonization scheme. Unlike other planners, however, the missionaries designated their colony primarily for converts.[3]

Mordecai Noah's proposal was in many respects similar to these other colonization efforts. He, too, advocated Jewish immigration from Europe and settlement in a religiously homogeneous agricultural colony. He too sought to send Jews to underdeveloped areas of the country. But he went beyond the other plans—he was familiar with them all—and undertook practical steps to bring his program to fruition.[4]

On January 16, 1820, Noah laid before the New York legislature a petition requesting that it survey, value, and sell him Grand Island in the Niagara River to serve as a colony for the Jews of the world. The petition seemed extraordinary: why not merely ask to buy the land? He certainly did not need legislative approval to turn it into a colony. But Noah sought maximum publicity for his plan, and as a journalist, he knew that only the extraordinary won attention. He may also have remembered the fanfare generated by a similarly grandiose project, the Grand Canal plan, filed a few years before by De Witt Clinton. Like Clinton, he may have hoped that his project's favorable publicity would redound to his own political advantage. Unlike Clinton, he did not have to worry about the legislature's fiscal conservatism. His plan required no state money at all. Still, he clearly hoped, although he was not overly sanguine, that the state would present Grand Island to him free of charge.[5]

The legislature initially reacted with caution. Various unfriendly members of the select committee which handled the bill opposed offering "preferences to any sect," fearing that "Dutch, Swiss, French &c. might wish similar assistance." Others warned that Christian–Jewish separation would be harmful. But Michael Ulshoeffer, chairman of the committee, along with several of his colleagues, expressed sympathy for the persecuted Jews in Europe—he had anti-Jewish riots in mind—and suggested a bill that simply transferred Grand Island to Noah in a normal way. The colonizer could then do with the island as he wished. As Ulshoeffer saw it, the sale of Grand Island was "a desirable object." The state had purchased the 17,381-acre island in 1815 from the Indians, and had watched idly while it filled up with squatters. In 1819, at considerable expense, the eight-mile-long island had been cleared. The squatters, however, threatened to return, and new battles loomed. Noah's proposal promised to solve the problem once and for all. Unfortunately, Ulshoeffer's "desirable object" soon faced an insurmountable barrier. Britain claimed ownership of Grand Island and demanded its return. The resolution of this diplomatic wrangle was left to a boundary commission; meanwhile, Noah's petition languished and died.[6]

Noah did not give up on his efforts to find what he termed a "New Jerusalem" for his brethren. Palestine, he thought, was not the answer, since many Jews "would not inhabit [it] if they recovered it tomorrow." Buoyed by the support of Christians who, a contemporary Jew (Benjamin Hart) observed, "wish[ed] the plan well," and called Noah "the Messiah of the Jews," Noah set out to find an American home for his coreligionists. He searched for a place where Jews could both own property in their own name, and enjoy the rights and privileges which "they [did] not possess in any other part of the globe." By December, Noah had decided that Newport, Rhode Island, was "the most eligible spot for Jewish emigrants." In an article in the *National Advocate* (December 1, 1820), he extolled its "harbor inferior to none in the Union," its "remarkably healthy" climate, and its moderate cost of living. He also reminded Jewish readers that the city had served as "the residence of respectable Jewish merchants" in colonial days, and that it still contained "a very spacious place of worship."[7]

Noah had apparently taken to heart the words of critics who attacked his plan claiming that "the Jews are not cultivators." In Newport, agricultural activities were unnecessary—indeed, impossible; Jews would have to live by commerce and industry. Noah had also apparently taken to heart the criticism of, among others, Isaac Harby (later famous for his effort, in 1824, to modify Jewish religious practice in Charleston's Beth Elohim synagogue) who felt that Jews should assimilate into the mainstream. But, while Noah agreed that Jews should "spread themselves over the Union and be amalgamated with other citizens," he still insisted that Jews maintain their separate identity as a people. He stressed that his was an effort to promote both identity and integration, and he correctly pointed out that other American groups maintained the identical set of goals:

> I certainly do admit that Jews should live among Christians and by thus mingling together endeavour to allay prejudices and become familiar with each others virtues; but even in extensive communities they form distinct associations—In fact all other religions do the same, and this establishment was only intended as a rallying point.[8]

Noah thought that Newport, even more than Grand Island, could further his dual objectives. Since it was a city, Jews could both mingle with non-Jews and remain distinct at the same time. But Newport offered potential immigrants none of Grand Island's major attractions. The city showed no signs of recovering from the devastating effects of the Revolutionary War, which had destroyed its port, and it therefore harbored only limited prospects for aspiring businessmen. Furthermore, the European Jews most interested in America were precisely those who sought agricultural careers. Struggling for emancipation, they fervently wished to disprove the canard that Jews were "unproductive" and unwilling to work with their hands. By becoming, as Noah suggested, American merchants and traders, they would be reinforcing the very stereotype which they so desperately wanted to refute. The original choice of Grand Island, which was poised at the mouth of the soon-to-be-completed Erie Canal, was a far better place for a colony. It offered both trade and agricultural possibilities, and promised a good return on investment. With Newport, Noah had no hope of success at all. Wisely, he did not pursue the plan.[9]

In order personally to stimulate Jewish immigration, Noah again sought a lucrative, secure, and prestigious consular post. He asked specifically for a post at Vienna; he offered, however, to accept any position which might help him to further his colonization project. He aimed to help his fellow Jews and to help himself at the same time. But his application fell on deaf ears, probably because his past diplomatic experience had not been forgotten. Stymied on all sides, he had no choice but to abandon his project, at least until a more favorable opportunity arose. Meanwhile, his plan piqued the interest of a group of young Jews in Germany.[10]

The first, somewhat confused reports of Noah's colonization ideas appeared in the *Koblenzer Anzeiger* of July 2, 1819. After Noah petitioned the state legislature in 1820, other German newspapers picked up the story. In the wake of the anti-Jewish *hep hep* riots, proposals for Jewish colonies abroad received much public attention. At least some Jews evinced interest. The *Verein für Cultur und Wissenschaft der Juden*, an association of young Jews in Germany dedicated to Jewish cultural development, discussed Noah's Ararat plan on April 30, 1820. Gerson Adersbach, a member of the society, boldly proposed that contact be made with the "educated, well reputed and patriotic man." But discussion was deferred. The subject of emigration from Germany proved too controversial for the fledgling and ardently patriotic organization. In late 1821, Noah's project was again discussed, this time by *Verein* member Eliezer Kirschbaum, who considered the planned colony a harbinger of the messianic era. Fearful that Noah might abandon his project for lack of European support, the *Verein* members, after some debate, agreed to elect him an extraordinary member of their organization. Delighted by their action, Noah, in 1822, printed his letter of appointment in the press. Neither he nor his readers knew that idealistic young Jews in their twenties had authored the letter. These men, like Noah, felt dissatisfied with Jewish conditions. Some even had visions of creating a brighter Jewish future. Despite what Noah thought, however, the *Verein* members were not, in any sense, leaders of

German Jewry. Nor did the *Verein* letter represent the kind of European Jewish mandate which Noah, in his ignorance, imagined.[11]

In spite of *Verein* recognition, and in spite of the boundary commission's 1822 award of Grand Island to New York State, Noah devoted almost no further effort to his project for the next two years. Presumably, his earlier experience had chastened him. Besides, local affairs occupied all of his energies. What finally roused him to action was the legislature's decision, in April 1824, to survey and sell Grand Island. Eager to purchase it, but short of means, Noah set out to find financial backing. General Peter B. Porter, an investor in nearby Black Rock, a hero of the War of 1812, and later Secretary of War, refused to finance the undertaking by providing the ten thousand dollars Noah needed—despite Noah's assurance that the sale of lots on Grand Island would yield "a princely fortune." Other New Yorkers found the opportunity more to their interest. By the time the sale took place, in June 1825, some of "the most spirited and enterprising" investors in New York State found themselves competing with one another for the land. Samuel Leggett represented Noah in the bidding and purchased land directly on his behalf. Eleven other merchants and lawyers—among them Jacob Barker, Levi Beardsley, James O'Morse, Alvin Stewart, John B. Yates, Archibald Mc-Intyre, and Peter Smith—speculated either for themselves or on behalf of a proposed private high school. In the end, Leggett managed to obtain 2,555 choice acres on the eastern shore of the island, for which he paid $16,985. The entire area brought in $76,230, considerably above the already somewhat inflated $50,000 value which Noah and Buffalo officials had earlier placed on the land.[12] On November 19, 1833, Noah wrote to New York State Comptroller Azariah Flagg: "Will you have the goodness to inform me how many acres I purchased in Grand Island[?]" The answer, unfortunately, is not extant, but the question demonstrates that Noah did purchase some Grand Island land, frequently cited reports to the contrary notwithstanding.[13]

Grand Island having been purchased, Noah now set about trying to induce "Jewish bankers or any wealthy and respectable persons of that denomination" to immigrate. Hearing that Churchill Caldon Cambreling, a wealthy one-time mayor of New York, was about to travel to Europe, Noah enlisted his aid in the effort "to induce the enterprising to embark in the project." But Noah knew that, in order to succeed, he needed far more publicity than that. Aided and advised by E. J. Roberts, his associate on the *New York National Advocate*, he commenced a vigorous promotion campaign for Grand Island. He also announced advanced plans for "suitable masonic, military and religious" dedication ceremonies. Shrewdly, he scheduled these exercises to take place just before the statewide observances celebrating the completion of the Erie Canal. He wanted as much attention as possible for his own project.[14]

Noah set out for Buffalo on September 8, accompanied by Abraham Benjamin Seixas, a nephew of his teacher, Shearith Israel's Reverend Gershom Mendes Seixas. With the aid of Isaac S. Smith, a friend and local resident, they made final preparations for the ceremony, arranged for a cornerstone, and issued invitations. Too late, they discovered that "a sufficient number of boats could not be procured in time to convey all those to the island who were desirous of witnessing the ceremony." Consequently, they shifted the ceremonies to St. Paul's Episcopal church, the only house of worship in Buffalo, and the only hall large enough for the expected crowd. The newly arrived rector of St. Paul's, Addison Searle, was acquainted with Noah and agreed to assist him. He likely knew that a precedent existed for lending his church to non-Protestants; four years earlier, St. Paul's had been lent for a worship service to Catholic families.[15]

The third day of the Hebrew month of Tishre, September 15, dawned brilliantly.[16] Cannoneers fired a rousing salute. The aged Seneca Chief, Red Jacket, came ashore. Crowds of spectators, most of them women, gathered to watch Noah's performance. The crowds hoped for good theater; they craved melodramas with exotic settings, impressive pageants, jubilant excitement, and holiday festivity. Noah, the accomplished dramatist, did not disappoint them. Resplendent in a Richard III costume, complete with a gold medallion neck chain—all lent by the Park Theater—Noah assumed his role as "Judge of Israel," and led a long procession from the masonic lodge to the church. There on the communion table lay the cornerstone, crowned with silver cups of wine, corn, and oil, and inscribed with the Hebrew words of the *Sh'ma* (Deut. 6:4): "Hear O Israel the Lord Our God the Lord is One." Soon, the music of the band's *Judas Maccabeus* and the organist's *Jubilate* gave way to the singing of "Before Jehovah's Awful Throne." The Rev. Searle conducted his "non-sectarian" morning service, an "ecumenical" service to dedicate a separatist Jewish colony. After a prayer, two prophetic lessons, the reading of a half-dozen Psalms (one of them in Hebrew), an ante-Communion Service and a benediction, Mordecai Noah rose to speak.[17]

Noah's address before the assembled at St. Paul's Church endeavored to "unfold the principles, explain the views and detail the objects" which were contained in the magniloquent "Proclamation to the Jews" issued "By the Judge," under the signature of "A.B. Seixas, Secretary Pro tem." earlier in the day.

The Proclamation had been directed to the widest possible audience. It announced the foundation of a city of refuge "to be called Ararat," proclaimed the reestablishment of the government of the Jewish Nation "under the auspices and protection of the constitution and laws of the United States of America," and declared Noah, "Judge of Israel."

Judge Noah then issued decrees:[18]

- A census and registration of all the world's Jews must be undertaken.
- Jews who so desired could remain in the diaspora, and should be faithful to the governments which protected them, yet they must aid other Jews to emigrate.
- Jews in military ranks must remain at their posts and "conduct themselves with bravery and fidelity."

- Jews must remain strictly neutral in the Greek-Turkish dispute, as many Jews lay "under the oppressive dominion of the Ottoman Porte."
- Annual gifts to "our pious brethren" in Jerusalem must be continued and aid should be increased to other seminaries of learning and institutions of charity.
- Polygamy must forever be abolished.
- Before they are married, all Jews must be able to read and write the language of the country which they inhabit.
- Prayers must always be said in the Hebrew language. Occasional vernacular discourses, however, are permitted as are other reforms which add "greater solemnity to our worship."
- Karaites, Samaritans (whose doctrines Noah erroneously considered essentially the same as those of other Jews), and small Jewish sects around the world, as well as "all who may partake of the great covenant and obey and respect Mosaical laws" must be admitted into the ranks of the Jewish people.
- Indians, "being in all probability the descendants of the lost ten tribes of Israel," must be made sensible of their condition and reunited with "their brethren".
- A head tax of three shekels of silver must be levied "upon each Jew throughout the world" to defray expenses of the Jewish government.
- A Judge of Israel must be chosen once every four years by the Paris Jewish Consistory based on proxy votes from every congregation of Jews in the world.

In a concluding substantive section of his Proclamation to the Jews, Noah, without obtaining their consent, appointed some of the most distinguished Jews in the world as his commissioners to further Jewish emigration. He authorized the Paris Consistory to investigate and report on Jewish conditions in the United States. He established "Roshhodesh [the new moon of the Hebrew month of] Adar, February 7th, 1826" as a special day of thanksgiving. Then he became humble. He pleaded with his fellow Jews to act properly, remember him in their prayers, and "keep the charge of the Holy God."[19]

Noah's Proclamation to the Jews reads basically like a series of orders. The "Judge of Israel" explained very little. In his Ararat Address, he went further. He reviewed the state of world Jewry and sought to provide an answer to the question which still puzzles historians today: why Ararat?

Noah always stressed the humanitarian aspects of Ararat. He called Ararat "an asylum for the oppressed," and inscribed on its cornerstone the words, "A City of Refuge for the Jews." Actually, the Jewish situation in 1825 was less urgent than when Noah first proposed his colony in 1820. But if riots and persecutions had died down, the overall condition of the Jews in 1825 still cried out for improvement: "The oldest of nations, powerful in numbers and great in resources, remains isolated, without a home, a country or a government." Jews, according to Noah, needed a "period of regeneration." In America, "under the influence of perfect freedom," he felt that Jews would study, acquire liberal principles, and qualify themselves to rule in the Land of the Patriarchs.[20]

Noah envisaged Ararat as a temporary refuge where Jews would be modernized. Among his goals were such typical Enlightenment reforms as: abolition of polygamy, encouragement of agricultural and mechanical arts, and the spread of complete literacy in the native language of the country. Noah even considered calling together a seventy-member Sanhedrin, an obvious imitation of Napoleon's method for modernizing Jews. But by whatever means, he resolutely determined to spread "intelligence and education." Future generations, he promised, would be "progressively improved and enlightened."[21]

Noah did not see Ararat as a surrogate Jerusalem. In 1820, he had felt that Jews would never voluntarily settle in the Holy Land, and that Grand Island would become the center of Jewry. At that time, he planned to name his colony "New Jerusalem," a name to which he still clung as late as 1824. But by 1825, perhaps influenced by new missionary interest in Palestine, he realized that no diaspora land could replace Jerusalem in the Jewish heart. His colony could at best serve as a temporary refuge, a happy if not promised land, an Ararat in the diaspora. The fact that the biblical Ararat was connected with the story of Noah only made this name more appropriate.[22]

Although Noah conceded that Ararat would be a temporary resting place for the Jews, he assigned it an important role in bringing about the ultimate, millennial restoration for which vast numbers of people earnestly prayed. He began his proclamation by observing that the period when "the race of Jacob... are to be gathered from the four quarters of the globe" was approaching. Ararat, he promised, would collect together and "improve" Jews, and thus speed "that great and final restoration to their ancient heritage which the times so powerfully indicate." As Noah knew, many Christians believed that Jewish restoration was the harbinger of the millennium. The opening paragraph of his address indicates that he was well aware of the worldwide implications of his scheme.[23]

Any benefits to the world from Ararat lay far in the future. America was more fortunate; as Noah saw it, the country would reap immediate benefits from the Jews. He promised that the wealthiest of his coreligionists (a group he had once identified as "enterprising merchants, silk and other manufacturers from France and Germany, mechanics wherever they are found, and agriculturalists from Poland and Ukraine") would come to America. Pending the millennium, America would have the use of their superior skills and ample capital. To make good on his promise, Noah in his writings wooed wealthy Jews and assured them of many opportunities. He reviewed Jewry's world situation, and sought to demonstrate that only in America would Jews escape oppression. He believed sincerely that Ararat would help wealthy Jews. But he believed just as sincerely that the project would have "the most important consequences to the country." As before, Noah wanted to prove that in aiding Jews he aided his country in ways that non-Jews couldn't match. Far from being a liability, he insisted that his Judaism served as an asset.[24]

Noah applied the same argument in discussing the effects of his project on New York State. In 1820, he had assured the legislature that Jewish immigrants would "give an impetus to a brisk trade," set up "settlements of a commercial character," and establish on Grand Island "a very important frontier post." He even suggested that Jews might be "induced to purchase and hold all the state stock and eminently benefit our fiscal concerns." Now, five years later, he was in a position to make good on his promises and to prove himself a valuable citizen. Consequently, he extolled the virtues of his state to foreign Jews, and urged them to invest as much as they could: "To men of worth and industry it has every substantial attraction; the capitalist will be enabled to enjoy his resources with undoubted profit, and the mechanic cannot fail to reap the reward of enterprise in a great and growing republic; but to the industrious mechanic, manufacturer and agriculturalist it holds forth great and improving advantages."[25]

In his public writings, Noah openly discussed the potential benefits of his project for his people, his nation, his state, and even for mankind's ultimate destiny. He said nothing at all, however, about the benefits which might accrue to himself. Grand Island, after all, was a prime location, one where most investors expected land values to rise. Privately, Noah once candidly admitted that he looked forward to "an immense profit." He also obviously enjoyed the accoutrements in office—the pomp, the ceremony, the title, and the speeches. He knew that if he succeeded, these and much more would be his for life. Yet, Noah did not undertake Ararat simply for reasons of fame and fortune; the sincerity of his interest in helping other Jews cannot be doubted. On the other hand, his was not a purely selfless endeavor either. Instead, both his own well-being and the well-being of others interested Noah. He was neither a complete altruist nor a complete egoist.[26]

From the perspective of Mordecai Noah, Ararat seemed like an ideal plan: everybody gained, nobody lost. This outlook was quite typical of early nineteenth-century colonizers. Irish, German, and black colonization advocates never mentioned just the benefits which a colony held open to settlers. Always, they went on to extol the numerous advantages a colony might bring to all governments and peoples remotely connected with it. Like Noah, these colonizers gave scant public attention to any but the high-minded altruistic motivations behind their schemes. Yet, personal concerns, while not necessarily of prime importance, never lay far from their minds.[27]

Despite these obvious similarities between Ararat and other colonization schemes, Noah adamantly insisted that he aimed "at higher objects than mere colonization." He aimed at melioration as well. In this sense, his colony resembled New Paltz colony, the Harrison, New York asylum set up for conversionist purposes by the American Society for Meliorating the Condition of the Jews. (Interestingly, one of Noah's letters of support came from

Erasmus H. Simon, an agent of that society who opposed the administrative policies of its colony.[28]) Both colonies called themselves asylums; both aimed at potential Jewish immigrants; and both sought explicitly to "ameliorate the condition of the Jews" by properly educating children and by providing agricultural and mechanical training to adults. Theologically, Noah and the missionaries also had much in common. Both agreed that America was destined to play a special role in the Divine plan. Both agreed that the millennium was imminent, but in some ways dependent upon Jews. Both agreed that Jews and Christians should respect one another. And both agreed that it was up to Jews to take immediate appropriate action to ensure that they qualified for final restoration to the promised land. Of course, Noah and the missionaries still disagreed about religious fundamentals. Noah believed in ultimate Jewish regeneration, while the missionaries believed in ultimate Jewish conversion. Still, the parallels are instructive. Noah's thinking had obviously been shaped by the evangelical Protestantism of his day—to such an extent, that he even shared many Christian views on the nature of world Jewry and how to improve it. Through Ararat, he sought to incorporate some of these Christian ideas into a framework which was staunchly Jewish.[29]

Important as Evangelical Protestantism was in the early nineteenth century, it was not nearly so powerful an ideological influence on Noah as American idealism. As a patriotic citizen and an influential politician, Noah could only advocate projects which were totally in harmony with freedom, democracy, and tolerance. Ararat posed a problem: it was both sectarian and undemocratic. Noah never resolved this problem. He may not fully have understood its implications.

In his Ararat Address, Noah brushed aside the idea that Ararat and America could be in conflict: "Conforming therefore to the constitution and laws of the United States, there is no difficulty in organizing and concentrating the Jewish nation." He did not, however, elaborate as to how he would reconcile the seemingly opposite goals of maintaining a separate Jewish identity and integrating the Jews into American society as a whole. Instead, he strove to obtain legitimacy for his project. He tied it to America's three most enduring myths: the Wandering Pilgrims, the Noble Savages, and the Revolutionary Fathers. Just as "a few pilgrims, driven to our continent by European persecution, have laid the foundation of a splendid empire," so, he claimed, "a few Jews in this happy land admonished by the past, and animated by anticipations of the future, may increase rapidly and prosperously." As for the Indians, he labeled them "the lineal descendants of the Israelites," the ten lost tribes. Finally, he termed his Proclamation to the Jews, a "declaration of independence." The comparison between July 4, 1776, and September 15, 1825, was a difficult one, and wisely he did not elaborate on it. But his rhetorical reference to peace and prosperity, as well as his call for a "new society" could not have been lost on the attentive audience.[30]

Unfortunately for Noah, neither his patriotic allusions nor his sweeping assertions could conceal the Ararat–America tensions inherent in his plan. If, as he claimed in his address, "in this free and happy country distinctions in religion are unknown," how could a separate Jewish colony be countenanced? How could a "government of the Jews" be organized if the constitution and laws of the United States were to be binding? How could Jews in Ararat be loyal to America if the asylum was "temporary and provisionary"?[31] Except for a vague reference to non-Jews being invited to settle in Grand Island, he ignored these questions. Inviting non-Jews was a standard method of avoiding charges of Jewish separatism. When, in 1843, Noah advocated a "Hebrew College" (boarding school) for the training of Jewish young men, there was again the assurance that "the school would be open to all denominations."[32]

By setting up a Jewish government on Ararat, Noah effectively negated his 1820 distinction between "mingling together [with Christians]" and "distinct associations [with Jews]." As the dedication ceremony demonstrated, however, the identity-assimilation problem remained unsolved. The service at St. Paul's Church seemed neither Jewish nor Christian, and it offended many. Efforts to resolve other areas of tension, particularly polity and foreign policy, proved no more successful.

Ararat needed a leader. In order to interest "enlightened" Jews in coming to Ararat, Noah believed that it needed an exceptional leader, one who would be colorful, charismatic, and above all, traditional. Tradition, however, prevented the democratic election of a sovereign. The Bible contained no democratic elections, and besides, who would have voted? On the other hand, an undemocratically elected sovereign was anathema to Americans, and certainly could not have been advocated by a Democratic politician. Noah found the solution to this problem in the Book of Judges. The Judges sprang from the people; they were not kings, and leadership did not pass to their sons. More importantly, "the manner and forms adopted in choosing the Judges of Israel" were "difficult... to decide with certainty." On the basis of so much ignorance, Noah had no trouble in convincing himself that the office of judge "conform[ed] in some respect to that of [American] Chief Magistrate." It followed that this form of leadership was "in accordance with the genius and disposition of the people of this country." Noah hoped that this explanation would satisfy his "enlightened" listeners. But he thought that the "unenlightened" abroad who read his proclamation might want something more simple. Consequently, in that document he boldly credited his office to "the grace of God."[33]

Foreign policy presented another clash between Ararat and America. As an American, Mordecai Noah advocated the Greek cause in its struggle for independence from Turkey. He even wrote a pro-Greek play, *The Grecian Captive, or the Fall of Athens*. Yet, as a Jew, he feared for the hundreds of thousands of his brethren living under Turkish rule "who would be instantly sacrificed by their relentless rulers upon the least succor being afforded to the revolutionists." Noah, therefore, struck a compromise: he enjoined Jews "not to mingle in this contest," and at the same time, he ordered them "not to throw obstacles in the way of its [Greece's] successful advancement."[34] The compromise was a weak one. Noah the "judge" could not even begin to resolve the tensions between Ararat and America. He ignored problems or resorted to mythic solutions. He never realized that it was impossible to integrate fully into the American mainstream, and to preserve perfectly Jewish ethnic identity at one and the same time. He never realized that the American Jew lived in a perpetual state of tension between "American" and "Jew."

Jews and ethnics generally were and remain sociologically ambivalent— torn between the demands of their group and the demands of their country. Colonizers often claim success in resolving this dilemma. But if they simultaneously promise the blessings of both integration and segregation they are doomed, like Ararat, to fail.[35] And no wonder. Structural polarities are resolved only in utopia and the world of myth. In the everyday world, basic irresolvable tensions remain.[36]

The response to Noah's 1825 extravanganza differed markedly from the reaction he had encountered in 1820. Then, the vast majority of newspapers supported him and wished his project well. After the Ararat dedication, reaction varied much more widely. Buffalo area newspapers understandably favored the project. Their region stood to gain from the endeavor, and they surely found Noah less visionary than some of the other radical and religious figures who kept western New York ("the burned over district") in a state of ferment. Elsewhere, many newspapers printed Noah's proclamation without comment, or, as in the case of the *New York Statesman*, confined their remarks to superficial praise of Noah's "liberal views." Noah's political opponents, however, had a field day. The *New York American* suggested that Noah find "a convenient apartment in the lunatic asylum," and then hinted darkly that Ararat might be designed "for swindling the wealthy Jews of Europe out of their money." The widely read and influential *Niles' Weekly Register* called Ararat a "land jobbing business," Noah, a potentially "great autocrat," and the entire project, nothing but "a very good business indeed." Even the *New York Mirror*, which was usually sympathetic to him, could not restrain its mirth: "Fall down! ye men of Israel, and worship this new Judge! Pay your capitation tax, and seven millions will forthwith enrich the treasury of your great Judge—Mordecai Manuel Noah."[37]

These criticisms were understandable, if not totally fair responses to Noah's theatrics. But they left the "judge" with an easy answer. His theatrics, he claimed, were designed for the "unenlightened" Jews of the world, not for sophisticated Americans. More important criticism came from the *American Atheneum*. Its learned editor wondered how Noah reconciled his support and defense of the Constitution with the undemocratic method by which he assumed his "ample and responsible" position of Judge of Israel. Perhaps, he suggested, Noah "considered himself the people," and therefore had "no other but himself to elect and to be elected." Isaac Harby in the *Charleston Courier* went further. Having opposed the colony scheme from the start, he now branded Noah as impious. Jews, he said, should wait for the Messiah, "who shall lead them to New Jerusalem not to New York and shall show his divine credentials in a guise somewhat different" from the one assumed by Noah. Harby held Noah's judgeship to be "contrary to scriptural authority," and he advised his fellow editor to reread the biblical books of Judges and Samuel. He next levelled his guns at Noah's ceremony and proclamation. He indicated that, according to his understanding of Judaism, to put a stone with the words of the Hebrew "Shemong" [Sh'ma] on a Christian Communion table "around which the sacrament is taken" was nothing less than blasphemy. To invite Jews to come to a pagan city was "profane." To call Ararat a city of refuge, when in fact it resembled the biblical cities of refuge not at all, was simply "ignorant." As for Noah's decrees, Harby ridiculed one after another.[38]

Noah dismissed Harby as a "new light" (referring, of course, to his role in the Charleston Reform Movement) and declared the southern editor "un-acquainted with the essential form of the [Jewish] religion." But Harby's criticisms were widely echoed by American Jews. Moses E. Levy attacked Noah for his "folly and sacrilegious presumption." Rachel Mordecai Lazarus doubted that anyone would submit "to the self-constituted 'governor' and 'judge of Israel'," and observed that most people deemed the entire scheme "visionary." Even eight years later, Benjamin Gratz still would have nothing to do with Noah: "his trick upon our nation to make money was too shallow to gull them: filthy lucre was his object."[39]

The critical reaction of his fellow Jews surprised Noah not at all. Back in 1824, he had told Peter Porter that his project was objectionable to American Jews "from the fear that the conduct of Jewish emigrants might possibly bring them into disrepute." Subsequent events did not alter his analysis. Despite the many substantive criticisms of Ararat, Noah continued to believe that status fears, fears which certainly affected later Jewish views on immigration, were the reason why "The Jews of the United States...have not been favourably inclined towards the project." Upon reflection, Noah conceded that his proclamation "should have been specifically directed to the European Jews;" it had no application or meaning to Jews living freely in the United States. Still, he remained convinced that those Jews who needed an asylum would avail themselves of the advantages which Ararat held forth.[40]

Noah was wrong. European Jews did not flock to Ararat. Nor was there any great support for Noah in the European Jewish press. Indeed, aside from the favorable response of some German *Verein* members, all Noah heard from abroad were words of ridicule. Judah Jeteles, a leader of the Austrian Jewish Enlightenment and the editor of the Hebrew journal *Bikkurei Haittim*, called Noah a "crazy man," and urged Jews to remain where they were. These sentiments were echoed privately by Rabbi Hayyim Joseph Pollak of Hungary. Abraham Andrade, Rabbi of Bordeaux, saw Noah as a simple charlatan. The poet Henrich Heine dismissed him as amusing. But none of these responses received nearly as much publicity as the letter sent to Noah by the Paris Chief Rabbi, Abraham de Cologna, representing himself and the Chief Rabbi of England. Cologna lampooned Ararat as "the chimerical consulate of a pseudo-restorer" and "a mere jest." He sternly warned Noah, whom he admitted was a "visionary of good intentions," that his project was "an act of high treason against the Divine Majesty."[41]

Perhaps, as Noah claimed, these rabbis merely acted on government orders. In Vienna, the police actually had seized the Ararat Proclamation. But the document received so much publicity in Europe (mentions of it have been found in newspapers from Britain, France, Germany, Austria, Russia, and Hungary) that word must have filtered down to ordinary Jews. The fact that Ararat nevertheless remained desolate indicates that Noah had misread the world Jewish situation. Jews, even "unenlightened" Jews, neither needed nor wanted an isolated asylum in a faraway land ruled by a self-appointed judge. To leave the uncertainties of Europe for an ill-conceived colony riddled with internal contradictions made no sense at all.[42]

A boat named *Noah's Ark* set sail from Grand Island in October 1825 to take part in the celebrations opening the Erie Canal. The five-ton boat was "handsomely fitted" and "freighted with all manner of animals and creepy things." It received considerable attention. Early in its journey, *Noah's Ark* ran into unspecified trouble. It turned back and never arrived in New York City.[43]

Noah's project soon went the way of *Noah's Ark*. Three weeks after Ararat's dedication, the "Judge of Israel" advised a friend to delay his purchase of land on Grand Island. A few months later, on January 24, 1826, the *Black Rock Gazette* sadly announced that "the probability of his [Noah's] success in getting together the Jews is at an end." For most people, Ararat became a source of amusement. Enemies trotted out Noah's proclamation with embarrassing regularity. As for Grand Island, Lewis F. Allen bought it very cheaply as timberland in 1833. In 1852, it was incorporated as a town. Today it houses over eighteen thousand people.[44]

All that remains of Ararat is a three-hundred-pound cornerstone. Like the wandering Jew whose condition the asylum was supposed to ameliorate, the stone has met ridicule and has been moved from place to place. Yet it has always been sought out and saved from destruction. In the late 1820s someone moved the stone from St. Paul's Church to the front lawn of Peter Porter's estate. There, Lewis Allen took a fancy to it, and in 1834 he arranged to have it set up in a little monument on Grand Island itself. But the monument became delapidated, and in 1850 it was torn down. For the next sixteen years, the cornerstone was a refugee, moved from place to place. It even spent a few months in an outhouse. The stone found a permanent home in 1866 when it was deposited in the building of the Buffalo Historical Society. But in Jewish history, even permanent homes turn out to be transient. In the 1930s, Julius Bisno, then international executive director of the B'nai B'rith Youth Organization, found the "dirty, grimy, almost unreadable cornerstone" in the basement of the Buffalo and Erie County Public Library. The cornerstone was rescued in 1958, and in 1965, it was moved to the new Grand Island Town

Hall. Today, the cornerstone sits as a tourist attraction, mounted on a pedestal and encased in glass. The monumental and venerable stone seems somehow to symbolize Noah's longstanding and deep concern for the fate of his people. But the inappropriate glass cover which "protects" the stone is also symbolic. It bespeaks the chimerical unreality, and deep inner contradictions which doomed Ararat from the very start.[45]

Chapter V

Independent Jacksonian

Noah's failure at Ararat had no damaging effects on his journalistic and political careers. To the contrary, he may have compensated for his setbacks in the religious realm by redoubling his efforts to succeed in the secular one. Cleverly manipulating his independent political status, he soon fell in line behind Andrew Jackson and shared in his patron's success. He attained, for the first time, a measure of financial security. He held high hopes for the future.

By rapidly reentering the world of journalism, this time as a proprietor rather than as a hireling, Noah revealed anew his characteristic mode of fighting adversity. He neither flinched nor despaired in the wake of his 1824 dismissal from the *National Advocate*. Instead, just as he had done after his Tunis recall, he marshaled his resources and started afresh. At the same time, he sought vindication and tried to cast his opponents in the worst possible light. Most basically, he aimed to drive the *National Advocate* out of business. To this end, he closely modeled his paper after his former journal: he copied its title; he published from the same address as formerly (48 Wall Street); he solicited from many of the same advertisers; he even sent his newspaper to the same set of subscribers. Noah hoped to prove that the *National Advocate* needed him at the helm in order to succeed. Thomas Snowden, who had paid $11,500 to purchase the *National Advocate*, fought back. First, he claimed ownership of Noah's premises and charged Noah's assistants with trespassing. When that claim failed (Noah held a lease to the building), he sought an injunction against Noah's *Advocate*. He lost again. The court agreed with Noah's attorney that "the point and spirit, the sprightliness, gaiety of heart and good humour" which characterized Noah's paper were not sold with the *National Advocate*. So long as he peddled his paper under a title that was uniquely his own, Noah was free to sell copies to whomever he pleased.[1]

For eighteen months, the *National Advocate* and the *New York National Advocate* coexisted, despite continuing problems caused by the similarity of their names. Unfortunately for Noah, his problems were compounded by his irresponsible associate, E. J. Roberts. Roberts had invested his lottery winnings in the *New York National Advocate*, and therefore assumed responsibility for the paper's finances. Since he had no financial skills, just money, he soon fell prey to swindlers and dropped deeply into debt, pulling his newspaper after him. Roberts resigned from the *New York National Advocate* on March 30, 1826, allegedly for political reasons. But he could not so easily resign from the financial imbroglios in which he and Noah were mired. By July 4, Noah found himself forced to close the *New York National Advocate* altogether. To satisfy creditors, the court had denied him the right to collect outstanding debts, and it announced plans to sell all the newspaper's assets for which Roberts had paid.[2]

Roberts briefly tried to publish the *New York National Advocate* himself, but he found very few supporters. Neither anti-Jewish slurs ("The Jews too have deserted us—well, they crucified our Saviour which was a much greater sin"), nor profuse subsequent apologies brought him readers. The "Jewish issue" became salient in New York only rarely, such as when a Jew ran for public office. Otherwise, citizens prided themselves on their tolerance. Roberts's efforts to build a circulation from among the prejudiced met with no success, and he lost, by his own estimate, a further twenty-five thousand dollars. Meanwhile, Noah, who as an insolvent debtor had lost nothing from Roberts's collapse, found new financial backers and a new newspaper, the *New York Enquirer*. The masthead insignia of the *New York Enquirer* pictured an ark sailing over the motto "A Free Press, The Ark of Public Safety." The ark reflected both Noah's name and popular interest in the new Erie Canal.[3]

The sequel came two years later, on June 20, 1828, when the embittered Roberts attacked Noah with a cowskin on the steps of the Park Theater. In a well-publicized trial, Roberts received a fine and a lengthy term on probation for assault. Convinced that Roberts had suffered enough, Noah refused to press civil charges.[4]

While Noah escaped other physical attacks, he could not protect himself from his opponents' base personal insults. Thomas Snowden once lambasted his "family of Jews" as "irresponsible in every respect." James G. Brooks, then an assistant on the New York *Courier*, tried to provoke Noah into a duel by plastering the city with wall posters reading "I publish M. M. Noah of the Enquirer as a coward." The hot tempered James Watson Webb, editor of the *Courier*, actually threatened Noah in writing with a "personal recontre." But unlike many New York journalists, particularly Webb, Noah felt no desire to fight his battles in the street. He battled with his pen, and lamented the brawls and "attacks in defense of honor" which debased the profession of journalism in his day. Unfortunately, his associate, William G. Graham, did not practice similar restraint. In December 1827, he was shot and killed in a private duel, much to Noah's shock and grief.[5]

Press battles were standard fare in all newspapers of the 1820s. Noah's *New York National Advocate* and *New York Enquirer* differed from the others mainly because of their journalistic quality. As before, Noah printed popular, lighthearted pieces on topics of human interest, and critical satires aimed at "good society." He also printed occasional "Post Office news"—items on brawls, crimes, and scandals similar to those later sensationalized by the penny press and yellow journalists. Still, he tried to maintain a delicate balance:

> It is the business of a newspaper, to tell its readers of everything *new*, which transpires in the world, and more especially of that sort of *newness*, which carries with it utility and value. It is well for the world to know that Simpkins drank himself to death; that Timpkins fell from the roof of a ten-story house and dislocated his neck; and that Pimpkins, in a fit of causeless jealousy, burnt up his house or throttled his better half. These are momentous *items*, and are detailed to the world in our daily columns, with a laudable industry. But as the Cambridge Professor said of Paradise Lost, they "prove nothing." All the possible fatalities of the whole family of the *kins*—(Simp, Timp, or Pimp) cannot have any imaginable influence on the fortunes and conduct of the other eleven million of souls, which make up the population of these free, independent and happy United States, which, by the by, are all going for Jackson. It is our business, as editors, to make known such occurrences as shall have an influence, and a beneficial influence too....

He thus tried to broaden the horizons of his newspapers without in any way cheapening the journals' quality. At the same time, he tried to expand his geographic coverage. He hired for his *New York Enquirer* a young Washington correspondent named James Gordon Bennett. Bennett never got along with his employer. Years later, he took his revenge in the pages of the *New York Herald*, which he founded in 1835. In spite of the enmity, however, Noah printed Bennett's columns. He deserves credit for encouraging the breezy, gossipy, "Horace Walpole" style of Washington reporting that many others conspicuously imitated.[6]

Noah also deserves credit for the investigative reporting which he introduced into his newspaper. "No one has been more actively and boldly engaged in exposing the unsound, stale and fraudulent practices of some of the institutions which have lately failed in this city," the *Evening Post* once exclaimed. Noah was equally interested in abuses outside the city. To be sure, politics and vindictiveness often lay behind Noah's revelations. It is always easier to investigate and condemn an opponent than to assail a friend. Still, the abuses which he uncovered were real. Real, too, were the risks which he took when he assailed the wealthy and powerful in the name of the people. Happily for him, his risks paid off. His efforts contributed to the mood of popular dissatisfaction which eventually elected Andrew Jackson to the presidency of the United States.[7]

The first of what a later generation would call "muckraking" pieces appeared in the *New York National Advocate* in 1825, when "Hancock" disclosed financial irregularities in the accounts of the Department of War. In printing the articles, Noah doubtless hoped to embarrass the Vice-President, and former Secretary of War John Calhoun, whose presidential ambitions he opposed at that time. But whatever the motivations, the charges of waste and corruption were accurate, even if Calhoun was not to blame. Revelations regarding the financial misdealings which led to the collapse of banks and insurance companies owned by Jacob Barker, Henry Eckford, and other powerful New Yorkers, proved similarly accurate. Again, Noah had old scores to settle with some of these men. But that should not obscure his crucial role as partial instigator of the investigations and judicial proceedings that subsequently took place. Curiously, Noah opposed levying criminal charges against those whom he exposed. He may have foreseen the legal maneuverings that would ultimately result in the defendants' vindication. He may also have succumbed to Tammany pressure against prosecution. Perhaps he merely believed that Barker and Eckford had suffered enough. Whatever the reason, Noah had already proved his point. By publicly exposing the financiers, he had demonstrated that an independent press, allied with the public, possessed more power than even the most important and wealthy men in New York City.[8]

Noah continually reasserted his journal's power. In 1826, he complained to the city corporation after receiving threats from the street inspector, John Bloodgood, who took umbrage at a Noah article. Noah properly demanded that the inspector be restrained. In 1829, he faced a ten-thousand-dollar libel suit after he accused financier George W. Brown of diverting funds from the Sharon Canal Company. The jury awarded Brown six cents in a judgment that everyone interpreted as a victory for Noah. As the *New York Enquirer* explained to Brown, "duty" required a journal "to expose the offender and bring him before the public." Noah occasionally solicited help from his readers, especially when he thought that the common man was being cheated. Once, for example, he asked if anyone knew why firewood had suddenly become so expensive. But he quickly learned that too many "assistants" could prove a hindrance. Eventually, he found it necessary to remind his readers that he had work to do. It took time to produce a newspaper that others praised as being "on the topmost round of the journalistic ladder." Besides, Noah had also to find time for politics.[9]

In his new politics, Noah displayed the same independent spirit that he demonstrated in his new journalism. He still allied himself with Tammany Hall, and he still maintained many of his old political friendships. But he no longer took orders. Nor did he receive Tammany patronage. The results of the 1824 election had finally convinced him that politicians were playing the political game according to a revised set of rules. "The time has gone by," he wrote in the *New York National Advocate*, "when leading and influential men are to be menaced with the anger of party for breaking through party discipline." The politics of the day were the politics of flux. Consequently, he felt free to oppose both the new National-Republican President, John Quincy Adams, and his own former mentor, Martin Van Buren. He edged instead toward Andrew Jackson, a politician whom he trusted both to win the election and to mold a new Jeffersonian party. Conveniently, he forgot the *National Advocate*'s old attacks on Jackson's "military despotism."[10]

Noah commenced his attacks on John Quincy Adams almost as soon as the President took the oath of office. While Van Buren and Tammany remained cautious and neutral, Noah lashed out at Adams' political appointments. He opposed the President's tactic of partially satisfying the patronage demands of each individual faction, and he charged that Adams aimed to destroy political parties altogether. Noah's opposition became particularly virulent when Adams appointed Rufus King ambassador to England. Noah had old scores to settle with King; besides, he considered the ex-Federalist both too old and too Anglophilic for the sensitive British post. He rested his principal attacks, however, on none of these arguments. Instead, he demonstrated anew his ability to uncover secret or long-forgotten incidents ("skeletons in the closet") which cast his antagonist in an unfavorable light. Most spectacular was his discovery—widely publicized by other journalists—that Rufus King had once discussed a proposal to invite Prince Henry of Prussia to become America's sovereign. Noah undoubtedly magnified the story out of all proportion. But there was a glimmer of truth to the report, and King could not deny it completely. Noah also somehow discovered that the executors of Alexander Hamilton's estate were demanding the return of some papers which King had in his custody. The vehement denial of Charles King (Rufus's son) proved to be a lie; a year later, after a court suit, King turned the papers over. Finally, Noah dug out a long forgotten anti-Irish quote attributed to Rufus King. As with his other discoveries, this one too had no effect on the Senate, which on December 20, 1825, confirmed the ambassador to his post by a wide margin. But Noah hoped that the voters would remember his crusade. While Martin Van Buren resignedly voted for Rufus King, Noah was already looking forward to the next election. He had in mind a new coalition which could defeat Adams, elect Jackson, and elevate Mordecai Noah to a position of glory.[11]

Governor De Witt Clinton played a vital part in Noah's calculations. He knew that as an early supporter of "Old Hickory," Clinton would play an important role in the Jacksonian campaign. To oppose Clinton would be to divide the Jacksonians and to risk defeat. Noah preferred to swallow pride and grasp for victory.

The governor was probably not surprised when his former nemesis approached him. For years there had been rumors that Noah privately respected Clinton, and opposed him vehemently only out of loyalty to Martin Van Buren. Writing under a pseudonym, Clinton in 1819 had himself alleged that Noah was "more than half Clintonian at bottom." Two years later, New York Surrogate Silvanus Miller had charged that Noah offered to support Clinton for a fee of seven thousand dollars. Of course, Noah had then ridiculed the allegation, calling Miller a "profligate old man." But Miller's subsequent libel suit disclosed that Noah's private opinion of Clinton diverged greatly from what he had said in public. The case ended in a hung jury.[12]

By 1826, Noah was ready to bring his private and public views into closer harmony. First, he stopped criticizing Clinton in his newspaper—a move which occasioned E. J. Roberts's abrupt departure from the *New York National Advocate.* Then he took the opportunity of a steamboat ride in honor of Mrs. Clinton to talk seriously with the governor. He hinted that he would support Clinton's bid for reelection in 1826, and wondered if the governor would in return support Van Buren's bid for reelection to the Senate. Noah politely refused Clinton's offer of a minor judgeship. The editor obviously did not plan to desert his old friends and his old party. He hoped instead to cement a coalition with Clinton, one similar to Van Buren's alliance with Rufus King, and he expected that Van Buren and his supporters would go along. They didn't. To Noah's unpleasant surprise, Van Buren arranged to support a strong challenger to Clinton: William B. Rochester, a Clay supporter and friend of the administration.[13]

Van Buren's "devious maneuver" reveals the chasm that had developed between the politics of the "Little Magician," as he was known, and the politics of the "fidgety editor." Van Buren, who was committed to no national candidate, concerned himself with state politics. He wanted the Bucktails to regain control from Clinton, and he believed—correctly, as it turned out—that the candidacy of the pro-administration candidate, Rochester, would divide Clinton's supporters and result in the defeat or isolation of the governor. Mordecai Noah, on the other hand, was already thinking ahead to the Presidential election of 1828. He wished to unite all Jacksonians and he had no interest in a temporary alliance with administration backers, for any purpose.[14] Consequently, he refused to support William Rochester. After some initial hesitation, he openly proclaimed himself neutral, which, in effect, helped Clinton, and he informed party members that he would promote them according to his "own convictions of what is right." When Rochester lost by a very narrow margin, the disappointed Bucktails understandably vented their rage at Mordecai Noah. Van Buren's relations with his old friend cooled noticeably.[15]

Martin Van Buren's ire had no effect on Noah's political course. Noah was over forty and sought both security and stability; the devious, mercurial Van Buren could provide him with neither. The political bandwagon of Jackson and Clinton, on the other hand, seemed to him well suited to his needs. Consequently, he jumped aboard, leaving the cautious Van Buren scheming in the background. Soon, Noah set to work trying to derail the presidential hopes of Daniel Webster. He ingratiated himself with De Witt Clinton by boosting him for vice-president over other potential candidates. He defended Andrew Jackson against the scurrilous attacks of his opponents. He even organized a large and successful pro-Jackson gala dinner. But amidst his bustling activity, he failed to give sufficient heed to Martin Van Buren's quiet realignment of New York State politics. Under Van Buren's coaxing, factionalized, per-sonality-centered politics were giving way to the politics of principle based on opposition both to John Quincy Adams and to Clintonian elitism. The Democratic Party was the name assumed by the new Van Burenites, and mass democracy—artfully managed from above—was what the Democratic Party advocated. Because he directed the party and its supporters, Van Buren had made himself—not Clinton—indispensable to any effort aimed at forging a nationwide Democratic Party around Andrew Jackson. His public support of Jackson, when it finally came, took on an aura of immense importance, and it received wide publicity. Jackson was extremely grateful.[16]

Jackson's gratitude proved the wisdom of Van Buren's earlier hesitant course. The New Yorker received greater respect from Jackson precisely because Jackson did not take his support for granted. In his subsequent maneuvers, Van Buren proved equally astute. Unlike Noah, he said nothing about the vice-presidency. He kept his options open, and did not immediately alienate John Calhoun's vice-presidential backers. Van Buren also demonstrated a remarkable ability to move with the political current. While Mordecai Noah, who was a Mason, dismissed anti-Masonic fever as "humbug," and urged that the movement "be put down," Van Buren wisely strove to accommodate the Antimasons. He urged Congressmen C. C. Cambreleng to convince Noah that change was necessary. "To run in the face of so irresistable a current of public feeling," Van Buren ominously warned, would be "reckless indiscretion."[17]

The same quest for stability which drove Noah toward Clinton and Jackson drove him also toward marriage. By coincidence, he again put his faith in a person named Jackson—Rebecca Jackson. Earlier, Noah had neither the time nor the money to get married, even assuming the right lady had come along.[18] The fledgling editor had enough trouble supporting his father and sister without having to worry about anybody else. But Noah did not give up hope. A few months after his father died, in 1822, he promised not to become an old bachelor: "I intend to get married when I have leisure," he assured his readers. As if to underline his interest, he joined and eventually led the Bachelor's Club, a society allegedly devoted to "perpetuate single bessedness," but in fact intended "to bring together youth, beauty, taste and character of both sexes [and] to place them in the most winning social intercourse."[19]

Whether Noah took a fancy to non-Jewish women at the Bachelors' Club is not known. The fact that Jews participated so freely in such a club, however, suggests one reason why the intermarriage rate in New York was so high. Whether Noah met Rebecca Esther Jackson at the Bachelors' Club is also not known. More likely, he met her through her father, Daniel Jackson, whom he knew both as a member of the Jewish community and as a political activist. Jackson was an Ashkenazi Jew and Noah identified more with the Sephardim, but that made no difference; Sephardi–Ashkenazi marriages were common among New York Jews. Nor did it matter that Noah and Jackson often differed over politics. Some of New York's great political feuds were carried on between relatives. Age also apparently proved to be no barrier to marriage. Even though Noah was forty-two and Rebecca was only seventeen, she accepted his offer. She probably agreed with her British uncle, David Aaron

Phillips, that it was "better to be the old man['s] darling than the young one's drugg [drudge]," especially in this case when the "old man" was, in Phillips' words, "a man of good sense and understanding and in every respect a gentleman." "Good sense," Mordecai Noah certainly demonstrated, for he had chosen as his wife a Jewish girl of "extraordinary personal beauty" who came from a well-respected family. Soon after their marriage, on November 28, 1827, Rebecca settled down to children and charitable pursuits. Her husband, meanwhile, went back to politics and the press.[20]

Now that he was a married man, Noah redoubled his quest for security. He asked Governor Clinton to appoint him "Director in any one of the Banks." In this way, he hoped both to guarantee his future and to benefit his newspaper's credit. In return, he promised to do his best for the "great cause." Unfortunately for Noah, his appointment was never finalized. On February 11, 1828, De Witt Clinton suddenly died at the age of fifty-eight.[21]

The death of De Witt Clinton simplified New York politics considerably. All New York Jacksonians, Noah included, united behind Martin Van Buren and the Democratic Party. Noah's newspaper, the *Enquirer*, soon became one of Andrew Jackson's most important unofficial party organs. Noah's newly found support became clear as early as April 1828 when, just before the state election, New York Democrats called upon him to write the party's official appeal for voter support. Andrew Jackson himself saw Noah's address praised as "very spirited" and sure to "produce a good effect."[22]

Not all of Noah's political writings demonstrated the same straightforward quality. Like too many of his fellow editors in 1828, he often placed politics above journalistic ethics. When, for example, John Quincy Adams's supporters produced a letter "proving" that Andrew Jackson had in 1813 perpetrated a "worse than savage attack" on Thomas Hart Benton (who later became an influential Missouri senator and Jacksonian supporter), Noah, basing his report on a personal interview with "Senator Benton," declared the whole story untrue. It only later emerged that he had mischievously interviewed an insignificant state senator from New York named Benton; the Missouri Senator had indeed brawled with Jackson, and Jackson had almost been killed in the encounter. Unlike the worst journalistic offenders, those who charged Jackson with murder and moral crimes, Noah avoided sensational appeals to base passions. But he certainly misrepresented facts, and he was not above using some scandal for political ends. On one occasion, he urged journalist Russell Jarvis to use "any means" to confirm reports that the pro-Adams New York Congressman, John W. Taylor, frequented the bed of a prostitute. He felt sure that the scandal, if proved, could "save Saratoga County" for the Jacksonians.[23]

Playing such an active role in the campaign as he did, it is not surprising that Noah himself became the subject of anti-Jacksonian attacks. Not a few journalists reminded the editor of his 1824 view of Andrew Jackson, and wondered what had made him change his mind. Others openly alleged that

Jackson bought Noah's support with a bribe. Still others used more primitive anti-Semitic attacks against the *New York Enquirer*'s editor. In appealing to the rising masses, Jacksonian-era journalists often descended to the gutter.[24]

Anti-Jewish attacks against Noah rose sharply after the Democratic Party once again nominated him for the post of sheriff. Although he assured Van Buren that he personally had "no feelings and no wishes" on the subject of the shrievalty, the still freshly married editor undoubtedly craved the financial security which the lucrative position promised him. Indeed, he hinted darkly that if he was not helped in some way, his *Enquirer* might "fall into hands having views foreign to the settled wishes of our friends." His veiled threat had an effect, and Noah received his nomination. But at great cost. It required five ballots to nominate him, and once nominated, he faced opposition from many Jacksonians, including James Watson Webb of the *New York Courier* (a paper which vied with Noah to represent the party) and his old nemesis, the ex-Federalist, William Coleman of the *New York Post*. Many Democrats, apparently, could not forgive Noah for opposing William Rochester just a year earlier.[25]

Noah's politics, controversial as they may have been, did not become an election issue. Instead, newspapers again concentrated on the candidate's religion. Editors knew that the epithet "Jew" hurt a candidate far more than the epithet "political independent." Webb thus attacked "Noah's· mob" of "Jewish friends" who allegedly threw opponents out of Tammany Hall. The *American* reprinted the Ararat proclamation with satiric comments. Noah's old paper, the *National Advocate*, went even further. This pro-Adams sheet "quoted" an uncle of Noah as hoping that, if elected, his nephew's first official act would be "to hang a Christian!" The paper then misquoted the Paris Sanhedrin of rabbis to "prove" that Jews pledged loyalty only to Jerusalem; they could neither render allegiance to the country in which they lived, nor act as full-fledged loyal subjects. This dual loyalty charge, common in Europe, made no sense in multiethnic America—though it likely succeeded in evoking passions. As the *National Advocate* itself demonstrated, politicians respected and reinforced ethnic loyalties when they could use them to advantage. Indeed, the same *Advocate* issue that questioned Jews' loyalty urged Catholics to support Noah's opponent, James Shaw, for no other reason than because he was Irish.[26]

Noah answered his opponents the same way he had answered them in 1822: he advocated tolerance and warned that other minorities too were vulnerable to prejudice. Religious freedom, he pointed out, was not just a Jewish concern. But his pleas were unavailing; James Shaw emerged the winner. His fifteen-hundred-vote margin of victory was one of very few favorable pieces of news that the Adamsites heard in the entire election. In 1828, Jackson, Van Buren, and the Democrats secured control over both the nation and the state.[27]

Why did the "common men," the "Jacksonian masses" who in 1828 supposedly rose up in revolt, pass Noah by? Noah after all, was a self-made man, a "venturous conservative," a moderate reformer, a believer in basic education, hard work, old-fashioned values and social equality, and, of course, a patriotic exponent of American virtue, destiny, and unique goodness. He was almost a prototypical Jacksonian. Yet, he was defeated by a little-known Adamsite. The party blamed the defeat on James Watson Webb and expelled him for insubordination. (He soon returned.) Noah, fairly or unfairly, blamed party leader Martin Van Buren, and proceeded to befriend Van Buren's arch-rival, John C. Calhoun. Others blamed Noah's character and former disloyalty to the party. But these reasons do not adequately explain why thousands of New York voters in all wards of the city, many of whom had never met Noah, took the trouble to deviate from the official Jacksonian slate in order to elect an opposition candidate. Something indubitably exceptional must have motivated voters to ignore Tammany's wishes on this office alone. As the anti-Jewish propaganda which the press fed the "common men" suggests, the "something indubitably exceptional" was Noah's religion. Voters discounted journalistic charges of immorality and aristocracy as election-time rhetoric. Noah's Judaism, on the other hand, was genuine and proudly displayed. The specter of a Jew hanging a Christian was frightening; it was, in shorthand terms, the age-old fear of Jewish revenge against Christianity. Many Jacksonians apparently preferred the safety of the church. As in 1822, they crossed party lines and voted for a Christian.[28]

"Major Noah has done his duty. He has been persecuted for the sake of the cause, and he should be rewarded for cause's sake." The words were those of Isaac Hill, editor of the pro-Jackson *New Hampshire Patriot*, after he learned of Noah's defeat. The feelings were Noah's own. With a wife to support and a newspaper to finance, Mordecai Noah needed patronage. Andrew Jackson and his party did not disappoint him. The first years of Jackson's presidency were the only years of Noah's life when he was well provided for.[29]

Noah's first political plum was a minor one. The New York City Common Council selected his *Enquirer* as one of five New York newspapers to be paid for printing the proceedings of the municipal corporation. As editor, he was no doubt pleased to see James Watson Webb's *Courier* denied city patronage. But he expected to receive something more for his years of service. Along with many well-informed politicians, he probably believed himself in line for the post of New York City corporation clerk. Although the *American* went so far as to lament that "an old citizen, a gentlemen and a Christian would be turned out" for a Jew, no nomination ever came through. Noah may have decided that he could do better in Washington. In February 1829, along with twenty other Jacksonian editors, he personally stated his claims before Andrew Jackson.[30]

Noah considered himself "too fat and in too good condition" to convince the president-elect of his penury. In the end, however, he must have made a good case for himself, for on April 25, Jackson appointed him "Surveyor and Inspector of the New York Port." The appointment was a stinging defeat for Martin Van Buren. The new Secretary of State had hoped that a Tammany stalwart, Jonathan Coddington, would be appointed surveyor, since Jackson had already appointed one Calhounite, Samuel Swartwout, as Collector of the Port. Van Buren would quite happily have relegated Noah to the less important post of municipal clerk. But Calhoun's friendship proved stronger than Van Buren's enmity. The lucrative position fell to Noah.[31]

Noah's chief task as surveyor was to record and certify all goods that were imported into the country via New York. He signed forms such as the following:

> I CERTIFY, That there was imported into this District, on the lst of September, 1830, by R.F. Allen & Co. in the American Ship Isabella, Leeds, Master, From Canton, one box of Hyson Tea, numbered and marked as per margin, containing Twelve Pounds.

He also collected fees (in addition to his hefty five-thousand-dollar salary) based on services rendered—or even, at times, those not rendered. Under the law, the collector, surveyor, and naval officer split between them the value of all goods seized at the port, regardless of who seized them. On July 28, 1831, for example, Collector Swartwout and High Constable Jacob Hays arrested Constant Polari, who had stolen the Dutch Crown jewels and escaped to New York. Noah received a third of the ten thousand dollars paid by the Dutch for the return of the jewels, even though, by his own admission, he played no part at all in either the theft's investigation or in Polari's capture. The Polari affair reemerged in 1850 when James Gordon Bennett of the New York *Herald* charged that Noah "salted down" the ten thousand dollars received from the Dutch government. Noah sued Bennett for libel, but the case was still pending when Noah died, and his relatives terminated the proceedings, much to the regret of Bennett's enemies.[32] While Noah did not keep for himself all of the money which he earned as surveyor—a portion of his emolument went to support Jacksonian politicians, and another large chunk went to cover the deficit of his newspaper—his income still was higher than it had ever been before.[33]

Noah saw no conflict of interest between his government post and his editorship of a newspaper. His *Enquirer* continued, albeit from an address closer to the Custom House. Many warned against this arrangement. Thomas Ritchie of the *Richmond Union* argued forcefully that "there should be as little connexion as possible between the press and the executive." He feared that patronage appointments such as Noah's would "bring down the lofty independence of the press." Several senators seconded these concerns. They opposed Jackson's policy of rewarding journalists with patronage, and made it clear that they could not confirm any editor unless he severed all journalistic ties. Surveyor Noah, who wanted both his newspaper and his senate confirmation, struggled with a dilemma. Journalistic independence doomed him to poverty, but rewarded him with respect and freedom. Political positions were more lucrative. But they demanded subordination, obedience, even silence.[34]

Happily for Noah, Andrew Jackson hinted at a way out of this dilemma. He declared that officers of government should not engage in politics openly. What they did privately was their own concern. In other words, the president would not be displeased if editors wrote anonymous pieces in favor of the administration so long as they did not maintain newspapers under their own name. Within a month of taking office, Noah moved to comply with this directive. He probably considered imitating other editors who removed their names from their newspapers while surreptitiously continuing to edit them as before. In the end, however, he followed the suggestion of James Gordon Bennett and Tammany Hall. On May 22, 1829, he sold his *Enquirer* for thirty-five thousand dollars to James Watson Webb and Daniel Tylee of the *Morning Courier.*[35]

Noah did not leave the field of journalism entirely. From the start, he promised to afford the new *Morning Courier and New York Enquirer* "all the aid" which his "editorial labor and experience" would permit. Under the arrangement, editorial responsibility lay entirely with Webb, who assumed blame for any item to which the administration took exception. Noah merely wrote articles and provided advice. Yet, he and Webb soon became fast friends. As Webb later admitted, they "daily almost hourly conversed freely on all the prominent issues of public interest." Other members of the large staff—including, at various times, James Lawson, Richard A. Locke, Prosper Wetmore, James G. Brooks, and Matthew L. Davis—helped to shape and enliven the *Courier and Enquirer.* James Gordon Bennett maintained the newspaper's connections with Tammany Hall. But Webb and Noah ran the paper. It is ultimately a tribute to their efforts (more to Webb's than to Noah's) that the *Courier and Enquirer* developed into one of the largest and most respected dailies in America.[36]

Perhaps because he spent less time than previously on his journalism, Noah found time to serve as a delegate to the New York City charter reform convention of 1829. New York's first ward elected him to the post, the only popular election which he ever won, and he took an active part in the proceedings. Chiefly, he concerned himself with three proposals. He wanted to strengthen the powers of the mayor, to abbreviate the term of common council members to one year, and to compel publication of all city messages and reports in the daily press. This latter cause bespoke an interest in open government, although it must have drawn smiles from the delegates. Ideology aside, Noah brought to the convention an intuitive feeling for language. He improved the wording of several amendments. He also displayed a lofty sense of history. It was at his insistence that the original 1657 charter of New Amsterdam was read into the record. As a Jew who had so recently been charged with dual loyalty, Noah may have had a special interest in demonstrating his association with his city's heritage. But eager as he may have been to belong, he refused to compromise his principles. He was one of only six delegates to oppose the report of the committee of the whole regarding redistribution of municipal powers, and he absented himself entirely from the final convention vote on the charter. The new charter created a Common

Council consisting of two houses, the Board of Aldermen and the Board of Assistant Aldermen, and it invested the mayor with somewhat greater power. In practice, however, many of the old abuses remained.[37]

The charter convention was one of Noah's rare forays into city politics. As a federal employee and a nationally recognized Jacksonian, the surveyor usually devoted most of his attention to matters pertaining to the government in Washington. In 1829, he served as unofficial advisor to Consul Charles Rhind, who undertook a secret mission aimed at concluding a commercial treaty with Turkey. Rhind praised Noah as "the best informed person" on the subject of Turkey to be found in the United States, and freely consulted him on highly secret diplomatic matters, a breach of confidence that disgusted Martin Van Buren. For his part, Noah provided Rhind with background information on Jewish bankers in the Ottoman Empire, and wrote him a Hebrew letter of introduction (cosigned by Naphtali Phillips), in which he asked Jewish leaders to aid Rhind in all his endeavors. Noah thought that Jewish bankers would be powerful enough to convince the Sultan to conclude a treaty "at a cheap rate." Van Buren feared that the loquacious Noah would undermine Rhind's cover (he was officially appointed consul to Odessa), and unwittingly compromise his mission. In fact, Rhind returned from Turkey with a treaty auspiciously favorable to the United States.[38]

Noah also gave advice regarding patronage appointments. He sought to make party loyalty the key criterion for a government post, and he brought many deserving office-seekers to the administration's attention. Years later, James Gordon Bennett charged in the *Herald* that Noah filled the Custom House with "a set of Jewish philosophers who with a very few exceptions, have helped to fleece the people of the United States of their money." He claimed that "many of these Hebrews" were even "related to the honest Major." As we shall see, Bennett made many such allegations and most proved completely false. Indeed, his charges reveal more about his own traditional stereotype of Jews as overt "philosophers" and covert "Shylocks" than they reveal about Noah's conduct in office. In this case, Noah actually did have three relatives in the Custom House, Naphtali Phillips and his sons Jonas and Aaron, but all held their positions before he came on the scene. He merely recommended that the collector of the port, Samuel Swartwout, keep his relatives at their desks.[39]

As surveyor, Noah had even more reason than before to maintain his interest in national politics. His job depended on the good graces of President Jackson. He therefore kept well informed. He exchanged letters with Duff Green, editor of Jackson's first "official" paper, the *Washington Telegraph*. He speculated with friends over Andrew Jackson's reelection plans in 1832. Finally, like all wise political employees, he carefully monitored the shifting fortunes of the Calhounites and the Van Burenites in the administration. He charted the moves of both warring factions carefully, sought diligently to determine the president's stance, and dexterously avoided committing to either side his wholehearted support.[40]

In spite of his caution, Noah almost lost his job. For a year, the surveyor had been serving at his post pending senatorial confirmation. He had carefully veiled his political views, and had published nothing under his own name. He therefore had every expectation that his commission would be approved, in spite of many senators' continuing hostility to the appointment of journalists to patronage posts. In March 1830, however, the increasingly pro-Calhoun *Washington Telegraph* alleged that a *Courier and Enquirer* article advocating a Jackson–Van Buren ticket in 1832 was actually written by Noah. James Watson Webb angrily denied the charge. He personally claimed responsibility for the article, and wondered out loud whether the *Telegraph* was not trying to poison the political atmosphere in advance of the vote on Noah's nomination. Noah also disavowed authorship of the offending article. In his open letter, however, he incautiously admitted that he maintained ties to the *Courier and Enquirer*. Even worse, he warmly endorsed in advance an Andrew Jackson bid for reelection. Unwittingly, the surveyor thus publicly confirmed many senators' worst fears of press–patronage connections. Despite the support of Vice-President Calhoun, the Senate, on May 10, 1830, defeated Noah's nomination by a vote of 25–23."[41]

The vote against Noah shocked many Democrats, infuriated Webb, and sent Noah scurrying off to Washington. Andrew Jackson, however, was unfazed. He simply sent Noah's appointment back to the Senate with the comment that "some of the members of the Senate voted against the confirmation of the appointment of Major M. M. Noah...through misapprehension." The misapprehension was actually Jackson's. When the angry Senate voted again on Noah, on May 29, not a single senator had changed his mind. What had changed was the composition of the chamber. Three of Noah's opponents (Senators Holmes, Tazewell, and Marks) were absent; meanwhile, all but one of his supporters (Senator Hayne) were on hand. The second vote thus ended in a 22–22 tie, and John C. Calhoun obligingly cast the decisive vote in Noah's favor. The surveyor's job was secure. Noah showed his gratitude by helping to set up Francis Blair's *Washington Globe* as the administration's new press spokesman.[42]

Andrew Jackson's unprecedented efforts on behalf of Noah encouraged the belief that the President had what Martin Van Buren called the "most friendly feelings" toward the surveyor. Those seeking power soon found him a good person to know. David Bailie Warden, who had helped Noah in his early days, now asked him for help in finding a new consulship. In reply, he heard indirectly that "Noah will keep fully his word, he loves you dearly, he honors you sincerely and he has the power of doing for you what no other person can nor will." Noah tried to be equally helpful to those seeking letters of introduction to the president and to those seeking favors from government. The surveyor did not neglect his friends just because he had suddenly come into power.[43]

Noah's new power may also have played a part in his association with the New York and Harlem Railroad, the first railroad in New York City. It was, perhaps, characteristic of Noah to be interested in an invention as new and as exciting as the locomotive. He quickly realized its enormous potential. In earlier years, however, he might have been paid to act as a publicist for the railroad; he certainly would not have been asked to act as an incorporator. Now that he was surveyor and a friend of Jackson, things were different. Even if he did not invest his own money in the railroad, he had sufficient influence to bring in money from friends, especially Jewish friends,[44] and from the state legislature. By making him an incorporator, the railroad bid for support in high places. Noah later severed his connections with the project, which took years to complete. Yet, he remained, with good reason, a proud pioneer. His efforts had helped to open up Harlem to the middle classes, and had begun to transform the upper New York City region from a declining "third or fourth rate country village" into a thriving ethnic community. Years later, the community would house many of Noah's coreligionists.[45]

In the midst of his public lobbying on behalf of the New York and Harlem Railroad, Noah was secretly also trying to raise funds to purchase half of the *Courier and Enquirer*. Daniel Tylee, co-owner of the paper with James Watson Webb, had made known his desire to sell; Noah, with great self-assurance, determined to buy. He needed twenty-thousand dollars, which he didn't have; but he did, at least, have access to power and patronage. On this basis alone, he managed to obtain funds. James Watson Webb's wealthy father-in-law, Alexander L. Stewart, put up five thousand dollars, and businessman Silas E. Burrows loaned the rest. Armed with this, Noah, on April 4, 1831, placed his own name alongside that of Webb on the mast of the *Courier and Enquirer*. Noah had not forgotten that President Jackson opposed overt political activity on the part of government officials. He privately admitted that he "risk[ed] much" in officially joining the paper. But the "serious and desperate" political fight facing the party in 1832—it was already clear that the president would face opposition from Henry Clay or John Calhoun—convinced him of the need to secure the powerful *Courier and Enquirer* for the Jacksonian. Presumably, he felt that Andrew Jackson would act like a Tammany man and forget his principles for the sake of political expediency.[46]

Andrew Jackson did not see things quite Noah's way. He was already drained by his battle with John Calhoun, the sensitive scandal over Peggy Eaton, and an extensive cabinet shakeup engineered by Martin Van Buren. Rather than having to face another chorus of opposition, the president thought it expedient to purge the new irritant by removing Surveyor Noah from office. Alarmed, James Watson Webb sent an appeal for help to Martin Van Buren, whom he erroneously blamed for Noah's troubles. But he worded his appeal so arrogantly that it only made matters worse. In desperation, Noah personally travelled to Washington. He hoped for a chance to plead his case before the president himself.

Noah first met with Martin Van Buren, whom he fortunately found in an ebullient mood. The Little Magician's recent political strategy had effectively purged Jackson's cabinet of its pro-Calhoun elements. Van Buren now saw himself as the president's natural successor. Soon the two veteran New York politicans understood one another. As Noah wrote to Webb, "I left him in a better humour towards me than for some years past." With Van Buren's blessing, the surveyor moved on to see the president. "He... will with his usual frankness declare to you what shall be done," Van Buren had promised. And so Jackson did. He told Noah to continue writing and to continue as proprietor. He warned him, however, to withdraw his name from the newspaper's mast. Jackson expressed confidence that Webb and Noah could somehow manage the legal arrangements between themselves.[47]

Noah left Washington convinced that "everything looked cheering." He was friends with Jackson and friends with Van Buren. He sat in the publisher's chair of James W. Webb and Co., the new dummy firm that produced the *Courier and Enquirer.* He sat, too, in the surveyor's chair of the New York Custom House. It was, as Noah admitted, his "moment of triumph." He had the best of all worlds. As he shortly learned, however, his good fortune rested on shallow ground. It depended for support on America's powerful and controversial central bank, the Bank of the United States, the very bank that Andrew Jackson had determined to destroy.[48]

Andrew Jackson's battle against the Bank of the United States forged the Jacksonian movement. It became the issue that divided politicians, inspired the masses, and led to the creation of the Whig Party. It also brought about the political downfall of Mordecai Noah. Noah was too sophisticated to view the Bank* as its enemies saw it: a sprawling monster extending its tentacles deep into the bowels of American society. On the other hand, he was too much a Jacksonian to ignore the very real abuses which the national Bank condoned. He therefore handled the Bank controversy as if it were an ordinary intra-party squabble: he sought to exact concessions from both sides and hoped that compromise and reconciliation would obviate the need for a difficult choice. Noah's hopes went unrealized. When the New York surveyor continued to vacillate on the Bank issue, others simply made his choice for him.[49]

Mordecai Noah's ambivalence toward the Bank went back many years. In 1818, his *National Advocate* had urged continued support for the central Bank, but had satisfied critics by calling for reforms of its management and powers. Later, he saw the Bank as more sinister: "the mammoth bank of the United States is prostrating the institutions of the state and the commerce of the city." Again, however, he urged extensive reforms rather than destruction. Merchants, bankers, and politicians (Martin Van Buren is a prime example) disagreed over the Bank's effect on the national economy. Noah, whose knowledge of finances was limited, saw no reason to take a firm stand on the issue.[50]

---

*In the following text, the capitalized form "Bank" refers only to the Bank of the United States.

Noah's position became more delicate once he was appointed to the post of surveyor. On the one hand, he felt attracted to the increasingly anti-Bank views of his patron, Andrew Jackson, who viewed the "monster" as an illegitimate and competing power.[51] On the other hand, he found himself pulled toward the firm pro-Bank views of his associate, James Watson Webb, whose frequent indebtedness made him a regular Bank customer. At the *Courier and Enquirer*, the politically and financially expedient anti-Bank stance generally won out, especially after Treasury Secretary Amos Kendall advised Noah in 1829 of President Jackson's decision to make the Bank a political issue.[52] But the newspaper continued to face pressure from the Bank's supporters, many of whom were prominent advertisers. Consequently, on this controversial issue, the *Courier and Enquirer* often remained diplomatically silent. When, in later years, it spoke up, it more often called for drastic reforms than for complete abandonment.[53]

The *Courier and Enquirer's* effort to satisfy backers of both sides of the Bank controversy continued until 1831. In that year, anti-Bank forces introduced into the state legislature the Morehead Resolution, a non-binding legislative declaration which urged Congress to oppose renewal of the Bank's charter when it came due. In response, both sides began to escalate their pressure on newspapers. Anti-Bank forces invoked the power of the state Democratic machine ("The Albany Regency") to whip newspapers into line; they threatened Bank supporters with loss of patronage. Pro-Bank forces, led by the wealthy, naive, scheming, and unstable merchant, Silas Burrows, adopted a more positive approach: they offered inducements. Hearing that his "old friend" Mordecai Noah sought to buy up Daniel Tylee's interest in the *Courier and Enquirer*, Burrows offered the surveyor a fifteen-thousand-dollar loan. The merchant assured Noah that he would immediately obtain funds for the loan from his own father. He warned Noah, however, that both Burrowses held very strong pro-Bank sentiments—and expected them to be noticed.[54]

The grateful Noah took Burrows's hint. Anti-Morehead editorials soon began to appear in the *Courier and Enquirer*. But Noah did not expect reprisals. He thought that the Morehead resolution went beyond the president's wishes—assuming, as did most people, that the president would sanction any means used to keep the *Courier and Enquirer* in friendly hands. Had he known the truth about the Burrows loans, Noah would have been more circumspect. As he discovered only later, Burrows had obtained the money for his loan, not from his father, but from the Bank itself (actually from the Bank's president, Nicholas Biddle, who recorded the loan nine months later in Bank records.) This deception was in line with Bank policy regarding influence buying: "The editor should believe that he is merely following friendly suggestions...no one connected with the paper should have any idea of the source from whence advances have been made."[55] The policy of putting important individuals in the Bank's debt without their knowledge did not only apply to newspaper editors. Three months after the Noah loan, Collector of the

Port Samuel Swartwout engineered a loan to Postmaster William T. Barry through the Bank's good offices. "Neither of the parties know the source where I have procured this loan," Swartwout assured Nicholas Biddle, "nor shall they until a *proper* time."[56]

Unfortunately for Silas Burrows, other newspapers had a good idea as to the source of Noah's advances. Within days, they charged Burrows, the Bank, and Noah with bribery. Although the charges met with disbelief, the *Courier and Enquirer* prudently resumed its silence on the Bank question. On so controversial and ramified a subject, it dared not risk the consequences of a firm position.[57]

Webb and Noah printed new pro-Bank editorials in August and December when they obtained additional Bank loans, this time openly and directly.[58] Previous pro-Bank editorials and an editorial campaign favoring the creation of an Albany branch of the Bank had alienated the paper from local sources of funds. It entered into an accommodation with the Bank of the United States in order to survive. Of course, the Bank never officially demanded editorial support as a condition of its loans. Indeed, it loaned money to many pro-Jackson and anti-Bank newspapers. But editors often independently concluded, for obvious reasons, that the Bank's friendship was worth cultivating. The potential benefits from playing both sides seemed to outweigh the risks. In Mordecai Noah's case, even the risks were limited, due to the multi-owner structure of the *Courier and Enquirer*. When, for example, administration officials warned Noah against his newspaper's pro-Bank stance, Noah simply denied "that he has written any article upon the subject of the bank," and he promised "to do his best to keep things right" in the future. He then proceeded to forward the letter of warning to Nicholas Biddle.[59]

The *Courier and Enquirer*'s game of duplicity was too delicate to escape detection for long—and the paper's editors knew it. When Congress began to investigate the Bank of the United States pursuant to the Bank's 1832 application for charter renewal, James Watson Webb panicked and immediately paid off one Bank loan. He simultaneously urged Nicholas Biddle "to keep our names and the name of our journal from appearing" in the investigation. Webb and Noah feared that even the Bank loans that they knew about might look to the committee like "an open case of bribery." Once they learned that the Burrows loan of 1831 was also from the Bank, they realized that corruption would most certainly be suspected.[60] Happily, Silas Burrows agreed "never… to desert a friend in the hour of trial." He remained mercifully silent. Only James Watson Webb appeared before Augustin S. Clayton's investigation committee. Aided by a letter from Mordecai Noah, he endeavored to justify all the newspaper's Bank loans as necessary and proper. Noah quite honestly swore that he had known nothing about Burrows's connections with the Bank, and was shocked to learn of them. A majority of the Clayton Committee, however, did not believe the editors, especially not after learning that Biddle had tampered with the Bank's books. In its final report, the committee concluded that the *Courier and Enquirer* had been bribed. Two minority reports, one of which was authored by John Quincy Adams, disagreed. Both cleared the newspaper of any misdeed whatsoever.[61]

The truth lay somewhere between these two extremes. The Bank had indirectly tried to influence the *Courier and Enquirer*, and the *Courier and Enquirer* had altered its editorial policy in response to Bank favors. But there was no prior agreement linking Bank loans, as distinct from Burrows's loan, to editorial support. Instead, the Bank, like any powerful politician of the day, used its power to its own best advantage. By the same token, Noah and Webb employed the politics of expediency to obtain maximum benefit for themselves and their newspaper.

The report of the Clayton Committee almost cost Mordecai Noah his job. The press and Tammany Hall believed the majority report and joined in censuring the surveyor. James A. Hamilton strongly advised Andrew Jackson that Noah was "unworthy of the confidence of the Government," and should be removed. Noah himself heard rumors "that I am to be requested to resign my office." But Jackson demurred. Noah's friends and the president's own high regard for the surveyor apparently saved him, for the time being. Still, Noah must have known that he would eventually have to choose between James Watson Webb and Andrew Jackson. He could not long continue his compromise course, which typically sought to satisfy everyone by proclaiming the Bank at one and the same time unconstitutional, necessary, in need of reform, and deserving of a new charter.[62]

The denouement came within days of Andrew Jackson's veto of the Bank recharter bill (July 10, 1832). It could not have come at a worse time. The *Courier and Enquirer* had just defaulted on one of its loans, owing to the large amount of advertising lost during the cholera epidemic that was then raging in the city. James Watson Webb's father-in-law, Alexander Stewart, grudgingly paid the debt, but demanded a large compensation for his trouble. The newspaper was in imminent financial peril. As for Noah, the veto had placed his paper and his president formally at odds. Wisely, he sided with the president and supported the veto.[63]

James Watson Webb solved both his problems with finances and his problems with Noah through a single ultimatum. He demanded from the Bank a loan sufficiently large for him to pay his debts and buy out Noah. He warned that if he didn't receive it, he would surrender entire control of the *Courier and Enquirer*'s editorial page to Bank opponents. Do "not be blind to your own interest and the interest of the bank," he sternly admonished the Bank's president. Nicholas Biddle, seething with rage at the Bank veto, needed no encouragement. He arranged for Webb to receive his loan. Immediately afterwards, on August 23, 1832, the *Courier and Enquirer* appeared without its banner of support for the Democratic team of Jackson, Van Buren, and Marcy. "Principles, not men" became the newspaper's new motto. The motto did not reflect reality. Actually, principles, men, money, and expedience lay behind Webb's actions. They also lay behind Noah's simultaneous decision to sell his share of the *Courier and Enquirer* and to retire from the press.[64]

In later years, Noah and Webb remained good friends. Although they later became competitors, and exchanged occasional invective in the press, they shared many of the same views and frequently worked together. In 1841, Noah recommended Webb for a patronage position under President William Henry Harrison. Five years later, he praised his tempestuous former colleague as "a very honorable man in all his dealings; always reliable in all his friendships and decided in his hostilities...possessing about as good a character generally speaking as his colleagues."[65]

Noah's retirement from the *Courier and Enquirer* preserved his job. He vowed eternal fealty to Andrew Jackson, and eagerly awaited the November election, certain that it would guarantee him his office for another four years. He must have looked forward, at age forty-seven, to a comfortable and secure life, one which would have permitted him the leisure to spend time with his family. But, as so often before, he was to be disappointed. Party leaders expressed understandable doubts about Noah's loyalty. They knew that he had supported, even if less than wholeheartedly, Andrew Jackson's two enemies: John Calhoun and the Bank of the United States. They knew that he continued to have friendly personal relations with Calhounite Duff Green and pro-Bank editor, James Watson Webb. They knew that the Clayton Committee had convicted him of bribery. On the advice of Vice-President-elect Martin Van Buren, who had opposed his nomination from the start, Surveyor Noah was not reappointed to a second term after he routinely resigned following the election. On January 10, 1833, a new, docile, and more consistently loyal Jacksonian, Horace Craig, succeeded him.[66]

Noah blamed Van Buren rather than Jackson for his misfortune. Even months later, he professed to be mystified as to why, "after having influenced Van Buren into the support of General Jackson," the new vice-president "thought it politic to punish me for it by pushing me out of office." The mystery, however, was no mystery at all. Van Buren served as a convenient scapegoat for Noah, who was unwilling to blame himself for his political errors. By setting himself a goal—"Van Buren must take the consequences"—Noah gave his life new direction. He found the strength to marshal his resources and join forces with other opponents of Van Buren. When he reemerged politically, it was as a Calhounite. He had become a firm critic of Jackson's inner circle of advisors, the "kitchen cabinet."[67]

Noah's new friends could not mitigate the shock of his surveyorship defeat. Even as late as 1841, Noah recalled with bitterness how "the crust" that had been thrown to him was "withdrawn before it was eaten." The bitterness is understandable. By 1841, Noah had been hungering for an entire decade just to get another taste of that delectable but elusive crust, the upper crust—the life of money, security, and power.[68]

Chapter VI

Conservative Whig

Mordecai Noah's new alliance with the enemies of Martin Van Buren, beginning in 1833, brought about a conservative shift in his politics. He expressed a new-found sympathy for states' rights advocates, southerners, and the rich, along with their causes. Yet, he did not suddenly abandon all his old principles: he still found deep satisfaction in helping others, and he still remained closely tied to the Jewish community. When his old and new principles clashed, however, he faced a dilemma. Usually, he sought somehow to harmonize his old and new views. He searched for synthesis, endeavored to find a middle ground, or attempted to play both sides of an issue. But he could not escape charges of inconsistency. Like most politicians of his day, he shifted parties, politics, and policies for reasons of both high principle and personal ambition. Noah the Whig differed appreciably both in politics and in thought from Noah the Jacksonian. America, too, had changed from the headstrong days of Jackson's first term. Yet, in both Noah's case and America's, differences are only part of the story; important continuities remained.[1]

One crucial difference between Surveyor Noah and ex-Surveyor Noah was confidence. Events had chastened the rambunctious politician. He became cautious. He seemed lost. He had to rebuild from scratch. At forty-seven, Noah was too old to learn a new trade or to enter a new profession. His thoughts turned rather to his old trade of journalism. He laid plans to begin a new daily newspaper.

A court suit gave Noah legal reassurance that James Watson Webb and the trustees who controlled the *Courier and Enquirer* could not sue him for breach of his 1829 merger agreement. His stint as co-owner of the *Courier and Enquirer*, according to the court, voided the earlier guarantees against his editing a competing New York newspaper. Noah also did not have to worry about finances. Since friends advanced money for the new paper and employed him as a salaried editor, he stood to lose nothing, even if his venture failed. Finally, he did not have to fear his own administrative incompetence. Thomas

Gill, a highly skilled newspaper manager (formerly on the *New York Post*), agreed to assume all non-editorial duties in the new paper. Noah had only to do what he did best: writing and editing. On September 25, 1833, the long-awaited newspaper finally appeared. Emblazoned on page one was the title: *The New York Evening Star*.[2]

The *Star* became one of the finest and most influential newspapers in the country. It developed a character of its own, and created features that others quickly imitated. Wiley Conner of the *Courtland* [Tennessee] *Herald* used the *Star* as a model, and proudly claimed to write "in the Mordecai Noah style." It was a formula for success. The *Star* appealed to merchants with its incisive editorials, and to women with its light hearted columns. Noah was a master of both genres. Meanwhile, Thomas Gill procured advertisements for the *Star* and kept the enterprise firmly, if not spectacularly, in the black. Partly because of this success, Noah never concerned himself with the two latest trends in journalism: increasing speed and decreasing price. The cautious and conservative *Star* stood aloof from the costly battle to get the news first. It did not invest in the boats and runners used by other newspapers to scoop the competition by several hours. Noah also stood firm against price reductions to one or two pennies. In the 1830s, Benjamin Day's *New York Sun* and James Gordon Bennett's *New York Herald* proved that a newspaper could cut its price substantially and still increase profits; but only if it appealed to the masses with crime, scandal, and salacious writing. Preferring to uplift the masses and "advance good morals" without being prudish, Noah contented himself with a smaller circulation (about three thousand) and smaller profits.[3] His six-penny paper proudly appealed to the "men that buy and sell and patronise and have the means to do so."[4]

In place of speed and low price, Noah claimed to offer quality. The *Star* employed talented reporters, among them Peter Townsend and Noah's nephew, Levi Laurens. It maintained stringers in Washington, and received news from around the nation. It boasted one of the first foreign correspondents of any American newspaper, R. Shelton Mackenzie of the *Liverpool Journal*. It published feature columns by William Dunlap, George P. Morris, and other leading cultural figures. It even printed occasional diagrams and plates, as long as they met high standards. The *Evening Star* stayed clear of penny-press gimmicks. Noah was the first to brand the *Sun*'s "discovery" of moon men a hoax. He also refused to exaggerate news for effect, although Bennett's use of this technique in his coverage of a murder investigation won him many new readers. But in advocating quality journalism, Noah ignored the potential of the penny press. He failed to realize that bargain-priced newspapers, once they accumulated profits, could afford to improve their coverage, employ more reporters, and stand firm against outside pressures. In Noah's own lifetime, the penny press would produce newspapers superior in quality to anything that American journalism had hitherto seen.[5]

Penny-press dailies, which depended for profits solely on advertising and sales, had no trouble maintaining their political independence; they prospered spectacularly without party subsidies. *The Evening Star* was less fortunate. Its profits were modest, never exceeding eight thousand dollars a year, and it depended for support on political allies. Noah was not, however, an editor for hire. He did not write as he was bidden. Rather, he solicited aid from those with whom he shared a common set of enemies. His patrons and readers joined in opposing Martin Van Buren, the "kitchen cabinet," and the New York State Democratic political machine (the Albany Regency).[6]

In the early days of the *Evening Star*, Noah sought to maintain a foothold in the Jacksonian camp, in spite of his opposition to these elements. In his *Prospectus of the Evening Star*, and in his later columns, he carefully distinguished between Jackson's aides and advisors, whom he opposed, and the "old hero" himself for whom he vowed undying support. "The people should rally round Andrew Jackson," he proclaimed, "they should all become his friends, his supporters and counsellors; they should aid all his patriotic views, bestow upon him an enlarged and liberal confidence, and thus separate him from the advances of a band of selfish speculators, immense stock jobbers, and ambitious politicians, who will attempt to trade upon his popularity for their own profit and advancement."[7]

Noah's distinction between the president and his advisors echoed earlier charges by supporters of John Calhoun. Still hoping to reconcile the president and his vice-president, Calhounites had blamed all misunderstandings between the two men on malevolent Van Burenite conspirators. When the "voice of truth" reached Jackson, they promised that he would "see and understand." But Jackson saw perfectly well. He was hardly the weak, naive, and dominated president portrayed by his erstwhile supporters. Instead, he was a president who ruled his cabinet, ruled his "kitchen cabinet," and sometimes overruled both. Former Jacksonians, including Noah, resorted to the artifice of a maladvised president to cover the gap between what Jackson promised and what Jackson produced. Rather than admit that Jackson, from their point of view, was "the god that failed," they invented a rationalization, "scheming advisors," that both justified their own former support for the president and explained why the hoped for millennium had not come about. In good conscience, they could thus ally themselves with anti-Jacksonians, all the while proclaiming that they truly believed in the Jacksonian gospel.[8]

Unfortunately for Noah, the justification that salved his conscience convinced his opponents not at all. Jacksonian newspapers merely charged him with crude deception, and labeled him a political foe. The *Albany Argus*, which Van Buren controlled, prophesied that Noah would "be as successful in getting the confidence of the friends of Jackson as he was in collecting shekels from the Jews." The *Washington Globe*, which Noah actually had helped to set up, urged the *Evening Star*'s editor to pursue "the honester calling of his tribe—the traffic of selling rags." A day later, editor Francis Blair apologized for the "ill-natured expression," and proclaimed that it was not to be understood "as applicable to Jews as a people."[9]

Anti-Jacksonians welcomed Noah with open arms. They encouraged the editor to oppose Jackson's removal of federal funds from the Bank of the United States, and goaded him to break with Jackson altogether. But though he fiercely attacked Jacksonian actions, Noah still hesitated to attack Jackson by name. In 1833, he supported the Independent Democratic ticket (also called the Independent Republican ticket), a slate which opposed Tammany Hall and Van Buren. Yet, he stubbornly maintained that the slate was completely Jacksonian, in spite of scornful Jacksonian opposition. A year later, following a surprisingly impressive showing at the polls, the Independents organized and assumed the trappings of a political party. Again, Noah supported them; again, he opposed the "cabinet," the "Regency" and Martin Van Buren; again, he obstinately insisted that his "opposition ha[d] been at no time to General Jackson."[10]

Noah's ritualistic devotions to Andrew Jackson did not survive the bitter 1834 election. Identified by outsiders as an anti-Jacksonian, he eventually assumed the proffered mantle, especially as the legion of "old Hickory's" opponents grew larger. Noah reneged on his promise that he would be "the last to abandon" Andrew Jackson. He finally accepted the inevitable and joined the burgeoning chorus of protest against the president's alleged misuses of power. Shortly thereafter, he became both a leading Whig—"Whig" was the evocative name that the anti-Jackson party chose for itself—and a leading administration critic. By 1835, the *Evening Star* spoke sneeringly of "King Andrew." It reminded readers about sordid aspects of Jackson's past that editor Noah had, just a few years earlier, striven mightily to cover up.[11]

Noah's conversion to the Whig cause seems at first glance to be surprising. He was not an old Federalist seeking to resurrect an aristocratic party; he was not a former Antimason; he was not of British or Protestant extraction; and he was not a supporter of a strong, active federal government. Yet a Whig he was, a prominent, if somewhat independent one. This seeming anomaly is explained by the peculiar nature of the nascent New York Whig Party. The party, in its early days, was almost an anti-party. It included a disparate group of variegated politicians, united by little more than their opposition to the policies of Andrew Jackson, Martin Van Buren, and their followers. Noah's political stance was typical of many. He avowed a primarily negative goal: "to prevent Martin Van Buren from becoming president." As for the few positive political reforms which Noah in 1833 had suggested—a one term presidency, direct election of the President, a ban on the appointment of congressmen to public office, and an end to nationwide, easily manipulated, party nominating conventions—he quickly abandoned them after they attracted no attention.[12]

Noah allied himself with the conservative (also called the conservative democratic) wing of the Whig Party, an unstable faction largely composed of ex-Tammany Hall members who found themselves in political disfavor. His was the faction closest to the merchants of New York; other factions, notably the Antimasonic and antislavery elements of the party, depended on other constituencies, looked to other leaders, and read other newspapers. Noah was also especially close to the Whig Party's Jewish supporters. Jewish Whigs presumably comprised the wealthier branch of the community, those who suffered from the economic dislocations attributed to the Bank War. Jews may also have voted Whig to identify with higher status ethnic groups which tended to vote in opposition to the pro-Catholic Democrats. Whatever the case, Jewish Whigs received surprising attention. "Let him [Martin Van Buren] take the followers of St. Peter," an 1838 Whig pamphlet proclaimed, "we are content with the followers of Moses." As it happened, in that particular 1838 election many of the "followers of Moses" refused to vote at all, since election day conflicted with Passover (April 10, 1838). The *New York Herald* thought that this might excuse Whig losses. It reported improbably that "the Pesach [Passover] diminished the Whig vote." But not for long. According to subsequent *Herald* reports, active Jewish support for the Whigs soon resumed. In 1840, the *Herald* predicted that "more than two thirds of the Jews in this state will vote for Seward and Harrison. They can bring to the polls in this city about eleven hundred voters." Six months later, the *Herald*'s political analyst gave further specifics. The Jews, apparently, were a force to be reckoned with: "Most of the Portuguese Jews are Whigs; of the German Jews, about half are Whigs; of the Pollakim [Polish Jews] about one third. There is still another sect of Jews in this city whose politics, etc. are but little if at all known."[13]

Most Jews, as well as most non-Jews, devoted their attention to politics only around election time. Not so Mordecai Noah. His was a ceaseless and usually futile quest to find the right candidate: the man who would unite the Whigs, inspire the electorate, bring the party a victory, and reward the faithful editor who supported him. State and local politics took up relatively little of Noah's time. Although he was an early supporter of Gulian Verplanck for the 1834 mayoralty race, and although he supported William Seward whenever he ran for office, he generally occupied his columns with presidential affairs. His goals, after all, were to take revenge on Martin Van Buren and to regain a slice of federal patronage.[14]

With the caution typical of this period in his life, Noah settled on no candidate in the prolonged 1836 presidential campaign. He did express concern that Daniel Webster would prove an unpopular sectional candidate, and he seemed to lean toward William Henry Harrison. Still, he had warm words also for Judge Hugh White, and until he dropped from the race, he praised Henry Clay. Noah's caution paid off when the Whigs allowed each state party to name its own opponent to Martin Van Buren. Their aim was to deny Van Buren an electoral majority, so as to eventually defeat him in the House of Representatives. But Whigs in New York and most other states nominated Harrison, and Noah approved of the choice. He boosted Tippecanoe lustily and foresaw certain victory at the polls. Unfortunately, his intense, personal desire for political revenge clouded his view of political reality. Even in retrospect, the *Evening Star*'s November 8, 1836 headline— *Pennsylvania Safe! Harrison Elected—Van Buren at Kinderhook*—seems almost as sad as it is ridiculous.[15]

"Betrayal" and "treachery" were terms that Noah used to explain the 1836 national Whig defeat. He did not refer to his own miscalculations. But all was not gloom. On the local level, there had been no "treachery"; the Whigs, in fact, had scored notable gains. The way Whig analysts read the election, everything augured well for the future. For once, these Whig analysts were right, but for entirely the wrong reasons. They certainly never imagined that, in 1837, a searing depression would descend upon the country. President Van Buren, who was not to blame for the depression, proved unequal to the economic challenge which it posed. He stood by timidly as privation and hardship spread throughout the country. Democrats watched helplessly as support for their party declined drastically. Sensing their chance, the Whigs organized and thrust for victory. They copied old Democratic tactics in quest of success. Yet, Whig efforts to organize a party structure led inevitably to disagreement and resistance. While the party demanded strict discipline, politicians and editors, Noah among them, frequently held out for their independence. Noah had faced the identical problem many times before.[16]

Noah justified his independence by rhetorically referring to his "long-standing principles" and by characterizing his *Star* as an "independent Whig Journal." He did not hesitate to oppose both his party's policies and its politics when he disagreed with them. When, for example, Whigs attacked state banking practices (notably those of the Phoenix Bank), defended abolitionists, advocated large spending projects, or crusaded for war, he dissented. He also parted company from Whigs who supported the presidential aspirations of Daniel Webster or Winfield Scott. Noah believed that the only Whig with any chance of winning in 1840 was Henry Clay. As for his party's newspapers, Noah often treated them (and they him) like sworn political enemies. Spurred by competition and the desire to prove his *Evening Star* unique, he fought press battles even over such trivial matters as his theatrical judgments and his devotion to the *New York Mirror*. Nevertheless, he generally proved loyal. He attacked Democrats with a vengeance, hated Martin Van Buren with a passion, and supported all party nominees at election time. Much as he rejected and repudiated all overt attempts to control or influence the *Evening Star*, Noah, on most occasions, accepted it as his "duty" to "blow the trumpet and obey orders."[17]

The Whigs, for their part, treated Noah the way that they perceived him: as a valuable, ambitious, and independent-minded supporter of the party's conservative wing. The *Star* received its share of patronage, and Noah received occasional honors, but neither the paper not its editor met with full acceptance. Both seemed too closely identified with the people Noah called his "old friends at Tammany Hall." Many Whigs thus viewed the *Star*'s editor neither as an insider nor as an outsider, a marginal position familiar for other reasons both to him and to his coreligionists. In April 1837, Noah was excluded. Whigs conspicuously neglected to invite him to a party dinner celebrating the election of New York's first Whig mayor. Several months later, he was excluded again. This time, Whigs denied him a patronage appointment as city comptroller. The fact that the previous Democratic comptroller, William Denman, supported his appointment probably helped the aspirant not at all. By the end of 1837, however, Noah finally was included. He played a prominent role in the Grand Whig Jubilee which celebrated the party's victories in the November election. In the ensuing years, Whig–Noah relations fluctuated wildly. The editor's place in the party depended on the outcome of the two protracted struggles in which he was involved: the political struggle between various factions of the Whig coalition, and the philosophic struggle between party discipline and self determination.[18]

Factional disputes generally found Noah allied with the conservative wing of the Whig Party. This group, more than any other, represented his emerging political philosophy. The middle-aged, married, and worldly editor had lost most of his youthful interest in social reform. He was in good company. The hard economic times had tempered the reform spirit all over the country. Yet, in Noah's case, conservatism was tinted by a continuing, if diminished, interest in human rights and social welfare. Noah could never long forget his own minority status and humble beginnings.[19]

Noah proudly identified with the "old school" of politics, a school he associated with Jefferson and the founding fathers. Perhaps in reaction to "King" Andrew Jackson, he called on Americans to "weaken the powers of the general government and to strengthen the powers of the state." In 1837, he went so far as to call for a constitutional convention aimed at curtailing the power of the executive branch. He thought that government should concern itself largely with peace and tranquility. He therefore lamented militaristic cries for war against France, Canada, and the Indians, and he attacked proposals for increased defense spending. The issues that vitally concerned him were "order," "good government," and the domestic threat caused by disorderly mobs.[20]

In keeping with his concern about domestic matters, Noah commented extensively and often in brilliant prose on social affairs and innovations. As befits a conservative, he expressed generally critical remarks. He thus described fashionable, late-hour parties as "the way our girls kill themselves prematurely." He even considered the soirées a cause of consumption. But woe to the young woman who swore off parties and took up sleighing! "One pleasant sleigh ride begets another," he warned, and in the end, "dissipation wears out the slender female frame." Unfortunately, Noah found auctions to be no better a pastime for women. "Pushing, squeezing, jostling each other—rumping the ladies ruffs, over bidding, getting excited by competition, buying things not wanted, and paying far above their value"—he condemned auctions as a waste of time and money. Men had more serious vices: speculation and gambling. Noah advocated hard work and thrift as better routes to fortune. Indeed, he now praised the wealthy, whom he himself had reviled in former years, because they set so fine an example: "almost all who are rich men began life as poor men, and by economy, industry, good fortune and integrity have become rich."[21]

Discipline had been a key factor in Noah's life. Without it he could hardly have pursued so many varied careers. Discipline is what Noah felt society lacked. Discipline, not surprisingly, became a cornerstone of his conservative social philosophy. "A sound whipping to every child that commits any thing wrong," he solemnly proclaimed. He opposed new views of leniency and educators' calls for a shorter school day. On the other hand, reforms that encouraged discipline met with his complete approval. He was an early and enthusiastic advocate of temperance; "a better reform, he claimed, "cannot exist." Once the movement became generally popular, in the 1830s, he made an important contribution to the cause by publishing a traditional Jewish recipe for "temperance wine"—unfermented raisin wine which many New York Sephardic Jews used on Passover:[22]

> Take a gallon demijohn, or stone jug; pick three or four pounds of bloom raisins, break off the stems; put the raisins in the demijohn, and fill it with water. Tie a rag over the mouth, and place the demijohn near the fire, or on one side of the fireplace, to keep it warm. In about a week it will be fit for use, making a pure, pleasant, and sweet wine free from alcohol.

Noah notwithstanding, raisin wine was neither biblical in origin, nor was it universally consumed by Jews at the Passover seder. Still, his recipe bespeaks the unselfconscious way in which he merged his religion and his social thought in an effort to achieve an American–Jewish synthesis.[23]

The same religious and human considerations which made Noah an advocate of temperance prevented him from taking the extreme stance of prohibition. He reminded his readers that his biblical namesake (the editor's favorite biblical character) "loved a drop of wine," and that even the Temple priests could drink when off duty. Besides, he observed, liquor in moderation helped the poor to keep warm in winter and helped everyone to cure mild cases of "indisposition." Abstinence, he darkly warned, would lead only to "reaction and concealment."[24]

Noah showed similar broad social concern in his reaction to the economic crisis of the 1830s. Although he refused to blame banks for the crisis, considered the workingman's (Locofoco) party "too ultra," and called for a cutback in spending, he condemned those who maintained that the poor "deserve to starve because they have earned nothing." He proposed, instead, intensive efforts aimed at finding the poor jobs. He advised Whig candidates to advocate an end to the use of convict labor, and he urged banks to lower their loan rates until the crisis passed.[25]

Yet another example of Noah's mixture of conservatism and conscience may be seen in his writings on Mormonism. Like most of his countrymen, he considered this new religion to be an "error and delusion." He referred to Joseph Smith's converts as "dupes" and worse. Yet, as a Jew, a humanitarian, and a firm advocate of peace and tranquillity, he censured the "intolerance and cruel bigotry" of those who persecuted the Church of Jesus Christ of Latter Day Saints. He urged Americans to leave the Mormons alone.[26]

More than many of his contemporaries, Noah recognized a central tension in the democratic system: the tension between individual rights and social stability. He found no simple solutions. Repelled as he was by what he called the "immoral" and deplorable doctrines of freethinker Frances Wright, he still conceded her the liberty to speak out freely. He lamented "religious imposters," but insisted that "freedom of religious toleration" prevented the state from acting against them. On the other hand, he found that the duty to "defend government and soil" transcended the "scruples" of Quakers. Much as he hoped for compromise with the pacifist religious group, he refused to support a bill exempting them from state service. Similarly, he found that law and order was more important than the just claims of "anti-renters." He sympathized with the plight of agrarians faced with landowners' enormous demands for back rent, and he called on the wealthy to show compassion. But he did not in any way countenance anti-renters' militant tactics.[27]

Broadminded as he often was, Noah certainly did not always see both sides of divisive issues. He had no sympathy at all for advocates of birth control and abortion, and, as we shall see, he took an increasingly hard-line stance against black rights. For the most part, however, his attitude was one of moderate conservatism. Fearful of social change, and eager to preserve the social order, he nevertheless respected minority rights, and lamented the occasional need for government coercion.[28]

Mordecai Noah's fear of social change, and his simultaneous interest in helping others and in preserving minority rights had a particularly strong impact on his attitude toward Irish Catholic immigrants. In the 1830s, these immigrants had become a central political concern in New York. Their number had grown markedly, due largely to the first Irish potato blight. Increasingly, their votes in the city had become a potent and adroitly manipulated political force.

Since the days of De Witt Clinton, the Irish had usually voted Democratic. After unsuccessfully wooing them, Mordecai Noah and his fellow Whigs concluded that Irish voters would continue to vote generally Democratic. The Whigs foresaw that the Irish, armed with both legal and illegal ballots, would ensure continued Democratic hegemony over all of New York City. Only a new coalition, one composed of anti-Irish Democrats and regular Whigs, had the potential to break this stranglehold. After months of articles bewailing "the changes which may be produced in the character and habits of native born citizens by the influx of foreigners," Noah, in June 1835, helped to bring this new coalition into effect. He joined in creating the Native American Democratic Association.[29]

Unlike many nativist organizations, the Native American Democratic Association was not avowedly anti-Catholic, a fact Noah stressed. The Jewish nativist scorned Protestants who lampooned Catholic ritual, and he urged all New Yorkers to "permit citizens to enjoy their religious belief and their ceremonies without attempting to bring them into ridicule." Noah himself was still suspicious of "popery," "priestcraft," and Catholic power. His own ancestors had suffered at the hands of the Spanish Inquisition, and he knew only too well that Jews in Rome and elsewhere continued to suffer under Catholic rule. He had also not forgotten Irish Catholic hostility to him when he ran for sheriff in 1828. Nor could he forget that his nemesis, James Gordon Bennett, was a Catholic. Yet, he also knew many liberal and tolerant Catholics. He befriended William Denman, editor of the pro-Democratic, Irish Catholic weekly, the *Truth Teller*. He praised Baltimore Catholics for their help in the battle to pass the "Jew Bill," the bill which enfranchised the Jews of Maryland. (Earlier, he had wrongly assumed that they opposed the measure.) He certainly saw no reason to join in any Protestant crusade. To the contrary, he branded as "disgraceful," "frauds," and "libels," books like *Six Months in a Convent* (1835), and *Awful Disclosures* (1836), which titillated the masses with lurid tales of convent secrets. He condemned the hate-mongering of the New York Protestant Association and similar militant groups. He even noted the irony that, of all people, a Jew had "to admonish Christians to live together in brotherhood and affection."[30]

Noah knew that anti-Catholicism held out great dangers to the Jewish people. Persecutions, after all, only bred further persecutions. It was a short step from anti-popery to anti-rabbinism. As the *Truth Teller* reminded Noah, a Jew, because he was a Jew, "ought to be the last man in the states" to be linked to religious prejudice. Noah evidently got the message. He occasionally condemned individual Catholic officials, and he lamented Rome's influence in America. But his pro-Catholic and pro-tolerance comments are far more striking. He never deviated from his 1824 view that "the Catholic religion in its purity is like all pure religions; it contains nothing revolting to piety, reason and common sense."[31] As for anti-Catholicism, he considered it "the precursor to bigotry and intolerance and a foe to liberty of conscience."[32]

Liberty of conscience did not enter into Noah's consideration of the immigrant problem. He, along with most nativists, did not want to shut the door against any immigrants, nor did he wish to treat "adopted citizens" differently from native American citizens. He supported measures aimed only at restricting the political activity of aliens. He hoped to prevent non-citizens from voting until they had accumulated twenty years (later changed to twenty-one years) residence in the country—the same number of years that a native-born resident had to wait before he could vote. The fact that the two situations were not parallel made no difference to nativists. Earlier, Noah had not hesitated to welcome alien voters when, for a brief period, he thought that they might support him. In 1827, for example, he had lauded immigrants as assets to America, and had bitterly lashed out against nativists: "to use the term 'foreigner' as a reproach is at once a libel upon the laws and customs of the country and an effusion of vulgar and spiteful malevolence." Yet, his course was not merely dictated by political expedience, despite the *Truth Teller*'s claim that "if Noah could command the support and vote of Irish men, he would discover a thousand qualities of their character." Noah was a nativist at heart. He believed, along with many native-born citizens, that an American birthright and upbringing were somehow superior.[33]

Noah had demonstrated his nativistic chauvinism as early as 1817, when he advised Columbia University to appoint only Americans to fill its academic vacancies. He warned that "we have no idea of permitting the minds of our children to be warped by foreign prejudices." In later years, he often employed nativism in his personal attacks against competing journalists, implying that their place of birth affected the quality of their reporting. He even once suggested that the Washington Monument be built strictly by native hands. The natives, Noah implied, were true believers in America. He claimed on their behalf the special rights and special status that others sought to accord only to Christians. Some New Yorkers called for a Protestant America; Noah, as if in response, insisted that "Native Americans must control the country."[34]

Noah promised that a nativist-controlled America would be benevolent—in spite of the demand that immigrants give up the vote for two decades. Even when he was at his most virulent, he stressed that "we are ready to extend the hand of friendship to *all* who may emigrate to our favoured country." He knew that his fellow Jews were among those immigrating to America, and he wanted to make sure that they would be in no way hindered. Noah also foreswore all oppression. In spite of occasional calls for job discrimination, he generally advocated equal opportunity. He offered immigrants "the full countenance and equal protection of the laws."[35]

Unlike most nativists, Noah persistently urged schooling—if necessary separate schooling—for all immigrant children. In 1840, when nativists roundly condemned Governor Seward for proposing liberal changes in the organization of the Protestant-dominated New York public school system, Noah supported his state's chief executive. He met privately with Catholic leaders, and he advised the Governor "to ascertain whether we cannot meet their views in some manner acceptable to them and beneficial to the cause of education." Like most New York Jews, Noah wanted to see a return to the pre-public school system, whereby every denomination received funds from the state for the education of its own children. But even after this scheme was defeated, he continued to support public school reform. He feared that otherwise immigrants would boycott the schools altogether. Education, as Noah saw it, was a means of insuring that the next generation of natives would be loyal. He could therefore advocate reforms in clear conscience, and stoutly maintain that he was a good nativist nonetheless.[36]

Noah's contemporaries wondered aloud how "one of the persecuted race of Israel" could justify his nativist stance. James Gordon Bennett of the *Herald* found it "very funny" that any member of "a tribe who have been aliens and renegades throughout the world" should even "talk of aliens." Yet, Noah's nativism, like his nationalism, his interest in American history, and his study of Indian origins (see Chapter Seven) may have stemmed precisely from a desire to escape the Jewish taint of foreignness. He wanted to prove that he was *more* loyal and patriotic than the average American. He claimed the mystical qualities associated with the title "Native American."[37]

Noah's strident nativist declarations sound strikingly similar to the chauvinistic testimonials pronounced by many emancipated, yet still insecure, European Jews. In their case, as in Noah's, nationalism, conservatism, and Judaism went hand in hand in defense of the state. Issues of Jewish concern, humanitarian questions, and other measures untainted by claims of loyalty had no trouble finding Jewish support. When loyalty became an issue, however, Jews trod far more cautiously. They feared, and still fear, having their patriotism called into question.[38]

"There are two questions which agitate...this country," Noah pointed out in 1835. "Naturalization laws" was one of them; "Southern rights" was the other. In both cases, he assumed a solidly conservative stance. Noah's nativism, as we have seen, was of the moderate variety; it was tempered by humanitarian and Jewish concerns. No similar concerns moderated his attitude toward blacks. By the end of his life, he had aligned himself with the most extreme, pro-slavery factions in the South. Even a friend admitted sadly in 1848 that Noah's "hostility to the whole negro race" was "boundless."[39]

In his early years, Noah had taken a different view. As consul, he had been impressed both with the increasingly humane racial policy adopted by Britain, and with the universal humanitarianism preached by France's Abbé Grégoire. The Algerians had taught him that whites, too, could be enslaved and harshly treated. In America, he therefore concluded, "every effort" should be made "to prevent slavery extending." He hoped that even in the South, blacks might be granted "a greater equality of rights." Noah did not talk about ending slavery altogether. But he did advocate colonization of blacks ("thus will amends be made for the original error, if not crime of enslaving a portion of our fellow creatures"), and he recommended meting out the stiffest of punishments to those who illegally engaged in the "revolting to humanity and disgraceful" slave trade.[40]

The Missouri question changed Noah's thinking on the whole slavery issue. Af first, he agreed with Congressman James Talmadge's amendment to bar further importation of slaves into the Missouri Territory and to plan for ultimate emancipation. He attended a public meeting favoring the proposal, and he pledged his support to efforts aimed at arresting "the evils of slavery by constitutional measures." As the debate proceeded, however, he learned, as others had learned in the debate over the Constitution, that slavery was more than just a humanitarian question. Slavery could not be considered apart from sectional politics, federal–state jurisdictional questions, and the problem of social order. Like Thomas Jefferson, Noah soon concluded that the Missouri bill was "a plot," a "ghost of departed federalism," or, as Jefferson called it, "a mere party trick." The plotters, he charged, aimed at "the erection of a northern party," and "the separation of the nation." He geared up to meet the challenge. "In union consists strength," Noah insisted, and though he continued to rail against the institution of slavery, he refused to countenance any compromises which even appeared to sanction federal intervention in Missouri's internal affairs. He knew that his extreme stance on the Missouri issue was unusual ("I stand alone in the North on this delicate point"); yet, contrary to his frequent practice, he neither played both sides of the issue, nor searched for a middle ground. As he saw it, the Union was paramount and not subject to compromise. Patriotism and national security demanded that antislavery forces yield in the face of southern hostility.[41]

Basically, Noah argued—and he was by no means unique—that slavery could only end with the permission of slaveholders and the South. Practically speaking, the Union thus became dependent upon slavery. One who threatened slavery threatened nothing less than America itself. In Noah's view, American freedom and American slavery had become inextricably linked.[42]

Noah's position on the Missouri Compromise allied him with southerners and pro-South elements in the North. He rejoiced at "social interchanges" between southerners and New Yorkers ("they tend to unite us by powerful ties"), and he supported a political alliance between the two regions—a move opposed by more abolitionist-minded, New England-oriented, rural New Yorkers. Noah received his backing from New York merchants who maintained extensive trade with the southern states. In the 1830s, as sectional tensions rose, he became one of the South's foremost spokesmen in the North.[43]

Mordecai Noah's 1833 prospectus to the *Evening Star* assured the South that its "voice must and will be heard." To fulfill this promise, his paper headlined on August 6, 1835, a notice, later much publicized, declaring itself the "medium of communication" through which southern views could be transmitted northward. The paper's editor justly claimed "a long, a sincere [and] a devoted attachment to the southern area of the country." His devotion brought him a subscription and a note of encouragement from the well known lawyer, James Henry Hammond, later South Carolina's governor and senator. In subsequent years, Noah warned repeatedly against abolitionist threats. He urged the South to support its own politicians. He called for stronger state governments and less federal control. He defended the South against its opponents. He even demanded generous northern concessions for the sake of the Union. All he asked of southerners in return were their votes for the Whig party.[44]

Both in 1836 and in 1840, Noah warned that a vote for Martin Van Buren was a vote for northern abolitionists. A vote against Van Buren, he promised, would protect the South's interests, institutions, and future. Noah also privately provided anti-Van Buren ammunition to Davy Crockett for use in his Whig-sponsored *Life of Martin Van Buren* (1835). The volume contains a slightly doctored letter from Van Buren to Noah (December 17, 1819) in which Van Buren is made out to be far more of an antislavery fanatic than he in fact was. In the original letter, Van Buren merely expressed support for the alliance with Rufus King and tried to calm Noah's fears regarding King's antislavery views.[45] Noah's political affiliations later changed; the move, however, had no effect at all on his allegiance to the South. He remained close to southern politicians, especially John Calhoun and William P. Mangum. He continued to explain the South's cause to northerners. In 1846, he actually offered to put up two-thirds of the capital necessary for him to publish a pro-Union, pro-South, and pro-Calhoun newspaper. Nobody, it seems, put up the remaining third. The paper became another one of Noah's many unfulfilled dreams.[46]

The idea of a pro-Union and pro-South newspaper seems somewhat contradictory. How could a newspaper be both sectional and national? Noah, however, saw no contradiction. Like many people of his day, he viewed northern fanatics as the main threat to Union. He supported the South very much as an antidote. He thus called David Wilmot's proposal, aimed at excluding slavery from territories captured in the Mexican War, a "firebrand" designed to "break down the influence of the South." He looked on other northern political moves, especially calls for free soil, with equal suspicion. The election of a northern, antislavery president, he warned in an open letter to antislavery "Barnburner" Democrats, would "endanger the existence of the Union or paralyze the compromises of the Constitution." Still, Noah did not hesitate to condemn southerners when they spoke of leaving the Union. He opposed both nullification and state interposition as sectional doctrines "too dangerous to recognize." In the same spirit, he praised as fair the Clay Compromise of 1850, in spite of southern opposition. Like most of America's Irishmen, Germans, and Jews—indeed, like most Americans of all nationalities—he feared to tamper with the political structure which had so successfully secured his rights and privileges. He continued to "go for the Union and the whole Union." He viewed everything else as of secondary importance.[47]

Among the issues which Noah relegated to a secondary level was the problem of slavery. In the 1820s, the pro-Union editor still termed the institutions a "misfortune" and an "evil." Though he saw no "safe" way of remedying the "evil," at least in the South, he continued, somewhat hesitantly, to support colonization efforts, "melioration" programs, and antislavery legislation in the North. In the 1830s, Noah changed his position and, following the lead of southern polemicists, became a full-fledged apologist for slavery.[48] At the same time, he developed an antipathy for free blacks everywhere. The two positions were complementary. Noah argued that freedom was dangerous both to the black man and to society. He termed slavery the "natural condition" of the race; the only condition under which it could be "happy and contented":

> There is liberty under the name of slavery. A field negro has his cottage, his wife, and children, his easy task, his little patch of corn and potatoes, his garden and fruit, which are *his* revenue and property. The house servant has handsome clothing, his luxurious meals, his admitted privileges, a kind master, and an indulgent and frequently fond mistress.[49]

Noah's change of heart on slavery mirrored a shift that had taken place all over the South. In the wake of heightened abolitionist agitation, southerners vigorously united in self-defense. They gradually stifled all doubts about slavery, doubts which they had freely expressed in earlier years. No longer did southerners speak of slavery as an evil necessity. They rather praised it as a positive good. As we have seen, Noah joined in this chorus of praise. He did so from conviction; not, as has so often been stated, because he was a southerner. He did have relatives in the South. He had even lived in Charleston for a few years of his youth. In those days, however, he had been opposed to slavery and had identified himself with the North. He came to support slavery later, and for reasons which had less to do with the South than with the Union as a whole.[50]

Along with many Americans, Noah in the 1820s developed a fear of blacks. At first, his fear was merely political: he worried that blacks, if enfranchised by New York State, would vote for the Clintonian candidates supported by their employers. Consequently, he urged the New York State constitutional convention to limit the franchise to white males, although he admitted that such a move had to be done "on grounds of *expediency*, because no one will deny their natural rights, or will believe that the mere 'tincture of skin' is to destroy claims which are unalienable."[51]

Revelations from the 1822 Charleston slave revolt trials transformed Noah's fears into a more general concern for social order. Like many whites, and like masters since at least the days of the biblical Pharaoh, he began to worry that the persecuted would seek revenge from their oppressors. He feared, as he later admitted, that the blacks might become "our masters" and might gain "possession of the country and its government." He reacted instinctively. He warned against "an excess of indulgence to the domestic black of the South," and "for the common safety" he advised tighter control. He soon sought tighter controls in the North as well. He cautioned New York City blacks that their actions were "becoming quite intolerable" and he warned that criminal, disruptive, and insolent behavior should be fully prosecuted. *Freedom's Journal*, the first black newspaper in America, responded by calling Noah the black man's "bitterest enemy."[52] It admitted, however, that he was only an enemy some of the time.

Incidents of black violence or purported violence in New York, in Haiti, and in the South (especially Nat Turner's revolt in 1831) fueled the "bitterest enemy's" hostilities and fears. The increasing tide of abolitionist-related disorders made him even more nervous. His response was to attack the symptoms rather than the cause. He glorified the status quo ("the bonds of society must be kept as they now are"), and condemned all who advocated ameliorative changes. "To emancipate slaves," he said menacingly, "would be to jeopardize the safety of the whole country."[53]

As Noah discovered, anti-abolitionist mobs could pose as grave a threat to the social order as militant abolitionists and violent blacks. In July 1834, a particularly ugly anti-abolitionist riot engulfed New York for several days. Spurred both by an "insulting" Independence Day rally of the American Anti-

Slavery Society, and deep-seated fears of white "amalgamation" with blacks, rioters terrorized the black community, torched several black churches, and vandalized or destroyed the property of some noted abolitionists. Noah was horrified. Unlike James Watson Webb, who helped to incite the riot and then blamed free blacks for bringing misfortune upon themselves, Noah condemned the rioters as "maniacs." He lamented that even in America "a man may be mobbed for his political and religious opinions," and he praised the "forbearance" and good behavior of the "innocent... colored people" throughout New York City. He even called for reparations to be paid to those who suffered damage. But though for a moment he had called himself "a friend of the blacks," his anti-abolitionism quickly reasserted itself. Blacks soon found Noah playing his more accustomed role of apologist for the South.[54]

In line with southern practice, Noah directed his primary attacks against abolitionist "fanatics," a group which he termed "a set of knaves whose sole object is to prey upon the credulous and unwary." He viewed abolitionists as a group already at war with America, and he fully supported new measures aimed at restraining them. First, he sought to ban the sending of abolitionist literature through the mail. He then urged that abolitionist petitions to Congress be "finally disposed of immediately on their being presented." Finally, he proposed that the New York State legislature pass an anti-abolitionist bill providing that:

> All writings or pictures, made, printed, or published, within this state, with a design or intent, or the manifest tendency whereof, shall be, to excite to, or cause insurrection, rebellion, riot, civil commotion, or breach of the peace, among the slaves, in any part of the United States of America, or with a design, or intent, or the manifest tendency whereof, shall be, to create on the part of the slaves an abandonment of the service, or a violation of the duty which the master has a legal right to claim, shall be deemed a MISDEMEANOR; and all persons who shall make, print, publish or circulate, or shall subscribe, or contribute money, or other means, to enable any other person to make, print, publish or circulate, any such writing or picture, shall be deemed guilty of the offence, and shall be punished by fine or imprisonment, or both, in the discretion of the Court.[55]

Several years later, when Noah was judge in the Court of Sessions, he unilaterally attempted to write his bill into law. He instructed the New York grand jury to indict anyone at the American Anti-Slavery Convention who suggested or discussed "a project embracing a dissolution of our happy form of government." He feared that such discussion "would inevitably tend to a disastrous breach of the public peace." As so often with Noah, the words and publicity were all-important. Nobody was in fact arrested.[56]

Though dissolution of the Union and breach of the peace were the twin dangers which motivated Noah's pro-South and anti-black stance, they were not the only arguments which he used to justify his position. He invoked biology to prove that blacks were an "inferior species to the white," and employed phrenology ("a study of vital importance and incalculable utility") to demonstrate "that the bump of destructiveness in that [black] race must

Four views of Mordecai Noah: the young writer, the utopian dreamer, the successful politician, and the somber old man. *(Photos courtesy Julius Bisno and American Jewish Archives)*

The Ararat dedication stone. The Hebrew words from Deuteronomy 6:4 read "Hear O Israel! The Lord our God, the Lord is One." *(Photo courtesy Julius Bisno)*

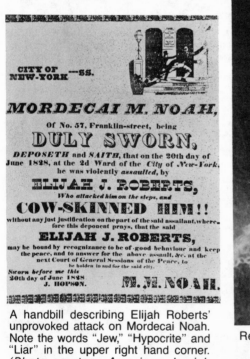

A handbill describing Elijah Roberts' unprovoked attack on Mordecai Noah. Note the words "Jew," "Hypocrite" and "Liar" in the upper right hand corner. *(Photo courtesy American Jewish Archives)*

Rebecca Jackson Noah *(Photo courtesy American Jewish Archives)*

possess hideous dimensions." No longer did he express faith in the power of social reformers to meliorate the condition of the blacks. "Science" had convinced him that innate, immutable, racial characteristics were responsible for the Africans' sorry plight. Nothing could change it. The Bible, as Noah read it, proved perfectly compatible with the word of science. Attacking those who condemned slavery as contrary to God's law, he averred that blacks suffered from an eternal biblical curse, one which doomed them forever to a separate and servile existence:

> God... has in his inscrutable wisdom made the distinction between the races in the distinction of color and they cannot be either reconciled or united by the conventional rules of society; he has in his commandments consecrated as property "the manservant and the maidservant"; he has surrendered that race to the whites, as "bondsmen for ever," and who will pronounce his divine will either "a curse" or "a sin"?[57]

Noah may have been convinced that slavery was justified by God, science, and the social order; still, one wonders why he glorified slavery. Why did he describe it as a benevolent institution which accorded blacks "all the comforts of life"? Why not simply call slavery "necessary" and leave it at that? Noah's military tactics suggest an answer. He saw himself engaged in a journalistic war, and as is so often done in war, he made a virtue out of necessity to spur on the troops. He knew that it was easier to fight for a "positive good" than for an "unfortunate necessity." Since the radical abolitionists couched their arguments in the language of holiness, perfection, goodness, and virtue, Noah in his counter-arguments did the same. The editor thus followed his own advice: "the successful usages and organizations of northern politicians should [be] engrafted on southern policy." He also followed an unstated corollary: the arguments and apologetics of southern defenders of slavery should be transmitted to the North. In both cases, he set himself up as the means of communication. As a result, he both influenced slavery's defenders and was influenced by them.[58]

Mordecai Noah's defense of slavery was unusually strident, even for a confirmed anti-abolitionist. But opponents found his religion still more curious than his views. Both abolitionists and blacks noted with surprise that Noah was a Jew. They proceeded to make the most of their discovery.

The *Liberator*, America's foremost abolitionist journal, used Noah's Judaism as a weapon of attack: "if this Judge be a fair specimen of the race," wrote abolitionist Edmund Quincy, "it is no wonder that they have been an insulted and despised people." Abolitionist William Lloyd Garrison went even further, calling the Jewish editor a "lineal descendant of the monsters who nailed Jesus to the cross." Happily, not everyone opposed to slavery fought Noah's prejudice by displaying prejudice of their own. *Freedom's Journal*, for example, tried to evoke from him "a fellow feeling" for slaves by suggesting that a Jew should learn from history to "sympathise with the oppressed of every hue." The *Colored American* also once reminded him of what it conceived to be his moral obligations as a member of an oppressed people. It was, however, a white man, editor Horace Greeley of the *New York Tribune*, who made the point most effectively. Taunted by Noah for having been seen eating with two black men, Greeley observed that men should be treated "according to what they are and not whence they spring." He then reminded Noah that "where there are thousands who would not eat with a negro, there are (or lately were) tens of thousands who would not eat with a Jew." The remark made an impression on New Yorkers; Noah, however, remained unpersuaded. He falsely charged Greeley with anti-Jewish prejudice, and continued to insist that Jews could not do "as the abolitionists atttempt to do: decry the will of God and trample on his divine laws." As far as Noah was concerned, Jewish law and American law were in agreement. Both "recognized, legalized and humanely regulated" the enslavement of human beings. In good conscience, certain that he was acting both as a good American and a good Jew, Noah declared his support for slavery, the South, and the Union as a whole.[59]

While Mordecai Noah called for union, stability, security, and order, his home life was undergoing rapid change. During the course of just fifteen years (1828–1843), Rebecca Noah presented her husband with seven bouncing children—six boys and a girl. The new family entailed Noah in new responsibilities and new expenses. He had to devote time, effort, and energy to the care, education and discipline of his children. He did his best. In letters, and no doubt in conversation as well, he urged his offspring to study diligently, to observe good habits, and to guard their health. He also worked hard to support his family, earning money both through his twenty-five hundred dollar salary, and through his free-lance writings in various journals, including the *New York Mirror*. Noah made more money from his investments. He earned a sizable sum—about twenty-five hundred dollars in 1838—from his part ownership of the *Evening Star* (business manager Thomas Gill owned the rest of the paper). He also made money, or tried to, from a land scheme in Texas.[60]

In the 1830s, many Americans saw Texas as the "Land of Promise." Although Mexico governed this land, Americans populated much of it, and talk of independence was rife. During 1834–5, "Texas fever" reached epidemic proportions in the United States. Most of the immigrants came from the southern and western states, but speculative money came from all over, particularly from New York. Collector of the New York Port Samuel Swartwout, editor James Watson Webb, and financier Joseph L. Josephs, all close friends of Noah, heavily invested in Texas. Noah invested too. More important, his *Star* became a mouthpiece for the speculators; it supported both independence and American intervention. Already in mid-June of 1835, Noah called for "some arrangements by which the Province of Texas could become the property of the United States." The editor defended the right of American citizens to fight on American soil, and he attacked those, many of whom also opposed slavery, who wanted the government to bar travel to the independence-minded area.[61]

The Children of Mordecai Noah[1]

MANUEL MORDECAI[2]	December 23, 1828–1873	Journalist	Named for Noah's father
JACOB JACKSON[3]	October 6, 1830–October 13, 1897	Journalist and lawyer	
ROBERT P.	December 4, 1832–1901	Journalist and lawyer	
ZIPPORAH	August 27, 1835–October 11, 1890		Named for Noah's mother
DANIEL JACKSON[4]	August 6, 1837–February 24, 1846		Named for Noah's father-in-law
	Died after accident		
HENRY	September 16, 1839–May 18, 1885		
LIONEL J.	September 25, 1843–September 23, 1897	Lawyer	

1. Unless otherwise noted, all information in this table is from: Isaac Goldberg, *Major Noah* (Philadelphia, 1938), 287–289; Malcolm H. Stern, *Americans of Jewish Descent* (Cincinnati, 1960), 167.

2. An obituary for Manuel Mordecai is in *American Israelite* (February 28, 1873), 6. See also Norton B. Stern and William M. Kramer, "The Historical Recovery of the Pioneer Sephardic Jews of California," *Western States Jewish Historical Quarterly*, 8 (October, 1975), 18–19.

3. W. Gunther Plaut, *The Jews in Minnesota* (New York, 1959), 16–21.

4. *New York Tribune* (September 9, 1845), p. 2:3 reported that "the second son of Major Noah was severely injured on Friday night [September 5, 1845]." It seems likely that the *Tribune* was referring to Daniel Jackson's accident.

The Texas declaration of independence and the bloody Battle of the Alamo confirmed Noah in his desire to "see Texas free." But he saw freedom as only the first step; his complete program called for Texas to be "annexed to the confederacy," and for Americans then "to step from Texas into Mexico." This jingoism was in line with both his pro-South policy and his nationalism. In this case, however, Noah also had an additional motive—his own speculations. James Gordon Bennett of the *Herald* noted the conflict of interest with a characteristic jeer: "Come out and show us a list of all you own in Texas." Noah responded with uncharacteristic silence; he continued to keep his investments secret.[62]

Notwithstanding the secrecy, it is safe to assume that Noah lost money in Texas. Unsettled military conditions, the uncertain legal status of land grants to foreigners, and the general economic collapse of 1837 combined to depress the value of all Texas investments. Still, Noah's loyalty to the cause remained undiminished. In 1844, he confidentially warned Secretary of State Calhoun that Mexico planned to march on Texas. At the same time, he again advocated immediate annexation of the Lone Star state. When annexation in 1845 led to war in 1846, he was undaunted; he supported the war as well. In spite of his sour speculation, he prided himself on being one of Texas's earliest and firmest supporters.[63]

Noah's failure to find fortune in Texas compounded the general economic woes which he suffered on account of the 1837 depression. He survived, although he claimed that his profits were less than they had been thirty years before, but his survival was dependent on the brilliant business management of Thomas Gill. When Gill died suddenly in April 1839, Noah's loss, by his own admission, was "irreparable." The *Star*'s gross income declined by twenty-five percent in a single year.[64]

As Noah had so often done before in times of financial crisis, he looked for a government patronage position, a post which would temporarily assure him of financial security. Since the Whigs had just assumed power in New York State, he had every hope of securing a position; indeed, he almost felt that he deserved one. Good-naturedly, Noah first recommended several of his friends to the attention of Governor Seward. With a false modesty which was typical of the period, he assured the chief executive that "I may battle to aid a friend but never for myself." This actually served to remind the governor that he was looking for a job. Noah proceeded to lobby for the governor's favor both by vigorously supporting Seward's programs, and by energetically campaigning for the Whig presidential team of William Henry Harrison and John Tyler. Henry Clay, Noah's personal choice for the nomination, had lost out at the Whig Party convention.[65]

Noah was no mere footsoldier in the bitterly contested 1840 presidential contest. He spared no effort to transform his 1836 anti-Van Buren headline from an embarrassing blunder into a glorious prophecy. He even undertook personally to organize a group of Democrats for Harrison, part of a larger grand scheme to make Harrison the "Candidate of the Nation." In spite of these efforts, many Whigs remained aloof and unimpressed. "I am sorry to say," wrote Simeon Dewitt Bloodgood (whose last name bespoke his aristocratic pretensions), "that Noah is influenced by improper motives. Were he satisfied all his grand schemes would fall to the ground." Bloodgood may have been correct; Noah, however, received the satisfaction that he desired. Governor Seward promised to nominate him an associate judge on the court of sessions as soon as the editor "could arrange to retire from the press."[66]

"Taking into consideration how zealously I have laboured in the ranks for thirty years, I think I am entitled to an honorable discharge." With these words, Noah advised Governor Seward that he was merging his *Star* into the *New York Times* (no relation to the present newspaper of that name) and retiring. The *Times and Star* soon itself merged with the *Commercial Advertiser*, and became one of New York's foremost conservative Whig papers. According to James Gordon Bennett, Noah received ten thousand dollars in cash and a seven-thousand-dollar note for his property—more than Bennett thought it was worth.[67]

On August 29, 1840, the last issue of the *Evening Star* went out to subscribers. It symbolized the end of an era. Both Mordecai Noah and the nation were set to embark on new and uncharted paths. Noah looked forward to a patronage position, financial security, and a return to upper-class life. The nation looked forward to a Whig administration, a reunited country, and a return to prosperity. After eight long, arduous Democratic years, Noah could almost taste sweet Whig revenge. Little did he know that, once again, his taste would be only a taste, and nothing more.

Chapter VII

A Jew in a World of Christians

The gyrations and vicissitudes of Mordecai Noah's political career did not affect his standing in the Jewish community. Jews continued to respect his political connections. Americans continued to view him as the most important Jew in the United States. Noah played his part to the hilt: he displayed his Judaism publicly, he answered questions about Jewish practices, and he defended the character of his people against all attacks. He also took an increasingly active role in Jewish communal activities. During the last quarter-century of his life, an impressive number of synagogues, schools, and philanthropies benefited from his advice, assistance, and leadership. But Noah was not content as an ethnic leader to be merely a "defender of the faith." Although he was concerned about Jewish identity, and although he was eager to protect his religion from hostile forces, he still believed that American Jews had to change in order to accommodate themselves to the outside world. He thus acted at one and the same time like two different types of ethnic leaders: the defender of the faith and the integrationist. His twin goals, just as they had been at Ararat, were, on the one hand, to preserve Jewish exclusiveness, and on the other hand to bring Jews and Christians closer together. Noah embodied but could not resolve the tension faced by all minority groups: the simultaneous search for the benefits of whole-hearted assimilation and the security of ethnic-roots identification.[1]

By the 1830s, Mordecai Noah was secure in his minority group position. Mild anti-Jewish slurs no longer fazed him; he was used to them. But he was unprepared for the tidal wave of anti-Jewish abuse unleashed by *Herald* editor James Gordon Bennett. Bennett, who disliked Noah as a person, as a competitor, and as a Jew, began attacking him for publicity reasons, to sell more newpapers, soon after he commenced the *Herald* in 1835. Within a few years, his collection of epithets included: "base Judean," "blasphemer," "Shylock," "a descendant, very likely of the family of Judas Iscariot," and finally "old clothes Jew," a taunt Bennett liked so well that he coupled it to Noah's name for over a decade. No *Herald* reader could long forget what religion Mordecai Noah professed! But Bennett did not confine his attacks to Noah alone. He magnified his opponent into a prototypical Jew, and proceeded to attack the Jewish people generally. According to Bennett, Jews were "a race of secret conspirators against [the Christian] religion," and a people "without a single redeeming feature."[2] Bennett purported to find hints of anti-Christian activities in an old edition of the Talmud. In April 1850, he went so far as to accuse the Jewish people of ritual murder.[3]

Noah, of course, had no choice but to respond, both in defense of himself and the Jewish people. He painstakingly rebutted those charges which he feared might be believed. Others he sloughed off with a supercilious taunt against Bennett the "foreigner" or Bennett the "blackmailer." Noah also resorted to ridicule. He printed a series of satires about life in Bennett's "blackmail family," and he urged Mrs. Bennett to keep her husband in order. Several times, he sought to punish Bennett in criminal proceedings. He hauled him into court on charges of libel at least twice, and in one case, he sued Bennett for nonpayment of debt (a one-hundred-dollar loan which Noah had years before made to Bennett's short-lived *New York Globe*). He even helped to organize two well-publicized "moral boycotts" of the *Herald* (1837 and 1840). But none of these countermeasures proved effective for long. Equally ineffective were Noah's periodic resolves to ignore Bennett. Always, some new controversy broke the calm, and Bennett's anti-Jewish animus flared afresh. It would continue to flare periodically, not only throughout Bennett's lifetime, but in the lifetime of his editor son as well.[4]

In the wake of James Gordon Bennett's well publicized effusions of prejudice, Mordecai Noah's writings became more than ever concerned with Jewish affairs. Perhaps he wanted to defy Bennett. Perhaps he was catering to a heightened popular interest in Jews generally and in his own Judaism in particular, an interest which Bennett had helped to spark. Perhaps he merely sought to serve New York's growing Jewish population (from 1825-1850, New York's Jewish population grew from five hundred to sixteen thousand). Whatever the reasons, Noah had far more items of Jewish interest in his later newspapers than in those dating back to his earlier Democratic days. During the 1830s and 1840s, he described synagogue consecrations, Holy Land expeditions, and Jewish disabilities in various parts of the world. He lamented Jewish infidelity (when freethinker Charles C. C. Cohen was blown to bits in his laboratory, Noah saw "divine interposition" at work), and took glory in Jewish power ("All the monarchies in the world are indebted to the Jews"). He urged everyone to study Hebrew and to learn about the Jewish past. As before, he also answered readers' questions about Judaism. Viewed as an expert on Judaism (European rabbis would have cringed at the thought) he responded to queries as well as he could. If he sometimes turned for assistance to Jews more learned than himself, he did not give them credit. Noah also expounded at length on Jewish marriage laws, Jewish views on baptism, and the Jewish observance of the Sabbath. He interpreted difficult biblical passages and elucidated obscure millennial prophecies. He presented the Jewish view of contemporary controversies like temperance and slavery. Most of all, he patiently responded to Christian proof texts and explained why he so obstinately refused to convert. To the end, he remained a conscious, loyal, and proud member of the Jewish community.[5]

By answering questions and dispensing information, Noah sought to protect the Jewish people. Like enlightened men of his day, the editor believed that ignorance bred intolerance. It followed that "a more general dissemination of learning" would improve the Jewish image in the world. Unfortunately, education proved to be a slow process. Noah often found that a venomous pen was a more effective tool of Jewish self-defense, at least in the short run. When Jewish bankers were maligned, Noah took their side and pointed out that a good many "New Testament Jews," also earned their living through banking. When he saw the word "Jew" used as a synonym for usurer, he courageously reminded Christians that they had "relieved Jews of all their ignominy" when it came to money lending. When, on the floor of the Senate, Daniel Webster used the word "Jew" as a verb meaning "to cheat," Noah protested again, although Webster was a prominent and well-respected member of his party. Noah made no personal allowances in condemning manifestations of anti-Judaism. He was as merciless with his friend, the poet N. P. Willis, as with his enemy, James Gordon Bennett. He did not hesitate to challenge even learned professors like George Bush (Professor of Hebrew at New York University), and Enoch Cobb Wines (then writing his *Commentaries on the Laws of the Ancient Hebrews*, but later a leading advocate of prison reform) when he thought that their portrayal of Jews was distorted.[6]

Noah defended individual Jews as earnestly as he defended Jews as a group. Though he privately admitted that the involuntarily retired naval captain, Uriah Phillips Levy, was "rough and uneducated [and] no favorite with many of the officers," he still fought strenuously to have him returned to active duty. As he wrote to Navy Secretary George Bancroft, "the friends of Captain Levy...are not without apprehensions that there may be some religious prejudices operating to his disadvantage." Noah also supported the highly eccentric convert to Judaism, Warder Cresson, when he faced trial for insanity (conversion was one of the bizarre acts cited in the prosecution's complaint). "That a Christian Court would decide that adopting Judaism as a religion would be a proof of insanity," Noah acidly exclaimed, "we never can believe." He proceeded to send Cresson an excessively laudatory deposition which the court admitted into testimony, although Noah had, in the meantime, passed away. Thanks in part to Noah, both Warder Cresson and Uriah Phillips Levy won ultimate vindication. The Jewish community was pleased; it had come to perceive both cases as symbolic tests of America's commitment to Jewish equality. But in stressing the Jewish aspects of the Levy and Cresson cases, Noah and other communal leaders displayed an all too common minority group disease known as "tunnel vision." They demonstrated a misleadingly narrow view of reality. Realistically speaking, Levy and Cresson might both have been found guilty for reasons which had nothing whatsoever to do with religion. What Jews would have misinterpreted as alarming anti-Semitism might merely have been a court's perception of the pugnacity of Levy or the insantiy of Cresson, and nothing more.[7]

Mordecai Noah was particularly prone to tunnel vision. When he returned in disgrace from Tunis, when he defended David Seixas against the Pennsylvania School for the Deaf and Dumb, and when he lost the shrievalty election, he also pointed only to reasons of religion. In each case, he blithely ignored other factors which came into play. Sometimes, he ignored these factors consciously: he feared that they would weaken his case. At other times, he simply failed to see the complexity of events; anti-Jewish charges clouded his view.

In retrospect, both forms of misrepresentation are understandable. Hypersensitivity to religious threats befits a member of a victimized people. Experience had taught Noah to take threats seriously. Manipulation of religious issues for personal or group ends was a similar manifestation of Noah's weakness. It reflected his desire to derive maximum benefit from the meager power resources then available to him. Other minority groups manipulated the issue of prejudice for exactly the same reason. Understandable as they may be, however, Noah's misrepresentations still were dangerous. By exaggerating the Jewish aspect of events, he ran the risk of misapprehending both America's view of the Jew and the Jewish role in the world. Noah's frequent public and private references to Jewish power exemplify these dangers. It was not long before non-Jews took exaggerated bombast like his "Jewish bankers...hold the purse strings of Europe," and turned it back upon Jews—at a terribly great cost.[8]

Noah's tunnel vision, lamentable as it may have been, should not obscure from view his real contribution to Jewish communal defense. He never failed, as the New York doctor, Daniel Peixotto, pointed out in 1830, "to resent the least aggression on the character of his people." Noah took the broadest possible view of the Jewish people. He retained a traditional belief in Jewish nationhood, and he concerned himself with manifestations of anti-Judaism all over the world. Many emancipated Jews, especially those in Germany and France, had renounced nationhood and pledged their sole allegiance to the country of their birth. Noah, while no less interested in trumpeting his patriotism, did not do so at the expense of the Jewish people. Rather, like Moses Montefiore of England, he sought to defend his people and to demonstrate his patriotism at one and the same time. From his earliest consular job, to his Jewish colony, to his last restorationist speech, the strategy was always the same. Noah searched for synthesis. He tried to prove by example that one could be a good American and a good Jew at the same time. Of course, Noah had an easier time proving his patriotism than did the average European Jew; he was a native in a land of immigrants. What's more, in

America, unlike in Europe, natives frequently retained their ethnic identities for generations. John C. Calhoun, for example, remained ever conscious of his Scotch-Irish forebears. America's nascent nationalism tolerated such "dual loyalties." In general, nativists only demanded that America be put first. They did not prevent an American from putting other loyalties second.[9]

Noah came face to face with the loyalties problem after the outbreak of Louis Papineau's 1837 rebellion in lower Canada. Many Anglophobic, freedom-loving Americans rejoiced that a movement of national liberation had sprouted so close to America's shores. Noah grieved. As far as he was concerned, the French Catholics in lower Canada were "from their nature and education intolerant." They had refused to allow Ezekiel Hart to take his seat in the Provincial Parliament (1808–1809) "on the ground that he professed the Jewish religion." "The idea of such people taking arms to sustain *Liberty* is preposterous," Noah informed critics who accused him of monarchism. He hoped that instead of rebelling, all Canadians would unite and prosper under liberal British rule. To be sure, in formulating his view, Noah took other than Jewish considerations into account. He feared that a free Canada would want to join the United States—a move that he had once heartily endorsed but now strenuously opposed, probably because he did not want to unbalance the ratio between free and slave states. He also had relatives in lower Canada; the rebellion would have hurt their trade with England. Finally, he had personally clashed with the hotheaded William Lyon Mackenzie, a leading proponent of Canadian independence, and himself the organizer of a rebellion in upper Canada. Still, the Jewish issue was the one which Noah stressed. He shifted his stance only after Canadian loyalist troops sank the American vessel *Caroline*, a move that made support of Canadian independence an inescapable patriotic duty. Yet, even while devoutly displaying his love of country, Noah did not neglect his people. He continued to advocate a Canadian settlement which would, in effect, have guaranteed Jewish rights.[10]

Jewish rights came to concern Noah again during the Damascus Affair of 1840. The affair, often considered a turning point in modern Jewish history, began when a Capuchin monk, Father Tomaso, and his servant disappeared in Damascus. Eager to increase his country's influence in the Middle East, Consul Ratti Menton of France incited Moslem officials to accuse Jews of ritually murdering the two men. Forthwith, an elaborate confession was bastinadoed out of an impoverished Jewish barber. Other Jews, alleged co-conspirators, suffered equally severe tortures, and the entire community was threatened with destruction. Meanwhile, blood accusations and anti-Jewish attacks spread throughout the East, the most serious outbreak occurring in Rhodes. Jews all over Europe joined to remonstrate against these unjust accusations. With Britain in the lead, several governments added their official voices to the chorus of protest. Never before had the western world and the Jewish people been so united in defense of Jewish liberty.[11]

American Jews did not stand aloof from this outpouring of indignation. On August 19, 1840, Mordecai Noah addressed a large Jewish protest meeting at

New York's Congregation B'nai Jeshurun.[12] In the ensuing days, protest meetings took place all over the United States. Yet, the American Jewish reaction seems strangely tardy. News of British protest demonstrations had appeared in the American press a full month earlier. During the nearly silent interim, even James Gordon Bennett had been moved to ask "what has Noah been doing in the affair, and what is he now doing?" In his Damascus Affair address, the American Jewish leader responded:

> When the news of the Damascus cruelty first reached me, and with it the impression it had made in every direction, I confess to you that I saw not the sufferings of the Jews—I heard not their groans—I felt not at the moment for the anguish they had suffered. I saw at once the finger of the Almighty in this—another sign shadowing forth the great events to come. I saw only results and said to myself, "God be praised—this is a great event—the Jews are accused of murder—accused of shedding Christian blood for the festival of the Passover. Enquiries will be set on foot—their innocence will be made known—their sacred religion defended—friends will be raised up for them in every direction—civilized governments will interpose a shield for their protection—the Musselmen finding them powerfully supported, will no longer oppress them—the sympathy of every good Christian will be exerted in their behalf—they will be free—they will appreciate this benevolent interference—they will feel as the nation felt of old—the promise God made to them will be fulfilled—they are his people and he has sworn to protect them—the Redeemer will yet come to Zion—everything is leading to this result.[13]

This appeal to predestination is not a wholly satisfactory excuse. Noah certainly did believe in the millennium, and he did grow up in a world where Jews accepted tragedy as an inevitable part of the redemption process. But he had often called on Jews to effect their own destiny. Why did he not at once do the same in 1840? In his Damascus Affair address, he hints at two reasons: first, he suspected British motives in leading the Damascus Affair protest. As a Jewish leader, he knew from personal experience that charges of anti-Semitism could be manipulated. He feared that British outcries might be designed more to embarrass imperialist France than to help suffering Jews. Being a Francophile and an Anglophobe, he preferred to wait until he was certain that the protest against the Damascus outrages was a truly universal one. Even then, in his public address, he went out of his way to mention non-British protests against the persecutions. He also underlined his belief that France was a "liberal, enlightened and tolerant" land. The villain, Noah explained, was not France, but French consul Ratti Menton; and Menton, he pointed out, was a Sicilian by birth.[14]

Noah's second reason for delay was an internal debate within Congregation Shearith Israel regarding the propriety of an American Jewish protest on the Damascus issue. Had American Jews the right to ask their government to intervene with a foreign nation on behalf of the Jewish people? Was it wise for Jews to publicize their ties to the unenlightened Jews of the East? The Sephardic Jews, like many enlightened Jews in Germany, said no to both questions. They also said no when asked to allow their sanctuary to be used for a Jewish protest meeting. Noah, who had long maintained strong ties to the Jews outside the United States, disagreed. He delivered his address at the Ashkenazic synagogue's protest, and used the occasion to insist again that one could be a patriotic American and a loyal Jew at the same time:

> Sir, it may be said...that we have no cause to interfere on behalf of our unhappy brethren, for we are exempt from such outrages, and can "sit under our own vine and fig tree, and there is none to make us afraid." We thank God that it is so, and in proportion to the great blessings that we enjoy should be our zeal to promote the safety of our people who are less happily conditioned. But sir, in every country on earth in which the Almighty has fixed the destiny of the Jew, spread as we are to the confines of the world—scattered by a wise Providence among every nation, we are still one people; bound by the same religious ties worshipping the same God, governed by the same sacred awe, and bound together by the same destiny, the cause of one is the cause of all...[15]

The Damascus Affair address brought Noah considerable public attention. It reinforced a popular view which cast the editor in the role of "defender of the faith." By 1840, other American Jewish leaders, especially immigrant leaders, may actually have been more active, more learned, and more concerned about defense of the faith then the native-born Noah. But Noah had become a symbol; whenever Jewish rights were abridged, the community called upon him to lead the protest. In 1846, New Yorkers staged a protest against the treatment of Jews in Czarist Russia; Noah participated. In 1851, Jews protested after America negotiated a treaty with Switzerland which included a clause discriminating against non-Christians; again, Noah participated. Only his death prevented him from continuing the struggle to have the treaty amended. Noah taught Americans that the battle for Jewish rights was not an internal battle, something of mere Jewish concern. He insisted rather that it be a national, even an international obligation, one which no country and no citizen could properly evade.[16]

As a Jewish communal leader, Mordecai Noah was not concerned only with defense against outside forces. He knew that the best way to truly safeguard the Jewish community was to strengthen the community internally. He therefore assumed an important role in religious, educational, and philanthropic activities. In his early years, when the Shearith Israel community and the New York Jewish community were still virtually synonymous, Noah's communal work centered around the synagogue. He served on synagogue committees, delivered several addresses from the pulpit and occasionally acted as a congregational trustee. Later, he became more involved in synagogue controversies. On at least two occasions, he supported unpopular minority viewpoints, and paid the price. In 1826 and 1841, synagogue members rejected his nomination for congregational office and elected another in his place.[17]

Noah's two election defeats were likely connected with his activities on behalf of a secessionist party within Shearith Israel. He lent his support to the Ashkenazi Jews who formed what later became Congregation B'nai Jeshurun. One might perhaps have expected Noah to oppose disunifying schisms; he surely knew that a community united by a single synagogue would be stronger than a fragmented community. But he also knew that Shearith Israel's European model of a *kehillah*—community control based on congregational coercion—had no place in voluntaristic America. His political experience allowed him to understand what motivated those who resisted enforced discipline and struck out on their own. An American synagogue, he realized, had to conform to the American religious pattern. Still, he did not himself join the Ashkenazic congregation. He proudly remained a "Sephardized" Jew. He did, however, sign petitions on behalf of the secessionists. He also addressed them from the pulpit in each of the first three years (1826–28) of their existence. In 1840, he addressed them again, this time on the occasion of the Damascus Affair mass protest meeting. By so often appearing in their midst, Noah in effect gave the secessionist synagogue a seal of legitimacy. He assured the non-Jewish world, and some doubting Jews as well, that worshippers at B'nai Jeshurun were recognized, fully bona fide members of the Jewish community. He demonstrated conclusively that the Jewish community and Shearith Israel were no longer synonymous.[18]

Noah, of course, did not have the power to decide who was and wasn't a member of the Jewish community. He merely served as a recognized central figure, a representative Jew, a Jewish spokesman. Still, Mrs. Benjamin F. Butler, wife of the noted New York lawyer, somewhat facetiously considered him "King and High Priest of the Jews." At the New York Hebrew Benevolent Society Anniversary Dinner, he once was toasted as the man who "gives the law to the Jew." A *Sunday Dispatch* obituary reported with considerable exaggeration that "among the Jews he was almost worshipped." In the eyes of the outside world, at least, a defined Jewish community existed, and Noah was its leader, if not, indeed, its king. Noah acted the part. He sought to span the growing multitude of diverse Jewish forms, institutions, and personalities developing below him. He perceived himself as the unifying figure recognized by Jews and Gentiles alike. In reality, Noah did not unify his people. To the contrary, the same voluntarism, individualism, and freedom which brought about the B'nai Jeshurun schism continued to divide American Jews into ever smaller and less organized fragments.[19]

Divided as they were, American Jews still formed a distinctive entity. They remained a community even without the threat of synagogue sanctions. When necessary, they somehow proved able to unite. Unity was perhaps most evident when the entire community faced a crisis like the Damascus Affair. On a smaller scale, however, Jews liberally furnished assistance to their kinsmen in need. When Noah needed help to obtain a government job, he requested and received recommendations from Jews all over the country. When he sought to borrow money, he again contacted Jews. Uriah Levy's sister, Ameliah, lent him three thousand dollars in 1834. Over a period of years, Rothschild's agent in America, the House of Joseph, lent him considerably more money. Noah occasionally even called on Jews for information. Jefferson Nones gave him exclusive reports on Colombian affairs after he returned from a military tour in that region. More spectacular were the faultlessly detailed reports from Paris which he received during the 1835–36 crisis over French payment of "spoliation claims" dating back to the Napoleonic era. Noah later admitted that his newspaper's information, which scooped the entire press, "uniformly derived from the House of Rothschilds Brothers & Co. in Paris and London, communicated in their confidential correspondence to their friends, Messrs. J. L. and S. Joseph & Co."[20]

Noah was at least as helpful to members of the Jewish community as they were to him. We have seen how, throughout his life, he derived pleasure and meaning from his ability to assist all those in need, Jews and Christians alike. Still, he maintained a special relationship with those of his own faith. They were in some senses, and often in all senses, members of his family. He wrote recommendations for at least two books by Jews: a children's anthology of literature by Isaac Gomez (1820) and a treatise on the history of money by Adolphus Hart (1851). He wrote personal introductions for many more Jews, the most interesting being a letter (May 1, 1848) to Ambassador Richard Rush in Paris introducing Dr. Simeon Abrahams who was on his way to the Holy Land. He also tended to employ Jews on his newspapers, although whether for ethnic or family reasons it is difficult to say. We can, however, be certain of one thing: American Jews formed a self-conscious and closely linked community. It was that community's interests which Mordecai Noah kept constantly in mind.[21]

Noah placed education at the top of his list of community priorities, the place reserved for it by most cultured men of his faith and era. Along with enlightened Jews and Christians throughout the western world, he was convinced that education held the key to Jewish modernization. He prophesied that intensive education would enable Jews "to assume and maintain a proper rank among their fellow-citizens." During his lifetime, he lent support to all who offered to bring his prophecy into fruition. He supported Moses E. Levy's "plan for the education of Jewish youth and ameliorating the condition of the Jews generally." He actively participated in the work of the Society for the Education of Poor Children and the Relief of Indigent Persons of the Jewish Persuasion. He presided over Lomde Torah, a society for the education of orphan children. He aided the educational work of the Association for the Moral and Religious Instruction of Children of the Jewish Faith. And he served as an examiner for the Polonies Talmud Torah School of Shearith Israel, the school where he had once studied. Noah's most important contribution to Jewish education came in 1843, when he announced plans to found a Hebrew College: a seminary where children over age six could "obtain a classical education, and at the same time be properly instructed in the Hebrew language." The aging editor—he was 58 and felt older—apparently envisaged living out his final years in a Jewish boarding school. He saw himself surrounded by students who "live[d] in conformity to our laws, and acquire[d] a liberal knowledge of the principles of their religion."[22]

Noah recognized in his Hebrew College proposal the basic dilemma of American Jewish education. On the one hand, Jewish parents were "naturally desirous that their children should be educated as Jews," something which could not be done in Christian boarding schools. On the other hand, Jewish parents wanted their children to integrate into American society, something which a traditional Jewish school could never tolerate. Characteristically, Noah strove for synthesis: he promised that his school, though strictly Jewish, would still "bear comparison with any college throughout the Union," and would guarantee "a thorough scholarship in every branch of study." No rules prevented non-Jews from attending the proposed Hebrew seminary. Presumably, they would have been treated the way Jews were treated in a Christian boarding school. Nevertheless, Noah emphasized that his seminary would be a Jewish institution, with Jewish prayers, Jewish dietary laws, and vacations on Jewish holidays. The "Hebrew College" project evoked little interest, despite support from Jewish newspapers in America and England. Under different auspices, however, the basic idea took hold. In the last years of his life, Noah found himself recommending at least three Jewish boarding schools: The Misses Palache's Boarding and Day School for Young Ladies of the Jewish Faith, the Hebrew and Classical School of E. Block, and Dr. Max Lilienthal's boarding school for boys, the boarding school where Noah sent his own ten-year-old son Henry to study. Each school imitated Christian forms while promising to preserve Jewish identity completely intact.[23]

Noah's educational interests were not confined to children. He realized that adults, too, needed Jewish education. He therefore served as an officer of the Hebrew Literary and Religious Library Association, perhaps the first Jewish adult education program in America. He also encouraged public lectures on subjects of Jewish interest, including the lecture series by E. C. Wines (with whom he later publicly disagreed). As a founding shareholder of New York University, Noah may even have played a role in sponsoring Hebrew studies at the highest educational level. His friend Isaac Nordheimer, a noted German Jewish classical scholar, served on the new university's faculty from 1836 until his untimely death in 1842. As a supplement to formal education, Noah supported Jewish newspapers. He realized that they could serve as an informal means of combating Jewish ignorance. Thus, he enthusiastically welcomed the publication of Isaac Leeser's monthly *Occident*; he heartily recommended Isidor Busch's short-lived German language weekly, *Israel's Herold*; and he gave considerable assistance to Robert Lyon's New York Jewish weekly, the *Asmonean*. As a journalist himself, Noah knew from experience how effectively a newspaper could defend the Jewish community. He also knew that newspapers could provide numerous invaluable services to communal leaders. Newspapers, like a growing number of other Jewish institutions, transcended the synagogue and served all Jews regardless of affiliation.[24]

Another institution which transcended the synagogue and served all Jews regardless of affiliation was the New York Hebrew Benevolent Society. Under Mordecai Noah's presidency (1842–1851), it became the most important Jewish philanthropy in the country, and a symbol of Jewish power in New York. Before he became its president, the society had limped along as the charitable arm of Congregation B'nai Jeshurun. Earlier still, it had maintained affiliations with Shearith Israel. Noah finally lifted the society above all synagogues, declaring it independent. His wife presented the society with its own symbol, a gold seal which the president wore around his neck at every meeting. Noah may himself have designed the seal. Like the Ararat stone, it included the *Sh'ma* (Deut. 5:4) in Hebrew. It also portrayed a dove with a twig in its beak, an obvious reference to Noah's biblical namesake. Noah also broadened the society. He invited non-Jews to take part in its functions. In addition, he set a new standard for donations by personally contributing $50— an amount far in excess of most previous gifts. Most important of all, Noah brought to the Hebrew Benevolent Society publicity. During his tenure, newspapers rarely ignored the society's activities.[25]

Noah's most spectacular triumph as Hebrew Benevolent Society president occurred in 1849, when he succeeded in momentarily uniting the fundraising efforts of his society with those of the German Hebrew Benevolent Society, a rival charity. The two philanthropies made a joint banquet which 350 Jewish and non-Jewish guests attended. Noah, as the newly named president of both organizations, presided. Unfortunately, the charitable union foundered after a year, probably because of personality differences. Still, Noah had demonstrated that a combined federation could increase the funds available to both charities by diminishing total administrative expenses. He anticipated the federation movement in American Jewish philanthrophy by a half-century. He also pioneered a community institution. He transformed the gala Hebrew Benevolent Society dinner into an annual ritual awaited by wealthy Jews and ambitious politicians alike. By attending the dinner, aspiring politicians demonstrated their support for the Jewish community; tacitly, they asked for Jewish support in return. The event also gave wealthy Jews the opportunity to demonstrate how they both preserved their identity (by supporting a Jewish charity), and integrated into society (by mixing with non-Jews). Reporters were available to publicize the achievement. Dignitaries who missed the annual banquet often felt compelled to send eloquent letters of regret. In 1849, Daniel Webster and William Seward both sent their highest praises to the "extraordinary people" and their charitable institution. A year later, the eloquent letters contained more tangible measures of praise. A hundred-dollar donation arrived from Governor Hamilton Fish. Jenny Lind, the renowned Swedish soprano (who later married a Jew) sent Noah a check for twice that amount. [26]

Noah quite naturally gave maximum publicity to such generous bequests. He realized intuitively that charity was more than just an exercise in altruism (although altruism there was aplenty). Charity was intertwined, as well, with considerations of status and honor. By publicizing generous gifts, Noah helped benevolent donors, particularly those who sought favors from the Jewish community. Free advertising also aided his society by bringing it both new bequests and a heightened sense of legitimacy and importance. Finally, Noah himself benefited from the publicity; it gave the public yet another reason to view him as leader of the Jews. In short, a symbiotic relationship developed between Noah, public figures, and the Hebrew Benevolent Society. All catered to the needs of the others, yet all in the process benefited themselves. In so catering to the needs of others, and opening his society to the outside world, Noah demonstrated again his abilities as an "integrationist" leader who could bring Jews and Christians closer together. While "defender of the faith" Isaac Leeser in Philadelphia lamented that the Benevolent Society displayed "so little of a Jewish character," Noah proudly pointed to the universal acclaim in which his society basked. He could also point to more concrete measures of success. Under his presidency, the Hebrew Benevolent Society's income multiplied, and ambitious plans were laid to build New York's first Jewish hospital, later to be known as Mount Sinai.[27]

We have so far seen Mordecai Noah as a Jewish leader speaking on behalf of the Jewish community. He identified as a Jew, defended the Jews, and played a prominent role in Jewish religious, educational, and philanthropic activities. He supported the movement away from a synagogue-directed community and toward one at once more modern and more pluralistic, one comprised of many synagogues and a few overarching organizations which transcended them all. He appealed to forces outside the Jewish community in order to further communal aims. He assumed the role of an "integrationist," but acted on behalf of an organization (the Hebrew Benevolent Society) designed to make the Jewish community stronger.

Many Jewish leaders would have been content with this. As rabbis, or communal functionaries, they had little direct knowledge of the outside world. They lived and worked exclusively within the narrow confines of the Jewish community. They never experienced at first hand the struggle of the average American Jew to maintain his identity in a Christian environment. Mordecai Noah, on the other hand, understood this struggle only too well. He spent his entire life in a world of Christians, and he never forgot—he was never permitted to forget—that he was different; he was a Jew. When his Judaism loomed as a barrier, when it seemed to deny him one of his goals, he refused to retreat. He proudly fought back. But viewed in the perspective of his sixty-six long years of life, these challenges fade in significance. Most of the time, Noah remained at peace with his neighbors. He sought their acceptance, their respect, and their love. He searched for a way of reconciling his Judaism with their Christianity. He tried to prove that he really wasn't so different, after all.[28]

Noah searched relentlessly for words adequate to describe the Jewish–Christian relationship. No illustration ever quite satisfied him. In his 1818 address at Shearith Israel he spoke of one true road, "the road to honour." Both Jews and Christians, he averred, "must pursue the same path to immortality." A later metaphor, one of the most beautiful he ever employed, suggested not one road, but two, yet roads so closely parallel as to be virtually indistinguishable: "There are two packets belonging to the New York and Boston line, one named *Jew* and the other *Gentile*. They carry equal freight, and sail with equal swiftness. They sail from the same port and arrive at the same destination. So it is with human *Jews* and *Gentiles* of the great world." Still another formulation hinted at a synthesis model, at least for social relations. Noah lavished praise on the then recently deceased Abraham Touro (brother of the famed philanthropist Judah Touro) for remembering in his will the interests of both Jews and Christians alike: "We thus perceive the munificent donor in his last moments blending Christian and Jewish charities, bearing in mind the claims of his religion, and not forgetting the illustrious institutions of charity by another faith, with the followers of which he lived in friendship and social affection."[29]

Noah, in a manner typical of enlightened Jews, exalted Christianity to a level above that held by any other religion, except his own. He gave no hint even of knowing that some medieval Jews had relegated Christianity to the level of idolatry. As far as he was concerned, Christianity had saved the world from paganism. He felt certain, based on his travels and reading, that the world would be much better off in Christian hands than in the hands of Moslems or Chinese. Unlike most Jewish polemicists, Noah never reviled either the Christian Bible or Christianity's founder. To the contrary, he showered praise upon Jesus' accomplishments and Christian morality in general—and no wonder. He argued that the best in Christianity really came from Judaism. Judaism, in other words, was the root; Christianity but a large offshoot: "We are much mistaken if every law or principle upon which Christianity now rests are [sic] not traceable in their origin to the Jewish people." Christianity was merely "*our* laws, *our* principles, *our* doctrines... beneficially spread throughout the world under another name."[30]

Noah convinced himself that, ultimately, Jewish–Christian similarities would become apparent to everyone. He predicted that Christians would renounce their belief in the divinity of Jesus and would become Unitarians, or would convert altogether. As harbingers of the future, he pointed to liberal Protestantism and to the conversion of Warder Cresson. He was certain that when the future came about, religious divisions would disappear completely. Mankind would finally enjoy "that great and happy union so long promised, predicted and cherished."[31]

Noah's grandiose vision sounds remarkably similar to a Protestant vision with which Americans were thoroughly familiar. Debts owed the Jews, the ultimate union of all believers, and harbingers of the future ("signs of the time") were standard fare in millennial and missionary magazines; only the conclusions differed. Protestants admitted that Christianity sprang from Jewish roots, but saw themselves as chosen inheritors and viewed Jews as accursed. They joined Noah in praying for an ultimate religious union, but they believed that it would be a reunion in Christ. Finally, they expectantly pointed, as Noah did, to millennial harbingers. But the favorable signs that they noticed were those of Reform Judaism and Jewish converts to Christianity. Examined within this Protestant setting, Mordecai Noah's millennial vision—indeed, his whole view of Christianity—takes on an entirely new perspective. On one level, it was what it appeared to be: a ringing integrationist endorsement of mutual tolerance, coupled with a hope for ultimate reunion. On another level, it was precisely the reverse: a powerful Jewish defense against the missionary challenge, a remarkable demonstration of how the Protestant vision could be turned on its head to suit Jewish ends.[32]

Neither the "defender of the faith" alone, nor the "integrationist" alone was the "real" Noah. The "real" Noah was ambivalent: sometimes the one, sometimes the other, and often both at once. The "real" Noah craved acceptance but demanded the right to maintain his identity. The "real" Noah praised Christianity but refused to become a Christian himself. Most New Yorkers accepted the "real" Noah on his own terms. Occasional bouts of prejudice notwithstanding, they allowed him to rise to considerable heights in New York society, and they quoted his newspaper widely. Christian missionaries, however, could never accept Noah on his own terms. They viewed America as a Christian land, and they viewed Jews as a degenerate people whose condition could be meliorated only through conversion. Noah, as a living symbol of Jewish enlightenment and potential, posed a dire threat to missionary ideology, the same kind of threat posed by Moses Mendelssohn in Germany. By the same token, the missionaries threatened Noah's ideology. They rejected his most basic and cherished belief by denying that he could be a good American and a good Jew at the same time.[33]

Noah and the missionaries waged war for over thirty years. The first stage of this battle was the fight against the American Society for Meliorating the Condition of the Jews (Chapter Three). The end of that battle, however, only brought Noah up against Joseph Wolff—a roving and highly eccentric missionary whose details of far-flung adventures entertained Christians for decades. During both of his visits to America, Wolff struggled valiantly to convert Noah. Noah, with less patience, called Wolff "a very ravenous and furious animal" and urged that he be "driven off."[34] Wolff was certainly the most colorful of Noah's missionary opponents, but he was far from the most persistent. New York-based missionaries made more tiresomely frequent overtures, especially after the American Society for Meliorating the Condition of the Jews resuscitated itself in the early 1840s. In general, Noah attacked the methods, expenses, aims, and at times, even the patriotism of missionaries. He then reminded the "pious frauds" that Judaism evinced no ill will toward any religion—and never proselytized at all.[35]

Despite the missionaries, or perhaps because of them, Noah continued to seek acceptance for himself and his beliefs. He sought more than mere social toleration. That status, he pointed out, presupposed that "one portion of [the] community has rights which are denied to others." He sought full equality. He desperately wanted to belong. His goal was to widen social parameters until they were broad enough to encompass Jews. He tried, in other words, to redefine the term "good citizen" so that he and his coreligionists might be included. He did not, of course, seek to write religion out of his definition entirely. Indeed, he equated atheism with immorality ("To suppose that a people can be moral without religion is to suppose a very improbable thing"). But, he argued that to believe in any divine-oriented religion was enough. The particular form of belief was less important than the fact that "we are all children of one great parent and are united by the same ties, controlled by the same destinies." Although he never used the term, Noah clearly advocated a civil religion: a basic theology broad enough to encompass all faiths. He agreed with Benjamin Franklin that any man who believed and practiced the essentials of religion could not but be a good man. He insisted that "the object of religion is good; no matter by what creed it may be reached."[36]

Although Noah sought acceptance for all creeds, he still called America a "Christian nation." In Tunis, like Joel Barlow before him, he had argued precisely the opposite: "the United States of America is not, in any sense founded on the Christian religion." But he made the statement merely in order to gain advantages from that country's Christian-hating ruler.[37] He subsequently assured readers of his *Travels* that he never for a moment forgot that he was "representing a Christian nation." In later years, Noah reiterated the point. He agreed with jurist James Kent that "the Christian religion was a part of the law of the land." He even clashed publicly with *Occident* editor Isaac Leeser, who claimed, based on the first amendment, that no religion at all was the law of the land. The clash, however, was basically semantic. Noah and Leeser defined the word "Christian" differently. When Noah invoked the word, he really meant "civilized" or "moral"—a standard and common meaning of the term at the time. His first, and still somewhat hesitant public use of "Christian" in this sense, his 1818 letter to Thomas Jefferson, proves the rule: "There are few in the Civilized, or if you please in the Christian world that can boast of having reached forth the hand of assistance towards these unfortunate and persecuted people."[38]

Noah felt that Christian values or, as we would say Judeo-Christian values, permeated America. They were the creed of America's civil religion. He certainly wanted to associate the Jewish people with that creed. He wanted to associate himself with that creed, as well. On one occasion, he modestly praised his own "Christian patience." Another time, he assured New York's Governor William Seward that he was "considered quite as good a Christian as the times will admit of."[39] Isaac Leeser, of course, reacted to a quite different meaning of the word "Christian." He favored radical church–state separation, and wanted America to be neither Jewish nor Christian. Acting as a "defender of the faith," the immigrant Leeser showed typical Jewish sensitivity to the broader connotations of the word Christian. Noah, in this case the "integrationist," simply used the word the way it was used by his neighbors.[40]

Noah followed his neighbors regarding other religious matters, as well. He supported Bible societies, since they taught "our common origin." He felt that the Bible, at least the Bible accepted by both Christians and Jews, could be the common holy book of America's civil religion. In 1840, he even tried to add a new dimension to the study of this holy book by publishing an English translation of what he supposed to be the Book of Jasher, a lost work twice referred to in the Bible (Joshua 10:13; 2 Samuel 1:18), and "discovered" in various versions periodically, from the Middle Ages onward. Noah's 1840 version was Moses Samuel's translation of a Jasher printed in Hebrew as early as 1625. What Noah contributed, besides a preface, was "a large sum of money for the original and translation," and considerable publicity, so that the volume would sell as many copies as possible. But the enterprise backfired. Instead of being Noah's contribution to Jewish and Christian understanding of the Bible, the volume became the center of controversy. It won a few friends—notably, Mormon prophet Joseph Smith and former President John Quincy Adams—but it also won many enemies, among them, not surprisingly, James Gordon Bennett. One anonymous "doctor" even called the book "a libel on the Christian Bible." The charge was ridiculous, but still fatal to Noah's original aim. Consequently, he reiterated that he "neither wrote nor translated" Jasher, and said nothing more about the book. He sought acceptance in more conventional ways.[41]

One way in which Noah sought acceptance was by advocating the nationwide observance of a common day of rest, a day when no business would be conducted and all could freely pursue private religious or social callings. To this end, he joined pious Christians in urging that Sunday, the Christian sabbath, be scrupulously observed by everyone. Though he was not a fanatical sabbatarian, and he opposed bans on Sunday mail and entertainment, he generally called for stricter sabbath law enforcement. He lamented the numerous violations which New York's grand jury overlooked. He even condemned those who sought special exemptions on the basis of their religion. Of course, Noah had no objections to Saturday, the Jewish sabbath. In theological debates, he insisted that it was the true Sabbath, and that Jews could never abandon it. But he argued that Jews should also uncomplainingly "respect...the laws of the land." He felt that for the sake of a national consensus, Jews and others who considered the seventh day of the week as holy, should resignedly agree to assume the burdens which two days of rest necessarily entailed. Clearly, Noah included widely observed Protestant rituals in his civil religion. He understood the first amendment to mean "abolition of all religious disabilities," and nothing more. If police regulations happened to stamp Protestant practice with the seal of law, that was perfectly legal; majority ruled. Isaac Leeser and others, alarmed at growing neglect of the Jewish sabbath, disagreed. They sided with liberals who termed Sunday laws religious coercion. To Noah this was heresy. He lectured his fellow Jews on the impropriety of even raising such an issue for debate. He worried that his carefully nurtured relationship with Christians might be fractured, and that Jewish loyalty and patriotism might again be called into question.[42]

What then was Noah's view of the Jewish–Christian relationship in

America? Much of the time, he agreed to submerge his Judaism under a vaguely defined, semi-secularized Protestant–American arch. Nevertheless, he emphatically insisted that his position under the arch be recognized, securely guaranteed, and subjected to no attacks. He sought to harmonize Jews and Christians. He did his best to forestall religious conflict. Even while seeking temporal peace, however, he proudly and boldly lay ultimate claims to the entire Protestant–American arch. The Protestant half of the arch, he insisted, sprang from Judaism, the mother of Christianity. The American half, he maintained with equal vigor, sprang from the lost ten tribes, the forefathers of the American Indians. In Noah's view, Protestant America thus owed everything to the Jews. Although he clung to the hope that at least a part of this debt would be paid off in the here and now, he understood that full repayment would come only in the millennium. Meanwhile, Noah bided his time, predicted the inevitable, and made the best of his interim situation.

Mordecai Noah certainly did not originate the notion that the Indians—the American half of his Protestant-American arch—sprang from the lost ten tribes of Israel.[43] Among both Jews and Christians, the idea had circulated for a quarter of a millennium, at least since Johannes Fredericus Lumnius's *De Extremo Dei Judicio et Indorum vocatione* in 1567. Subsequently, the theory went through numerous versions, especially as missionaries and inquiring visitors gleaned new information. But scholars did more than just debate whether Indian languages, relics, and customs reflected Hebraic origins or spontaneous developments. On a deeper level, their inquiries were tinged with ideological significance. Would the discovery of the tribes serve the cause of Christian theology or that of Jewish theology? Could the presence of tribes in America signal that America truly was God's new Israel? Would conversion of the Indians bring on the millennium? Would the millennium more readily be hastened by allowing Jews to spread unmolested "from the one end of the earth even unto the other" (Deuteronomy 28:64)? The questions divided believers from unbelievers, Jews from Christians, those who prepared for imminent millennium from post-millennial scoffers who eschewed speculation altogether.[44]

Mordecai Noah was thoroughly familiar with the basic literature on the lost ten tribes. As late as 1820, however, he cast doubt on purported similarities between the Jews and the Indians. He rather adopted as his own the position of more skeptical scholars, assuring his readers that "we have never believed that the American Indians are descendants of the nine and a half tribes of Israel that crossed the Euphrates [sic]." Noah did have considerable sympathy for the Red Men. In his *She Would be a Soldier* (1819), he presented the most fair-minded Indian that the American stage had yet seen. But his concern in all cases was with the contemporary Indian, and his plight. He did not deal with ancestors of the Indians until his Ararat address of 1825. In that famous speech, Noah summarized all standard proofs previously adduced on behalf of the Judaic origins of the Red Men: their monotheism, tribal configurations, symbols, and customs. He then invited the Indians, who held significant power in upstate New York, to join his Ararat experiment. If the Indian chief Red Jacket made any response, it was not recorded.[45]

Noah certainly did not convert to the lost ten tribes theory of Indian origins merely to secure Ararat's safety. His new convictions may actually have stemmed from more recent scholarship, or from further reading. Whatever the case, he was not blind to the ramifications of his new ideas. He understood that if the Jews and the Indians were one people, the Jews were then both "the first people in the old world"—the ancestors of Christianity—and "the rightful inheritors of the new." Jews could proclaim proudly, "we were here first." They could enjoy the same smug self-satisfaction and false security enjoyed by founders and pretended founders everywhere in the world.[46]

Noah promised at Ararat that he would pursue the subject of Indian origins "by every means in [his] power." He kept his word. On February 14, 1837 (the day after New York's flour riot), he delivered, under the auspices of the Mercantile Library Association, a lecture on "Jewish Antiquities," or the lost ten tribes. The lecture took place at Clinton Hall before a large and distinguished audience. Noah was well received and his lecture much praised. Soon, it was printed, translated into German, and reprinted. Yet, in his lecture, Noah said nothing that had not been said before. Like Protestant evangelicals, he praised Indians as virtuous and noble. Quoting published research, he linked the red men to numerous aspects of Jewish ritual and custom. He also adduced many similarities between Indian languages and Hebrew. The numerous comparisons, however, were no more convincing in Noah's formulation than in those of his predecessors. It still takes considerable imagination to transform *Cha hakeet Kana* into a Hebrew phrase meaning "you resemble those reproved in Canaan." More interesting was Noah's argument that only North American Indians descended from the Jews, while the rest descended from Canaanites and Phoenicians. When the "Jews"—the North American Indians—arrived on the scene, Noah believed that they doomed the southerners to the very fate which Joshua had meted out to the southerners' ancestors: "Fifteen hundred years after the expulsion of the Canaanites by Joshua...the descendants of Joshua a *second* time fall on the Canaanites on another continent, knowing them as such, and burn their temples and destroy their gigantic towers and cities." The new world was thus linked symbolically—even typologically—with the old. Jews played the crucial role in both places. They embodied both the pious "Christian" values of the white men, and the quintessential American values of the red men. Destiny, Noah believed, would inevitably propel his people to the front ranks: "the Jews...will stand forth, the richest, the most powerful [and] the most intelligent nation on the face of the globe."[47]

Noah's Judeo-centric view of the future contrasted sharply with the standard Christian view of his day. While one viewed the sorry state of Indians as proof of Jewish accursedness, the other employed the same evidence to prove Jewish strength. According to Noah, the existence of the lost ten tribes demonstrated that God still loved his people Israel and would ultimately restore them to their former glory ("all the prophecies relative to their future destination will in due time be strictly fulfilled"). Christians were thus not "God's new Israel," for God's chosen people still flourished. They formed the basis of Protestant America, and they still merited divine blessings. Yet, even as he distanced himself from Christian interpretations, Noah allied himself with Christian piety. He insisted that the lost ten tribes proved both the veracity of scriptures and the special status accorded America in the heavenly schema. In later years, Noah tried to strengthen both of these premises. He searched for new evidence to support his Indian origins theory, and he stoutly maintained that California was the site of the biblical Ophir (he spelled it "Ofir" in order to show that all of its letters were found in the word "California").[48]

In tracing parallels between past and present, Noah demonstrated anew his hearty conservatism and his fear of change. He wanted history to move in recurrent, predictable, and safe patterns. He therefore linked the new world with the old world. He compared the Puritan fathers with the ancient Hebrews.[49] He presented the City Charter Convention with the original New York charter. Yet, Noah still realized that history was "of essential importance to the *progress* of learning and civilization and the successful advancement of governments." He saw movement toward a millennium and he insisted that human agency played a role in influencing the development of events. He both desired change and feared it. He took comfort in history—supporting many historical societies and museums—and sought to transcend history. Like all human beings, he was caught between a receding past and an unknown future. He ran down both paths, searched for a middle way, or sought to create his own synthesis. If at times only confusion emerged, it was at least the confusion of a man who did not fear to grapple with the tensions of his day, even if he could not always resolve them.[50]

The tensions between tradition and change, identity and assimilation, independence and group discipline—the same tensions, in short, which affected so many other facets of his life, affected Noah's personal religion, as well. His was the era when emancipated Jewry began to be buffeted by the winds of doctrinal and ceremonial reform. Jews sought to prove both their unswerving loyalty and their unencumbered modernity. They wanted a religion which they could proudly display to their ever curious, non-Jewish neighbors. Still, many Jews hesitated to reform too much of tradition. They feared that Jewish unity might be permanently fractured. They worried that Jews' distinctive identity might be eternally lost.

Influenced by evangelical Christianity, Mordecai Noah evinced particular concern that religious beliefs—the basics of religion—not be altered. "No community ever yet prospered without religion and morality," he thundered. He therefore invoked the teachings of Benjamin Franklin and warned that "it is safest to believe." He expounded the Bible's literal meaning and looked forward to an imminent millennium. He stoutly maintained his faithfulness to every miracle and put off doubters by pointing to history's miraculous preservation of the Jews. He even condemned the "rabbi" (actually, two rabbis, Gustavus Poznanski and Isaac Mayer Wise) who, in 1850, publicly renounced faith in a personal messiah and resurrection of the dead. Such a rabbi, he said, "played the hypocrite as to his own beliefs." Noah's beliefs sometimes verged on the incredible. He once insisted that Jewish marriage rites went back to the patriarch Jacob. On another occasion, he claimed that Torah scrolls dating back to pre-Solomonic times still could be found. Yet, on other occasions, he stridently attacked fanaticism. He ridiculed those who saw the hand of God in particular events ("heaven acts by general not by special laws"); doubted that animal sacrifices would ever be restored; deprecated biblical procedures in the case of a woman's suspected infidelity; and dated three biblical prophets (Haggai, Zechariah, and Malachi) to post-Second Temple days. More boldly, he praised human reason as the "highest gift which Providence has bestowed upon man," and, according to Isaac Mayer Wise, he once even went so far as to deny the existence of "the devil, hell and brimstone together with all popular absurdities of this kind."[51]

Again, neither Noah the believer, nor Noah the rationalist represents the "real Noah." Torn between tradition and change, the "real Noah" took an ambivalent stance, one that varied with his audience and his mood. He showed similar ambivalence in his discussions of Jewish ceremonial law. In his Ararat address of 1825, he insisted that "there is no part of our religion which should be altered, nothing should be taken from the law, for if the power of innovation existed, there would be no end to the pruning knife." Nine years later, in an address at the consecration of the Crosby Street synagogue of Shearith Israel, he advocated many alterations, especially those which he thought had proved successful in Germany. Unfortunately, the address, while highly praised in the press, was never printed, possibly at the request of the highly embarrassed traditionalist leaders of Shearith Israel. From his later writings, however, it is clear that Noah opposed what he called "excrescences in Rabbinical writings." He approved of lectures, music, and vernacular prayers, and disapproved of redundancies in the service. But Noah had not abandoned his earlier staunch traditionalist stance. As he demonstrated in an 1848 address, he sought both orthodoxy and reform at the same time. Again, he simultaneously desired change and feared it:

> The Jewish religion should never change its original form or type, reforms create schisms, and promote divisions; besides impairing the unity of our faith.... I must confess that I should like to see some changes in our ritual and ceremonies. While admiring the beauty and sublimity of the Hebrew language, I should still be gratified, if we could introduce in our prayers, a portion of the language of the country in order that we may better comprehend the great responsibilities of our faith. We might also curtail many repetitions, and introduce some beneficial changes; but where are the limitations and boundaries to these reforms, when we once introduce the pruning knife?[52]

The reforms which Noah suggested were not nearly so extensive or radical as those practiced by Charleston's Reformed Society of Israelites, 1825–1833. Still, the Society, like Noah, stressed ceremonial and behavioral changes; it insisted that Jewish identity symbols be maintained. While originally opposed to the Charleston reformers, Noah later became far more sympathetic to their aims. Never, however, did he connect himself with any formal Jewish reform movement.[53]

Noah examined ritual reform from the standpoint of utility and survival. He wondered whether Jewish unity and tradition were more valuable than the benefits which reform promised. He questioned whether reform, once started, could be properly managed. He feared that reform would ultimately lead to complete assimilation. The fact that Talmudic law might be violated by reformers worried Noah not at all. Unlike European Jews, he did not debate the merits of Reform Judaism based on learned quotations from rabbinic literature. Rabbinic literature was to him a closed and uninviting world. What little he knew of this world, he knew only through translated or secondary sources, and probably Christian ones, at that. The Sephardic-Marrano tradition with which he associated, the rationalism which he advocated, the Protestant literature which he read, and the Jews with whom he interacted, all maintained that the essence of Judaism lay in the Bible. The Talmud and its commentaries were compared to Catholic doctrine: an excrescence filled with "many crudities." Some of these crudities, Noah once exclaimed, struck "at the pure principles contained in the Bible." He felt sure that those who understood the law thoroughly, "seldom or ever" referred to the Talmud. He therefore had no hesitation about telling Isaac Leeser to "shut the Talmud and open the Bible." God's word, he insisted, was "our safest guide." To be sure, Noah sometimes defended the Talmud against Christian attacks. He did not mind using rabbinic citations when he knew of them and agreed with them. His Judaism, however, was very much a biblically centered Judaism. He considered basic laws regarding circumcision, vernacular Hebrew ("the antedeluvian language used no doubt by Adam"), the seventh day (Sabbath), and women all to be equally sacred and immutable. Noah admitted that proselyte circumcision, unintelligible Hebrew prayers, the Christian sabbath, and the subordinate role accorded women in Jewish law, all posed serious problems for faithful Jews. But he preferred the problems to the radical solutions proposed by some reformers. He hesitated to tamper with recognized benchmarks of Jewish identity.[54]

The same concern for Jewish identity lay behind Noah's strong stance against intermarriage. He knew that others considered Jews illiberal, even tribal, for spurning marriage with non-Jewish lovers. Were not all children of the same God? Nevertheless, he understood that this alleged Jewish illiberalism was really nothing less than Jewish survivalism. Children of mixed marriages, at least in his day, almost invariably became Christian (Moses Dropsie and the children of Solomon Jackson are notable exceptions). Noah did not go so far as some in Shearith Israel who wished to deny intermarried

Jews their long-held seats in the synagogue. Nor did he support any government ban on interreligious marriage. But he did make known his belief that followers of different religions should coexist and comingle without cohabiting. As long as he was alive, none of his children married outside of the faith.[55]

Noah's desire to maintain and strengthen Jewish identity had seemingly little impact on his personal religious observance. Hungering for acceptance in the non-Jewish world, he often violated even stringent biblical laws when compliance might have resulted in monetary loss, isolation, or ostracism. As the *Asmonean* sadly lamented, he was not "a rigid ceremonialist." Still, he never denigrated the ceremonies. He certainly never defended his infractions, as would later reformers. He just deviated, and he tried to do so as quietly as possible. In his ritual observance, as in his social interactions, he sought to integrate without compromising his Jewish identity.[56]

Noah did not observe the Jewish Sabbath in the traditional Jewish manner. In 1818, his assistant happened to mention in court that the editor did "not attend to business on that day." But Noah still visited the office on the Sabbath. Later, as publisher of an evening paper that appeared on Saturday afternoon (the *Evening Star*), his Sabbath labors increased. They increased further when he began to publish a Sunday paper, an undertaking on his part which *Tribune* editor Horace Greeley found rather peculiar. Yet, Noah still joined in lamenting the general decline in Jewish Sabbath observance. He was especially troubled by Jewish storekeepers whose Sabbath violations were so much more public and blatant than his own.[57]

Like most other Jews, Noah observed the high holidays far more scrupulously than he did the Sabbath. Although he knowingly placed himself far from a Jewish community on the Rosh Hashanah (Jewish New Year) before his Ararat dedication, his presence at Shearith Israel services in later years was often noted. He also seems to have observed most other major Jewish holidays, as well as the fast of the ninth of [the Hebrew month of] Ab, but how scrupulous he was in his observance is not known. In general, Noah preferred rituals which were performed annually or infrequently to those which demanded daily observance. He thus observed Jewish festivals and Jewish rites of passage, but found thrice-daily prayers far too arduous. He once described phylacteries, worn by traditional Jews at weekday morning services, as something worn by the "Israelites of old."[58]

The same effort to compromise between total observance and no observance can be seen in Noah's approach to Jewish dietary laws. In his home, he ate kosher meat. He wanted his children brought up observing kashruth as well. He also urged non-Jews to eat kosher meat—he later claimed that many "old New Yorkers" did so—because, he said, the meat was hygienically superior. Once he even suggested that rabbinic laws of meat inspection be introduced in all of New York State in order to prevent the spread of disease. Whether his own concerns went beyond the purchase of kosher meat, and included adherence to such provisions of the dietary laws as the separation of milk and meat, is not known.[59]

Noah was vitally concerned that food brought into his home not contain lard, a swine product. When he purchased kosher foods, of course, this posed no problem. But when he bought commercially prepared foods, or imported items, he worried that they might be impermissibly tainted. This fear became particularly serious in the case of olive oil, which French suppliers reputedly diluted with lard. Isaac Leeser characteristically suggested that rabbis inspect the preparation of the oil, and certify it for Jewish use. Noah, in strikingly modern fashion, proposed a technological solution. With the aid of a professor at the New York College of Pharmacy, he found a chemical test for lard, and printed the formula in the *Occident* for the benefit of Jewish readers. As it turned out, the printed formula contained an error which had later to be corrected. But Noah had shown that technology might be used to bridge the gap between the demands of Jewish law and desires born of the modern world—in this case, the desire to purchase commercially produced foodstuffs unsupervised by rabbinic authorities. Technology enabled him to enjoy modern conveniences in clear conscience.[60]

Noah could not satisfy all of his "modern world" desires with technological solutions. He enjoyed dining out with non-Jews, and when he did so, he violated dietary laws undisguisedly. "Hermippus" of Philadelphia knew his fellow journalist as "one of your truly good fellows," who loved "a turtle dinner and a glass of wine," and could sing "an admirable song." Turtles, of course, are not kosher. Nor, for that matter, are oysters, although Noah, along with many other nineteenth-century Jews (incuding Rabbi Isaac Mayer Wise) enjoyed them. So delectable a food, they apparently told themselves, could not but be kosher. Yet, even in public, Noah retained one easily identified food taboo: he abstained from eating pork or pork products. The Bible actually makes no distinction between a pig and other nonkosher animals—rabbits, for example. All alike are prohibited. As early as Hasmonean times, however, the prohibition of pork had become a symbol of Jewish dietary distinctiveness. Perhaps this development occurred because swine products played so important a part in the non-Jewish diet. Perhaps its deeper cause was that the pig carries what Mary Douglas calls "the odium of multiple pollution"—that is, it violates dietary prohibitions in three ways instead of the normal one. Whatever the reason, the pig, long before the nineteenth century, had become a synechdoche, if not indeed a replacement for the entire kashruth code. Noah once complained that "the very mention of pork, cooked or raw, makes my stomach heave at any time." His ample belly must have gyrated wildly when, as chief officer of Tammany Hall, "he distinguished himself in the dissection and dislocation of a heathen pig, distributing the particles thereof to his surrounding compeers." Noah did not, however, partake of the feast himself. According to the contemporary description, he "delicately declined... lest the daughters of the uncircumcised should titter."[61]

Noah's ritual practice typifies not only American Jewish religious observance in his day, but also the Judaism practiced by a great many diaspora Jews in all of the modern period. Jewish folk religion, as distinct from the Judaism laid out in rabbinic codes, has always mediated between the lure of the external world and the countervailing desire to identify with one's own people. Mordecai Noah was certainly far from the first Jew to be more observant of dietary laws at home than outside. He was also anything but unique in adopting easy, infrequent, and seemingly modern rituals—those not difficult to justify—over those which might have proved more restrictive and more open to ridicule. Only his specific ritual choices distinguished Noah from other Jews. Though not a "rigid ceremonialist," and though far less traditional than most "defenders of the faith," he was still probably more observant than the average American Jew of his day, or of our own.[62]

Once he had small children, Noah faced a new problem connected with his religious observance: the problem of Christmas. By the 1840s, Christmas had become a nationwide celebration. Trees, lights, gifts, glitter, and Christmas stockings created a merry holiday, one which held enormous allure for Jewish children. Hanukkah possessed no similar magic. An unimportant Jewish holiday, it was then unconnected with gifts and merriment. Were it not for a few extant Hanukkah lamps, we might not know that the holiday was celebrated in early America at all. Noah's problem was thus the perennial problem of American Jewish parents: his children were jealous of their Christian friends. Later, Jews would magnify Hanukkah in an effort to create a Jewish functional alternative to Christmas. They instituted gift-giving, songs, parties, and decorations all designed to counteract the Christian challenge. Noah's solution was entirely different. He reinterpreted Christmas into the celebration of "a great event worthy of being commemorated among civilized communities." He urged everyone to celebrate it as the birthday of that religion which spread monotheism throughout the world. His family followed his advice. "Henry and Linny [Lionel] are making arrangements to hang up their stockings to night for Christmas," Noah wrote to his daughter Zipporah in 1848. He did not mention how his two young sons had celebrated Hanukkah.[63]

Noah had certainly not become a Christian. In 1848 he was still an honored and influential member of the Jewish community; but he wanted recognition from Christians. He associated with Christians in his political and social activities. He catered to a Christian audience in his press. In his declining years, as in his earlier years, he sought to act as a good Jew, to be recognized as a "good Christian," and to identify as a good American—all at the same time.

CHAPTER VIII

Declining Years

"Our friend Noah...seems mellowing into a type of the patriarchs of old," remarked the editor of *Home Journal* in 1850. He had made a shrewd observation. During his last decade, Mordecai Noah evolved into "old Noah." Increasingly, he was respected and pitied, honored and ignored, heard and forgotten. At first, he strove to stave off the inevitable. He made a final stab at the kind of status and power which he had tasted but never long enjoyed. By his sixtieth birthday, however, he realized that these hopes were illusory; he settled down to the role of oracle. Sometimes his pronouncements still set off controversy. He continued to fight occasional press battles with James Gordon Bennett. But, like two more famous men of his era, Henry Clay and John C. Calhoun, he called in his old age for peace, harmony, and reconciliation. He warned, as others had warned, that "the union is in danger." Unfortunately, he could offer no effective means of setting things right.[1]

Governor William Seward kept his promise to Mordecai Noah. In January 1841, he nominated him to a judgeship in the New York Court of Sessions, the five-man municipal court (four judges and the recorder) responsible for civil and criminal cases not requiring a jury trial. The position, in the words of fellow journalist David Lambert, was "very inconsiderable." It did pay two thousand dollars a year plus legal fees, and it did confer on its holder the august title of "judge." But it really offered little status and even less power. In the wake of the Whig presidential victory, Noah had hoped for something better. He wanted to turn the clock back seven years, and to resume his lucrative, prestigious and powerful job as surveyor of the New York port. North Carolina senator Willie Person Mangum and several New York congressmen supported his application to President William Henry Harrison. But their appeals to "reason and justice" fell on deaf ears, perhaps because the president soon took ill. Consequently, Noah received no federal post, and had to settle for what Seward had offered him.[2]

It proved more difficult than Noah had imagined to win confirmation of his judgeship. His political enemies—the same people who had opposed him when he ran for sheriff and when he was appointed surveyor—determined to defeat him once again. The fact that they were fellow Whigs made no difference. The Whigs were a divided party. Leader of the opposition, as usual, was Charles King—this time aided by Gulian Verplanck. They and their supporters questioned Noah's legal and moral competence, resurrected a twenty-three-year-old charge of mail opening, alleged that Noah maintained secret press connections, and invoked religious prejudice against the idea of a Jew judging Christians. But Governor Seward, who may have remembered Noah's devoted loyalty on the issue of Catholic education, countenanced no party opposition to his nominee. Contrary to expectations, therefore, the nomination passed on a unanimous vote. On May 6, 1841, Judge Mordecai Noah made his debut as probably the first Jew to sit on a criminal court bench in modern times.[3]

Noah had the makings of an excellent municipal court judge. He had adequate legal knowledge, a vast store of intuitive human knowledge, an understanding of his city and its people, an appreciation of the problems of minorities and immigrants, a respect for the rights of individuals, a concern for public order and social morality, a jolly sense of humor, and a genuine desire to help people. While the unreliable and sensational newspaper law columns make it difficult to know whether he lived up to this potential, they do suggest that he brought human qualities to the bench. One example, even if overdramatized, speaks volumes:

> In the Court of Special Sessions yesterday, a man named John Fisher was brought up for some trifling offense for trial. His wife, a beautiful young woman not more than seventeen years of age, appeared at the bar with an infant in her arms, as the advocate of her husband. She was dressed plainly, and by no means in the height of fashion. Her fashion, her child and her tears had a softening effect upon the Court. The husband was discharged and left the room. The young wife lingered behind to sob out a few sentences of gratitude. Judge Noah spoke to her a few kind words, and enquired of her "are you really so destitute as you appear, and is that your child?" "As there's a God," replied the poor creature, "it is all true. Since my husband has been in prison for triflingly offending against the dignity of our landlord, the latter has turned me and my child out of doors, and retained for his rent, as he claims our all—little all. For four days I have with my child subsisted in the open air, depending wholly upon the cold charity of such as chanced to pass by."
>
> This was more than Judge Noah could stand: with his face concealed from the gaze of the spectators, to conceal an evident emotion, he beckoned to the poor woman, and as she approached him, slipped into her hand a *five dollar note*, wishing her better success and happiness hereafter. She left the Court with an altered countenance. The Judge adjusted his spectacles, called the Court to order, and the business proceeded.[4]

Noah was not just sensitive to the needs of others. He worried too about his own image. One lure of the judgeship, after all, had been the honor attached to the accompanying title. In place of honor, however, Judge Noah soon found himself the butt of ridicule. Predictably, the scoffer was the cynical James Gordon Bennett, a man who first made his reputation by extracting material of broad popular interest from dry courtroom scenes. Bennett, a supporter of the governor, had carefully avoided voicing any unfavorable comment about Noah's appointment to the bench. Instead, he engaged in "double-speak," dutifully reminding his readers that "Mr. Noah formerly held the office of a 'Judge in Israel' on Grand Island." Gleefully, he anticipated many "a funny scene" if, as he professed to hope, Noah won confirmation. When the hope was realized, the funny scenes followed close behind. Bennett sent his liveliest reporter, William H. Attree, to satirize the court proceedings, and Attree spared no one, least of all Noah. The *Herald* lampoons were replete with double entendres (Noah warned a loafer accused of pork stealing "never to touch pork again"), vicious personal attacks ("Judge Noah...is so fat and sleek and slippery that he frequently almost tumbles asleep on the bench") and outright libels ("Noah is as much the editor of the *Star* now as ever he was"). Noah's colleague on the bench, Judge James Lynch, had editor Bennett indicted on contempt charges just for printing such material. But the damage to Noah's prestige had already been done. By the time Bennett came to trial, eight months later, Noah had graciously acceded to the desperate plea of *Herald* lawyer John Morrill, and in return for a written apology (for a while Bennett talked of his "old friend Noah") he agreed to ask the court to drop all charges.[5]

As in the Barker case of fifteen years before, Noah's motives in abandoning a strong *prima facie* case are difficult to understand. Contemporaries too were mystified. Privately, the judge did explain that he held "no personal feelings in the matter," and blamed Attree, not Bennett, for the offending articles. He pointed out, as well, that as an editor he had himself often apologized his way out of libel suits. But outright contempt of court was surely different from ordinary libel. Furthermore, Bennett was no ordinary foe. The cause of Noah's actions seems, therefore, to lie beneath the surface. Evidence is lacking; still, his sense of justice may have been tempered by his desire to avoid having himself unflatteringly compared to Shakespeare's Shylock. The "pound of flesh" spectre, often invoked against Jews, perhaps prevented him from demanding his due. If so, he was saved by the court. Judge Nathan Kent ignored Noah's *nolle prosequi* [do not prosecute] plea and fined Bennett three hundred and fifty dollars.

Although Bennett's conviction brought a temporary halt to the *Herald*'s attacks against Judge Noah, the Judge's dissatisfaction with his job did not diminish. For a long time, city aldermen refused to pay him his salary, less because they disliked him than because they opposed the 1840 court reform law under which he had been appointed. Formerly, Sessions Court justices had been city aldermen who earned extra money on the side as judges. Adding to Noah's misery were his opponents, who heckled him with incessant charges of conflict of interest. They claimed, rightly or wrongly, that while serving on the bench he continued to write anonymous partisan articles in conservative Whig journals; his indignant denials were not believed. Finally, Noah felt personally frustrated over his low status and lack of visibility. Except for an occasional headline, such as when he instructed the grand jury to indict anyone at the American Anti-Slavery Convention who suggested or discussed "a project embracing a dissolution of our happy form of government," he was relegated to that insignificant corner of the newspaper reserved for court proceedings. He hungered for more front-rank status and more behind-the-scenes power. Presented with the opportunity to achieve both goals, he seized it. In July 1842 he vacated his seat on the bench.[6]

Noah left the bench for the opportunity to take an active role in the political organization of President John Tyler, the little known vice-president who succeeded to the White House upon the untimely death of William Henry Harrison. It was one of Noah's poorer political decisions. Tyler had long since been abandoned by most Harrison supporters. Henry Clay's faction of the Whig Party, the group with which Noah had earlier associated himself, read Tyler completely out of the Whig Party. By 1842, the only major Whig support for the embattled president came from Secretary of State Daniel Webster, and Noah had opposed him for years. As for the Democrats, they showed little interest in seeing Tyler return to their midst after a ten-year hiatus. It therefore seemed safe to assume, as most politicans did, that "His Accidency" would be a one-term president, and a bad one at that.

Noah subbornly disagreed. He saw possibilities in Tyler's plan to unite conservative Democrats and conservative Whigs into a new, pro-Union Coalition. He may also have been impressed by Tyler's cordial treatment of Jews. In his first fourteen months in office, the president had assured Richmond's Jacob Ezekiel that a presidential reference to "Christian people" did not exclude Jews, for whom he professed to have "none other than profound respect". He had also overturned the court-martial conviction of Captain Uriah Phillips Levy, who was somewhat maliciously accused of improperly punishing a recalcitrant seaman. But, while these actions may have justified his decision in his own mind, they surely were not determining factors. Basically, Noah supported Tyler because he believed that the president still had the ability to win the voters over to his side. All Tyler needed, he thought, was a good newspaper, a more active political organization, and better advice. Noah confidently assumed that he could fill all three needs, and he expected to be handsomely rewarded for his efforts.[7]

Noah published the first issue of his new Tylerite newspaper on July 18, 1842. *The Union* was the name of the paper, and union was precisely what the editor called for: a union of the divided fragments of "the old Republican party which elected Jefferson, Madison and Monroe." "The Whig Party," Noah proclaimed, "cannot in its present temper... be kept together any longer." He called instead for a return to the early, pre-Jackson party system. After several blasts at Tyler's opponents, and an ambitious promise of journalistic excellence, *The Union* appealed for public support. It was to be disappointed. "The people have so great a veneration for it that they won't touch it," the *New Haven Herald* wryly observed. Following an initial printing of fifty thousand copies, *The Union* settled down to a paltry circulation of between five hundred and a thousand. It depended for survival on government patronage and political contributions, many of them involuntary.[8]

The first issue of *The Union* had piously declared that "a journal should rather lead than follow party." But follow is all that Mordecai Noah was permitted to do. Paul R. George, Tylerite leader in New York, maintained a tight rein on *The Union*'s editorial page. As in his early *National Advocate* days, Noah found himself forced to toe the line. George allowed him no criticism of Daniel Webster, and he even had to remain silent in the face of James Gordon Bennett's usual unpleasant attacks. Bennett supported Tyler and was a personal friend of the president's son, Robert. *The Union* also paid obeisance to the *New York Sun.* That successful penny paper assumed responsibility for *The Union*'s printing and distribution, as well as for much of its news. Noah left his personal stamp on his newspaper only through feature articles, many of which received wide publicity through republication in other journals. Nevertheless, his brief tenure as editor was basically an exercise in timidity and subservience. Where he had hoped for power and prestige, he encountered only insecurity and frustration.[9]

Noah had good reason to feel insecure. His appointment as editor and chairman of the Tyler General Committee met opposition from the start by a large group of Tyler's supporters: New York Postmaster John L. Graham, party stalwart John Fowles, editor James Gordon Bennett, and a host of their followers. According to a pseudonymous memoir,[10] this faction soon commenced a letter-writing campaign to President Tyler, in which "Major Noah was assailed in every possible shape and at every point." "His Hebrew origin and religion, was represented to be odious to the great mass of the People; and it was further advanced and urged that he had, in consequence of his eccentric political career and advanced age, outlived his talents, his influence and his friends." Unless Noah was deposed, these letters claimed, Tyler would lose the vote of the entire state of New York. The president's opinion of his New York editor surely did not improve when he saw the *Union*'s dismal circulation figures. Noah's controversial advice—remove Daniel Webster and elevate New Yorker Silas Wright to the post of key advisor—made him no better liked. He then made further enemies by trying to whip political appointees into line. That move proved as unpopular in 1842 as it had been two decades earlier. In the end, Noah had but one major supporter, Paul R. George. And George, who faced troubles of his own, left him defenseless. A scant five months after he appointed Noah, Tyler therefore consented to his removal. As consolation, the President promised him a better job. He also agreed that Isaac Phillips, Noah's nephew, could succeed to the editor's chair. But the *Union* continued, now as a morning paper, for only a few weeks more. Then it was killed outright, and Phillips was fired. Noah, meanwhile, took over temporary leadership of the New York branch of Tyler's newly formed third party. He confidently expected to hold this job only until a surveyorship or consulship opened up.[11]

Noah rapidly lost faith in Tyler's ability to win a second term. A trip to

Richmond taught him that Thomas Ritchie, influential editor of the *Richmond Enquirer*, had deserted the president. A disastrous pro-Tyler rally (March 15, 1843) at New York's Tabernacle taught him that New Yorkers had deserted the president, as well. Amid cries of "Put Out That Jew," anti-Tyler forces captured control of the crowd from the presiding Noah. They proceeded to vote nine cheers for Henry Clay, nine cheers for Martin Van Buren, three hurrahs for "a celebrated lady who conducted a harem in one of the streets which radiate from Broadway," and nothing but groans for John Tyler. A week later, Noah disbanded the Tyler Party in New York, and quietly abandoned all thoughts of a Tyler reelection. But he did not abandon Tyler himself. While he realized that the chief executive could offer him no political power, he still hoped that he would keep his political promises. Noah therefore continued to expect that Tyler would reward him with a lucrative, prestigious, and secure position in which to live out his remaining days.[12]

Noah almost received what he wanted. Several New York newspapers heard "unofficially" that he was again to be appointed surveyor of the port. At the last minute, however, his opponents blocked the move. He never enjoyed the satisfaction of revenging himself on those who drove him from office in 1832. Noah next sought to be nominated chargé d'affaires at Constantinople, an appointment which in his mind would doubtless have vindicated his consular actions back in Tunis. He was well suited for the Ottoman post, and he would no doubt have enjoyed the diplomatic corps' pomp and status. The proximity to Palestine and the potential for helping needy Jews made the job even more appealing. An opening even existed in Constantinople, since minister David Porter had recently died. But the position was not to be his. "The President has not noticed my application," Noah lamented to his friend Duff Green, "he apprehended my religion would not be acceptable to the Sultan and his Ministers." Noah had persuasively argued—as he had argued thirty years before—that his Judaism would be an asset to America, since Jews held great power in Turkey. He also had hinted that his coreligionists would look kindly on his appointment, and on the wise president who made it. But Tyler had heard disturbing reports from other sources about the Sultan's intolerance. By the time Noah had collected contrary evidence (including a letter from Moses Montefiore), Tyler's administration was nearing an end, and no appointment could be made. Noah applied for the Turkish post again soon after James Polk entered the White House, but the letters he had so laboriously collected had in the interim been lost. Yet another of Noah's goals would remain forever unfulfilled. As it turned out, no Jew received appointment as American minister to Turkey until Oscar Straus won the job in 1887. After that, Constantinople became for years the "Jewish post" in the diplomatic corps, the only Jewish post.[13]

In 1842, Noah had abandoned his secure but trivial judgeship for the promise of a newspaper, and the hint of much more. Many of the goals that he had sought for himself throughout his life—a consulship, political power, and the surveyor's chair—had seemed suddenly within his reach. President Tyler, deserted by most Americans, had become his messianic hope personified. But the secular messiah proved false, a delusion born of despair and old age. Noah felt "most disgracefully and villainously cheated, swindled [and] bamboozled." In late spring of 1843, he belatedly abandoned Tyler and returned to Tammany Hall, the nest of his youth. The old, war-weary, battle-scarred politician had come home. Slowly, he began to fade away.[14]

Noah returned to Tammany Hall without fanfare. He was an errant son; accepted, but granted no favors. He would have to survive on his own. Too old to change professions, Noah, on July 6, 1843, announced a new journalistic venture: a three-cent Sunday newspaper entitled *Noah's Weekly Messenger*. The first issue received a hearty welcome, probably because it contained a damaging attack on President Tyler's associates and policies. After the second issue, however, the newspaper verged on collapse. Happily for Noah, the *Sunday Times* (partly edited by the then unknown Walt Whitman) agreed to merge with his *Messenger*. United, the *Sunday Times and Noah's Weekly Messenger* flourished all the way up to 1892.[15]

Sunday newspapers still aroused controversy when Noah started his, and he therefore faced his share of pious evangelical opposition. He responded, ironically enough, by demonstrating that he did the work for his Sunday paper on Saturday. He then made sure to mold the *Times and Messenger* into a family newspaper, one which could be "received and approved in circles where no Sunday publication had penetrated before." The *Times and Messenger* contained an abundance of moralizing tales and affecting historical sketches. One reader called the weekly "the paper par excellence in everything that relates to old times in New York and revolutionary matters." Noah also spiced the journal with witty reviews, amusing court notices, occasional reminiscences, and lively barbs at James Gordon Bennett. Even his editorial and news columns seemed somehow less ponderous than those in the dailies. Noah's most striking innovation, however, was undoubtedly his column of "answers to correspondents." Sometimes, he merely provided information to the curious: "O'Connell was born in 1775." Other questioners received helpful advice: "if the debtor cannot pay, the case is a hopeless one, and an expense of a suit can do no good." To still others, he dealt mild reproof: "criminal intercourse previous to marriage on the part of the person you have married gives you no right to a divorce. It was your business to find out the character of the woman." A final group of questioners received detailed responses to religious queries and challenges. The very last answer he wrote before his death is typical:

> If Christianity had not been established, there would have been nothing but the darkest paganism extant... [But] if Jesus were the promised Messiah, he did not bring with his advent all the good and power promised to the Jews in the Messianic kingdom. They were to be gathered together as a nation when the Messiah appeared. Alas! They are still dispersed without a home, a country, or a government!

The "answers to correspondents" column received favorable notice in other publications, and grew longer as the years went by. It was an important factor in the rapid growth of the *Times and Messenger* from a circulation of a few hundred in 1843 to a booming circulation of fifteen thousand in 1851.[16]

For all of its eventual success, the *Times and Messenger* was never able to support Noah adequately—certainly not in the journal's fledgling days. To provide for his family of nine, he had no choice but to find additional sources of income. He made several efforts to begin a new daily New York newspaper—four numbers of the *Independent* actually appeared in December 1843—but because of his age and his enemies, neither city Democrats, nor supporters of John Calhoun, nor even southern pro-slavery forces agreed to back him financially. His efforts to make money in the publishing world fared only slightly better. He tried to purchase for publication Aaron Burr's secret love letters, but Matthew Davis, Burr's executor, resolutely refused to sell them; they were too personal. He also tried to put together a book entitled *The National Volume*, "a work comprising an essay, paper or literary offering from every distinguished Statesman, Historian, Poet, or writer of eminence or reputation in the Country." This project too came to nothing. In the end, all Noah published was a new edition of his old *Essays of Howard*, now retitled *Gleanings from a Gathered Harvest*. Although the book did prove popular—it went through two editions (1845, 1847)—the volume hardly sold well enough to make Noah financially independent. When his Hebrew boarding school plan also fell through, the ex-Judge swallowed his pride and accepted an anonymous job on the editorial staff of Moses Beach's penny paper, *The New York Sun*, which he knew from his days with *The Union*.[17] Unfortunately, his precise role in the development of that enormously successful newspaper remains unclear. One contemporary credited him with being "political, financial and literary editor," as well as "Washington correspondent over the signature of Montgomery." Others called him general editor. James Gordon Bennett, on the other hand, considered him nothing but a glorified "penny a liner." Whatever the case, it must have been depressingly difficult for Noah, after so many years in the limelight, to work barely recognized backstage. The fact that the *Sunday Times and Noah's Weekly Messenger* had his own name right up on the title line served only as limited compensation.[18]

Noah's *Times and Messenger* claimed not to have a "partisan character." It wanted to attract readers of every political stripe. But the newspaper's editor also candidly admitted that he was "not strictly neutral." In fact, he consistently supported the conservative, "Hunker" wing of the Democratic party, a faction comprised of men who, generally speaking, were more wealthy, more tolerant of slavery, and more eager for banks and unrestricted expansion than the "Barnburner" radicals who comprised the party's other faction. Of course, Noah was only a political follower; his Whig and Tylerite past barred him from any leadership role. When he sought a more important position, as he did from John Calhoun and Secretary of War (also Hunker leader) William Marcy, he met with firm rebuffs. It thus became Noah's role to serve as self-appointed party oracle. Like many an oracle, he found himself frequently ignored. Nevertheless, he continued to remind the faithful of damaging past divisions, and he called upon them to unite, at least at election time. He set a personal example by supporting his old enemy, Martin Van Buren, when he became the state party's presidential choice in 1844. Once James Polk became the Democrats' national nominee, he supported him, as well. After the election, Noah cheerfully returned to a more partisan, conservative stance, one which he considered best for the country as a whole. He opposed changes in the state constitution, opposed antislavery measures such as the Wilmot Proviso, and opposed calls for a third party. When, much to his regret, the radical Barnburners abandoned the Democratic Party in 1848 and nominated Martin Van Buren on a third-party presidential ticket, he feared for the Union itself. But after Whig candidate Zachary Taylor won the election (Noah had been one of the first to predict that he would be nominated), the oracle did not join in the general cry of the Democratic vanquished for party reunion. He rather called to mind the punishment meted out to Tammany's other errant sons—a punishment with which he was most intimately familiar— and he joined the so-called "Hard Hunkers," who opposed readmission of the Barnburners except on extremely severe terms. For a brief moment, Noah basked again in glory. He assumed a leadership role among Hard Hunkers, and he ran on a factional slate for the post of Tammany Hall Grand Sachem. But his moment passed. Noah and the Hard Hunkers lost the election despite challenges of vote tampering. The aged oracle closed out his political career with yet another bitter disappointment, and yet another stinging defeat.[19]

Why was Noah so singularly unlucky in his four decades of politics? Certainly, the policies he espoused, his own public image, and his frequently ill-considered alliances hurt him in many cases, especially late in life. Such a consistent pattern of disappointment, however, suggests a more fundamental problem, as Noah himself may have recognized. "Whenever there is a fierce battle to be fought, I am called upon. The moment victory ensues, I am shelved," he complained at age sixty-two to his old friend, theater manager Sol Smith. He never understood why. He did not realize that, in America, combative journalists and governing politicians were drawing ever further apart. The public saw journalists as rowdy, vituperative, and unprincipled— hardly men fit to govern. Noah suffered from guilt by association. He also suffered from the very real but dimly perceived burdens which a journalistic tie imposed upon a politician. First, there was an ethical problem: the natural conflict of interest between those who zealously watched over government and those who actively participated in its daily functions. Then, there was a structural problem: the very act of writing made it difficult for a journalist to engage in political maneuvering. Martin Van Buren could withhold comment on sensitive subjects, tell different people different things, easily shift his views to conform with public opinion, and explain away all inconsistencies and harsh words with clever rhetoric. When Mordecai Noah changed his mind or expressed an unflattering judgement, it was in black-and-white, and impossible to deny. Still, those who refused Noah political advantage rarely cited as reasons his journalistic ties. They usually blamed personal factors, often religious ones. As justifications, these sufficed. They were easily understood and evoked sympathetic responses. As explanations, they sufficed not at all. Similar men, Jews included, faced far fewer obstacles on their paths to power. Perhaps Noah would have advanced further had he been a wealthy Protestant aristocrat with a Dutch last name. But he might also have advanced further had he not simultaneously tried to involve himself both in the making of events and in their journalistic coverage.[20]

Whatever problems Noah may have had advancing in America did not affect his standing in the Jewish community. In the last decade of his life, as journalism and politics occupied a smaller fraction of his day, he gave increasing amounts of time to his fellow Jews. He involved himself in Jewish charities, and spoke out for Jewish rights. More than anything else, he dedicated himself to the cause of Jewish restoration.

While many call Noah a Zionist, the term is actually an anachronism. The current meaning of the word Zionist originated in 1890. Noah can also not be considered a "forerunner of Zion." As defined by Jacob Katz, a forerunner is one who led a movement to Palestine. Noah had no followers at all. He was a restorationist": he advocated a program of action designed to bring about the return to Zion. Most Jews believed that God would restore the Jewish people only in His own good time.[21]

Noah had talked about restoration since his 1818 Consecration Address at Shearith Israel. But until the 1830s, he held a traditional, deterministic view of the subject. He talked about "signs," "prospects," and what "will" happen, rather than about "efforts," "movements," and what "should" happen. Sometimes, as in 1818, promising signals of emancipation made him optimistic: "Never were prospects for the restoration of the Jewish nation to their ancient rights and dominion more brilliant than they are at present." At other times, as in 1824, instability and war made him pessimistic: "There is much to be done before the period of restoration arrives." In all cases, external forces generated his optimism and pessimism. He made no personal contributions to the cause. When he did act, it was to bring Jews to New York, not to Jerusalem. Ararat, of course, did have restorationist implications. Noah saw America as the land beyond the sea where Jews would gather prior to their ultimate return. But the "Grand Judge of Israel" viewed restoration as only a "just hope." Had he considered the millennium to be any more imminent, he could hardly have justified so ambitious a project as a Jewish colony.[22]

Noah became a restorationist advocate of immediate return to Zion in the 1830s. He did not suddenly abandon his old belief in ultimate messianic, millennial redemption; he rather merged it with his equally old secular espousal of self-help: "The Jewish people must now do something for themselves; they must move onward to the accomplishment of that event long foretold—long promised—long expected." He concluded, as had Christian reformers, that man could be the instrument of his own redemption, even while redemption itself still remained the affair of the Lord. He saw man as affecting his own destiny, but only affecting it in part. Torn between a determinism that he could no longer accept, and secular notions of free will that he viewed as heresy, Noah, like many men of his age, strove to synthesize these two things into an acceptable middle ground. At the same time, he put forward a restorationist scheme designed to be acceptable to Jews and Christians alike.[23]

Noah's intellectual shift on the question of restoration was intimately connected with rapidly unfolding events in the Middle East. The Holy Land, remote and forbidding in the 1820s, had by the 1830s become a center of world attention. Missionary organizations had set themselves up in Jerusalem. Holy Land news pushed its way into the religious and secular press. Improved sailing vessels sent tourists and pilgrims scurrying to religious shrines. The same vessels brought a growing stream of Palestine emissaries back to the United States. Meanwhile, behind the scenes in the Middle East, the great powers competed for influence, often with tacit missionary assistance. Turkey, which had dominated the region for centuries, seemed in danger of imminent collapse. As other countries gathered around eager to pick at the spoils, war loomed ominously on the horizon.[24]

Mordecai Noah believed that even so highly dangerous a situation could be beneficially exploited. He therefore suggested that Christians and Jews jointly purchase the Holy Land, either as a unit or in discreet parcels of land, in order to aid persecuted Jews, the same kind of Jews whom he had unsuccessfully tried to help at Ararat. He proposed to set up for these Jews a Jewish buffer state, and to place this new "Judea" (as he once called it) under the protection of either Britain or the great powers. A "Judea," he felt, would eliminate international rivalry, strengthen Turkey financially, endear Christians to Jews, and, of course, bring about the Jewish restoration for which he prayed. What he needed, Noah realized, was money and Christian cooperation. A post in America's Turkish consulate would also have been helpful, but he held little hope of receiving one. Heavily involved in politics, and chastened by experience, he pondered his plan alone for nine long years, only sharing it occasionally with his readers. At last, in 1844, he found the time and courage to present his idea before New York Christians. His address received close attention, wide distribution, and lasting fame. It was, by general agreement, the most important address that he ever delivered.[25]

Noah presented his *Discourse on the Restoration of the Jews* twice, both times before distinguished audiences at the large New York Tabernacle. Those in attendance at his lectures included Bishop Hughes, the Catholic prelate of New York, and many Protestant missionaries, whose interest had already been piqued by new restorationist ideas emanating from Britain. The president of the London Society for the Promotion of Christianity Amongst the Jews, Lord Shaftesbury, and other evangelicals had concluded that Jewish restoration was a necessary precondition both for conversion and redemption. American evangelicals, who had trouble converting Jews anyway, found the doctrine alluring. Noah aimed to convince these Christians that their new restorationist interests and his interests were thoroughly compatible. To this end, he praised Christianity's founder, denied Jewish culpability in the crucifixion, and found many kind words for "that religion which is calculated to make mankind great and happy." He had his criticisms of Christianity, and he pointed out many examples of Jewish persecution. But his basic goal was "to promote human happiness equally among all faiths." He therefore fervently called for tolerance, and patiently explained why Jews would not voluntarily convert. Then, at his climax, he asked Christians to "unite in efforts to promote the restoration of Jews in their *unconverted* state, relying on the fulfillment of the prophecies and the will of God for attaining the objects they have in view after that great advent shall have arrived."[26]

Noah believed that his program for setting up an independent Jewish state in Palestine invited just the sort of Christian–Jewish cooperation that he had in mind. As a politician, he had no qualms about making common cause with any group that could further his immediate aims. The founder of modern Zionism, Theodore Herzl, who like Noah was a politically aware journalist, demonstrated the same kind of goal-oriented pragmatism. Noah felt that ultimate questions—who would convert and which Messiah would come—could be put off until the end of time. Pending that, he pointed out, all could live happier lives. Jews could benefit from having their own state. Christians could pay their debts to the Jewish people while basking in the rewards reserved for those who furthered millennial aims. Meanwhile, all Americans could enjoy the satisfaction of knowing that theirs was the land described by Isaiah (18:1) as that land destined by God to play a crucial role in the restoration process.[27]

Noah's restoration plan proceeded along a course charted two decades earlier at Ararat. Again, he borrowed a new, exciting, and still developing idea, one being discussed, for various reasons, all over the English-speaking world. Again, he recast the idea into a form thoroughly beneficial to Jews, but still, he hoped, acceptable to Christians. Again he propounded the newly modified idea as his own and sought out the widest possible number of supporters. His strategy was the same strategy which American Jews would often adopt in trying to win over allies to their side. He insisted that support should stem as much from self-interest and patriotism as from benevolence and charity. Abundant experience had taught him that a cause couched in general terms, one which appealed to different people for different reasons, had a better chance for success than even the most worthy of causes couched in parochial language.

In his restoration address, Noah predicted (based, of course, on a prophecy by Ezekiel) that "Russia, in its attempt to wrest India from England and Turkey from the Ottomites, will make the Holy Land the theatre of a terrible conflict." He then reassured his audience that "Great Britain, with her allies, will come to the rescue." In private, however, Noah was much less sanguine regarding the direction of British policy. He feared that "England is playing a deep game for the exclusive right of way across the Isthmus of Suez," and he worried that if she won that right, America's Far East trade might suffer grievously. His suggestion, one remarkable for its time, was that America agree to build a railroad, "from Cairo in Egypt to Suez on the Red Sea." In return, he thought, Egypt would grant the United States rights equal to those granted Great Britain. American trade would thus be rendered safe; at the same time, British power would be held in check. Noah basically wanted two separate groups, entrepreneurs (the American government and American railroads) and restorationists (American Jews and American Christians), both to become involved in the Middle East. Each, he knew had its own goals to pursue, and each, he assumed, would work independently. Yet he doubtless believed that each would indirectly help the other. All alike, he hoped, would benefit in the end.[28]

Noah's railroad plan received no known response. In its waning days, the Tyler administration cared little about the Middle East and less about Noah. On the other hand, the Restoration Address received abundant press comment, especially after it appeared in a handsomely published booklet in January 1845. Nathan Peabody Rogers, editor of the abolitionist paper *Herald of Freedom*, condemned the speech for showing insufficient devotion to America: "New England or New York is as good as Palestine, and a great deal better... the Jews had better stay where they are." The *New York Albion* found the "Jewish conception of the mere humanity of the Saviour," to be "prejudicial to the cause which Judge Noah is advocating." James Gordon Bennett, ever eager to stir up the rabble, condemned the same section of the speech as "the most insulting attack on Christianity that has ever been attempted." Noah did have his defenders, and many praised his spirit and tone. His call for Christian aid, however, went completely unheeded. Restoration came about in other ways.[29]

Jews proved as sensitive as Christians to those sections of the Restoration Address which dealt with Christianity. Yet, in Jewish eyes, Noah's comments seemed, as London's *Voice of Jacob* put it, "anti-Judaic... tenable neither on historical nor on scriptural grounds." Sympathetic as many Jews were to Noah's aims, they could neither understand nor tolerate such comments as: "The second advent, Christians, depends upon you. It cannot come to pass, by your own admission, until the Jews are restored, and restored in their unconverted state. If he is again to appear, it must be to his own people, and in the land of his birth and his affections—on the spot where he preached and prophesied and died." Nor could they agree with his sympathetic portrayal of Jesus. Isaac Leeser, editor of the *Occident*, went even further. He cast doubt on practical aspects of Noah's plan, particularly the idea that the great powers would guarantee Jewish safety. He then condemned all talk of cooperation with missionaries in any form whatsoever: "With conversionists, as such, we cannot, as Jews enter into any league; the Jews are abhorrent to them, and if they grant us any favors, they do it for the sake of a return." Noah defended himself aggressively against Leeser's attacks, and earnestly proclaimed his good intentions. But he had as little understanding of Leeser's objections as Leeser had of his aims. Their battle ended in a vitriolic draw.[30]

The acerbic clash between Noah and Leeser provides a striking example of the dichotomy between "integrationists" and "defenders of the faith." Noah, in this case the integrationist, looked out, and tried to bring his group into line with Christian America. He graciously called for ecumenism and harmony, and glowingly portrayed the benefits of unity and cooperation. Leeser, in this case the "defender of the faith," took an opposite stance. He looked inward, and strove to preserve Jewish group identity. He fearlessly battled to strengthen his people's cultural defenses and grimly warned against the twin dangers of assimilation and conversion. Both the integrationist and the defender of the faith provided valuable service to the Jewish community. Noah stimulated discussion and attacked closed-minded insulation. Leeser maintained vigilance and prevented fawning accommodation. In between lay a broad middle ground of innovations with appropriate security. To be sure, this middle ground was the ground which Leeser and Noah both usually occupied. Leeser instituted many an integrationist reform; Noah rallied to many a Jew's defense. But the Restoration Address, perhaps because it so openly dealt with historically sensitive and evocative questions, raised extreme passions in both men. Chastened by the experience, they each subsequently altered their views and adopted more moderate positions.

The series of events which brought Leeser and Noah closer together were the nationalist revolutions that spread throughout Europe in 1848. Both Jewish leaders instinctively saw a parallel between demands for German, Polish, and Italian statehood, on the one hand, and the age-old promise of a Jewish state, on the other. Both men wondered whether the time had finally arrived for purposeful Jewish action. Yet, Leeser was too wrapped up in domestic concerns to advocate anything concrete. He merely suggested, with more than normal awkwardness, that "the patriotic Hebrew also look proudly forward to the time (even without revelation) when he may again proudly boast of his own country." As for Noah, he characteristically wanted to begin building at once. Happily for him, a project was at hand. As he outlined it in his last major restorationist address—this one delivered at Shearith Israel on Thanksgiving Day (November 23) 1848—the project was nothing less than a plan "to aid in the erection of the temple at Jerusalem." Honesty compelled Noah to admit that the "temple" was Jerusalem's projected Beth El synagogue, and he was only assisting Palestine emissary Yechiel Cohen to collect funds for its construction. He had helped many other charity-gathering emissaries over the years, and he would shortly aid a group urging a more efficient central collection for Palestine. But the Beth El cause was different. Noah envisaged a link between the "temple" and The Temple. He noted recent archeological finds on the Temple site, and he predicted that human construction of even a small temple would be both a sign and a spur toward God's inevitable construction of the real thing. Once again, he linked self-help and determinism in order to appear both active and orthodox at the same time. In this speech, however, no provocative calls for Christian aid cast doubt on his orthodoxy. Bowing to custom, he refused even to accept Christian donations for the Jerusalem synagogue. He did mention Christianity in his speech, but only to contrast it unfavorably with Judaism. He proudly proclaimed that Judaism would triumph in the end.[31]

Predictably, Noah's temple speech received far less attention than his discourse on the restoration. The *New York Tribune* reprinted the text of the oration, and a few newspapers ridiculed Noah for things he never said. Basically, however, the address was ignored. It was too parochial to be of wide interest. Isaac Leeser also devoted little attention to Noah's speech; he saw it as an exaggerated appeal for funds. He may also have taken umbrage at the use of the world "temple" to mean synagogue, a usage hitherto employed only by German Reform Jews. But in England, the *Jewish Chronicle* trumpeted the speech, reprinting it with the warmest of comments. Its views of restoration and Noah's were congruent: both appealed for new forms of Jewish action; both still held many traditional views on Divine intercession; both wanted Jews to imitate Christian restorationist efforts; and, both formulated programs with an eye to events in the rest of the world. "A few more sincere and enthusiastic patriots like Mr. Noah," the *Chronicle* gushed, and Jews "would soon rouse... from their present apathy." The "sincere and enthusiastic patriots" did not emerge for another half-century. When they did emerge, they were men who resembled Mordecai Noah in only limited and superficial ways.[32]

Restoration of the Jews was the last major cause Noah espoused before he died. He was old and he knew it. He hoped to leave a final, lasting legacy to the Jewish people. Strangely, Noah had been considered old for many years. "He is in his dotage," the *Truth Teller* had reported in 1834. Noah was then forty-eight, and he had many vigorous years ahead of him. Other newspapers also prematurely cast the then Whig editor into the ranks of the senescent. Much as he protested that "our son and heir is short of six years old and our youngest scarcely walks," he could not escape the stigma of old age. And stigma it was. By his day, the cult of youth had conquered America. Many agreed with Nathaniel Hawthorne that the elderly were "a set of wearisome old souls, who had gathered nothing worth preservation from their varied experience of life."[33]

Why was Noah prematurely characterized as "old Noah?"[34] A bout of temporary paralysis (probably a mild stroke) in the early 1830s may have altered his visage somewhat. Many long years of highly visible journalistic service may also have contributed to popular misapprehensions of his age. But the honest errors were few. Most of those who commented on his age did so in more malicious contexts. They intended to relegate Noah to oblivion by declaring him old-fashioned and all used up. Younger editors, calling themselves "new" wanted to enter and alter the journalistic profession. They endowed Noah with extra years in an effort to widen the gap between traditional editors, and those who espoused the mass popular journalism associated with the penny press.[35]

Time, of course, changed "old Noah" from an ugly epithet into a universally acknowledged statement of fact. By 1846, he was one of the oldest editors in the United States, second only to Thomas Ritchie, then of the *Washington Union*. His old age began to tell. Slowly, he disengaged himself from his arduous labors, and set to work on his memoirs. Unfortunately, he never completed them. In 1848, having left the *New York Sun*, probably after its editor retired, the Democratic Party awarded him a traditional old-age pension. It appointed him to a "no work" post as inspector of customs in the port of New York (his salary was $1,095). Still, he continued to write for the *Times and Messenger*—how much he wrote and how much his able assistants wrote cannot be known—and he continued to call for Union, southern rights, Jewish–Christian reconciliation, and good, old-fashioned values. But he was more venerated than heeded. His oracular pronouncements sounded stuffy and out of date: "Everything is changed—business habits, manners and systems. Our tailor sports a mustache, takes a seat next to us in the parquette of the opera, and cries, 'Brava! Brava!' and is a good judge of Italian music when he should be only a judge of broadcloth and a neat fit."[36]

In his old age, Noah gave many public addresses for the benefit of Jewish and secular charities. He also presided over joint meetings, like the one called by immigrants and natives to hail the restoration of the French Republic in 1848. On all these occasions, however, his symbolic importance loomed far larger than his real authority. Initiative and drive came from other directions; he provided his name and whatever influence he could muster. Noah also employed his influence and connections on behalf of his children. He helped his son Manuel gain entry into the world of journalism, and he tried to obtain a "personal favor" from Governor Henry Anthony of Rhode Island for his son Jacob. But as he watched his oldest children go out into the world, his own world contracted. Rheumatism enfeebled his movements, and dampened his usually ebullient spirit. He knew that his days were numbered.[37]

In February 1851, Mordecai Noah suffered a damaging stroke. He remained alert, and he even continued to dictate answers for the correspondence column of the *Times and Messenger*. But he never recovered. A second stroke, on March 16, deprived him of speech, memory, and movement. He rallied briefly, and raised a few false hopes. But the end had come. On March 22, 1851, he breathed his last.[38]

Epilogue

The newspapers of Monday, March 24, 1851, contained a special column of notices urging members of New York synagogues and societies "to attend the funeral of the late M. M. Noah Esq.... at 4 o'clock P.M. at the residence of the departed, 624 Broadway." A large concourse of citizens—one of the largest to attend a New York funeral in years—gathered on the spot. "Representatives of the bench, the bar, and the mart...doctors, authors, musicians, comedians, editors, mechanics, professionals and non-professionals" all accompanied the hearse to the Twenty-first Street Cemetery of Shearith Israel. A brief ceremony, an eloquent address by Rabbi Morris J. Raphall, and the body was lowered to rest. Months later, after burials within the city limits had been banned, the family erected a memorial stone. Its message, fittingly modest and memorable, read: "The warm hand is cold, the kindly eye is dimmed, the generous heart has ceased to beat; for beneath this monument lie the mortal remains of M. M. Noah. He died in 1851."[1]

Obituaries bountifully praised Mordecai Noah. Many traced his successes in journalism, politics, diplomacy, and drama. Others acclaimed his personal characteristics: his irrepressible good humor, abundant good works, and munificent, often anonymous donations to charity. Still others extolled his Jewish activities: his vigorous defense of Jewish rights; his leading role in synagogue, educational and philanthropic affairs; and his tireless efforts on behalf of oppressed Jews all over the world. But only Rabbi Raphall captured Mordecai Noah's supreme achievement—the achievement that raised him above his contemporaries and transformed him into an historical figure of enduring importance: "Mordecai Noah took upon himself the pleasing duty of proving to his country, that its children professing the Jewish faith were as able, as faithful, as zealous in her cause and service as any of her other children."[2]

Noah was the first Jew to confront openly—in articles, lectures, and well-publicized activites—the challenge of American freedom. He was the first to demand continuous recognition as both a devoted American and as a devoted

159

Jew. He was the first to explore seriously the profound problems faced by Jews in an America composed largely of Christians. He was, in short, the first Jew in American history to gain a national hearing; the first American Jew with sufficient ambition, status and talent to be a leader, an Americanizer, a spokesman and a guardian all at once.

Ultimately, Noah found no viable solution to the American Jewish dilemma. He offered no real guidance to the Jew who sought total acceptance at a cost of less than total assimilation. His own life offered many pos-sibilities—on the one hand militant Judaism and self segregation, on the other, unity with Christians and religious imitation—but his personal efforts were not crowned with success. To most Americans he remained a Jew; to many Jews he seemed disconcertingly untraditional. While both groups accepted him, both assumed that he fully belonged in the other's sphere. Noah thus never discovered the supreme synthesis for which he so longingly yearned. But he spent a lifetime searching.

Noah's dilemma remains a dilemma thirteen decades after his death. Jews still strive to harmonize minority identity with national allegiance. They still seek a golden mean between wholehearted assimilation and ethnic-roots identification. They still struggle to befriend Christians without betraying their own religion. Overall, the American Jewish search has always been a search for synthesis, a longing for utopia, a quest for an ideal, tension-resolving unity. It is a millennial rather than a realistic hope. It is a search fated forever to continue. But it is by no means a futile search. In looking for what they can never find, American Jews have always found a great deal. They produced works of unparalleled vibrance and creativity. They carved out a vital place for themselves in science, technology, culture, and politics. They became a readily distinguishable intellectual community.

And so the muse of Jewish history enjoys yet another strange and wondrous irony. For in trying to prove how much they had in common with everyone else, Jews demonstrated their uniqueness once again.

Notes

For more extensive annotation, see Jonathan D. Sarna, "Mordecai M. Noah: Jacksonian Politician and American Jewish Communal Leader—A Biographical Study" (unpublished Ph.D. dissertation, Yale University, 1979).

Abbreviations

AJA—American Jewish Archives, Clifton Avenue, Cincinnati, Ohio 45220
AJA—American Jewish Archives
AJHQ—American Jewish Historical Quarterly
AJHS—American Jewish Historical Society, 2 Thornton Road, Waltham, Ma. 02154
Barnburner Letter—A Letter Addressed to the Southern Delegates of the Baltimore Democratic Convention, on the Claims of "Barnburners" to be admitted to Seats in that Convention (New York, 1848)
C&E—Morning Courier and New York Enquirer
Consecration Address—Mordecai M. Noah, *Discourse Delivered at the Consecration of the Synagogue K.K. Shearith Israel in the city of New York on Friday, the 10th of Nisan, 5578, corresponding with the 17th of April, 1818* (New York, 1818)
Corresp. and Docs.—Correspondence and Documents Relative to the Attempt to Negotiate for the Release of the American Captives at Algiers; including remarks on our relations with that regency (Washington City, 1816)
DHJUS—Morris U. Schappes (ed.), *A Documentary History of the Jews in the United States 1654–1875* (New York, 1971)
EJ—Encyclopedia Judaica (Jerusalem, 1971)
Enq.—New York Enquirer
Enq.-Country—New York Enquirer for the Country
ES—Evening Star
ES-Country—Evening Star for the Country
Jews of Philadelphia—Edwin Wolf II and Maxwell Whiteman *The History of the Jews of Philadelphia From Colonial Times to the Age of Jackson* (Philadelphia, 1975)
JUSDH—Joseph L. Blau and Salo W. Baron (eds.), *The Jews of the United States 1790–1840: A Documentary History* (New York, 1963)
LC—Library of Congress, Washington D.C.

Lost Tribes Discourse—Mordecai M. Noah, *Discourse on the Evidences of the American Indians Being the Descendants of the Lost Tribes of Israel* (New York, 1837)

Major Noah—Isaac Goldberg, *Major Noah: American Jewish Pioneer* (Philadelphia, 1938)

Marcus-Festschrift—Bertram W. Korn (ed.), *A Bicentennial Festschrift for Jacob Rader Marcus* (Waltham, 1976)

NA—National Archives, Washington D.C.

Nat.Adv.—*National Advocate*

N.Y. Nat. Adv.—*New York National Advocate*

PAJHS—*Publications of the American Jewish Historical Society*

"Ararat Address"—"Address of Mordecai M. Noah...Delivered at the Laying of the Corner Stone of the City of Ararat," reprinted in *PAJHS*, 21 (1913), 230–52

Restoration Discourse—Mordecai M. Noah, *Discourse on the Restoration of the Jews* (New York, 1845)

Temple Address—Mordecai M. Noah, *Address Delivered at the Hebrew Synagogue in Crosby-Street, New York, on Thanksgiving Day to Aid in the Erection of the Temple at Jerusalem* (Jamaica, 1849)

T&M—*Sunday Times and Noah's Weekly Messenger*

Travels—Mordecai M. Noah, *Travels in England, France, Spain and the Barbary States in the Years 1813–14 and 15* (New York, 1819)

Note: Newspapers are cited where possible by date, page, and column, and if published in New York the place of publication is usually dropped [e.g. *Herald* (January 10, 1839), 2:1].

Chapter I. Formative Years

1.   Jacob R. Marcus, *The Colonial American Jew* (3 volumes, Detroit, 1970).

2.   Ira Rosenwaike, "An Analysis and Estimate of the Jewish Population in the United States in 1790," *PAJHS*, 50 (1960), 23–35. Jacob R. Marcus, ed., *Jews and the American Revolution* (Cincinnati, 1975), 103.

3.   Noah's middle name is often given as Manasseh. Manuel, however, is undoubtedly correct as it is the name used by Noah in his "Proclamation to the Jews" (on other occasions he called himself simply M.M. Noah), and, of course, it was his father's name. In Hebrew accounts, Noah's middle name is usually given as Immanuel. This is an error: Manuel Noah's Hebrew name was Menahem. Henry S. Morais, *The Jews of Philadelphia* (Philadelphia 1894), 396; *JUSDH*, 385; see also *Asmonean*, 3 (1851), 188. For Noah's Hebrew name, see David de Sola Pool, *Portraits Etched in Stone: Early Jewish Settlers 1682–1831* (New York, 1952), 409, and the only Hebrew document signed by Noah (November 13, 1829) in Phillips Family Papers, Box 1, AJHS translated in Moshe Davis (ed.) *With Eyes Toward Zion* (New York, 1977), 205–6.

4.   Isaac Goldberg reprints a letter from Zipporah Noah to her sister (ca. 1789) in which Zipporah mentions two other children: Samuel and Uriah. These were the children of Elias Noah, probably Manuel Noah's brother. Since Elias is not listed as having any wife, it may be conjectured that Zipporah undertook to bring up these children. Isaac Goldberg, *Major Noah* 16–

17; Malcolm Stern, *Americans of Jewish Descent* (Cincinnati, 1960), 167; Joseph Rosenbloom, *A Biographical Dictionary of Early American Jews: Colonial Times Through 1800* (Kentucky, 1960), 134. Here and elsewhere, Goldberg cites letters which have now vanished. Happily, Goldberg printed many of these letters, and I have used his transcriptions throughout. Hans Reissner in *Eduard Gans: Ein Leben Im Vormärz* (Tuebingen, 1965) 80n.35, and in personal correspondence, concludes that the original letters were burned.

5. Quote is from *Nat. Adv.* (September 8, 1823), 2:2. For the date of Noah's birth, see *T&M* (March 30, 1851); *American Biographical Sketch Book* (New York, 1848), 402; Stern, *Americans of Jewish Descent*, 167; and *Major Noah*, 15. On Manuel Noah, see Pool, *Portraits Etched in Stone*, 409-10; Rosenbloom, *Biographical Dictionary*, 134, and works cited therein; and *Jews of Philadelphia*, 174, 177, 440. Wolf and Whiteman claim (p. 177) that Manuel Noah left for Europe in 1797 leaving his wife with a young son and daughter. Since, in 1797, Manuel's wife had been dead for five years, I suspect that Manuel Noah left in 1791. It is, after all, quite unlikely that he continued paying Mikveh Israel dues for six years after he left Philadelphia. The 1791 date would also agree with information in *T&M* (April 6, 1851), 2. The Noah family tradition claiming that George Washington was present at the wedding of Manuel and Zipporah Noah has been disproved by Malcolm Stern, *AJHQ*, 65 (1976), 373. On Zipporah Noah's death, see Barnett A. Elzas, *The Old Jewish Cemeteries at Charleston S. C.* (Charleston, 1903), 82.

6. On Phillips, see *JUSDH*, 22, 243, 513-15; *DHJUS*, 63, 68-9, 584; *Jews of Philadelphia*, *passim*; *Major Noah*, 8-13; Samuel Rezneck, *Unrecognized Patriots* (Westport, 1975), *passim*; and works cited in Rosenbloom, *Biographical Dictionary*, 141.

7. Quote is from Hannah Adams, *The History of the Jews From the Destruction of Jerusalem to the Present Time* (London, 1818), 394. (The volume was first published in Boston in 1812.) See *Jews of Philadelphia*, 62. David de Sola Pool, *Old Faith in a New World* (New York, 1955), 461-2; Malcolm Stern, "New York's Early Jews: Some Myths and Misconceptions," A Lecture Delivered Before the Jewish Historical Society of New York (New York, 1976); Jacob R. Marcus, *The Colonial American Jew* (Detroit, 1970), II, 966-67; and H. J. Zimmels, *Ashkenazim and Sephardim* (Oxford, 1958).

8. *T&M* (April 6, 1851), 2; *Consecration Address* (1818), 46n.18; *Travels*, 60-194, esp. 125; George White, *Statistics of the State of Georgia* (Savannah, 1849), 619-20; and *New York Mirror*, 14 (April 1, 1837), 316-17, all include Noah's comments on his Sephardic ancestors or on Spain. See also Richard D. Barnett, "Zipra Nune's Story," in *Marcus Festschrift*, 47-61 which reprints Noah's account of his relatives, first published in White. Barnett's comment: "it was not published until fifteen years after Mordecai Manuel Noah's death," (p. 47) is in error. White first published Noah's account in 1849. For other comments on Noah's relatives, see Pool, *Old Faith*, 162, 437; and N. Taylor Phillips, "Family History of the Rev. David Mendez Machado," *PAJHS*, 2 (1894), 45-61.

9. On Noah's relatives, see Phillips, "Family History of the Rev. David Mendez Machado" and Stern, *Americans of Jewish Descent*, 167, 169, 174.

10. Quotations are from *Nat. Adv.* (September 8, 1823), 2:2 and *T&M* (November 7, 1847), 1:2. For other details of Noah's schooling, see *Nat. Adv.* (November 4, 1827), 2:3; *PAJHS*, 27 (1920), 55, 57; and *T&M* (May 13, 1849), 1:5; (March 30, 1851), 2.

11. On Noah's early employment, see quoted comments: *T&M* (August 19, 1849), 2:3; (May 13, 1849), 1:5; (March 30, 1851), 2; and *Commercial Advertiser* (May 20, 1823), 2:1; as well as *N.Y. Nat. Adv.* (June 3, 1826), 2:1; *Tribune* (March 21, 1851); and *Boston Museum* (April 26, 1851), 1.

12. These ties with Canada may have led to the almost certainly false accusation that Noah was a Canadian "and never was naturalized in this country." *Charleston Investigator* (February 3, 1813), 3:1; and *Herald* (October 16, 1842), 2:1; and (May 13, 1850), 2:3, all contain this report. I suspect that a common source is responsible for the story.

13. Quotations are from *Boston Museum* (April 26, 1851), 1; *New York Evening Post* (April 21, 1821), 2:2 which should be compared with S. B. H. Judah, *Gotham and the Gothamites* (New

York, 1823), pp. xvii, xxxix; and Citizens of the United States to James Madison (August 25, 1810), General Records of the Department of State (R.G. 59), Applications and Recommendations for Public Office Under President Madison (M438 roll 6).

14. On Naphtali Phillips, see *PAJHS*, 21 (1913), 172–4. The basic work on Federalist anti-Semitism is Morris U. Schappes, "Anti-Semitism and Reaction, 1795–1800," *PAJHS*, 38 (1948), 108–37, which should be modified by *Jews of Philadelphia*, 218. The quoted Nones letter is from the *Philadelphia Aurora* (August 11, 1800) reprinted in *DHJUS*, 95.

15. Philip S. Klein and Ari Hoogenboom, *A History of Pennsylvania* (New York, 1973), 112–13; Sanford W. Higginbotham, *Keystone in the Democratic Arch* (Harrisburg, 1952), 147–76; Sidney M. Fish, *Aaron Levy Founder of Aaronsburg* (New York, 1951) 34–39; *Jews of Philadelphia*, 218–19. For Noah's role, see *Philadelphia Aurora* (September 16, 1808), 3:3; (September 19, 1808), 3:5; *Boston Museum* (April 26, 1851), 1:1; *New York Columbian* (August 30, 1820), 2:2; *New York Atlas* (March 30, 1851), and J. Thomas Scharf and Thompson Westcott, *History of Philadelphia 1609–1884* (Philadelphia, 1884), II. 1137.

16. There is no history of Jews in American journalism. On various individual Jewish journalists, see *PAJHS*, 21 (1912), 172–4 (Naphtali Phillips); *American Israelite*, 20 (February 28, 1873), 6 (Manuel Noah); W. Gunther Plaut, *The Jews in Minnesota* (New York, 1959), 16–21 (Jacob Noah); Charles Reznikoff and U.Z. Engleman, *The Jews of Charleston* (Philadelphia, 1950), 80–86 (Isaac Harby); Bertram W. Korn, *The Early Jews of New Orleans* (Waltham, 1969), 182–83, 321 (Samuel Harby); Alexander Brody, "Jacob Newton Cardozo: American Economist," *Historia Judaica*, 15 (April 1953), 135–66; John A. Forman, "Lewis Charles Levin: Portrait of an American Demagogue," *AJA*, 12 (October 1960), 150–90; *DHJUS*, 291–3, 643 (Abraham G. Levy); Henry Cohen, "The Jews in Texas," *PAJHS*, 4 (1896), 9–15 (Jacob De Cordova); Helen Kohn Hennig, "Edwin De Leon," Unpublished Masters thesis, University of South Carolina, 1928; Ira Rosenwaike, "Levy L. Laurens: An Early Texas Journalist," *AJA*, 27 (April 1975), 61–66; and Isaac M. Fein, *The Making of an American Jewish Community (Philadelphia*, 1971), 22–24 (Jacob I. Cohen Jr.).

17. The best broad study of Jews in the early American theater remains Leon Spitz, "Pioneers of the American Theater," *The American Hebrew*, 160 (September 8, 1950), 75; and in *American Jewish Times Outlook* (October 1950). See Isaac M. Fein, *Boston: Where It All Began* (Boston, 1976), on Michael Hays; Samuel Oppenheim, "Jews Who Helped to Finance the New or Park Theater in New York in 1793 and 1794," unpublished ms. in Samuel Oppenheim Collection, box 255, AJHS; and Harby's "Defense of the Drama," reprinted in *JUSDH*, II 405–10. See also, E. Z. Melamed, *Breaking the Tablets* (Chicago, 1930), 211–18; "Theater," *EJ*, XV, 1049–78; M.J. Landa, *The Jew in Drama* (New York, 1969 [1926]); and Adeline Pierce, "Early Intolerance Toward the Theatre in America," *The Drama*, 18 (1928), 146.

18. Noah's quoted memoir of his theatrical activities to 1832 may be found in his letter to William Dunlap, conveniently reprinted in Jacob R. Marcus, *Memoirs of American Jews* (Philadelphia, 1955), I, 120–24. See also *T&M* (November 7, 1847), 1:2; *The Atlas* (March 30, 1851); A. H. Smyth, *Philadelphia Magazines and Their Contributors* (Philadelphia, 1892), 182; and Noah's *The Fortress of Sorrento: A Petit Historical Drama in Two Acts* (New York, 1808).

19. Quotations are from *Nat. Adv.* (May 26, 1820), 2:1; (July 18, 1820), 2:3 and Noah to Dunlap in Marcus *Memoirs*, 120–24.

20. Charlotte [Ramsay] Len[n]ox, *Shakspeare Illustrated, or the Novels and Histories on which the Plays of Shakespeare are Founded With Critical Remarks and Biographical Sketches of the Writers* by M. M. Noah (Philadelphia, 1809), vi, 308, On the popularity of Shakespeare in America, see David Grimsted, *Melodrama Unveiled* (Chicago, 1968), 252. Mrs. Lennox's original work was published during 1753–54 and comprised five volumes.

21. Noah to Thomas P. Barton (December 28, 1842), bound in Boston Public Library edition of *Shakspeare Illustrated*, partly reprinted in *Major Noah*, 37. On Gesta Romanorum see *Shakspeare Illustrated*, p. viii, and Geoffrey Bullough (ed.), *Narrative and Dramatic Sources of*

Shakespeare (London, 1957), I, 445–514. For the Gomez and Harby critiques, see *JUSDH*, III, 973–6, and remarks of Louis Harap, *The Image of the Jew in American Literature* (Philadelphia, 1974), 260, 268–9.

22. Ellery C. Stowell, "Consular Service," *Encyclopedia of the Social Sciences* (New York, 1938), IV, 279–82; and William Barnes and John H. Morgan, *The Foreign Service of the United States* (Washington, D.C., 1961), 57–65.

23. Citizens of the United States to James Madison (August 25, 1810); and the quoted letter, Noah to Robert Smith (January 7, 1811) in General Records of the Department of State (R.G. 59), Applications and Recommendations for Public Office Under President Madison (M438 roll 6).

24. Quote is from Noah to Smith (January 7, 1811) cited in n.23.

25. Noah's letters of recommendation are found in R.G. 59, Applications and Recommendations for Public Office Under President Madison (M438 roll 6); see also, Noah to Naphtali Phillips (June 10, 1811) in Isaac Goldberg, "Mr. Noah, American," *The Menorah Journal*, 24 (Autumn 1936), 285–87. The date of Noah's appointment as consul is from the introductory note to microcopy 485, Despatches From United States Consuls in Riga, National Archives. The appointment was reported in *The Columbian* (July 2, 1811), 2:4 and Noah accepted on the same day: Noah to Madison (July 2, 1811), Despatches From Riga (microcopy 485). Noah revealed his plans in his quoted letter to Phillips (June 10, 1811) in Goldberg, "Mr. Noah, American," 286 (orthography modernized).

26. Noah's confirmation is detailed in *Journal of the Executive Proceedings of the Senate of the United States of America* (Washington, D.C., 1928), II, 188, 190, 193. Subsequent quoted correspondence: Noah to James Graham (December 18, 1811), and Noah to James Monroe (February 18, 1812), as well as the later history of the Riga consulate is in Despatches from United States Consuls in Riga (microcopy 485); see also *Travels*, 182.

27. *Atlas* (March 30, 1851); *Charleston Investigator* (April 14, 1813), 3:1; *Evening Post* (September 5, 1817), 2:1; *Columbian* (August 30, 1820), 2:2; *Herald* (May 13, 1850), 2:3; *Spectator* (September 1, 1820), 1:2–3, and Barnett A. Elzas, *The Jews of South Carolina* (Philadelphia, 1903), 38.

28. The extract is from the *Charleston Times* (May 9, 1812); other extracts are printed in *Major Noah*, 54–55. I do not agree with Goldberg that "Caled the Elder" and "Yusef Kahn" are merely masks for Noah. More likely, they are enemies of Noah. They imitate "Muly Malak's" style poorly.

29. *Charleston Times* (June 2, 1812), 2, contains the offending Muly Malak article. For details of Noah's duel, see Noah to Naphtali Phillips (June 8, 15, 1812) in Goldberg, "Mr. Noah, American," 288–91; Noah's "My First Duel," *The Union* (July 20, 1842), 2:1 (reprinted in *The Dollar Magazine*, 2 [September 1842], 277–79); and E. S. Thomas, *Reminiscences of the Last Sixty-Five Years* (Hartford, 1840), 58–61 (all quoted). My identification of William Crafts (1787–1826) is based on E. S. Courtenay, *Eulogy on the Hon. William Crafts* (Charleston, 1826). On Canter, see Rosenbloom, *A Biographical Dictionary of Early American Jews*, 19; and Joseph Gutman, "Jewish Participation in the Visual Arts of Eighteenth and Nineteenth Century America," *AJA* 10: (October 1958), 24. The prevalence of dueling in Charleston is recounted in Mrs. St. Julien Ravanel, *Charleston the Place and the People* (New York, 1925), 410–15.

30. On Clinton and New York politics, see Jerome Mushkat, *Tammany* (New York, 1971), 45–50, and Dorothie Bobbé, *De Witt Clinton* (New York, 1933), 180–89. For Noah's response, see Noah to Phillips (June 8 and June 15, 1812) in Goldberg, "Mr. Noah, American," 288–91. Noah admitted to the authorship of the Clinton letter in *Nat. Adv.* (August 29, 1820) 2:5; (February 6, 1822), 2:2; his name appears on the Yale edition of the work which was formerly owned by Jacob I. Cohen. Earlier, Noah had been linked with the pamphlet in *Charleston Investigator* (May 19, 1813). Robert J. Turnbull's alternate hypothesis, quoted in J. Blanck, *Bibliography of American Literature*, VI, 453 is unfounded.

31. *A Letter Addressed to the Members of the Legislature of South Carolina Examining the*

Claims and Qualifications of De Witt Clinton to the Presidency of the United States (Charleston, 1812), quotes are from pp. 28, 18, 22, 26 and 33.

32.   John Kerr [attributed author], *The Wandering Boys or the Castle of Olival* (Boston: 1821); Noah to Dunlap in J. R. Marcus, *Memoirs*, 122; *Major Noah*, 68–70 and Harold Schoenberger, *American Adaptations of French Plays on New York and Philadelphia Stages from 1790 to 1833* (Philadelphia, 1924). The play was produced in America 37 times between 1816–31, and 25 times in New Orleans alone between 1823 and 1838; see Grimsted, *Melodrama Unveiled*, 252, and B. W. Korn, *Early Jews of New Orleans*, 313.

33.   Noah to Naphtali Phillips (March 11, 1813), in Goldberg, "Mr. Noah, American," 291–92. Noah's boasting is recounted in *Charleston Investigator* (May 19, 1813), 2. On the political nature of diplomatic appointments, see Warren F. Ilchman, *Professional Diplomacy in the United States 1779–1939: A Study in Administration* (Chicago, 1961), 1–40.

34.   The dispute is best followed in the contemporary press: *Charleston City Gazette* (April 1–30, 1813), quotes from issues of April 1, 30 and *Charleston Investigator* (April 10–May 19, 1813), quotes from April 10, 14, 1813. See also E. S. Thomas, *Reminiscences*, 69, 77–78, and John H. Wolfe, *Jeffersonian Democracy in South Carolina* (Chapel Hill, 1940), 242–73, esp. 269–71. Wolfe misidentifies "Argus."

35.   *Charleston City Gazette* (March 29, 1813); *Charleston Investigator* (May 19, 1813); Thomas; *Reminiscences*, 69, 77–78.

36.   Thomas, *Reminiscences*, 58.

Chapter II.   Consul Noah

1.   The basic works on Noah's consulship remain those which he himself wrote: *Correspondence and Documents Relative to the Attempt to Negotiate for the Release of the American Captives at Algiers Including Remarks on our Relations with that Regency* (hereafter cited as Corresp. and Docs.) (Washington, 1816), and *Travels in England, France, Spain and the Barbary States in the Years 1813–14 and 15* (New York, 1819). I have greatly profited from Esther Cember's "Mordecai Manuel Noah: American Diplomat in Barbary 1813–1815: A Reappraisal," (unpublished M.A. thesis, Columbia University, 1968), and am very grateful to Ms. Cember for making it available to me. Also of value, primarily for its source material, is Gilbert S. Rosenthal, "Mordecai M. Noah, Diplomat," unpublished essay in AJA biographies file. The history of Jewish involvement in diplomacy has been neglected. See, however, Lucien Wolf, "The Jew in Diplomacy," *Essays in Jewish History* (London, 1934), 385–410.

2.   H. Z. Hirschberg, *A History of the Jews in North Africa* (Jerusalem, 1965). Morton Rosenstock, "The House of Bacri and Busnach: A Chapter from Algeria's Commercial History," *Jewish Social Studies*, 14 (1952), 343–64. On the use of Jews as intermediaries between North Africa and the West, see David Cazés, *Essai Sur L'histoire des Israelites de Tunisie* (Paris, 1888), 123. *Travels*, 380–81, and Cecil Roth, "Jacob Benider: Moroccan Envoy at the Court of St. James," *Miscellanies of the Jewish Historical Society of England* 2 (1935), 84–90. Americans were well aware of the importance of Jews in North Africa, see Edward D. Coleman, "Plays of Jewish Interest on the American Stage, 1752–1821," PAJHS, 33 (1934), 175, 180; Louis Harap, *The Image of the Jew in American Literature from Early Republic to Mass Immigration* (Philadelphia, 1974), 35–36; the Bacri Letters in volume 601 and Tobias Lear to William Shaler (April 23, 1815), in volume 603 of RG84, Algiers Legation Archives, NA; and Ray W. Irwin, *The Diplomatic Relations of the United States with the Barbary Powers 1776–1816* (Chapel Hill, 1931), esp. 72, 75, 172, 199. For evidence that Noah's religion was a factor in his appointment to Tunis, see Noah to John Graham (June 17, 1811), RG59, Applications and Recommendations for Public Office Under President Madison (M438 roll 6), NA; *Corresp. and Docs.,* 117; *Travels*, 378–79; and *C&E* (October 12, 1830), 2:2.

3.   On American relations with Barbary, see Irwin, *Diplomatic Relations*; Gardner W. Allen, *Our Navy and the Barbary Corsairs* (Cambridge, 1905); Edgar S. Maclay, *A History of the*

United States Navy from 1775–1901 (New York, 1901), 2: 3–22; and for the earlier period, Louis B. Wright and Julia H. Macleod, *The First Americans in North Africa: William Eaton's Struggle for a Vigorous Policy Against the Barbary Pirates 1799–1805* (Princeton, 1945). Noah opposed Tobias Lear's tributes policy, see below and *Travels*, 385.

4.   Allen, *Our Navy*, 278–79; Irwin, *Diplomatic Relations*, 172–73; and Maclay, *History of the U.S. Navy*, 2: 4–5.

5.   An additional person, one Mr. Pollard of Virginia, was later removed from a Spanish vessel and also enslaved. Later documents therefore talk about twelve captives. On reaction to the enslavement of American seamen, see Harley Harris Bartlett, "American Captives in Barbary," *Michigan Alumnus*, 61 (Spring 1959), 238–254. Monroe's charge to Noah is in Monroe to Noah (April 13, 1813), James Monroe Presidential Papers, (series 1, reel 5), LC; reprinted in *Travels*, 70, and *Corresp. and Docs.*, 7. I agree with Jacob R. Marcus, *Memoirs of American Jews* (Philadelphia, 1955), 1: 129 on the reasons why secrecy was necessary.

6.   *Noah to Monroe* (July 29, 1813), RG59, Despatches From the United States Consuls in Tunis 1797–1906 (T303 roll 4), NA; and *Travels*, 1–59; see also, H. G. Barnby, "Noah at Sea," *Mariner's Marine*, 59 (November 1973), 443–48.

7.   Noah to Richard S. Hackley (October 2, 1813); Hackley to Noah (October 3, 1813); Noah to Monroe (October 7, 1813) in Despatches from Tunis (T-303), NA; *Travels*, 69–76, *Corresp. and Docs.*, 11–15.

8.   The best sketch of Keene is in Cember, "American Diplomat in Barbary," 97–100. For the administration's view of Keene, see Littleton W. Tazewell to Monroe (November 9, 1815), Monroe Papers, LC; and Richard Raynal Keene, *A Letter of Vindication to his Excellency Colonel Monroe President of the United States* (Philadelphia, 1824). See also Paul S. Clarkson and R. Samuel Jett, *Luther Martin of Maryland* (Baltimore, 1970), 196–7.

9.   Monroe to Hackley (October 2, 1813); Hackley to Noah (October 3, 1813); Instructions to Raynal Keene (January 20, 1814), and other documents, all found in Despatches from Tunis (T-303); *Travels*, 71–76; 91. *Corresp. and Docs.*, 16–21.

10.   For Noah's account of what happened in Gibraltar, see *Travels*, 107, 149; Keene's similar account is in his *Letter of Vindication*, 37; Norderling's account is in his letter to Tobias Lear (April 9, 1814) in Monroe Papers (series 1 reel 5), LC; Richard Rush's analysis is reprinted in *Travels*, appendix, pp. xiv–xvi. Keene detailed what happened to him in Algiers in Keene to Noah (May 22, 1814), Despatches from Tunis (T-303), NA reprinted in *Travels*, 141–158 and *Corresp. and Docs.*, 21–50. See also Norderling to Lear (April 9, 1814). Norderling's anti-Semitism is demonstrated in the second line of his letter to Lear where he sneeringly refers to Noah's "sweet Jewish name," and in Norderling to Hackley (June 18, 1813), RG59, Despatches from Algiers (M23 roll 10), NA. On Aaron Cardozo see EJ, 5:163. Noah later appointed Cardozo as a commissioner to supervise his Ararat colony.

11.   Most accounts of Keene's activities in Algeria are based on his own very detailed letter to Noah (May 22, 1814) in Despatches from Tunis (T-303), and reprinted in *Travels*, 141–58; *Corresp. and Docs.*, 21–50. See also Noah to Monroe (May 31, 1814), Despatches from Tunis, reprinted in *Corresp. and Docs.*, 63–75; and Rush's Report in *Travels*, appendix, pp, xi, xvii–xviii.

12.   See sources listed in n.11 as well as *Travels*, 158–62; and *Corresp. and Docs.*, 57–80. Noah justified his large bill for the mission by comparing it with the enormous expense account of Tobias Lear.

13.   Cember, "American Diplomat in Barbary," 95–96.

14.   *Travels*, appendix, pp. xiii–xvi; see Noah's defense on p. xx.

15.   *Travels*, pp. xi, xiv–xv, Norderling to Lear (April 9, 1814), Monroe Papers, LC.

16.   Norderling to Lear (April 9, 1814), Monroe Papers, LC. For evidence of Lear's importance in Washington, see Madison to Monroe (April 10, 1815; May 4, 1815), Monroe Papers, LC. See *Travels*, 415: "I have heard it rumored that Col. Lear was the prominent cause of that letter having been written to me."

17.   George Smith to William Crawford (October 19, 1814), forwarded by Crawford in his letter of December 19, 1814, Monroe Papers, LC. Keene explained his treatment of Norderling in his letter to Noah (n.11); *Travels*, 144.

18.   Smith to Crawford (October 19, 1814), Monroe Papers, LC. Affidavits of citizenship for all released hostages may be found in Despatches from Tunis (T-303); Rush's analysis is printed in *Travels*, appendix, pp. xvii–xviii, and Noah's defense is in *Travels*, 159–60. For a repetition of the charges see *Columbian* (January 28, 1818), 2:3. Noah first mentioned that his claims were disallowed in Noah to Monroe (June 14, 1815), Despatches from Tunis (T-303), see also *Travels*, 269–70; *Corresp. and Docs.*, 63–80.

19.   David Bailie Warden (1772–1845) served as consul to Paris until removed on June 10, 1814, allegedly for assuming without permission the role of consul-general after the death of Joel Barlow. Upon his removal, Warden settled in France and promoted the interests of America, both personally and through his writings. Herbert H. Fiske, "David Bailie Warden," *Dictionary of American Biography*, (New York, 1936), 19:493–4.

20.   *Travels*, 195–242; Crawford to Monroe (December 19, 1814), Monroe Papers, LC; Noah to Albert Gallatin (October 28, 1814), Gallatin Papers, New York Historical Society; Noah to Warden (September 24, 1814; and December 29, 1814), Warden Papers, Maryland Historical Society, Baltimore, Md. (available on microfilm); Noah to Warden (February 10, 1815), vol. 16, Warden Papers, LC; and "Ararat Address," 241. On Grégoire, see Ruth Necheles, *The Abbè Grègoire 1787–1831: The Odyssey of an Egalitarian* (Westport, 1971); Professor Necheles advises me that she knows of no references to Noah in Grégoire's papers, but see his *Histoire des Sectes Religieuses* (Paris, 1828), 376–79. *Major Noah*, 129–30, dismisses the story of Noah's father as a legend, for "not a word of this is to be found in any of Noah's writings." The "legend," however, was printed in Noah's own paper after his death, as well as in Simon Wolf's biographical sketch: *T&M* (April 6, 1851), 2; Simon Wolf, "Mordecaid Manuel Noah: A Biographical Sketch," *Selected Addresses and Papers of Simon Wolf* (Cincinnati, 1926), 109. We can now confirm that Manuel Noah went to Tunis with his son and also departed with him: "Noah's Journal," December 17, 1814, in Despatches from Tunis (T-303) and "Journal of the American Charge d'affairs at Tunis [Ambrose Allegro], September 21, 1815" in RG84, vol. 601, Algiers Legation Archieves, NA. For other mentions of Noah's father see Ambrose Allegro to Noah (November 3, 1815), RG59, Miscellaneous Letters of the Department of State (M179 roll 40) in correspondence of March 18, 1818, NA; and Richard B. Jones to Noah (October 7, 1815), in Despatches from Tunis (T-303). In *Travels*, 380. Noah misleadingly claimed to be "without family or relatives" in Tunis.

21.   *Travels*, 243–61; Noah to Monroe (December 28, 1814); (January 12, 1815) and Noah's Journal (December 1814), all in Despatches from Tunis (T-303); Noah to Warden (December 29, 1814), Warden Papers, Md. Historical Society; and *Baltimore Literary Monument*, 2 (September 1839), 228. In his published writings Noah claimed to have visited the Bey just a day after he assumed power (*Travels*, 256). Noah's journal indicates that the coup took place on December 21, 1814 and he was received at the palace on December 24. The consuls who followed Noah refused to acquiesce peacefully to the order requiring them to kiss the Bey's hand. Consul Anderson's refusal is mentioned in RG84 vol. 601, Algiers Legation Archives, NA; Consul Folson's is discussed in his journal and in his letter to John Quincy Adams (May 21, 1818); see also the Bey's letter to Adams on this subject (September 2, 1817), all in Despatches from Tunis (T-303 roll 5). The first to kiss the Bey's hand was probably William Eaton; see Wright and MacLeod, *First American in North Africa*, 31. Noah's conciliatory posture is spelled out in his letter to Warden of July 26, 1816, Warden Papers, Md. Historical Society; see also *Travels*, 386.

22.   Noah to Warden (December 29, 1814), Warden Papers, Md. Historical Society; financial accounts found in RG84, Tunis Legation Archives; Despatches from Tunis (T-303); Noah to John Quincy Adams (March 4, 1818), RG59, Miscellaneous Letters of the Department of State (M179), NA; Richard Jones to Noah (October 7, 1815), Despatches from Tunis; Noah to Monroe (January 12, 1815), Despatches from Tunis; and Noah to Warden (December 29, 1814), Warden Papers, Md. Historical Society. William Eaton also used to complain and

demand recall, Wright and Macleod, *First American in Barbary*, 121; so did Richard Jones, Jones to Monroe (June 12, 1814), RG84, Tripoli Legation Archives, NA. Several years after his recall, Noah proposed that ambassadors and consuls be compensated at the rate of $15,000 to $20,000, *Nat. Adv.* (January 1, 1819), 2:1.

23. Quote is from Noah to Warden (December 29, 1814), Warden Papers, Md. Historical Society.

24. *Travels*, 307–14 (quote is from p. 309); Noah to Warden (February 10, 1815), vol. 16, Warden Papers, LC.

25. Leopold Zunz, in his epoch-making work on the Jewish sermon, claimed that while serving as consul, Noah attempted unsuccessfully to establish Jewish schools in Tunis. I know of no evidence to support this assertion. The only other comment on this matter belongs to Grègoire, who claimed that Noah hoped to establish Jewish schools, but never had the opportunity. Leopold Zunz, *Die gottesdienstlichen Vortrage der Juden* (Berlin, 1832), 475; Hebrew edition (Jerusalem, 1947), 218; Grégoire, *Histoire des Sectes Religieuses*, 379. On divisions within the Jewish community of Tunis, see also [anon] *Zedek Ovichalom: Notes sur l'histoire des Deux Communautes Israelite...*(Tunis, 1897).

26. *Travels*, 303–307, quotes are from pp. 304, 307. A different version of this story appears in *The Atlas* (March 30, 1851). In this version, Curadi was a blasphemer, not a debtor.

27. On the *Abaellino* affair, see the secondary sources cited above in n.3; *Travels*, 264–68, 286; Noah to Monroe (February 20, 1815) and other documents in Despatches from Tunis (T-303); Noah to Warden (February 10, 1815), Warden Papers, LC. Rush suggested that Noah may not legally have been permitted to serve as agent for the *Abaellino* in his report, *Travels*, appendix, p. xix; see also on this point, Cember, "American Diplomat in Barbary," 17. Noah argued that with regard to the sale of captured vessels America should not be treated like a Christian nation; see below chapter VII, n. 36.

28. In addition to sources cited in n.27 see Noah's affidavit (July 30, 1815), *American State Papers: Naval Affairs, Class VI*, #135 (Washington: 1834), 397; Noah to Monroe (May 20, 1815), Despatches from Tunis (T-303) and *Travels*, 286–88.

29. Noah to Monroe (May 20, 1815), Despatches from Tunis (T-303); *Travels*, 385; Irwin, *Diplomatic Relations*, 159.

30. Cember, "American Diplomat in Barbary," 65–70, Monroe is quoted on p. 68; *Travels*, 370–75, and secondary sources cited in n.3.

31. In his manuscript autobiography, Joseph Nones claimed that Decatur had sent him as envoy to Noah, and that Noah had opened Monroe's letter in his presence. I prefer Noah's account since it was written soon after the event. It would also seem to be quite doubtful that Nones could know what was in any secret letter which he might have delivered to the consul. Joseph B. Nones autobiography, fasc. 32, pp, 6, 10, Nones Papers, AJHS; on Nones see Abram Kanof and David Markowitz, "Joseph B. Nones: The Affable Midshipman," *PAJHS*, 46 (1956), 1–19.

32. Decatur was very angry when he discovered just how self-serving Noah's advice had been. Apparently, Decatur had been most eager to bring the $46,000 back to the United States withhim, and he felt that Noah had misled him. For his part, Noah called Decatur "one of the most gallant and patriotic men that ever lived." Years later, he urged that a congressional pension be awarded to Decatur's widow. See *Travels*, 385 and the interesting comment on how a Mr. Price saved Noah from "personal chastisement" by Decatur in *Herald* (October 10, 1839), 2:1. Noah's positive comments on Decatur and his wife are in *Nat. Adv.* (March 27, 1820), 2:1 and *ES* (February 10, 1837), 1:2.

33. *Travels*, 375–86; the letter of recall is on pp. 376–77, and in *Corresp. and Docs.*, 82. (I have deleted Noah's italics), and may also be found in Noah's handwriting, in slightly different form and without Monroe's last sentence in Noah to Warden (October 9, 1815), Warden Papers, Md. Historical Society. The original of this letter has never been found. On the government's refusal to pay Noah's bills see above, n. 18.

34. In addition to items cited in n.33, see Noah to Decatur (August 4, 1815), and Journal of

the American Charge d'Affaires in Tunis, RG84, Tunis Legation Archives, NA, and *Corresp. and Docs.*, 82–89. On Noah's return to France, see *Travels*, 403, and Noah to Warden, (December 8, 1815), Warden Papers, Md. Historical Society; and on Noah's return to the United States, see *Travels*, 411. Monroe announced his appointment of Thomas Anderson in a letter to Anthony Morris (July 18, 1816), RG59, State Department Instructions to Diplomatic Representatives 7:412 (M28 roll 7).

35.   Quotes are from *Travels*, 412 and Noah to William Lee (September 5, 1820), Gratz Collection, Case 6, Box 33, Historical Society of Pennsylvania, Philadelphia, Pa. (also found on AJA microfilm 1156 and Rosenthal, "Mordecai M. Noah, Diplomat," 14–15).

36.   Noah later claimed that his religion "was not known in Barbary." Perhaps it was not generally known, but if Aaron Cardoza, who had many ties with Tunis, knew of Noah's religion, and if all the consuls in Algiers knew that he was Jewish, the Bey was probably informed as well. *Travels*, 378 and Norderling to Lear (April 9, 1814), Monroe Papers, LC.

37.   On Joel Hart, see Joel Hart Correspondence File in AJA and *DHJUS*, p. 595; for information on Nathan Levy see *JUSDH*, II, 325–34, 611–13. Noah proudly boasted of his good relations with the Bey in *Travels*, 386; the problems of later consuls are amply documented in Despatches from Tunis (T-303, reel 5), especially Bey to John Quincy Adams (September 2, 1817). Norderling's comments on Jews are in Norderling to Lear (April 9, 1814), Monroe Papers, LC; Porter's are quoted in Monroe to Madison (April 22, 1815), Madison Papers (Series II, reel 26), LC. I am indebted to Professor R. Rutland for helping me to decipher Monroe's illigible handwriting. On Porter's views, see also *DHJUS*, 621.

38.   Quotes are from *Travels*, 70, 378 and Madison to Monroe (April 24, 1815), Monroe Papers (series I reel 6), LC; see also *Corresp. and Docs.*, 105. In the continuation of this letter, Madison suggests a possible replacement for Noah. According to Esther Cember, this indicates that the "main reason" for Noah's recall may have been political—the desire to open up a consular vacancy in an election year. Unfortunately, Cember's theory suffers from the "post hoc propter hoc" fallacy: Madison moved to replace Noah, therefore the replacement was the cause of the dismissal. In fact, there is no indication of a political motive lurking behind Noah's recall. To the contrary, Noah's removal had the potential for alienating Noah's friends in Pennsylvania and South Carolina, and was open to misinterpretation by Jews all over the country. Cember, "American Diplomat in Barbary," 109.

39.   The case of Uriah Phillips Levy is detailed in Abram Kanof, "Uriah Phillips Levy: The Story of a Pugnacious Commodore," *PAJHS*, 39 (1949), 1–65. See below Chapter VII, n.7.

40.   *Travels*, 413–16; Noah to Warden (December 8, 1815, July 26, 1816), Warden Papers, Md. Historical Society; *Corresp. and Docs.*, esp. 89–128. On the suppression of *Correspondence and Documents*, see also *Nat. Adv.* (October 1, 1817), 2:2; *Columbian* (July 20, 1817), 2:3; (November 15, 1820), 2:2 and *Evening Post* (September 5, 1817), 2:1.

41.   Letters of support from diplomats are in Despatches from Tunis (T-303) and *Travels*, appendix, pp. i–iv; Gaillard's letter, Gaillard to Monroe (April 17, 1816) is in RG59, Applications and Recommendations for Public Office Under President Madison (M438 roll 6) and in *Travels*, 413 where Gaillard's name is not mentioned. Letters from Jewish leaders include Naphtali Phillips to Monroe (August 22, 1816), Despatches from Tunis (T-303); Phillips to Monroe (October 20, 1816) in *JUSDH*, II, 322, and Harby to Monroe (May 13, 1816), in *JUSDH*, II, 318–22.

42.   Quotes are from Monroe to Phillips (October 26, 1816), Noah Papers, AJHS; and A. A. Massias to Stephen Pleasanton (December 15, 1816) in *JUSDH*, II, 323–24. Interestingly, Massias's own father came from Tunis and was a diplomat in the service of the Bey, see *Travels*, 381.

43.   Carey McWilliams also considers the use of anti-Semitism as a mask, but his analysis differs from mine. See his *A Mask for Privilege: Anti-Semitism in America* (Boston, 1948). For a twentieth-century case with certain similarities to Noah's recall—including Jewish exploitation of anti-Semitism—see Wayne A. Wiegand, "The Lauchheimer Controversy: A Case of Group Political Pressure During the Taft Administration," *Military Affairs*, 40 (1976), 54–59.

44. *Travels*, appendix, pp. xi–xii; George Williams to Monroe (January 26, 1816); Bloomfield to Monroe (February 1, 1816); W. Smith to Monroe (February 10, 1816); handwritten note of James Monroe (February 27, 1816); Smith to Monroe (April 4, 1816); Sullivan to Monroe (April 25, 1816); Smith to Monroe (July 15, 1816), and Smith to Monroe with enclosures (July 18, 1816), all in RG59, Miscellaneous Letters of the Department of State (M179, reel 33), NA.

45. On the Rush Report, see Rush to Monroe (December 31, 1816), Miscellaneous Letters of the Department of State, and *Travels*, appendix, pp. ix–xix which reprints the Rush report (quote is from p. xix). On the Lewis claim, see also *Travels*, appendix, pp. xxii, xxiii; *American State Papers*, vol. IX, #359, 527; Noah to Pleasanton (July 23, 1816), Despatches from Tunis; and Pleasanton to Noah (July 30, 1816), RG59, Consular Instructions of the Department of State (M78 roll 1), NA.

46. Quotes are from John Quincy Adams to Noah (February 20, 1818), RG59, Domestic Letters of the Department of State (M40 reel 15), NA; Noah to Adams (March 4, 1818; March 18, 1818), Miscellaneous Letters of the Department of State (M179 roll 40); see also C. F. Adams (ed.) *Memoirs of John Quincy Adams* (Philadelphia, 1875), IV, 63.

47. Quotes are from (in order): Noah to Warden (February 10, 1815; November 24, 1818), Warden Papers, LC; *Travels*, 135, 164, 169, 58, 241, 125. On Noah's view of Islam, see *Travels*, 133, 295–99, and *American Monthly Magazine and Critical Review*, 4 (March 1819), 354. Cf. *Nat. Adv.* (December 23, 1823), 2:2 and *T&M* (June 3, 1849), 2:1.

48. There is a fragmentary letter in the Noah Papers of the American Jewish Historical Society, in which one Louis Kinloch advises a friend to read Noah's *Travels* before applying for a consulship in South America. If Judaism proved a barrier in Tunis, Kinloch argues, how much more likely was it to prove a problem in Catholic South America?

49. Critical reaction to *Travels*, includes: *American Monthly Magazine and Critical Review*, 4 (March, April, 1819), 341–55, 431–38; and *Niles Weekly Register*, 16 (August 28, 1819), 433. See Noah to Alden Spooner (n.d., likely May, 1819), New York Historical Society; and *Columbian* (September 20, 1819), 2:4 for evidence that *Travels* sold out its entire edition; and *American* (March 17, 1821), 2:3 for mention of a second edition.

50. John Adams to Noah (March 15, 1819) reprinted in Moshe Davis, ed., *With Eyes Toward Zion* (New York, 1977), 19; Edgar E. MacDonald, ed., *The Education of the Heart: The Correspondence of Rachel Mordecai Lazarus and Marie Edgeworth* (Chapel Hill, 1977), 33–34; C. D. Coxe to Henry Clay (April 28, 1825), Despatches from Tunis (T-303, roll 5); James F. Hopkins (ed.) *The Papers of Henry Clay* (Lexington, Ky: 1972), IV, 307. S. M. Fitch, in *New York Evening Post* (August 19, 1822), 2:5, claimed that *Travels* prevented Noah from being nominated to the New York Assembly. Other Noah attacks on Monroe include *Nat. Adv.* (August 7, 1822), 2:2, and *Enq.-Country* (October 20, 1826), 1:2. On Noah's later efforts to obtain a consulship, see *Travels*, 216; *Columbian* (July 31, 1819), 2:3; Noah to John Q. Adams (July 24, 1820), RG59, Applications and Recommendations for Public Office under President Monroe, (M439 roll 12), NA, reprinted in *JUSDH*, III, 886; David Brent to Noah (February 28, 1831), Domestic Letters of Department of State (M40 roll 22), NA; and Noah's bitter comments in *Nat. Adv.* (February 6, 1822), 2:2 and (October 6, 1823), 2:2. Noah had no further contact with Richard R. Keene. In 1819, Keene wrote to his "old and worthy friend" and asked for help on a volume opposing ex-President Madison. Noah did not reply. Instead, he passed the letter on to the State Department with the request that President Monroe be informed of his action. Noah to J. Q. Adams (May 21, 1819), Miscellaneous Letters of the Department of State (M179 roll 44).

51. *Major Noah*, 117; Hyman B. Grinstein, *The Rise of the Jewish Community of New York 1654–1860* (Philadelphia 1945), 453; Marcus, *Memoirs of American Jews*, I, 118.

Chapter III. National Advocate Years

1. Daniel J. Levinson, *The Seasons of a Man's Life* (New York, 1978), 71–135; Gail Sheehy, *Passages* (New York, 1976), 28, 138–50. The only study of Noah's *National Advocate*

years is William Louis Shulman, "The National Advocate, 1812–1829" (Unpublished Ed.D. thesis, Yeshiva University, 1968).

2. It is difficult to date exactly when Noah took over as editor of the *National Advocate*. *Columbian* (May 27, 1817), 2, may contain an oblique reference to him; certainly by June the secret was out (see especially June 23, 1817). He later claimed that he was not editor on April 28, 1817, see *Nat. Adv.* (October 19, 1821), 2:3. With the exception of Shulman, "The National Advocate," 26, most secondary works are in error regarding when Noah assumed the editor's chair. On Henry Wheaton, see Elizabeth F. Baker, *Henry Wheaton* (Philadelphia, 1937).

3. Noah republished these essays in 1820 as a separate volume, *Essays of Howard on Domestic Economy*. He republished the essays with certain changes in 1845 and 1847 under the title *Gleanings From a Gathered Harvest*. The most notable alteration was the deletion of an essay opposing the slave trade. [Mordecai M. Noah], *Essays of Howard* (New York, 1820); see reviews in *American* (July 8, 1820), 2:5 and *New York Literary Journal and Belles Lettres Repository*, III (1820), 76. For editions of *Gleanings from a Gathered Harvest* see *National Union Catalog Pre-1956 Imprints* (Washington, D.C., 1975), vol. 420, 282. *Nat. Adv.* (October 2, 1818), 2:1 suggests that Noah may not have authored all of these essays.

4. Noah published a particularly damaging revelation about Thomas L. McKenney, see Charles F. Adams (ed.), *Memoirs of John Quincy Adams* (Philadelphia, 1875), VI, 66.

5. Noah's trial for publishing the *Observer* letter is reprinted in John D. Lawson (ed.), *American State Trials* (St. Louis, 1914), I, 671–98. See Noah to Gulian Verplanck (February 26, 1841), New York Historical Society; S. B. H. Judah, *The Buccaneers* (New York, 1827), I, 84; and *NY. Nat. Adv.* (November 12, 1827), 2:5.

6. Noah and Coleman clashed over the Mitchill letter in October 1822, see *Nat. Adv.* and *Evening Post*, especially October 11–17, 1822. On Noah's ignorance of English history, see *Evening Post for the Country* (September 23, 1820), 1:2, 2:3.

7. Quotes are from the [Philadelphia] *Columbian Observer*, III (July 31, 1824), 2:4–7 and *Nantucket Inquirer* (January 10, 1825), 2:4; see also retrospective praise in *Tribune* (March 27, 1851), 4:3. On Noah's importance in the history of New York journalism, see I. C. Pray, *Memoirs of James Gordon Bennett and his Times* (New York, 1855), 45. Frank L. Mott, "Facetious News Writing 1833–1882," *Mississippi Valley Historical Review*, 29 (1942), 36–7 is incorrect in dating this genre to James Gordon Bennett in the 1830s. Circulation figures for early newspapers are notoriously inaccurate, but for 1816, Frederick Hudson, *Journalism in the United States from 1690 to 1872* (New York, 1873), 226, listed 875 *National Advocate* subscribers, and in 1823, Noah in *Nat. Adv.* (November 6, 1823), 2:1 claimed 1200 daily and 1200 bi-weekly subscribers.

8. On the political dependence of early American newspapers, see James L. Crouthamel, "The Newspaper Revolution in New York, 1830–1860," *New York History*, 45 (April 1964), 91–114; and Elwyn B. Robinson "The Dynamics of American Journalism from 1787 to 1865," *Pennsylvania Magazine of History and Biography*, 61 (1937), 435–45. Noah admitted to Bucktail support in his letter to Gulian Verplanck (February 26, 1841), New York Historical Society. Noah's salary was revealed in *Columbian* (October 16, 1817), 2:3.

9. On Tammany Hall and Tammany Society, see Jerome Mushkat, *Tammany: The Evolution of a Political Machine 1789–1865* (New York, 1971), a volume on which I have heavily relied; and Gustavus Myers, *The History of Tammany Hall* (New York, 1917). For an incomplete list of Jewish officers in Tammany Hall, see *PAJHS*, 27 (1920), 394. Noah was the only Jewish Grand Sachem before the Civil War. On his election to the post, see *American* (June 3, 1824), 2:5 and Shulman, "National Advocate," 27–28. Noah's Tammany address was printed: *Oration Delivered by Appointment Before Tammany Society of Columbian Order... United to Celebrate the 41st Anniversary of American Independence* (New York, 1817), quotes are from pp. 20, 24. See also Fred Somkin, *Unquiet Eagle: Meaning and Desire in the Idea of American Freedom* (Ithaca, 1967), 12–14. Noah's anniversary address to Tammany Society in 1823 was not published, but see *Nat. Adv.* (May 7, 1823), 2:4. Calhoun's comment is

in his letter to Ninian Edwards (June 12, 1822) in W. Edwin Hemphill (ed.) *The Papers of John C. Calhoun* (Columbia, S.C., 1973), III, 159–60.

10.　Michael Wallace, "Changing Concepts of Party in the United States: New York, 1815–1828," *American Historical Review*, 74 (1968), 453–91; quote from the *Albany Argus* (February 27, 1826) is on p. 461. See also Robert V. Remini, "The Albany Regency," *New York History*, 39 (October 1958), 341–55; idem, *Martin Van Buren and the Making of the Democratic Party* (pb. ed. New York, 1970); and Alvin Kass, *Politics in New York State 1800–1830* (Syracuse, 1965). The Noah quote is from the *Nat. Adv.* (October 31, 1823), 2:1.

11.　Wallace, "Changing Concepts of Party," 464–65; Kass, *Politics in New York*, 34; William L. Mackenzie, *The Life and Times of Martin Van Buren* (Boston, 1846), 168, 195, 197, 200, 234 and idem, *The Lives and Opinions of Benjamin Franklin Butler and Jesse Hoyt* (Boston, 1845), 38–40; quote is from Noah to Jesse Hoyt (February 23, 1823) on p. 40. Years later, Noah conceded that Martin Van Buren oversaw his early editorials, see *T&M* (March 25, 1849), 2:1. His earlier comments, quoted here, are in *Nat. Adv.* (August 8, 1822), 2:2. Noah asked Azariah Flagg for patronage based on his loyalty, see Noah to Flagg (January 18, 1824), Flagg Papers, New York Public Library. On Alexander Hamilton's control over the *Evening Post*, see Allan Nevins, *The Evening Post: A Century of Journalism* (New York, 1922), 25–26, 32–33; De Witt Clinton's control over the *Columbian* is revealed in Charles Haines to Alden Spooner (June 27, [1818]), Spooner Papers, New York Historical Society. Noah's interest in publishing a commercial paper is revealed in Noah to J. M. Sanderson (August 8, 1824), Historical Society of Pennsylvania; and he discussed his thoughts of resignation in *Report of the Trial of an Action on the Case Brought by Silvanus Miller...Against Mordecaid Noah* (N.Y., 1823), 27, 30; *Nat. Adv.* (September 6, 1824), 2:1 and (September 24, 1824), 2:4 from where quote is taken.

12.　For the Eckford quote see *Niles' Weekly Register*, XXVII (September 11, 1824), 25 and on the whole issue see Noah's *A Statement of Facts Relative to the Conduct of Henry Eckford esq. as connected with the National Advocate* (New York, 1824).

13.　Wallace, "Changing Concepts of Party," 456. Dorothie Bobbé, *De Witt Clinton* (New York, 1933) remains the standard biography.

14.　On Van Buren, see Denis T. Lynch, *An Epoch and a Man: Martin Van Buren and His Times* (New York, 1929); Holmes Alexander, *The American Talleyrand: The Career and Contemporaries of Martin Van Buren* (New York, 1935); William E. Smith, "Van Buren, Martin," *Dictionary of American Biography*, 19 (1930), 152–157; and Remini, *Martin Van Buren*. On the relations between Noah and Van Buren, see Albert M. Friedenberg, "The Correspondence of Jews With President Martin Van Buren," *PAJHS* 23 (1914), 71–100, quote is from Noah to Van Buren (July 13, 1819) on p. 72. Others noted the Van Buren-Noah connection, see Peter Porter to Henry Clay (September 30, 1822) in James F. Hopkins, *The Papers of Henry Clay* (Lexington, Kentucky, 1963), III, 290 and Charles R. King (ed.), *The Life and Correspondence of Rufus King* (New York, 1900), 509.

15.　*Nat. Adv.* (July 8, 1817), 2:1; (August 14, 1818), 2:2; (April 10, 1819), 2:1–2; (February 25, 1820), 2:1.

16.　My analysis of Bucktail identity formation has been influenced by Wallace, "Changing Concepts of Party"; George Devereux, "Ethnic Identity: Its Logical Functions and its Dysfunctions," in George De Vos and Lola Romanucci-Ross (ed.) *Ethnic Identity* (Palo Alto, Cal., 1975), 42–70; and David L. Horowitz, "Ethnic Identity," in Nathan Glazer and Daniel P. Moynihan (eds.) *Ethnicity: Theory and Practice* (Cambridge, 1975), 11–40.

17.　Kass, *Politics in New York State*, and Mushkat, *Tammany*, 67 deal with the themes of expediency and opportunism. On Noah's "all's fair" comment, see *Evening Post* (November 4, 1817), 2:1; *Nat. Adv.* (November 7, 1817), 2:2, *Columbian* (November 8, 1817), 2:3; and De Witt Clinton and Pierre Van Wyck, *The Martling Men* (New York, 1819), 21.

18.　On the canal, see Ronald E. Shaw, *Erie Water West: A History of the Erie Canal 1792–1854* (Lexington, Ky., 1966); Shulman, "National Advocate," 49–60; and Bobbé, *Clinton*, 145–69.

19. Noah to Van Buren (December 19, 1820) reprinted in Friedenberg, "Correspondence with Van Buren," 76; Cadwallader C. Colden, Memoir...*Presented to the Mayor of the City at the Celebration of the Completion of the New York Canals* (New York, 1825), Appendix, pp. 126, 325. Quotes are from *Nat. Adv.* (August 18, 1818), 2:1; (April 9, 1819), 2:1; and (May 24, 1820), 2:4. Noah later took blame for his false analysis of the canal project, see *Nat. Adv.* (October 4, 1823), 2:1; *ES* (November 6, 1833), 2:1 and (March 7, 1837), 2:1.

20. *Nat. Adv.* (April 26, 1824), 2:2. Cf. (October 27, 1824), 2:1 and (November 8, 1824), 2:1.

21. The Council of Appointment had the responsibility to appoint most nonelected officials in New York State. It often served as a patronage arm of the executive, although it claimed to be and at times was independent. The Council of Revision was modeled on the English House of Lords. It consisted of the Governor, Chancellor, and Supreme Court justices who were empowered to veto any bill within ten days of its passage. A two-thirds vote of both legislative houses was required to overturn a council vote.

22. On the convention, see Mushkat, *Tammany*, 69–73; Shulman, "National Advocate," 60–97 and generally Merrill D. Peterson, *Democracy, Liberty and Property: The State Constitutional Conventions of the 1820s* (Indianapolis, 1966).

23. Quote is from *Nat. Adv.* (October 22, 1821), 2:4; see also (October 20, 1821), 2:4.

24. George Dangerfield, *The Era of Good Feeling* (New York, 1952); Ronald Formisano, "Deferential-Participant Politics: The Early Republic's Political Culture 1789–1840," *American Political Science Review*, 68 (1974), 473–87; Charles S. Snydor, "The One Party Period of American History," *American Historical Review*, 51 (April 1946), 439–51; and more specifically for New York, Mushkat, *Tammany*, 75–101; and Remini, *Martin Van Buren*, 12–29. Quotes are from *Nat. Adv.* (April 21, 1821), 2:2 and (August 23, 1820), 2:3.

25. DeAlva S. Alexander, *A Political History of the State of New York* (New York, 1909) I, 267–72; Mushkat, *Tammany*, 64, 70; *Columbian* (July 13, 1819), 2:1; *Nat. Adv.* (July 2, 1819), 2:2; (July 12, 1819), 2:2; *True Sun* (August 29, 1848), and the two quoted letters, Van Buren to Noah (December 17, 1819) and Noah to Van Buren (December 19, 1819), both in Friedenberg, "Correspondence with Martin Van Buren," 73–75.

26. On the Missouri Compromise see below Chapter VI; Glover Moore, *The Missouri Controversy 1819–1821* (Lexington, Ky., 1953); and *Nat. Adv.* (July 28, 1820), 2 which is quoted. See also *Nat. Adv.* (April 24, 1823), 2:2 where Noah regrets ever having supported King.

27. James F. Hopkins, "The Election of 1824," in Arthur M. Schlesinger, ed., *History of American Presidential Elections 1789–1968* (New York, 1971), 349–412 cites earlier literature. Noah urged Monroe to take an active role in the campaign in Noah to Monroe (June 23, 1823), Monroe Papers, Library of Congress. Noah may have had some early hesitations about Crawford, see John Calhoun to Ninian Edwards (August 20, 1822), *Calhoun Papers*, VII, 248–9; Peter Porter to Henry Clay (September 30, 1822; October 22, 1822); *Clay Papers*, III, 290, 356. Noah's quoted comments on the other candidates are from *Nat. Adv.* (June 7, 1823), 2:1; (September 6, 1822), 2:3; (September 16, 1822), 2:3 and (February 21, 1824), 2:2.

28. Quotes are from *Nat. Adv.* (October 10, 1823), 2:2; (September 16, 1822), 2:3; cf. (January 28, 1819), 2:1–2. For earlier invocations of this myth, see *Hartford Courant* (January 28, 1788), 3 quoted in Moshe Davis, *With Eyes Toward Zion* (New York, 1977), 19; [Pittsburgh] *Tree of Liberty* (May 25, 1805) quoted in Carl E. Prince, "John Israel: Printer and Politician on the Pennsylvania Frontier, 1798–1805," *Pennsylvania Magazine of History and Biography*, 91 (1967), 52; Myer Moses, *An Oration Delivered Before the Hebrew Orphan Society* (Charleston, 1807), 7.

29. Noah retrospectively viewed his feud with Sharpe in *Nat. Adv.* (November 8, 1822), 2:1 and (January 3, 1823), 2:1–2. Quote is from Friedenberg, "Letters to Martin Van Buren," 77.

30. On Noah's poverty, see Noah to Van Buren (December 19, 1819), in Friedenberg, "Letters to Martin Van Buren," 75. His role as city printer is described in New York [City] Common Council, *Minutes of the Common Council of the City of New York 1784–1831* (New

York, 1930), X, 143, 484; *Nat. Adv.* (July 28, 1819), 2:1; *Columbian* (July 29, 1819), 2:2; and *Evening Post* (July 30, 1819), 2:2. Regarding the shrievalty, see *Columbian* (June 10, 1820), 2:1; (November 9, 1820), 2:1 and Noah to Van Buren (December 29, 1820), in Friedenberg, "Correspondence with Van Buren," 76. For reaction to the appointment, see *Columbian* (February 26, 1821), 2:4 (quoted). The date of Noah's appointment is in Edgar A. Werner, *Civil List and Constitutional History of the Colony and State of New York* (Albany, 1889), 524.

31.   Novelist James Fenimore Cooper in *Notions of the Americans* (1828) called attention to the fact that "the sheriff of the city of New York... was a few years ago, a Jew" to prove that in America, church and state were separated. Cooper erroneously believed that New Yorkers elected Noah to his office. He might better have observed that New York's longtime policeman, Jacob Hays, was a Jew, albeit a non-practicing one. James F. Cooper, *Notions of the Americans Picked Up By a Travelling Bachelor* (Philadelphia, 1848), II, 246; see Louis Harap, *The Image of the Jew in American Literature from Early Republic to Mass Immigration* (Philadelphia, 1974), 191. On Jacob Hays, see *Cyclopedia of American Biography*, XII (1904), 354; Samuel I. Prime, *Life in New York* (New York, 1847), 149; and Noah's own epitaph in *T&M* (June 23, 1850), reprinted in Jerome Mushkat, "Epitaphs by Mordecai Noah," *New York Historical Society Quarterly*, 55 (July 1971), 263–65.

32.   Peter J. Coleman, *Debtors and Creditors in America* (Madison, 1974); *Nat. Adv.* (March 25, 1818), 2:2; Shulman, "National Advocate," 139–43. Noah described his first visit to the debtors prison in *T&M* (January 6, 1850), 1. On his actions during the yellow fever epidemic, see *Evening Post* (August 31, 1822), 2:1 and the biography of Noah in *New York Mirror*, 4 (July 25, 1846), 250, written by Noah's friends. Simon Wolf's account, according to which Noah lost $200,000 in debts, is fantastic; see *Selected Addresses and Papers of Simon Wolf* (Cincinnati, 1926), 120.

33.   The idea that (in Noah's words) "a Jew ought not to hang a Christian" became an important issue in the election. As Noah analyzed the voting: "those that expected to be hanged voted against me, and those who believed they ought to be hanged voted against me." According to three different sources, Noah confronted the hanging issue with a characteristic bon mot. "It would be a damned poor Christian that would want to be hanged" is the Samuel Lockwood version. "Pretty Christians, forsooth, whose crimes have sent them to the gallows" is the sentence remembered by George P. Morris. The most elegant version was recalled by Evart A. Ducykinck: "Pretty Christians to require hanging at all." *Nat. Adv.* (November 8, 1822), 2:2; Samuel Lockwood, "Major M. M. Noah," *Lippincott's Magazine*, I (1868), 668; *New York Mirror*, 15 (July 1, 1837), 6; Evart A. Ducykinck, *Cyclopedia of American Literature* (Philadelphia, 1875), I, 768. See also S. B. H. Judah, *Gotham and the Gothamites*, (New York, 1823), pp. x, xiii; and Philip Hone's diary, XIII, p. 393 as quoted in Leonard Gappelberg, "M. M. Noah and the Evening Star: Whig Journalism 1833–1840," (Unpublished Ed.D. Thesis, Yeshiva University, 1970), 221.

34.   Early efforts to dump Noah were mentioned by *Evening Post* (February 12, 1822), 2:3; (September 24, 1822), 2:3–4 and *American* (October 1, 1822), 2:3–4. For the nomination of Noah and Wendover see *Nat. Adv.* (November 1, 1822), 2:2. Quotes are from *Evening Post* (November 2, 1822), 2:2–4 and *Commercial Advertiser* (November 6, 1822), 2:1; see also *American* (December 2, 1823), 2:2 on Noah's Jewish support. Lynch, *Epoch and a Man*, 243, curiously explains the 1822 Noah-Sharpe dispute by referring to an 1823 dispute over who should be state printer.

35.   In January, 1821, soon after *Israel Vindicated* was published, George Houston was serving as an assistant writer on the *National Advocate*. Noah later claimed that he had "no agency" in writing *Israel Vindicated*, but he clearly knew the author's identity. Jonathan D. Sarna, "The Freethinker, The Jews, and the Missionaries: George Houston and the Mystery of *Israel Vindicated*," *AJS Review*, 5 (1980).

36.   Quotes are from *Evening Post* (November 5, 1822), 2; *Nat. Adv.* (November 8, 1822), 2:2; and "An Israelite" [George Houston], *Israel Vindicated* (New York, 1820).

37.   Quotes are from *Nat. Adv.* (November 4, 1822), 2 and (November 6, 1822), 2. The *New*

Jersey Eagle's comments were reprinted in the *American* (November 8, 1822), 2:4. For other comments on the sheriff race, see *New York Spectator* (November 12, 1822), 1:1; *Evening Post* (November 7, 1822), 2:1; and editorial opinions reprinted in *Nat. Adv.* (November 10, 1822), 2:2–3 and (November 29, 1822), 2:3.

38.   *Nat. Adv.* (November 7, 1822), 2:1.

39.   Excerpts from Strong's sermon are in *Evangelical Witness*, I (1822–23), 311–12; for Noah's reply see *Nat. Adv.* (November 22, 1822), 2:2–3; see also (December 20, 1822), 2:2 and (August 7, 1822), 2:4 on death of Rachel Phillips. Other comments on Strong's sermon are in *Evening Post* (December 20, 1822), 2:3; *New York Statesman* (December 24, 1822) and the sarcastic comments of John Neal in *Blackwood's Magazine* reprinted in John Neal, *American Writers: A Series of Papers Contributed to Blackwood's Magazine* (1824–1825), ed. F. L. Pattee (Durham, 1937), 88. For the debate over the cause of the yellow fever epidemic, see William Gribbin, "Divine Providence or Miasma? The Yellow Fever Epidemic of 1822," *New York History*, 53, (1972), 283–98.

40.   Quotes are from *Nat. Adv.* (November 7, 1822), 2:1; Noah to Jesse Hoyt (February 23, 1823) in Mackenzie, *Lives and Opinions of Butler and Hoyt*, 39–40; see also pp. 89, 439; and Noah to Azariah Flagg (January 18, 1824), Flagg Papers, New York Public Library.

41.   John C. McCloskey, "The Campaign of the Periodicals after the War of 1812 for Native American Literature," *Publications of Modern Language Association*, 50 (1935), 262–73. *Travels*, p. vi; *Nat. Adv.* (November 3, 1818), 2:1; (May 11, 1819), 2:1; (December 11, 1820), 2:1; (February 24, 1821), 2:2; and (November 12, 1825), 2:3–4. *New York Literary Journal and Belles Lettres Repository*; and Noah to C. De Witt (May 26, 1819) in Noah Papers, New York Public Library.

42.   The psychohistorian might write volumes about Noah's fondness for this motif. It seems most likely, however, that the motif reflected less on Noah and more on the actresses for whom he wrote his plays. As careerwomen in a society which relegated women to the home, actresses must have envied their male competitors. The "woman in man's clothes motif," like tomboyism, allowed women to play out their fantasies without breaking society's norms. Janet S. Hyde, B. G. Rosenberg and Jo Ann Behrman, "Tomboyism," *Psychology of Women Quarterly*, 2 (Fall 1973), 73–75; Juanita H. Williams, *Psychology of Women* (New York, 1977), esp. p. 81.

43.   Jacob R. Marcus, *Memoirs of American Jews* (Philadelphia, 1955), I, 120–24. James Rees, *The Dramatic Authors of America* (Philadelphia, 1845), 328; Charles P. Daly, *The Settlement of the Jews in North America* (New York, 1893), 123; Arthur H. Quinn, *A History of the American Drama from the Beginning to the Civil War* (New York, 1923), 151–53, 193; *Major Noah*, 164–88; Lee M. Friedman, "Mordecai Manuel Noah as a Playwright," *Pilgrims in a New Land* (Philadelphia, 1943), 221–32; Richard Moody, *America Takes the Stage: Romanticism in American Drama and Theater 1750–1900* (Bloomington, Indiana: 1955), 90, 143, 152, 155, 192; and *idem*, *Dramas From the American Theater 1762–1909* (New York, 1966), 115–22. See also items cited above, Chapter I, nn. 17–19, and Louis Harap, *The Image of the Jew in American Literature* (New York, 1974), esp. pp. 263, 266.

44.   The play was first produced on June 19, 1819. See Moody, *America Takes the Stage*, 90, 155–6; and for attendance figures, David Grimsted, *Melodrama Unveiled: American Theater and Culture 1800–1850* (Chicago, 1968), 252. *She Would Be A Soldier* is reprinted most conveniently in Moody, *Dramas From the American Theater*, 115–42. For reviews and notices, see Bertram W. Korn, *The Early Jews of New Orleans* (Waltham, Ma., 1969), 161; Allan Nevins, *The Evening Post: A Century of Journalism* (New York, 1922), 115; *Columbian* (June 21, 1819), 2:2; (November 30, 1821), 2:1; and (March 29, 1822), 2:3.

45.   The play was first performed on May 15, 1820; the Park theater burned on May 25, 1820. An extensive review of *Yusef Caramalli* is in *New York Literary Journal and Belles Lettres Repository*, 3 (1820), 70–71, 141–43, which also includes correspondence relative to Noah's return of the benefit money. See also Grace Seixas to Mrs. I. B. Kursheedt (June 5, 1820), Grace Seixas Nathan Papers, AJHS; Charles H. Haswell, *Reminiscences of an Octogenarian of the*

City of New York (New York, 1896), 110–11; and Noah's reminiscence of the fire in *T&M* (June 6, 1847), 2:2. *American (March 19, 1821), 3:1* reports on a production of *Siege of Tripoli* in Boston.

46. M. M. Noah, *Marion, or the Hero of Lake George: A Drama in Three Acts,* (New York, 1822); *Evening Post* (November 28, 1821), 2:6; *Nat. Adv.* (November 29, 1821), 2:4.

47. *Nat. Adv.* (April 26, 1819), 2; Rees, *Dramatic Authors,* 19.

48. The play was first produced on June 17, 1822. See Harold W. Schoenberger, *American Adaptations of French Plays on the New York and Philadelphia Stages from 1790 to 1833* (Philadelphia, 1924), 69–71; *American* (June 15, 1822), 2:4; *New York Spectator* (June 18, 1822), 2:1; Stephen Larrabee, *Hellas Observed: The American Experience of Greece 1775–1865* (New York, 1957). Quote is from *Nat. Adv.* (October 22, 1822), 2:2.

49. Mordecai M. Noah, *The Grecian Captive, or the Fall of Athens* (New York, 1822); Joe Cowell, *Thirty Years Passed Among the Players in England and America* (New York, 1845), 63–64; *Nat. Adv.* (June 19, 1822), 2:3; *Evening Post* (June 19, 1822), 2:1.

50. *Major Noah,* 182, 186 and Cadwallader, *Memoir... Presented to the Mayor of the City at the Completion of the New York Canals,* 325 deal with the interludes; on *Natalie* see *Major Noah* 284–5; *Herald* (May 22, 1840), 2:3; (May 30, 1840), 2:5; and the *Natalie* poster in the Theater Collection of Harvard University. The *Herald* claimed that the Park Theater paid Noah six hundred dollars for *Natalie.*

51. Quote is from Noah, *Grecian Captive,* p. iv. On the reasons why literary creativity in America was discouraged, see Grimsted, *Melodrama Unveiled,* 146; John Paul Pritchard, *Criticism in America* (Norman, Oklahoma: 1956), 10; "American Drama," *American Quarterly Review,* 1 (June 1827), 331–57 and the theoretical discussion in Vytautas Kavolis, *History on Art's Side: Social Dynamics in Artistic Efflorescences* (New York, 1972).

52. Noah played an active role in benefits for, among others, Thomas A. Cooper, Thomas S. Hamblin, James W. Wallack, and Samuel Woodworth. He also sat on the committee of arrangements to honor Charles Dickens in 1842. *American* (November 1, 1830), 2:6; *Herald* (November 7, 1836), 2:3; (September 27, 1837), 1:1; (January 10, 1839), 2:3; *C&E* (October 4, 1839), 2:5; *ES* (October 12, 1839), 2:4; (November 6, 1839), 2:3 and "Old New York Revived," *Historical Magazine,* 2nd Series, 2 (August 1867), 111.

53. Henry D. Stone, *Personal Recollections of the Drama or Theatrical Reminiscences* (Albany, 1873), 81; Montrose J. Moses, *The Fabulous Forrest* (Boston, 1929), 68; Raymond FitzSimons, *Edward Kean,* (New York, 1976), 146, 151, 153, 206. Other quotes are from Weed, *Autobiography of Thurlow Weed,* 59; and *The Union* (July 18, 1842), 1:3. See also, "A Jew and A Christian," *International Magazine,* 3 (May 1851), 162; and John T. Townsend, *My Own Story* (New York, 1902), 95–101.

54. *ES-Country* (April 24, 1835), 2:2 is quoted. See also *ES-Country* (November 20, 1835), 2:2 for Noah's interest in railroads; and Noah to Charles B. Moss (November 21, 1844), John Tyler Papers, Library of Congress for Noah's interest in a Red Sea canal and fan propellers.

55. Quotes are from *Nat. Adv.* (October 9, 1821), 2:2; *Evening Post* (January 29, 1824) reprinted in Isaac N. P. Stokes, *The Iconography of Manhattan Island 1498–1909* (New York, 1926), V, p, 1636; cf. *Minutes of the Common Council,* XIII (January 26, 1824), 511; and *Nat. Adv.* (June 6, 1823), 2:2.

56. Quote is from *Nat. Adv.* (August 23, 1816); 2:1; See also, Shulman, "National Advocate," 104–15.

57. Noah's grand jury report to the city is reprinted in *Nat. Adv.* (August 22, 1820), 2:3–5; and *American* (August 23, 1820), 2:4–5. His humanitarian pronouncements are in *Nat. Adv.* (December 7, 1818), 2:2; (March 19, 1821), 2:2 and (March 30, 1821), 2:2. Regarding capital punishment, see his series of articles in *NY Nat. Adv.* (January 21–February 4, 1826).

58. Noah might have taken his own advice on this last point, for in 1823 he arranged—through political connections, his opponents charged—to have himself certified as a lawyer. He never

succeeded in building up a practice. Attacks on the exceptional manner in which Noah was admitted to the bar include *American* (May 17, 1823), 2:3; (June 7, 1823), 2:3; *Evening Post* (May 24, 1823), 2:2; (May 30, 1823), 2:1; (June 3, 1823), 2:2 and *Columbian Observer*, 3 (July 31, 1824), 2:4; see *Nat. Adv.* (May 27, 1823), 2:2. Noah was admitted to practice before the United States Supreme Court on February 16, 1829, see *Enquirer* (February 24, 1829), 3:2.

59.   The best sources for Noah's views are his two speeches before the Society of Mechanics and Tradesmen: *An Address Delivered Before the General Society of Mechanics and Tradesmen of the City of New York on the Opening of the Mechanic Institution* (New York, 1822), an address which members of the Common Council attended, see *Minutes of the Common Council,* 12 (November 14, 1821), 112; and *Address Delivered at the Re-Opening of the Apprentices Library* (New York, 1850). This address is reprinted in Thomas Earle and Charles T. Congdon (eds.) *Annals of the General Society of Mechanics and Tradesmen of the City of New York From 1785–1880* (New York, 1882), 273–79.

60.   Quote is from *Address Delivered at the Re-Opening of the Apprentices Library,* 14.

61.   Quotes are from [Philadelphia] *Columbian Observer,* 3 (July 31, 1824), 2:4; Rachel Mordecai Lazarus to Maria Edgeworth (December 20, 1823) in Edgar E. MacDonald, ed., *The Education of the Heart: The Correspondence of Rachel Mordecai Lazarus and Maria Edgeworth* (Chapel Hill, 1977), 45; *Albany Argus* (August 15, 1820), 2:5; *Evening Post (May 24, 1823), 2:2; Nantucket Inquirer* (January 10, 1825), reprinted in Bayrd Still, "New York City in 1824: A Newly Discovered Description," *New York Historical Quarterly,* 46 (April, 1962), 155; and *Columbian* (August 18, 1819), 2:1. On Noah's character, see also Judah Zuntz to Samuel Myers (January 3, 1820), Myers Family Papers, Box 2327, AJA; *Columbian* (April 14, 1820), 2:3; *Evening Post* (January 6, 1821), 2:3; (May 24, 1823), 2:2; and Judah, *Gotham and Gothamites,* 92. Edward Pessen has written the most important works on class and social mobility in this period, see his *Riches Class and Power Before the Civil War* (Lexington, Ma., 1973) and "Who Has Power in the Democratic Capitalist Community? Reflections on Antebellum New York City," *New York History,* 58 (April 1977), 129–56.

62.   Carl E. Prince, "John Israel: Printer and Politician on the Pennsylvania Frontier 1798–1805," *Pennsylvania Magazine of History and Biography,* 91 (January 1967), 46–55. *Columbian* (May 21, 1817), 2:1 and *Nat. Adv.* (August 5, 1817), 2:2 deal with anti-Jewish attacks on other journalists. Newspaper references to Noah's religion are far too numerous to list. Quotes are from *Columbian* (December 7, 1819), 2:3; (December 15, 1819), 2:3; *American* (November 3, 1823), 2; and (November 6, 1823), 2:3. An earlier use of the phrase "de monish" is found in an 1800 attack on Benjamin Nones, see *DHJUS,* 92.

63.   Quotes are from *Nat. Adv.* (July 28, 1817), 2:2; (October 6, 1817), 2:3; see (August 26, 1817), 2:4. Noah's role in the Jewish community is examined below in Chapter VII.

64.   *Consecration Address,* partially reprinted in *JUSDH,* I, 82–85. See David and Tamar de Sola Pool, *An Old Faith in the New World* (New York, 1955), 50; and Louis Ruchames, "Mordecai Manuel Noah and Early American Zionism," *AJHQ,* 54 (March 1975), 197–200; Noah expressed many of the themes in this address earlier, *Nat. Adv.* (July 9, 1817), 2:2.

65.   Noah probably never saw what may be the most interesting response to his discourse. John Myers of Norfolk, Virginia, sent a copy of the address to Attorney General William Wirt, and in a private letter, Wirt expressed his indebtedness. He found Noah "a just and comprehensive as well as a liberal thinker," and termed Noah's address informative and amusing. Wirt then went on to wonder out loud whether persecution, rather than Divine Providence, was not the key to Jewish unity: "They have not been persecuted as individuals, but as a nation; what was more natural than that the reaction of resentment and indignation should have been national, too.... I believe that if those persecutions had never existed, the Jews would have melted down into the general mass of the people of the world." Carrying his logic further, Wirt wondered whether enlightenment would not prove a bad thing for the Jewish people: "Let us suppose these persecutions at an end throughout the earth... how long would the children of Israel [continue to exist] as a separate nation? Could they be discriminated at the end of a century and a half?" William Wirt to John Myers (June 12, 1818), Myers Family Papers, AJA. Wirt's comments may

be compared with those of Thorstein Veblen, "The Intellectual Pre-eminence of Jews in Modern Europe" (1919), reprinted in Max Lerner, *The Portable Veblen* (New York, 1948), 467–79. See also the critical comments in Isador Twersky, *Jewish Studies in American Universities* [in Hebrew] Jerusalem: Institute of Contemporary Jewry, 1970), 15ff.

66. The letter Noah sent to Jefferson accompanying his address is preserved: Noah to Jefferson (May 7, 1818), Jefferson Papers, Coolidge Collection, Massachusetts Historical Society; see also *JUSDH*, I, 241. Letters of notables to Noah are printed in *Travels*, appendix, pp. xxv–xxvi, and have been frequently reprinted. Noah's address was noticed as far away as Georgia, see *Columbia Museum and Savannah Advertiser* (April 30, 1818), 2:2. Jacob de la Motta's correspondence is reprinted in *DHJUS*, 156–157.

67. Quotes are from Judith Zuntz to Samuel Myers (January 3, 1820), Myers Papers, AJA; *Nat. Adv.* (November 17, 1819), 2:2; (May 14, 1819), 2:3. On the Maryland Jew Bill, see *Nat. Adv.* (January 23, 1819), 2:1; (February 8, 1820), 2:3–4; (October 17, 1820), 2:2; (December 12, 1820), 2:5; (February 6, 1821), 2:2; (January 28, 1823), 2:3; (September 17, 1823), 2:1–2; *NY Nat. Adv.-Country* (January 10, 1826), 3:2. See also *JUSDH*, I, 33–55 and Edward Eitches, "Maryland's 'Jew Bill,' " *AJHQ*, 60 (March 1971), 258–79. On David G. Seixas, see *Nat. Adv.* (March 3, 1820), 2; (March 10, 1822), 2:2–3; (March 18–19, 1822); (April 27 1822), 2:3; (June 18, 1822), 2; *Documents in Relation to the Dismissal of David G. Seixas from the Pennsylvania Institution for the Deaf and Dumb* (Philadelphia 1822) and *Letter to C. C. Biddle... Connected With the Dismissal of David G. Seixas...* (Philadelphia, 1822) and *NY Nat. Adv.* (December 13, 1825), 2:1. Noah expressed his opposition to listing a criminal's religion in *Nat. Adv.* (August 26, 1817), 2:4; (December 23, 1822), 2:3; (July 28, 1823), 2:1–3; and *American* (July 28, 1823), 2:2. He answered a question about Judaism in *Nat. Adv.* (May 5, 1821), 2:1. In his weekly newspaper, *Sunday Times and Noah's Weekly Messenger*, he answered questions about Judaism almost weekly. See also *Nat. Adv.* (May 1, 1824), 2:3–4, for George Bethune English's report to Noah on Jews in the Ottoman Empire.

68. Noah's comments on missionaries include *Nat. Adv.* (July 9, 1817), 2:2; (January 6, 1820), 2:3; (January 9, 1822), 2:3; (December 23, 1822), 2:3; (February 1, 1823), 2:2; (February 20, 1823), 2:3; (March 4, 1823), 2:4; (May 14, 1823), 2:2; (October 23, 1823), 2:2; and (March 30, 1824), 2:4. On the American Society for Meliorating the Condition of the Jews, see David M. Eichorn, "A History of Christian Attempts to Convert the Jews of the United States and Canada" (Unpublished Ph.D. thesis, Hebrew Union College, 1938); Lee M. Friedman, "The American Society for Meliorating the Condition of the Jews and Joseph S. C. F. Frey, *Early American Jews* (Cambridge, 1934), 96–112; Lorman Ratner, "Conversion of the Jews and pre-Civil War Reform," *American Quarterly*, 13 (1961), 43–54. My reading of Noah's *National Advocate* has been influenced by the thesis of Leo Strauss in his *Persecution and the Art of Writing* (Glencoe, Ill., 1952).

69. Quote is from *NY Nat. Adv.* (May 13, 1826), 2:1; see also (April 22, 1826), 2:2 and *Enquirer for the Country* (May 18, 1827), 2:5; (May 29, 1827), 1:1; (August 19, 1828), 2:4.

70. Mushkat, *Tammany*, 80, 84; Dixon R. Fox, *The Decline of Aristocracy in the Politics of New York* (New York, 1919), 271–301; James F. McGuire, *The Democratic Party of the State of New York* (New York, 1908), I, 90–91; and J. A. Kehle, "The Delegate Convention: Agent of the Democratic Process," *South Atlantic Quarterly*, 72 (1973), 53–65.

71. King displayed his anti-Jewish feelings in many of his replies to Noah. One example suffices: "Jews are in fact a nation rather than a sect, and whether born in England, France or the United States, answer more readily to an appeal made to them as Jews, than as Englishmen, Frenchmen, or Americans.... I doubt the propriety of placing them at the head of any political journal. Deficient as they must be in that single national attachment, which binds a man to the soil of his nativity, and makes him the exclusive patriot of his own country; they would be more apt to consult their own personal views than the public good... the sanctity of the Christian religion, and the glorious right of private judgement to them are nothing." "An American Jew" replied to King in a pamphlet which attacked both Charles King and his father as opponents of liberty. If the pamphlet was not actually written by Mordecai Noah, it used many of the arguments against the

Kings which had appeared in Noah's newspaper. *A Letter to Charles King From an American Jew* (New York, 1823), quote is from pp. 3–4. See also *Nat. Adv.* (July 30, 1823), 2:3; and Daly, *Settlement of Jews in North America*, 125–6. For Rufus King's similar views, see John W. Pratt, *Religion, Politics and Diversity* (Ithaca, 1967), 144.

72. On Noah's opposition to the convention, see *Nat. Adv.* (May 31, 1822), 2:1; (December 24, 1822), 2:1; (June 4, 1823), 2:2; (July 24, 1823), 2:1; (February 11, 1824), 2:2; (February 24, 1824), 2:3.

73. *American* (June 3, 1823), 2:3; (November 1–8, 1823); and *Nat. Adv.* (November 15, 1823), 2:3. The pro-Calhoun *Patriot* was published specifically against Noah, see Calhoun to Michael Sterling (April 28, 1823) in Hemphill (ed.), *Papers of John Calhoun*, VIII, 36. Noah discussed his support for Governor Yates versus Samuel Young in *Nat. Adv.* (October 13, 1824), 2:2; see Mushkat, *Tammany*, 86 for another view. The decline in Bucktail support for Crawford is evident from the letter of Benjamin Butler to Jesse Hoyt (January 29, 1824) in Mackenzie, *Lives and Opinions of Butler and Hoyt*, 38–39.

74. Thomas Gibbons of the New York Steamship line and Stephen Price of the Park Theater also helped to finance the paper while Collector of Customs John Thompson and silversmith John Targee oversaw the *National Advocate*'s accounts.

75. The major source on this dispute is Noah's *Statement of Facts Relative to the Conduct of Henry Eckford, esq. as connected with the National Advocate* (New York, 1824) and the response printed in *Niles' Weekly Register*, 27 (September 11, 1824), 24–29. See also *National Advocate* and *Evening Post* (September 2–6, 1824); and the subsequent court cases: *Thomas Snowden v. M. M. Noah, John D. Brown, and others*, I. Hopkins 347 (1825); and other cases reported in *New York Statesman* (January 18, 1825), 3:1–2, and (February 25, 1825), 4:2.

76. On Noah's return to the *National Advocate* see *Nat. Adv.* (September 7, 1824), 2:3 and (September 20, 1824), 2:1; *Niles' Weekly Register*, 27 (September 25, 1824), 53; *New York Statesman* (September 21, 1824), 3:3–4; *New Hampshire Patriot and State Gazette* (September 27, 1824), 3:2; *American* (September 10, 1824), 2:2; and (October 9, 1824), 2:4. On the sale of the newspaper, see *Nat. Adv.* (December 8, 15, 16, 1824). See also *NY Nat. Adv.* (December 16, 1824) and *Nat. Adv.* (November 11, 1824), 2:1 where E. J. Roberts' association with Noah is mentioned. The most detailed account of this entire dispute is Shulman, "National Advocate," 34–43, but Shulman ignores the evidence found in court cases.

Chapter IV: An Asylum for the Jews

1. Samuel Ettinger's notion of conflicting centripetal and centrifugal currents in modern Jewish history is, in some respects, the debate over Jewish colonies writ large; see *A History of the Jewish People*, ed. H. H. Ben-Sasson (Cambridge, 1976), 727–32. Questions of separatism vs. assimilation were argued most forcefully in the French Enlightenment [see Arthur Hertzberg, *The French Enlightenment and the Jews* (New York, 1968)], and in the debate over Zionism.

2. On the various colony schemes, see Jacob R. Marcus, *The Colonial American Jew* (Detroit, 1970), I, 361–6; Simon Dubnow, *History of the Jews in Russia and Poland* (New York, 1975 [1916]), I, 364; James Parkes, "Lewis Way and His Times," *Transactions of the Jewish Historical Society of England*, 20 (1964), 189–201; Marcus L. Hansen, *The Immigrant in American History* (pb. ed., New York, 1964), 131–33; and *Nat. Adv.* (November 29, 1817), 2:1–2. Moses Shulvass has an interesting comparison of Ararat and the contemporaneous Decembrist Movement in Russia, "The Jewish States of Mordecai Noah and the Decembrists," *Hadoar* (March 5, 26, 1976), 276, 277, 324, 325 (in Hebrew). For Noah's positive view of Robert Owen's New Harmony Colony, see *NY Nat. Adv.* (November 12, 1825), 2:3; (November 30, 1825), 2:1–2; (March 7, 1826), 2:1; *T&M* (August 15, 1847), 2:2.

3. Leon Huehner, "Moses Elias Levy, an Early Florida Pioneer and the Father of Florida's First Senator, *Florida Historical Quarterly*, 19 (April 1941), 319–45; Samuel Proctor, "Pioneer Jewish Settlements in Florida 1764–1900," *Proceedings of the Conference on the Writing of*

Regional History in the South (Miami, 1956), 81–113; and Jacob Toury, "M. E. Levy's Plan for a Jewish Colony in Florida—1825," *Michael*, 3 (1975), 23–41; all deal with Levy. Myers's plan is revealed in Myers Family Papers, Box 2327–2327b, esp. Judah Zuntz to Samuel Myers (January 3, 1820), bx. 2327b, AJA, Cf. *JUSDH*, III, 879. On Robinson, see *JUSDH*, III, 879–84; *DHJUS* 141–47; and Lee M. Friedman, *Pilgrims in a New Land* (Philadelphia, 1948), 233–47. The missionary colony is discussed below, and in S. Joshua Kohn, "Mordecai Manuel Noah's Ararat Project and the Missionaries," *AJHQ*, 55 (December 1969), 210–14; and Max J. Kohler, "An Early American Hebrew Christian Agricultural Colony," *PAJHS*, 22 (1914), 184–6.

4.   Noah's knowledge of other colonial schemes is clear from correspondence in the Myers Family Papers, AJA. On Noah and Robinson, see *National Advocate* (December 1, 1819) 2:1; (March 4, 1820) 2:4; (March 24, 1821) 2:2; and New York County Clerk Records, Insolvent Debtors, reel IV, pp. 69–79 (1824), AJHS, where Robinson is listed as an endorser for one of Noah's notes. See also Chapter II, nn. 68–69 on Noah and the missionaries.

5.   The basic work on Ararat is Lewis F. Allen, "Founding the City of Ararat on Grand Island by Mordecai M. Noah," *Buffalo Historical Society Publications*, I (1879), 305–328, reprinted in *PAJHS*, 8 (1900) 98–118; in A. B. Makover, *Mordecai M. Noah His Life and Work from the Jewish Viewpoint* (New York, 1917), 36–64; and with new matter in *Buffalo Historical Society Publications*, 25 (1921) 113–44. Other studies are listed in the bibliography.

6.   Noah's memorial to the legislature is in *Nat. Adv.* (January 24, 1820), 2:3, and he reported on the legislative debate in *Nat. Adv.* (March 6, 1820), 2:1–2, which is quoted. For other documents and reactions, see G. Herbert Cone, "New Matter Relating to Mordecai M. Noah," *PAJHS*, 9 (1903), 132–33; *Niles' Register*, 17 (January 20, 1820), 371; Elkanah Watson, *History of the Rise and Progress of the Western Canals* (New York, 1820), 104; *Nat. Adv.* (March 3, 1820), 2:1; (March 6, 1820), 2:1; *New England Palladium and Commercial Advertiser*, 50 (March 7, 1820), 2:3; The [Philadelphia] *Union*, 20 (March 10, 1820), 2:4; and *Columbian* (January 22, 1820), 2:1.

7.   On "New Jerusalem," see note 22 below. The Hart quote is from Benjamin Hart to Moses Hart (May 4, 1820), Hart Family Papers, file J-E-6/2, microfilm 916 at AJA. Other quotes are from *Nat. Adv.* (December 1, 1820), 2:2 reprinted in *Providence Patriot* (December 20, 1820), 1:2; and in Seebert J. Goldowsky, "Newport as Ararat," *Rhode Island Jewish Historical Notes* 6 (November 1974), 604–9.

8.   *Columbian* (February 7, 1830), 2–3; *Charleston Patriot* (February 3, 1820), reprinted in *Evening Post* (February 16, 1820), 2:3; and *Nat. Adv.* (March 6, 1820), 2:1–2; cf. (February 11 1820), 2:1.

9.   Morris A. Gutstein, *The Story of the Jews of Newport* (New York, 1936), 173–255; *A History of the Jewish People* (ed. Ben Sasson), 787; *Columbian* (November 6, 1818), 3:1 and Cadwallader C. Colden, *Memoir... Presented to the Mayor of the City at the Celebration of the Completion of the New York Canals* (New York, 1825), 85–88.

10.   On Noah's consular application, see Charles F. Adams (ed.) *Memoirs of John Quincy Adams* (Philadelphia 1875), V (September 7, 1820), 173–4; *JUSDH*, III, 885–90.

11.   I have not seen the *Koblenzer Anzeiger* article and I find its date puzzling. I must, however, rely on Nathan M. Gelber, "Mordecai Emanuel Noah: His Dream of a Jewish State in America," *SURA: Israeli American Annual*, 3 (1957–8), 396–401; and Bernard D. Weinryb, "Noah's Ararat Jewish State in its Historical Setting," *PAJHS*, 43 (1954), 172–3, 181–5. On the *Verein*, see Hans C. Reissner, "Ganstown—U.S.A.: A German-Jewish Dream," *AJA*, 14 (April 1962), 20–31; *idem, Eduard Gans: Ein Leben im Vormaerz* (Tuebingen, 1965), 83–102; Eliezer S. Kirschbaum, *Hilchot Yemot Hamashiach* (Berlin: 1822), chapter 14 (in Hebrew); and Michael A. Meyer, *The Origins of the Modern Jew* (Detroit 1967), 169, 179. The *Verein* letter is reprinted in *JUSDH*, III, 891–93. See *New York Spectator*, 25 (October 18, 1822), 2:2, and *Boston Recorder (November 2, 1822), 2:3.

12.   Robert V. Bingham, "The History of Grand Island," *Buffalo Historical Society Publications*, 34 (1974), 59–78 is the best secondary account. See *Nat. Adv.* (April 10, 1824), 2:4; and Noah to ? (September 27, 1824), Noah Papers, Houghton Library, Harvard University,

Cambridge, Ma.; another copy in Lee K. Frankel Collection, AJA. A photograph of this letter may be found in Friedman, *Pioneers and Patriots*, p. 109. On Noah's correspondence with Porter, see Noah to Peter B. Porter (August 17, 1824), Peter A. Porter Collection, Buffalo and Erie County Historical Society, Buffalo, N.Y., item HH-26; typescript on p. 4 of item HH-11: Peter A. Porter, "Noah's Dream: A New Jerusalem in America" (unpublished article). Porter delayed his answer to Noah. See Noah's follow-up letter, Noah to Porter (September 13, 1824), Norton Collection, Buffalo and Erie County Public Library and Jonathan D. Sarna, "The Roots of Ararat," *AJA*, 32 (April 1980). The standard account of the Ararat purchase is Lewis F. Allen's "Founding of the City of Ararat." Allen was not a contemporary to the events he described, and I have modified his account on the basis of the following: Levi Beardsley, *Reminiscences* (New York, 1852), 156–7; *Black Rock Gazette* (June 21, 1825), 3:4–5; *Evening Post* (March 8, 1826), 2:5–6; and *NY Nat. Adv.* (October 1, 1825), 2:2; cf. Hugh G. J. Aitken, "Yates and McIntyre," *Journal of Economic History* 13 (1953), 36–57.

13.   Noah to Flagg (November 19, 1833), Noah Papers, AJHS. See also Noah to Porter (August 17, 1824) Porter Papers, Buffalo & Erie County Historical Society. Contrary reports are likely all based on Lewis Allen's account.

14.   Quotes are from Noah to Churchill Caldon Cambreleng (June 15, 1825), Noah Papers, Houghton Library, Harvard University, Cambridge, Ma.; *NY Nat. Adv.* (September 7, 1825), 2:2. See also *NY Nat. Adv.* (June 24, 1826), 2:3 and *Black Rock Gazette* (June 21, 1825), 3:4–5.

15.   The standard account of the dedication ceremonies, which I quote, was written by Noah and appeared in the *Buffalo Patriot-Extra*, (September 17, 1825), 1–2. It is largely reprinted in Allen, "Founding of the City of Ararat," and is faithfully followed by *Major Noah*. In my account, I have also used the *New York National Advocate* (September 1, 1825), 2:3; Malcolm Stern to Louis Ruchames (March 1, 1973), correspondence regarding A. B. Seixas in AJA Correspondence file: "A. B. Seixas"; and Charles W. Evans, *History of St. Paul's Church* (New York, 1903), 168–69, 361–69. Goldberg's comment, "Noah's latitudinarian friend-in-need [Searle] was censured" (*Major Noah*, 193–4) is without foundation and is based on a misreading of Evans.

16.   In his proclamation, Noah erroneously called September 15 the second day of Tishre. This error became particularly embarrassing later on when his enemies, noting that the second of Tishre was Rosh Hashana (the Jewish New Year), belatedly accused him of impiously violating the sanctity of the day. Gordis, "Mordecai Manuel Noah," 122 n.14; see *Herald* (May 5, 1838), 3:1; (June 23, 1838), 2:2.

17.   In addition to *Buffalo Patriot-Extra* (September 17, 1825), 1–2; see *Herald* (October 27, 1842), 2:1; for a sneering retrospect, and *American* (September 21, 1825). On the theatrical aspects see David Grimsted, *Melodrama Unveiled: American Theater and Culture* (Chicago: 1968), 42, 78. Compare the account of the Erie Canal dedication in Colden, *Memoir... at the Celebration of the Completion of the Canals.*

18.   Franz Kobler suggests that Noah's dictatorial tone reflects the influence on him of Napoleon Bonaparte, whose own efforts to modernize Jews Noah had surely watched in his youth. Some aspects of Ararat do indeed suggest French influence, and Napoleon's indirect effect on Noah is a fascinating, but unfortunately unanswerable question. Yet to claim, as Kobler does, that Noah's Francophilism and "megalomaniacal" tendencies make it "obvious to any observer" that Noah was "imbued with a Napoleonic spirit" is, it seems to me, to claim far too much. Franz Kobler, *Napoleon and the Jews* (New York, 1975), 190–195.

19.   The Proclamation is most conveniently reprinted in *JUSDH*, III, 894–900. This edition will be used throughout and will be referred to as "Proclamation to the Jews." *Weekly Herald* (June 13, 1840), 212 claimed that George Houston (above, Chapter III, n.35) authored this proclamation, but it seems unlikely.

20.   "Ararat Address," 230–3. On the American reaction to the *hep hep* riots, see *Columbian* (October 28, 1819), 2:3; (December 29, 1819), 2:4; *North American Review*, 12 (January 1821), 226–7; *DHJUS*, 149; and the early numbers of *The German Correspondent* (1820),

available on reel 130 of the American Periodical Series. For the comment of the New York Legislature, see Cone, "New Matter Relating to Mordecai Noah," 132.

21   Monogamy and civilization were closely linked in American thought. Missionaries to the Indians also stressed the need to end polygamy; see Louis Filler and Allan Guttmann, *The Removal of the Cherokee Nation* (New York, 1962), 56. In France, polygamy was also an important issue among Jews and non-Jews, see Francis Malino, *The Sephardic Jews of Bordeaux* (University, Ala., 1978), 35, 75. On the Sanhedrin plan, see Noah to Porter (August 17, 1824), Porter Collection, Buffalo & Erie County Historical Society; "Ararat Address," 251.

22.   The name "New Jerusalem" is found in E. Watson, *History... of the Western Canals in the State of New York*, 104; Benjamin Hart to Moses Hart (May 4, 1820), Hart Family Papers, file J-E-6/2 microfilm 916, AJA; Noah to Porter (August 17, 1824), Porter Collection, Buffalo & Erie County Historical Society. Noah knew of the tradition linking Ararat to the homeland of the lost 10 tribes, based on a misinterpretation of "Arzareth" in IV Ezra (2 Esdras) 13:45, see *T&M* (March 3, 1850), 2:1. Considering his views on the Indians and the lost ten tribes, this might have served as added inducement to use this name. On Arzareth, see W. A. Wright, "Note on Arzareth," *Journal of Philology*, III (1870), 113–14. Marrano interest in Esdras is discussed in Ronald Sanders, *Lost Tribes and Promised Lands* (Boston, 1978), 15, 77–79, 195.

23.   "Proclamation to the Jews," 895. For more on Noah's restoration views, see below Chapter VIII.

24.   Quotes are from Noah to John Q. Adams (July 24, 1820), in *JUSDH*, III, 888–9; and Noah to ? (September 5, 1820), Gratz Collection, Case 6 Box 3, Historical Society of Pennsylvania, also on AJA microfilm 1156; see also "Ararat Address," 236–245.

25.   Quotes are from *Columbian* (January 22, 1820), 2:1; and *JUSDH*, 897; see "Ararat Address," 247; and Jacob R. Marcus, *American Jewry Documents: Eighteenth Century* (Cincinnati, 1959), 204–5, for an eighteenth-century example of the same argument (Alexander Cuming).

26.   Noah to Porter (August 17, 1824), Porter Collection, Buffalo & Erie County Historical Society. See also Erik Erikson's discussion of "optimum ego synthesis to which the individual aspires," *Young Man Luther* (New York, 1962), 254.

27.   There is no good study of early American immigrant colonization efforts, but see Hansen, *Immigrant in American History*, 131–33. Many of these conclusions could be equally well applied to utopian communities, see Charles Nordhuff, *The Communistic Societies of the United States* (New York, 1965 [1864]); Mark Holloway, *Heavens on Earth* (New York, 1966); and on the Colonization Society, see Philip J. Staudenraus, *The African Colonization Movement, 1816–1865* (New York, 1961), esp. 119–22.

28.   S. Joshua Kohn, *The Jewish Community of Utica, New York, 1817–1948* (New York, 1959), 7 and *idem*, "Noah's Ararat Project," reprint this letter.

29.   Quotes are from "Ararat Address," 230, 234. On the missionary colony, see works cited in note 3 *supra* as well as *JUSDH*, III, 714–57. For Noah's direct response to missionaries, see Chapter III, nn. 68–69 and VII nn. 32–35.

30.   "Ararat Address," 233, 235, 249, 230.

31.   "Ararat Address," 244, 232; "Proclamation to the Jews," 896.

32.   *Occident*, I (September, 1843), 301–7, esp. 302; Gordis "Mordecai Noah," 128; see below Chapter VII, n. 23.

33.   "Ararat Address," 234; "Proclamation to the Jews," 895.

34.   Mordecai Noah, *The Grecian Captive, of the Fall of Athens*, (New York, 1822); Richard Moody, *Dramas From the American Theater 1762–1909* (New York, 1966), 117–20; "Ararat Address," 248. See also, Gelber, "Noah," 402.

35.   According to John A. Hostetler, "of hundreds of recorded attempts to establish communal societies in North America, the Hutterites are the only group that has managed not only to survive but to expand and prosper." The Hutterites are anomalous precisely because they

reject all integration into the larger society. They maintain their identity via strict segregation and studied isolation. John A. Hostetler, *Hutterite Society* (Baltimore, 1974), quote from p. 1.

36. My analysis owes much to Claude Levi-Strauss, *Structural Anthropology* (New York, 1963); and Robert K. Merton, *Sociological Ambivalence and Other Essays* (New York, 1976).

37. *Erie Gazette*, 6 (September 22, 1825), 2:5; *Albany Arguş* (September 23, 1825), 2:4; *Buffalo Emporium* (September 17, 1825), 2; *Black Rock Gazette* (June 21, 1825), 3:4–5; *New York Statesman* (September 24, 1825), 2:2 (quoted); *The Telescope* (October 1, 1825), 70; [Harrisburg, Pa.] *Oracle of Dauphin* (October 1, 1825), 2:1–4; *Evening Post* (September 24, 1825), 2; *American* (September 21, 1825), 2 (quoted); *Niles' Weekly Register*, 29 (October 1, 1825), 69, reprinted in *JUSDH*, 900–902 (quoted); *New York Mirror*, 3 (October 1, 1825), 79 (quoted). On ferment in Western New York, see Whitney R. Cross, *The Burned Over District* (New York, 1950).

38. *American Atheneum*, 1 (1825), 223; *Charleston Courier* reprinted in *The Literary Chronicle and Weekly Review* [London] #339 (November 12, 1825), 732–33; see *NY. Nat. Adv.* (September 30, 1825), 2:1 for Noah's standard response.

39. Quotes are from *NY. Nat. Adv.* (October 18, 1825), 2:2–3; Moses E. Levy to Isaac L. Goldsmid (November 18, 1825) quoted in Jacob Toury, "M.E. Levy's Plan for a Jewish Colony in Florida—1825," *Michael*, 3 (1975), 29; Edgar E. MacDonald (ed.), *The Education of the Heart: The Correspondence of Rachel Mordecai Lazarus and Maria Edgeworth* (Chapel Hill, 1977), 93; Benjamin Gratz to F. B. Blair (February 21, 1833), Blair-Lee Papers, Princeton University, Princeton, N.J.; see also 'Hertz ben Pinchas' in *London Jewish Chronicle* (August 6, 1847), 216b–217a for a retrospective view of American Jewish reaction to Ararat.

40. Noah to Porter (August 17, 1824), Porter Papers, Buffalo & Erie County Historical Society; *NY. Nat. Adv.* (September 30, 1825), 2:1.

41. *Bikkurei Haittim*, 7 (1826), 45–9, translated in part in *JUSDH*, III, 902–5. A. R. Malachi, "Hebrew Sources for Mordecai Manuel Noah's Ararat," *Bitzaron* 41 (December 1959), 78–89. Copies of the Cologna letter were widely reprinted after it appeared in *NY Nat. Adv.* (January 12, 1826), 2:3–4.

42. *NY Nat. Adv.* (September 30, 1825), 2:1; Gelber; "Noah," 394–404 is the best account of world Jewish reaction to Ararat; see also Reissner, *Eduard Gans*, 83–102.

43. *NY Nat. Adv.* (October 4, 1825), 2:1; (October 31, 1825), 2:2; *Evening Post* (October 6, 1825), 2:1; Colden, *Memoir... Canals*, 296, 313; Ronald E. Shaw, *Erie Water West: A History of the Erie Canal 1792–1854* (Lexington, Ky., 1966).

44. Noah to Albion Stewart (October 5, 1825), Noah Papers, AJHS; and the quoted article, *Black Rock Gazette*, (January 24, 1826), 3:5. Later notices of Ararat include *Truth Teller* (February 25, 1826), 62; *American* (November 3, 1828), 2:5; *Niles' Weekly Register*, 41 (November 26, 1831), 287; *New Hampshire Journal (October 1, 1827)*, 2; and Alexander S. Mackenzie, *The American in England* (New York, 1835), II, 25. Even Noah's son Jacob later made sport of Ararat: "The King of the Jews," *American Jews Annual (1888–89), 29–30*. On the later history of Grand Island, see Bingham, "The History of Grand Island." For recent population figures see *1978 Commercial Atlas and Marketing Guide* (Chicago, 1978), 384.

45. Samuel Rezneck, "A Travelling School of Science on the Erie Canal in 1826," *New York History*, 40 (1959), 264 (on Asa Fitch); William L. Stone, "From New York to Niagara: Journal of a Tour, in Part by Canal in 1829," *Historical Society of Buffalo Publications*, 14 (1910), 251; E. S. Abdy, *Journal of a Residence and Tour in the United States of North America from April 1833 to October 1834* (London, 1835), I, 287; James G. Bennett in *Herald* (February 6, 1838), 2:1; (August 21, 1840), 2:2; and A. Nevins (ed.) *Diary of John Q. Adams* (New York, 1928), 552 regarding a July 26, 1843 visit. See also W. D. Howells, *Their Wedding Journey* (ed. John K. Reeves, Bloomington, Indiana, 1968), 89–90. On the history of the shrine, see Lewis F. Allen to Peter B. Porter (May 22, 1834), Peter A. Porter Collection, Buffalo & Erie County Historical Society, document X-5; Allen, "The Founding of Ararat;" Julius Bisno to author (February 22, 1978); and Marion E. Klinge to author (October 7, 1978).

CHAPTER V. Independent Jacksonian

1. Court battles between the two *Advocates* include *Thomas Snowden v. Mordecai M. Noah, John D. Brown and Others*, I Hopkins 347 (1825); and *Snowden v. Mckee and Bell, Evening Post* (January 24, 1825), 1:5–6. See also *Statesman* (February 25, 1825), 4:2; *NY Nat. Adv.* (December 16, 1824), 2:3 and *American* (January 28, 1825), 2:2.

2. Josephus Stuart to Henry Clay (March 15, 1825), and Daniel Brent to Mordecai Noah (September 1, 1825) in James F. Hopkins (ed.) *The Papers of Henry Clay* (Lexington, Ky., 1974) IV, 111, 614; *The People v. E. J. Roberts* printed in *Evening Post* (July 21, 1828), 2:3 and *New York Statesman* (July 23, 1828), 3:2–3; and *August Greele v. M. M. Noah and E. J. Roberts*, printed in *Journal of Commerce* (March 21, 1832), 1:3–4. See also William L. Shulman "The National Advocate 1812–1828" (Unpublished D.Ed., New York, Yeshiva University, 1968), 42–46.

3. Sidney Kobre, *The Development of American Journalism* (Dubuque, 1969), 166.

4. Roberts's attacks are in *NY Nat. Adv.* (July 7–17, 1825). A contemporary wall poster portraying the Noah-Roberts fight is described in Albert M. Friedenberg, "An Interesting Item Concerning Major Mordecai M. Noah," *PAJHS*, 18 (1909), 212 and is portrayed in *PAJHS*, 30 (1926), 251.

5. For Snowden's political and personal attacks on Noah, see *Nat. Adv.* (August 9, 1825), 2:2; (November 20, 1827), 2:1; (July 14, 1828), 2:3; (July 26, 1828), 2:2; (September 19, 1828), 2:3; and (November 15, 1827), 2:2 which is quoted. See also Shulman, "The National Advocate," 47. Noah-Webb battles may be followed in both the *New York Courier* and the *New York Enquirer* (June-November, 1828). See especially *Enq-Country* (June 29, 1828), 1:1, for Noah's fear of an assassination attempt; and *Herald* (May 14, 1836), 1:1 for James G. Bennett's reminiscence of the squabble. James G. Brooks's posters are described in I. C. Pray, *Memoirs of James Gordon Bennett and his Times* (New York, 1855), 94; Webb's threatening letter, Webb to Noah (November 20, 1828) is preserved in Box 1a, Webb Papers, Yale University, New Haven, Ct. See also James L. Crouthamel, *James Watson Webb, A Biography* (Middletown, Ct., 1969), 22, 208–9. Noah responded to personal anti-Jewish attacks from other editors in *NY Nat. Adv.* (September 24, 1825), 2:3 and (October 21, 1825), 2:1. On the Graham duel see *Enq-Country* (December 4, 1827), 1:1; Charles H. Haswell, *Reminiscences of an Octogenarian of the City of New York (1816–1860)* (New York, 1896), 223 which has an incorrect date; and Pray, *Memoirs of Bennett*, 79.

6. Kobre, *American Journalism* 166–67; Crouthamel, *Webb*, 18; and Benjamin Perley Poore, *Perley's Reminiscences of Sixty Years in the National Metropolis* (Philadelphia, 1886), I, 58. The quote is from *Enq.-Country* (November 17, 1827), 2:2.

7. Quote is from *Evening Post* (July 25, 1826), 2:3.

8. "Hancock" pieces appeared in *NY Nat. Adv.* (September–October, 1825). On the *Barker-Eckford* cases, see *N.Y. Nat. Adv.* (February 27–March 1826): *Enq.-Country* (July 28, 1826), 2:3; (August 4, 1826), 2:3; (September 22, 1826), 1:2; *Herald* (June 5, 1849), 4:1; (July 12, 1850), 8:2.

9. On Bloodgood, see *NY Nat. Adv.* (June 7, 1826), 2:1; and *Evening Post* (June 7, 1826), 2:3. The Brown case is reported in *Evening Post* (January 19, 1829), 2:2 which is quoted; and *Enq.-Country* (January 20, 1829), 2:4. Noah inquired about firewood in *NY Nat. Adv.* (May 5, 1826), 2:2 and complained about disturbances in *Enq.-Country* (March 23, 1827), 2:5; (July 27, 1827), 2:2. Praise for the *Enquirer* is quoted from Poore, Perley's *Reminiscences*, 58.

10. The political background for this period is portrayed in Jerome Mushkat, *Tammany: The Evolution of a Political Machine* 1789–1865 (Syracuse, N.Y., 1971), 92–115; and Robert V. Remini, *Martin Van Buren and the Making of the Democratic Party* (New York, 1959), 58–198; see also the more general treatment in *idem, The Election of Andrew Jackson* (New York, 1963). Quote is from *NY Nat. Adv.* (October 5, 1825), 2:2. For Noah's earlier opposition to Jackson, see *Nat. Adv.* (July 15, 1823), 2:1, see also Isaac Harby, "The Presidency," reprinted in *JUSDH* II, 361–66 for Harby's earlier support of Jackson.

11.   For Noah's attacks on the candidates, see *NY Nat. Adv.* (March–October 1825); Hopkins, ed., *Clay Papers*, IV 843, 853, 855; Charles F. Adams, ed., *Memoirs of John Q. Adams Comprising Portions of his Diary from 1795 to 1848* (Philadelphia, 1875), VII, 55; Charles R. King (ed.) *The Life and Correspondence of Rufus King* (New York, 1900), VI, 627–28, 643–44, 647, and Richard Kravel, "Prince Henry of Prussia and the Regency of the United States, 1786," *American Historical Review*, 17 (1911), 44–51.

12.   Noah's private views of Clinton are alluded to in *Columbian* (August 22, 1817), 2:5; *Nat. Adv.* (June 24, 1822), 2:2; and De Witt Clinton, *The Martling Men; or Says I to Myself How is This?* (New York, 1819), 21. The Miller trial was published by L. H. Clarke: *Report of the Trial of an Action on the Case Brought by Silvanus Miller, Esq. Against Mordecai M. Noah, Esq. Editor of the National Advocate for an Alleged Libel* (New York, 1823).

13.   *NY Nat. Adv.* (April 20, 1826), 2:1. Jesse Hoyt to Martin Van Buren (June 11, 1826), Van Buren Papers, reprinted in Albert M. Friedenberg, "The Correspondence of Jews with President Martin Van Buren," *PAJHS*, 22 (1914), 79–80; *NY Nat. Adv.* (June 19, 1826), 2:4.

14.   This dispute has its counterpart in the literature on Jacksonian era politics. Some scholars claim that the presidential race dominated all political maneuverings of the day. Others see state politics as predominant. As in so many cases, both are partly in the right and both are in the wrong. Richard M. McCormick, *The Second American Party System* (Chapel Hill, N.C., 1966); and Alvin Kass, *Politics in New York State 1800–1830* (Syracuse, N.Y., 1965).

15.   *Enq.-Country* (November 14, 1826), 3:3 is quoted; see *Evening Post* (November 3, 1826), 2:3; *ES* (June 28, 1838), 2:1; *Union* (July 28, 1842), 2:1; Hopkins (ed.) *Clay Papers*, VI, 207, 764, 876, 885; R. V. Remini, *The Age of Jackson* (New York, 1972), 3–7; and William L. Mackenzie, *The Life and Times of Martin Van Buren* (Boston, 1846), 201, 203.

16.   On Noah's opposition to Webster, see the *Boston Courier* and *Enq.* (June–September 1826) as well as William Lloyd Garrison's comment in Walter Merrill (ed.) *The Letters of William Lloyd Garrison*, vol. I (Cambridge, 1971), 43. *Evening Post* (December 24, 1827), 2:5 describes the Jackson dinner.

17.   Quotes are from *Enq.-Country* (March 30, 1827), 1:1; and Van Buren to C. C. C. Cambreleng (October 23, 1827) reprinted in Friedenberg, "Correspondence with Van Buren," 80–81, cf. Remini, *Van Buren*, 158, 191 (Professor Remini erroneously believes that the *Courier and Enquirer* had already merged in 1827). The recent literature on Antimasonry is summarized in Robert Formisano and Kathleen S. Kutolowski, "Antimasonry and Masonry: The Genesis of Protest, 1826–1827," *American Quarterly* 29 (Summer 1977), 139–65. For evidence that Noah was a Mason, see Samuel Oppenheim, "The Jews and Masonry in the United States before 1810," *PAJHS*, 19 (1910), 1 n.1. Noah later adopted a more prudent, negative view of Masonry, see *ES-Country* (January 2, 1836), 1:1.

18.   The same practical constraints prevented James Gordon Bennett of the *New York Herald* from getting married until he was forty. Oliver Carlson, *The Man Who Made News: James Gordon Bennett* (New York, 1942), 208.

19.   For Noah's discussion of bachelors, see *Nat. Adv.* (March 5, 1821), 2:3; (February 11, 1826), 2:3; *Enq.-Country* (February 2, 1827), 3:2; *Norwich Courier* (February 7, 1827), 5; *Sun* (January 24, 1835), 2:1; "A Bashful Man," *New York Mirror*, 12 (March 7, 1835), 282–3; "The Bachelor and the Married Man," *New York Mirror*, 14 (December 17, 1836), 199; *ES-Country* (February 19, 1836), 2:2; quotes are from *Nat. Adv.* (April 4, 1822), 2:1; and *T&M* (April 5, 1846), 2:3.

20.   On Daniel Jackson, see *DHJUS*, 611; Malcolm H. Stern, "The 1820s: American Jewry Comes of Age," in *Marcus Festschrift*, 548 n. 15; Israel Goldstein, *A Century of Judaism in New York* (New York, 1930), 53–55, 58, 60, 70, 90; William L. Mackenzie, *The Lives and Opinions of Benjamin Franklin and Jesse Hoyt* (New York, 1845), 88, 100, 127–8 (which may also refer to another Daniel Jackson); and I Edwards Chancery 605 where a Noah-Jackson business connection is revealed. On marriage patterns among early New York Jews, see Malcolm H. Stern, "Two Studies in the Assimilation of Early American Jewry," (Unpublished D.H.L. thesis,

Hebrew Union College, 1958),69–93; *idem*, "The Function of Genealogy in American Jewish History" in Jacob Marcus, (ed.) *Essays in American Jewish History* (Cincinnati, 1958), 69–93; and for a notice of Noah's marriage, see Barnett A. Elzas, *Jewish Marriage Notices from the Newspaper Press of Charleston, S. C. (1775–1906)* (New York, 1917), 14. The Phillips' quotes are in *Major Noah*, 220. Comments on Rebecca Noah's beauty are from *Atlas* (March 30, 1851).

21. Noah to Clinton (November 27, 1827), Clinton Papers, Columbia University, N.Y.

22. *Enq.-Country* (February 22, 1828), 2:2; W. R. Swift to Andrew Jackson (April 8, 1828) in John S. Bassett (ed.) *Correspondence of Andrew Jackson* (Washington, 1928–33), III, 397–98. See also Remini, *Van Buren*, 167–69; Mushkat, *Tammany*, 109–11.

23. Bassett (ed.) *Correspondence of Jackson*, III, 455–57 and *The New London Gazette and General Advertiser* (July 16, 1828), 3:1. Noah's letter to Jarvis (August 21, 1828) is in the Russell Jarvis Papers, Manuscript Division, LC.

24. For attacks on Noah, see the broadside entitled "A Mirror for Politicians," found in the Massachusetts Historical Society, as well as *New Hampshire Journal* (October 8, 1827), 1:6; *Nat. Adv.* (September 14, 1827), 2:1; *American* (March 22, 1828), 2:3; (December 15, 1828), 2:1; and William C. Bryant II and Thomas G. Voss, *The Letters of William Cullen Bryant* (New York, 1975), I, 268. On the general subject of journalism in the 1828 election, see Remini, *Van Buren*, 164; *idem*, *The Election of Andrew Jackson*, 76–80; and Culver H. Smith, "Propaganda Techniques in the Jacksonian Campaign of 1828," *East Tennessee Historical Society Publications*, 6, (1934), 44–46.

25. Quote is from Noah to Van Buren (October 2, 1828) in Friedenberg, "Correspondence with Van Buren," 81–2.

26. *American* (October 24, 1828), 2:3; *New York Courier* quoted in Crouthamel, *James Watson Webb*, 22 and *National Advocate* (November 3, 1828), 2:2. See also all New York papers, October 29–November 4, 1828.

27. *Enq.-Country* (October 28–November 7, 1828), and Mushkat, *Tammany* 113–14.

28. Marvin Meyers, *The Jacksonian Persuasion Politics and Belief* (New York, 1957). On the reaction to Noah's defeat, see Crouthamel, *Webb*, 22; Mackenzie, *Martin Van Buren*, 205; and John C. Hamilton to Martin Van Buren (March 3, 1829), in Friedenberg, "Correspondence of Van Buren," 83.

29. "Major Noah," *New Hampshire Patriot and State Gazette*, 20 (November 10, 1828), 3:4.

30. New York [City] Common Council, *Minutes of the Common Council of the City of New York 1784–1831* (New York, 1930), XVII, 633 (February 9, 1829); *American* (December 29, 1828), 2:5, Bryant, ed., *Letters of Bryant*, I, 271 and Bassett (ed.) *Correspondence of Jackson*, IV, 27 all deal with Noah's pre-surveyorship patronage.

31. The story of the Jacksonian editors' visit to Washington is frequently told; see, for example, Pray, *Memoirs of Bennett*, 100. Noah's appointment is listed in Edgar S. Werner, *Civil List and Constitutional History of the Colony and State of New York* (Albany, 1889), 180. Van Buren's attitude toward Noah's appointment is disputed by historians. For other views, see Mushkat, *Tammany*, 115–16, and Mackenzie, *Van Buren*, 214. My account is based on Duff Green to Noah (April 21, 1829), Green Papers, LC; Martin Van Buren to Andrew Jackson (April 23, 1829), Bassett (ed.) *Correspondence of Jackson*, IV, 27; Jonathan I. Coddington to Jesse Hoyt (February 13, 1829; March 29, 1829) in Mackenzie, *Van Buren*, 209, 213; Noah's retrospect in *ES* (June 23, 1834), 2:2; and *Enq.-Country* (May 1, 1829), 2:1, in which Noah announced his nomination for the office. On Calhoun's friendship for Noah, see Coleman to Hamilton (March 18, 1829) in James A. Hamilton, *Reminiscences of James A. Hamilton* (New York, 1869), 127.

32. I have published documents dealing with this case in my "A German-Jewish Immigrant's Perception of America, 1853–54: Some Further Notes on Mordecai M. Noah, A Jewel Robbery, and Isaac M. Wise," *American Jewish History*, 68 (1978), 206–12.

33. Leonard White, *The Jacksonians: A Study in Administrative History* (New York, 1954), 106–7; *ES* (June 23, 1834), 2:3; *New Hampshire Patriot and State Gazette* (November 10, 1828), 3:4; William Price, *Clement Falconer, or the Memoirs of a Young Whig* (2nd ed., Baltimore, 1847), II, 7. The quoted document is from the private collection of Mr. Julius Bisno, who was kind enough to place it at my disposal.

34. *Enq.-Country* (May 5, 1829), 1:1; Ritchie to Noah (March 25, 1829; April 11, 1829) in Mackenzie, *Van Buren*, 214–15; Pray, *Memoirs of Bennett*, 116; and Claude G. Bowers, *The Party Battles of the Jacksonian Period* (New York, 1828), 80–86; cf. B. R. Brubaker, "Spoils Appointments of American Writers," *New England Quarterly*, (1975), 556–64.

35. *ES* (August 5, 1834), 2:2; Noah to Webb (n.d.), Webb Papers, box 1a, Yale University; Culver H. Smith, *The Press, Politics and Patronage: The American Government's Use of Newspapers 1789–1875* (Athens, Ga., 1977) especially 95–96; *Noah v. Webb*, I Edwards Chancery 604; Pray, *Memoirs of Bennett*, 105–6, 207; Mushkat, *Tammany*, 120; and Crouthamel, *Webb*, 30.

36. *C&E* (May 23, 1829), 2:1; (March 22, 1830), 2:1; (October 11, 1832), 2:2 which is quoted; Noah-Webb correspondence in Webb Papers (esp. May 27, 1830), Yale University; and Duff Green to Noah (August 20, 1829), Green Papers, LC. The organization and staff of the *Courier and Enquirer* is briefly discussed in Haswell, *Reminiscences*, 265; F. L. Mott, *American Journalism 1690–1960* (New York, 1962), 225; Crouthamel, *Webb*, 30–33; and Thomas Govan, *Nicholas Biddle: Nationalist and Public Banker 1786–1844* (Chicago, 1959), 155.

37. James Kent, *The Charter of the City of New York With Notes Thereon Also a Treatise on the Powers and Duties of the Mayor, Alderman and Assistant Alderman and the Journal of the City Convention* (New York, 1836), 223–347; Mushkat, *Tammany*, 120.

38. Nathan M. Kaganoff, "Observations on America-Holy Land Relations in the Period Before World War I," in Moshe Davis (ed.) *With Eyes Toward Zion* (New York, 1977), 79–80, 202–6; James Hamilton, *Reminiscences* 144–5, 173; Walter L. Wright Jr. "Rhind, Charles," *Dictionary of American Biography* VIII (1935), 529–30.

39. *Herald* (January 28, 1839), 2:1; Mackenzie, *Van Buren*, 216.

40. Noah to J. N. Barker (October 5, 1829), Collection 8983, University of Virginia; Noah to Duff Green (March 28, 1830); Mackenzie, *Van Buren*, 216, 219.

41. *New York Public Library Bulletin*, 3 (1899), 331–2; Solomon Lincoln Jr., "Letters to John Brazer Davis," *Proceedings of the Massachusetts Historical Society*, 49 (1916), 220; James Campbell to Nathan Sanford (April 27, 1830); Stephen Allen to Nathan Sanford (April 27, 1830) in RG59, Letters of Application and Recommendation During the Administration of Andrew Jackson (microcopy 639 roll 5), NA; Daniel Webster to Marion Dutton (May 7, 1830), Webster Collection, Dartmouth College; Duff Green to Noah (March 24, 1830), Green Papers, LC; *Niles' Weekly Register* (1830), 105–12, 169, 229; Noah-Webb Letters, mostly undated, in Webb Papers, Yale University; and *Journal of the Executive Proceedings of the Senate*, IV, 46, 78, 82, 90, 101.

42. *Journal of the Executive Proceedings of the Senate* IV, 106–7; 113–4; *Lincoln*, "Letters to J. B. Davis," 222; *PAJHS*, 23 (1915), 120; Mackenzie, *Butler and Hoyt*, 88; and Smith, *Press, Politics and Patronage*, 129.

43. Andrew Jackson's view of Noah is evident from the quoted letter of Noah to James Watson Webb (n.d. [May 1831]), Box 1a, Webb Papers, Yale University; see also Andrew Jackson to J. A. Hamilton (April 16, 1832) in Hamilton, *Reminiscences*, 244–45. For Noah's efforts to help his friends, see the quoted letter of Charles Sealsfeld to David B. Warden (May 29, 1831), Warden Papers, Md. Historical Society; also, Noah to W. B. Lewis (November 1, 15, 1831), Noah Papers, Morristown National Historical Park, Morristown, N.J.; Noah to E. Hayward (April 6, 1832), printed in Robert F. Batchelder, *Autograph Catalogue #16* (1976), 1; Noah to R. Livingston (July 7, 1831) in RG59, Miscellaneous Letters of the Department of State (M179), NA; and Abram Kanof "Uriah Philips Levy: The Story of a Pugnacious Commodore," *PAJHS* 39 (1941), 58.

44. The *Troy Budget* once referred to the railroad as a plan "begotten by a Jew, born of a Jew, owned by Jews." Mordecai Noah denied this charge, but it is nevertheless true that among the petitioners for the railroad one finds the names of Daniel Jackson, J. Phillips, David S. Lyon, Jacob Isaacs, John I. Hart, and, of course, Noah's own. *ES* (April 16, 1835), 2:3; *Evening Post* (April 3, 1833), 2:2.

45. *Acts of Incorporation of the New York and Harlem Railroad Co. 1831–1853 With Proposals for Preferred Stock 1848 and Report on the Albany Extension 1850* (New York, 1855); Noah to Azariah Flagg (May 7, 1831), Noah Papers, AJHS; James W. Webb to Martin Van Buren (April 12, 1831) in Friedenberg, "Correspondence with Van Buren," 85; Joseph R. Greene Jr., "New York City's First Railroad, the New York and Harlem 1832 to 1867," *New York Historical Society Quarterly Bulletin*, 9 (January 1926), 107–23.

46. Noah to Azariah Flagg (May 7, 1831), Noah Papers AJHS (quoted); Noah to Judge Moran (April 9, 1832), Gratz Collection, Historical Society of Pennsylvania, also on AJA microfilm 1156; *C&E* (April 4, 1831), 2:1; *Niles' Weekly Register* (April 9, 1831), 95; *Report of the Committee of the House of Representatives at the 1st Session of the 22nd Congress*, IV (1831), report #460; and Crouthamel, *Webb*, 37–8.

47. Noah to Webb in Box 1a, Webb Papers, Yale University; see also James Watson Webb to Martin Van Buren (April 12, 1831) in Friedenberg, "Correspondence of Van Buren," 85–6 (note that the editor mistakenly printed Tyler for Tylee).

48. Noah to Webb (n.d.) Webb Papers, Yale University, and Noah to Judge Moran (April 9, 1832), Gratz Papers, Historical Society of Pennsylvania, also on AJA microfilm 1156, which is quoted. For Van Buren's earlier view of Noah, see Hamilton, *Reminiscences*, 144; *ES* (August 3, 1834), 2:2; and Bennett's diary as cited in Mushkat, *Tammany*, 135.

49. Works on the Bank War which are of particular relevance to Noah include: Ralph C. H. Catterall, *The Second Bank of the United States* (Chicago, 1903), 258–63; Frank O. Gatell, "Sober Second Thoughts on Martin Van Buren, The Albany Regency and the Wall Street Conspiracy," *Journal of American History*, 53 (June 1966), 19–32; Thomas Govan, *Nicholas Biddle: Nationalist and Public Banker 1786–1844* (Chicago, 1959), 144–204; James L. Crouthamel, "Did the Second Bank of the United States Bribe the Press?" *Journalism Quarterly*, 36 (1959), 35–44; *idem*, Webb, 34–47; the far more negative treatment in Leonard I. Gappelberg, "M. M. Noah and the Evening Star: Whig Journalism 1833–1840" (Unpublished Ed.D. thesis, Yeshiva University, 1970), 102–48; and Bruce I. Ambacher, "Urban Response to Jacksonian Democracy: Philadelphia Democrats and the Bank War 1832–1834," in Margaret F. Morris and Elliot West (ed.) *Essays on Urban America* (Austin, 1973), 21–54.

50. For Noah's earlier views, see *Nat. Adv.* (December–January, 1818–19, especially December 24th) and (May–July 1822, especially July 29th); quote is from (July 10, 1822), 2:3. For Van Buren's changing views on the Bank, see Mackenzie, *Van Buren*, 88, 113 and R. L. Colt to Nicholas Biddle (December 14, 1829), Biddle Papers, LC (microfilm edition has been used throughout).

51. R. L. Colt, a Baltimore friend and relative of Bank president Nicholas Biddle, believed that Noah was also influenced by the fact that the "Cohen Brothers Israelites are not friendly to the Bank." I know of no evidence suggesting that Colt was actually correct. R. L. Colt to Nicholas Biddle (April 15, 1830), Biddle Papers.

52. While most people believed that Noah wrote the anti-Bank editorials in the *Courier and Enquirer*, they were actually authored by James Gordon Bennett. When Bennett proudly revealed this fact, in 1832, he failed to disclose that while reviling the Bank publicly, he secretly served as a paid informer for Bank president Nicholas Biddle. For over a year Bennett provided Biddle with valuable political information; he even suggested to Biddle ways of thwarting anti-Bank forces. Bennett admitted to the authorship of the articles in *C&E* (February 2, 1832), 2:2; see also Pray, *Memoirs of Bennett*, 178. On Bennett's secret relationship to Biddle, see Govan, *Biddle*, 153–4; Mushkat, *Tammany*, 119; and Bennett's letters themselves, especially Bennett to Biddle (September 25, 1830), Biddle Papers.

53.   On the early attitude of *C&E* to the Bank, see Pray, *Memoirs of Bennett*, 111, 148; Govan, *Biddle*, 125; Gappelberg, "M. M. Noah," 103; and William Stickney (ed.) *Autobiography of Amos Kendall*(Boston, 1872), 178.

54.   *C&E*'s later attitude toward the Bank is detailed in Crouthamel, *Webb*, pp. 36—38 (the date "April 1831" on p. 36 should read April 1830); Alexander Hamilton to Nicholas Biddle (April 9, 1830), Biddle Papers; *C&E* (April 13, 1831), 2:2; *C&E-Country* (December 3, 1831), 2:2; (December 22, 1831), 2:2; and (March 15, 1832), 2:1. On the Burrows loan see above and the Burrows-Biddle Correspondence (1830) in the Biddle Papers.

55.   Quote is from W. B. Lawrence to Nicholas Biddle (February 10, 1831), see also Lawrence to Biddle (April 16, 1831), both in Biddle Papers.

56.   Samuel Swartwout to Nicholas Biddle (June 15, 1831, see also May 31, 1831 and December 17, 1831) in Biddle Papers.

57.   On the charges levelled against the *Courier and Enquirer*, see Silas Burrows to Nicholas Biddle (April 12, 15, 1831), Biddle Papers; James W. Webb to Martin Van Buren (April 12, 1831) in Friedenberg, "Correspondence of Van Buren," 85–6; Noah to Webb (n.d.) in Webb Papers, Yale University; *C&E* (April 16, 1831), 2:2; and *Niles' Weekly Register* (May 14, 1831), 183.

58.   Richard Latner hypothesizes that pro-Bank forces wanted Noah to replace the anti-Bank Francis Blair as editor of the *Washington Globe* during this period. While I know of no evidence to support this allegation, it is true that anti-Bank editor James Gordon Bennett was invited to purchase one half interest in the financially ailing *Globe* in late 1832. Nothing came of the deal. Richard B. Latner, "A New Look at Jacksonian Politics," *Journal of American History*, 61 (March 1975), 943–69; James G. Bennett to Nicholas Biddle (December 1, 1832), Biddle Papers.

59.   22nd Congress, *House Report 460*; Noah to Charles J. Ingersoll (August 5, 1831), Historical Society of Pennsylvania; *C&E-Country* (November 21, 1831), 2:1; Mackenzie, *Van Buren*, 230; Nicholas Biddle to James W. Webb (November 13, 1831); James W. Webb to Nicholas Biddle (January 4, 1832), Biddle Papers; Hamilton, *Reminiscences*, 235–6.

60.   On April 16, 1832, Andrew Jackson wrote to James A. Hamilton: "I received your last of the 11th instant and sincerely regretted to hear of the melancholy attack of Mr. Noah—hope he has recovered, as I have heard nothing from him since." Gappelberg has ingeniously suggested that Noah's melancholy attack was brought on by his discovery that the Bank lay behind the Burrows loan. Unfortunately, there is no other evidence to support this theory; nor is it clear to me that a "melancholy attack" is the same as an attack of melancholy. More likely, Jackson was referring to an attack of paralysis that Noah retrospectively described several years later. Gappelberg also notes that Noah remained on good terms with Burrows in spite of the deceptive loan. Burrows later received a free subscription to Noah's *Evening Star*. Hamilton, *Reminiscences*, 244; Gappelberg, "M. M. Noah," 112, 117; *ES* (February 4, 1834), 2:2.

61.   Quotes are from (in order) James Watson Webb to Nicholas Biddle (March 15, 1832; March 5, 1832) and Silas Burrows to Nicholas Biddle (March 19, 1832) all in Biddle Papers.

62.   On the reaction to the Clayton Report, see Crouthamel, *Webb*, 43; Mushkat, *Tammany*, 138–9; *Evening Post* (April 11, 20, May 2, May 4, 1832); (October 26, 1832), 2:1–2; and the quoted letters, James A. Hamilton to Andrew Jackson (May 7, 1832), in Bassett (ed.) *Correspondence of Jackson*, IV, 437; Noah to Judge Moran (April 19, 1832), Gratz Collection, Historical Society of Pennsylvania, also on AJA Microfilm 1156. Noah summarized his former view of the Bank in *C&E* (October 18, 1832), 2:2.

63.   Noah to James W. Webb (July 2, 1832), box 1a, Webb Papers, Yale University; A. Stewart to Webb (July 3, 1832) and Webb to Biddle (July 8, 1832) in Biddle Papers.

64.   Webb to Biddle (July 13 [quoted], July 16, August 1, August 5, August 12, August 14, August 19, August 24, 1832), Biddle Papers; *Niles' Weekly Register* (September 1, 1832), 11–12; Allan Nevins (ed.) *The Diary of Philip Hone 1828–1851* (New York, 1927), 72; Hudson, *Journalism in the United States*, 345; and Crouthamel, *Webb*, 33, 43–47. The *U. S. Telegraph*

(September 11, 1832), 3:4 prints Noah's negative reply to a petition inviting him to begin a new newspaper.

65. *C&E* (October 18, 1832), 2:2; *Herald* (December 5, 1836), 2:3; *C&E* (January 27, 1837), 2:1; (February 1, 1837), 2:1; (December 12, 1837), 2:3. Noah to Webb (n.d. [1839]). Noah to William Henry Harrison (February 16, 1841), in Webb Papers, Yale University; and Noah's quoted comment in *New York Mirror* 4 (June 20 1846), 171.

66. John S. Jenkins, *History of Political Parties in the State of New York* (New York, 1846), 388; Mushkat, *Tammany*, 143; and Edgar Werner, *Civil List and Constitutional History of New York*, 180.

67. Noah to Abner Dickins (July 15, 1833), Miscellaneous Papers, New York Public Library; see also *ES* (June 23, 1834), 2:3; *Truth Teller* (July 16, 1836), 230.

68. *American* (May 4, 1841), 2:2.

CHAPTER VI. Conservative Whig

1. Leonard I. Gappelberg, "M. M. Noah and the Evening Star: Whig Journalism 1833–1840," (Unpublished Ed.D thesis, Yeshiva University, 1970); and Leo Hershkowitz, "New York City, 1834–1840: A Study in Local Politics" (Unpublished Ph.D. thesis, New York University, 1960) are basic secondary sources for this period in Noah's life.

2. *Noah and Another v. Webb and Others*, I Edwards 604; *Dairy of William Dunlap* (New York, 1930), III, 667–8, 680; Gappelberg, "Noah," 96–7.

3. A penny paper called the *Morning Star* appeared from March 21–May 1, 1834, and another of the same name published in late 1836. There is no evidence that Noah had any connections with either of these unsuccessful ventures. In 1836, Noah did suggest that he might begin to produce a penny sheet called *Noah's Ark*, but he soon abandoned the idea, and instead commenced a campaign of attacks against cheap newspapers. A file of the 1834 *Morning Star* is in the American Antiquarian Society. On the 1836 *Star*, see Gappelberg, "Noah,' 48; and Frank M. O'Brien, *Story of the Sun* (New York, 1918), 134. See also *ES* (October 3, 1836), 2:2.

4. On Noah's journalism during this period, see Gappelberg, "Noah," 25–59; James L. Crouthamel deals with what he calls the "newspaper revolution in New York," in an article under that title in *New York History*, 45 (April 1964), 91–113 and in his book, *James Watson Webb: A Biography* (Middletown, Ct., 1969), 67–81; see also T. H. Giddings, "Rushing the Transatlantic News in the 1830's and 1840's," *New York Historical Society Quarterly*, 42 (1958), 47–58. On the *New York Sun*, see O'Brien, *The Story of the Sun*, 1–24; and on the *Herald*, see below Chapter VII, as well as Wallace B. Eberhard, "Mr. Bennett Covers a Murder Trial," *Journalism Quarterly*, 47 (Autumn, 1970), 457–63. More generally, see Harvey Saalberg, "Bennett and Greeley, Professional Rivals, Had Much in Common," *Journalism Quarterly*, 49 (Autumn, 1972), 538–46. Quotations are from Henry S. Foote, *Casket of Reminiscences* (Washington, D.C., 1874), 41; *ES-Country* (September 15, 1836), 2:2 and (March 10, 1837), 2:2.

6. On the profits of the *Star*, see Gappelberg, "Noah," 99.

7. Quote is from M. M. Noah and Thomas Gill, *Prospectus of the Evening Star*, (New York, 1833), 16; see *JUSDH*, II, 370–75.

8. Richard B. Latner, "The Kitchen Cabinet and Andrew Jackson's Advisory System," *Journal of American History*, 65 (September 1978), 367–88; Leon Festinger, *When Prophecy Fails* (New York, 1956).

9. Quotes are from *Albany Argus* (September 17, 1833); and *Washington Globe* (October 3–4, 1833) both in Gappelberg, "Noah," 6, 20; and from *ES* (September 25, 1834), 2:2.

10. On politics in this period see Jerome Mushkat, *Tammany: The Evolution of a Political Machine 1789–1865* (Syracuse, N.Y., 1971), 143–57. Gappelberg, "Noah," 5–6, 19–20.

11. *United States Telegraph* (September 11, 1832), 3:4–5; *ES-Country* (June 5, 1835), 2:2;

ES (January 18, 1837), 2:1; and *ES-Country* (March 7, 1837), 2:6. For Jackson's view of Noah, see John S. Bassett (ed.) *Correspondence of Andrew Jackson* (Washington, D.C., 1933), V, 183, 481 and VI, 53.

12. Elliot R. Barkan, "The Emergence of a Whig Persuasion: Conservatism, Democratism and the New York State Whigs," *New York History*, 52 (October, 1971), 376–95; R. P. Formisano, "Political Character, Antipartyism and the Second Party System" *American Quarterly*, 21 (1969), 383–409; Lynn L. Marshall, "The Strange Stillbirth of the Whig Party," *American Historical Review*, 72 (1966–67), 445–68; G. G. Van Deusen, "Some Aspects of Whig Thought and Theory in the Jacksonian Period," *American Historical Review*, 63 (January 1958), 305–22; and *idem*, "The Whig Party," in Arthur M. Schlesinger (ed.) *The History of the United States Political Parties* (New York, 1973), 333–63. The quote is from *Diary of William Dunlap*, III, 667–8 (orthography modernized). For Noah's suggested political reforms see Noah and Gill, *Prospectus of Evening Star*, 12, 15.

13. Noah discussed the schism in Whig ranks most clearly in an undated letter to James W. Webb (wrongly dated to 1839) in Webb Papers, Yale University; as well as in Noah to Seward (November 30, 1839), Gratz Collection, Historical Society of Pennsylvania (also AJA microfilm 1156) and in Noah to Bloodgood (April 30, 1840), Seward Papers, University of Rochester; see also *ES* (October 28, 1839), 2:1; and *Herald* (January 27, 1840), 2:1. On Jewish Whigs, see the quoted sources, Jonathan Punkin, *Downfall of Freemasonry* (New York, 1838), 21–2; *Herald* (April 16, 1838), 2:4; (October 15, 1840), 2:3 and (April 13, 1841), 2:4; as well as *ES* (April 4, 1834), 2:1. See also Frank O. Gatell, "The Anti-Jacksonian Animus of Rich Men," in Edward Pessen, *New Perspectives on Jacksonian Parties and Politics* (Boston, 1969), 104 which notes that all seven Jews listed in Moses Beach's 1845 directory of the wealthiest men in New York were Whigs.

14. Robert W. July, *The Essential New Yorker: Gulian Crommelin Verplanck* (Durham, N.C., 1951), 190; *ES* (September 14, 1834), 2:2; Noah to Seward (March 15, 1838), Gratz Collection, Historical Society of Pennsylvania, (also on AJA microfilm 1156).

15. *ES* (February 1835–November 1836). Noah's headline appeared on November 8, 1836 and was reprinted in *ES-Country* (November 11, 1836), 2:1. See also *Erie Gazette* (September 15, 1836), 2:3.

16. Quote is from *ES* (November 29, 1836), 1:1; see Marshall, "Strange Stillbirth of the Whig Party"; Peter Temin, *The Jacksonian Economy*, (New York, 1969); and James C. Curtis, *The Fox at Bay: Martin Van Buren and the Presidency 1837–1841 (Lexington, 1970).*

17. *Quote is from ES* (April 13, 1839), 2:1; cf. *ES-Country* (November 15, 1836), 1:1; *ES* (June 23, 1834), 2:3; and *ES* (March 19, 26, 28, 1838).

18. *ES*, 1838–39; Noah to S. D. Bloodgood (April 30, 1840) in Seward Papers, University of Rochester; *Herald* (July 20, 1839), 2:3; *Truth Teller*, 8 (1837), 223, 246; Noah to Richard P. Smith (December 10, 1837), Rare Book Collection, University of Pennsylvania Library, Philadelphia, Pa.; and *American* (November 30, 1837), 2:1.

19. E. Malcolm Carroll, *Origins of the Whig Party*, (Durham, 1925), 187; Van Deusen, "Some Aspects of Whig Thought," and Barkan, "The Emergence of a Whig Persuasion." Cf. Arthur C. Cole, *The Whig Party in the South* (Washington, D.C., 1913).

20. For Noah's identification with the old school, see *Enq.-Country* (January 25, 1828), 2:7. Noah's calls for a weaker central government include *ES* (November 27, 1833), 2:1 and (August 23, 1834), 2:1 which is quoted. On constitutional change, see *ES-Country* (May 12, 1837), 2:1; and (July 4, 1837), 1:3. Noah's articles supporting peace and opposing mobs include *ES* (February 20, 1835), 2:1; (March 2, 1835), 2:2; (January 9, 1836), 2:2; (November 29, 1837), 2:1; and the quoted article *ES-Country* (August 14, 1835), 2:1. See also Gappelberg, "Noah," 188–218, and Noah's earlier views on war in *Nat. Adv.* (July 24, 1817), 2:1; (October 11, 1817), 2:1 and (October 19, 1817), 2:1.

21. Quotations are from M. M. Noah, "Fashionable Parties and Late Hours," *Poughkeepsie Casket*, 1 (February 13, 1836), 27, also in *Southern Literary Messenger*, 1 (February 1835),

357–8; *ES-Country* (February 5, 1836), 2:2; M. M. Noah, "Attending Auctions," in Walter Percival (ed.) *Friendship's Gift* (Boston, 1848), 146, also in *Poughkeepsie Casket*, 1 (April 23, 1836), 70; *ES* (November 11, 1834), 2:2.

22. The noted reformer, Arthur Tappan, used Noah's writings on unfermented wine to corroborate his theory that "the wine created at the marriage at Cana must have been unfermented." Interestingly, the issue of raisin wine arose again in the twentieth century during prohibition. The great rabbinic authority, Louis Ginzberg, cited the raisin wine practice as part of his responsum permitting Jews to use unfermented grape juice for ritual functions which called for wine. From the point of view of Jewish law, however, raisin wine is by no means required on Passover. Its use may reflect a residual marrano tradition brought to New York from Holland. Lewis Tappan, *The Life of Arthur Tappan* (New York, 1870), 105. For Louis Ginzberg's responsum, see *American Jewish Year Book*, 25 (1923–4), 401–25, esp. 415, 423, 425; and *Conservative Judaism*, 8 (April 31, 1952), 23–4; see also Eli Ginzberg, *Keeper of the Law* (Philadelphia, 1966), 221. Professor Haym Soloveitchik advises me that he knows offhand of no rabbinic sources alluding to the custom of raisin wine on Passover. Indeed, several rabbis opposed the use of nonfermented wine for ritual purposes.

23. Quotations are from *ES-Country* (July 24, 1835), 3:2; (February 19, 1836), 2:6; *Tri-Weekly Journal*, Augusta, Maine (February 25, 1836), 3:2 and Philip S. White and H. R. Pleasants, *The War of Four Thousand Years* (Philadelphia, 1846), 293–5.

24. *New York Mirror*, 17 (1839), 285 and *ES-Country* (February 12, 1836), 2:2, both quoted, as well as *ES-Country* (February 19, 1836), 2:1; and *T&M* (August 8, 1847), 2:2. On the general debate over the biblical view of temperance, see William A. Butler, *A Retrospect of Forty Years, 1825–1865* (New York, 1911), 21–25.

25. Quotes are from *ES-Country* (September 11, 1836), 1:3; and (March 31, 1832), 1:1; see also Noah to Seward (September 18, 1834), Seward Papers, University of Rochester; and Samuel Rezneck, "The Social History of an American Depression 1837–1843," *American Historical Review*, 40 (1935), 622–87.

26. *ES-Country* (May 22, 1835), 2:2; (January 20, 1837), 2:2; Gappelberg, "Noah," 229, 233; and *T&M* (March 21, 1847), 2:4 which is quoted. More generally, see David Brion Davis, "Some Themes of Counter-Subversion: An Analysis of Anti-Masonic, Anti-Catholic and Anti-Mormon Literature," *Mississippi Valley Historical Review*, 47 (1960–1), 205–24; as well as Thomas O'Dea, *The Mormons* (Chicago, 1957), 41–75.

27. On Fanny Wright, see *ES* (October 22, 1838), 2:1; on religious imposters, see *ES-Country* (April 21, 1835), 3:4; cf. *Union* (September 9, 1842), 2:1; and on Quakers, see *T&M* (May 3, 1845), 2:1. The anti-rent controversy is discussed in *ES-Country* (November 1, 1836), 1:1; *ES* (December 12, 1839), 2:3; *Herald* (February 9, 1837), 2:2 as well as Thomas P. Govan, "Agrarians and Agrarianism: A Study in the Use and Abuse of Words," *Journal of Southern History*, 30 (1964), 38–9. More generally, see Henry Christman, *Tin Horns and Calico* (New York, 1945); and David M. Ellis, *Landlords and Farmers in Hudson-Mohawk Region* (New York, 1946). *New York Municipal Gazette* (November 30, 1842), 1:2 mentions Noah's sympathy with municipal anti-rent forces.

28. *Herald* (December 25, 1839), 3:5; *Union* (August 19, 1842), 2:2 and *T&M* (September 26, 1847), 2:4. Noah expressed mixed feelings about copyright reforms in Noah to A. Hart (January 14, 1838), Beinecke Library, Yale University.

29. Quote is from *ES-Country* (April 7, 1835), 2:1. From among the vast literature on American nativism during this period, see Ira M. Leonard and Robert D. Parnet, *American Nativism 1830–1860* (New York, 1971) which lists earlier sources; and Ray A. Billington, *The Protestant Crusade 1800–1860: A Study of the Origins of American Nativism* (pb. ed., New York, 1964, 1st ed. 1938).

30. The quotations in this section are from *ES* (October 11, 1833), 2, reprinted in *Truth Teller* (October 19, 1833), 332; and *ES* (March 19, 1835), 2:2. On Noah's knowledge of Catholic persecutions of Jews, see Chapter I, n. 8; as well as *Consecration Address*, p. 46, n. 18;

Truth Teller (May 13, 1826), 150; *Nat. Adv.* (September 19, 1823), 2:1–2; and *Truth Teller* (February 25, 1826), 62. On the Maryland Jew Bill, see *JUSDH*, 44–46; *Nat. Adv.* (January 28, 1819), 2:1; *NY Nat. Adv.* (February 21, 1826), 2:4; Rudolf Glantz, *Jew and Irish* (New York, 1966), 68; and Edward Eitches, "Maryland's Jew Bill," *AJHQ* 60 (March 1971), 274. Noah opposed anti-Catholic tracts in *ES* (March 28, 1835), 2:4; *ES-Country* (April 24, 1835), 2:1; (February 19, 1836), 1:4; (November 1, 1836), 2:2; (January 17, 1837), 2:3; and (April 14, 1837), 2:1. His position was attacked in *Spirit of '76* (April 13, 1835), 10:3, and he drew praise from *Truth Teller* (February 13, 1836), 59; see also Ray A. Billington, "Maria Monk and Her Influence," *Catholic Historical Review*, 22 (October 1936), 283–96. Noah lashed out against anti-Catholic hate mongers in *C&E* (August 8, 1831), 2:1 and *ES* (March 19, 1835), 2:2; and he opposed nativist Samuel Morse's mayoralty bid in *ES-Country* (April 15, 1836), 1:1. Morse's anti-Catholicism, which contrasts sharply with that of Noah, is discussed in Carleton Mabee, *The American Leonardo: A Life of Samuel F. B. Morse* (New York, 1969, 1st ed., 1943), 162–80.

31. Rudolph Glanz, who failed to read Noah's own writings on Catholicism, and Leo Hershkowitz, who misread Noah's writings on the subject declared Noah to have been an anti-Catholic. Hershkowitz writes: "Having fanned the fires of religious bigotry by accounts of a 'holy week' in Rome where 'the scarlet whore is making a great parade of her wardrobe,' Noah reiterated charges that the 'corruptible' Irish were selling their votes...." The original sarcastic paragraph, in Noah's *Evening Star*, reveals Noah's true attitude toward anti-Catholicism:

> Very Decent—The *Post*, which is the dear friend of the Catholics, and begs all their votes for *the* party, published a letter from Rome, from which the following extract is made: "This is holy week, and the 'scarlet whore' is making a great parade of her wardrobe."

Glanz, *Jew and Irish*; Leo Hershkowitz, "The Native American Democratic Association in New York City, 1835–1836," *New York Historical Quarterly*, 46 (1962) 48; *ES* (June 16, 1836), 2:2.

32. Quotations are from *Truth Teller* (May 13, 1826), 150, reprinted in Glanz, *Jew and Irish*, 62; *Nat. Adv.* (March 27, 1824), 2:2; *Truth Teller* (April 24, 1835), 2. For evidence of Noah's awareness of links between the persecution of Catholics and the persecution of Jews, see *Nat. Adv.* (November 6, 1822), 2:2; and *NY Nat. Adv.* (February 21, 1826); as well as the comments in *Truth Teller* (April 4, 1835), 110. The general subject of early Jewish attitudes toward Catholicism has been insufficiently studied. See Moses Hart's "The Ten Commandments of the Roman Catholic Church," file A–F, Hart Family Papers, Three Rivers, Quebec, microfilm at AJA; Charles Reznikoff and Uriah Engelman, *The Jews of Charleston* (Philadelphia, 1950), 108 on M. C. Mordecai; Isaac Leeser, *The Claims of the Jews to an Equality of Rights* (Philadelphia, 1841), 46; Bertram W. Korn, "The Know Nothing Movement and the Jews," *Eventful Years and Experiences* (Cincinnati, 1954), 58–78; and James G. Heller, *Isaac M. Wise: His Life, Work and Thought* (New York, 1965), 622. Noah's views on Catholics and immigrants may be contrasted with those of another Jew, Lewis C. Levin, see John A. Forman, "Lewis Charles Levin: Portrait of an American Demagogue," *AJA*, 11 (October, 1960), 150–90.

33. Quotes are from *Enq-Country* (August 31, 1827) and *Truth Teller* 11 (1835), 197, in Glanz, *Jew and Irish*, 57.

34. Quotes are from *Nat. Adv.* (September 11, 1817), 2:1; and *ES* (October 1, 1835), 2:1; cf. *Nat. Adv.* (July 29, 1820), 2:1; and *Truth Teller* (August 15, 1835), 262.

35. Quotations are from *ES-Country* (June 22, 1835), 1:1; and (June 9, 1835), 2:6. On Noah's interest in Jewish immigration, see *Consecration Address*, 30; *ES-Country* (September 9, 1836), 1:4; *T&M* (June 27, 1847), 2:1 and Chapter IV, *supra*.

36. Regarding the public schools, see Noah to William Seward (August 28, 1840), Historical Society of Pennsylvania, which is quoted; and Seward to Noah (August 29, 1840), Seward Papers, University of Rochester, also reprinted in part in William H. Seward, *An Autobiography from 1801 to 1834*, (New York, 1891); *Nat. Adv.* (April 6, 1824), 2:2; *ES* (March 10, 1840), 2:3; (August 22, 1840), 2:2; *Herald* (October 1, 1840), 2:4 and (October 15, 1840), 2:3. More

generally, see Diane Ravitch, *The Great School Wars* (New York, 1974), 3–78; Vincent P. Lannie, *Public Money and Parochial Education* (Cleveland, 1968), esp. 33, 72; Glyndon G. Van Deusen, "Seward and the School Question Reconsidered," *Journal of American History*, 52 (1965), 313–19; Henry J. Browne, "Public Support of Catholic Education in New York, 1825–1842: Some New Aspects," *Catholic Historical Review*, 39 (1953), 1–27; and Edward Connors, *Church State Relationships in Education in the State of New York* (Washington, D.C., 1951). On the general question of Jews and public schools, see Lloyd P. Gartner, "Temples of Liberty Unpolluted: Jews and Public Schools, 1840–1875," in *Marcus Festschrift*, 157–90.

37. Among those who commented on the peculiarity of a Jew being a nativist were *Columbian* (June 7, 1820), 2:3; *Herald* (September 16, 1842), 2:1, both quoted; and William Mackenzie in *Workingman's Advocate*, 22 (August 24, 1844), 4. See a contemporary response by humorist Jack Downing in *The Rover*, 3 (1844), 351; as well as Crouthamel, *Webb*, 58, 59, 101; and *Truth Teller* (June 27, 1835), 205–6.

38. H. H. Ben Sasson (ed.), *A History of the Jewish People* (Cambridge, 1976), 825–833.

39. The best treatment of this subject is Grappelberg, "Noah," 149–87. Quotes are from *ES-Country* (October 6, 1835), 1:1 and *Sunday Atlas* (May 21, 1848) in Lyons Scrapbook, III, 776, AJHS.

40. Quotations are from *Nat. Adv.* (November 18, 1819), 2:1–2; *Travels*, 40, cf. 423; *Nat. Adv.* (November 22, 1819), 2:1 and (June 3, 1820), 2:3. Noah's earliest mention of race is in his *Shakspeare Illustrated*, I, 76, where he discusses Othello; see also Louis Harap, *The Image of the Jew in American Literature From Early Republic to Mass Immigration* (Philadelphia, 1974), 548. His comments on blacks in England, recorded in *Travels*, were, in later years, quoted back to him, see *Rights of All* (October 9, 1829), 43:3. Noah's views on colonization fluctuated but remained generally positive, see *Nat. Adv.* (October 22,–27, 1817); *NY Nat. Adv.* (June 29, 1826), 2:1; *ES-Country* (May 19, 1835), 1:2; *T&M* (January 23, 1848), 2:6; and (May 5, 1850), 2:1. On colonization generally, see Philip J. Staudenraus, *The African Colonization Movement 1816–1865* (New York, 1961). Noah's opposition to the slave trade never wavered, see his *Essays of Howard*, 210–14; and *Union* (August 25, 1842), 2:1.

41. The basic work on the Missouri Compromise remains Glover Moore's *The Missouri Compromise 1819–1821* (Louisville, Ky., 1953), esp. 190–192; see also Richard H. Brown, "The Missouri Crisis, Slavery and the Politics of Jacksonianism," *South Atlantic Quarterly*, 65 (Winter, 1966), 55–72; Mushkat, *Tammany*, 68–9; and David B. Davis, *The Problem of Slavery in the Age of Revolution* (Ithaca, N.Y., 1975), 163, 340–42. Noah's views may be traced in *Nat. Adv.* (November 1819–February 1821). Quotes are from *Nat. Adv.* (August 24, 1820), 2:2; (June 2, 1820), 2:2; and (April 11, 1820), 2:2; as well as Noah to? (September 5, 1820), Gratz Collection, Historical Society of Pennsylvania (also on AJA microfilm 1156). For Jefferson's view of the Compromise see M. Peterson, *Thomas Jefferson and the New Nation* (New York, 1970), 996; and for that of Martin Van Buren, see, John C. Fitzpatrick, *The Autobiography of Martin Van Buren* (Washington, D.C., 1920), 101, 138. On the question of national union, see Noah's early comment in *Charleston City Gazette* (April 30, 1813), 2:2; as well as his *Oration Delivered by Appointment Before Tammany Society of Columbian Order...* (New York, 1817); *Nat. Adv.* (April 11, 1820), 2:2; (July 11, 1820), 2:1; (November 18, 1820), 2:1; (February 8, 1821), 2:2; (June 7, 1823), 2:1 and (November 8, 1823), 2:2.

42. The freedom/slavery paradox is most fully explored in Edmund Morgan, *American Slavery, American Freedom* (New York, 1975); see also Noah's comment in *ES-Country* September 15, 1835), 1:1.

43. On at least two occasions Noah sided openly with the North, see *Nat. Adv.* (November 20, 1820), 2:1; and *NY Nat. Adv.* (February 18, 1825), 2:1. His pro-South writings are far more voluminous; see particularly, *Nat. Adv.* (October 3, 1821), 2:3; *C&E-Country* (May 14, 1830), 2:6; *ES-Country* (April 14, 1835), 2:1; (August 11, 1835), 3:1; (September 11, 1835), 4:3; (September 18, 1835), 2:1; (September 22, 1835), 2:2; (October 6, 1835), 1:2; (February 23, 1836), 2:1; (February 20, 1837), 2:6; *T&M* (August 6, 1848), 2:3; as well as the quoted comments, *Nat. Adv.* (June 20, 1823), 2:1.

44. Noah and Gill, *Prospectus of the Evening Star*, 14–15; and *ES* (August 11, 1835), 1:1. See also Noah to Asbury Dickins (July 15, 1833), Miscellaneous Papers, New York Public Library; Hammond to Noah (August 19, 1835), Hammond Papers, LC, container 5 (reel 3); and Students of the University of Virginia to Noah (December 8, 1836), University of Virginia Library, Charlottesville, Virginia.

45. Richard W. Smith, "The Career of Martin Van Buren in Connection with the Slavery Controversy Through the Election of 1840," (Unpublished Ph.D. thesis, Ohio State University, 1959), 165–68; *Autobiography of Martin Van Buren*, 101, 138; and Noah to Jesse Hoyt (April 14, 1840) in Van Buren Papers, reprinted in *PAJHS*, 23 (1914), 87–88.

46. On Noah's opposition to Martin Van Buren see *ES-Country* (November 3, 1835), 2:3; (November 13, 1835), 1:2; (October 28, 1836), 1:1; and (November 1, 1836), 2:1. Noah's relationship with Calhoun and Mangum are revealed in *ES-Country* (February 3, 1837), 1:2; Noah to William Seward (February 22, 1839), Gratz Collection, Historical Society of Pennsylvania; and Henry Thomas Shanks (ed.) *The Papers of Willie Person Mangum* (Raleigh, N.C. 1952, 1953), index s. v. "Noah". Noah discussed his proposed paper in Noah to M. C. Mordecai (October 21, 1846), AJA Correspondence Files, AJA, reprinted in *Major Noah*, 265.

47. Noah opposed the Wilmot Proviso in his *T&M* (May 23, 1847), 2:1; (December 5, 1847), 2:2 and in his *Barnburner Letter*, 9, 11 which is quoted. See also Mushkat, *Tammany*, 233; and Chaplain W. Morrison, *Democratic Politics and Sectionalism: The Wilmot Proviso Controversy* (Chapel Hill, 1967). In 1848, Noah and Russell Jarvis engaged in a journalistic fray over free soil. Jarvis' surviving letters are in the *Daily Globe* (July 31, August 18, September 2, September 14, September 26, 1848). Noah's surviving replies are in the *True Sun* (August 19, 29, 1848). See also Jarvis's *Facts and Arguments Against the Election of General Cass* (New York 1848), and, on the dangers of a northern president, Noah's *Barnburner Letter*, 13 which is quoted. Noah's praise for the Clay Compromise is in *T&M* (May 26, 1850), 2:3; (June 23, 1850), 2:1; and (August 25, 1850), 2:1. The immigrant view of slavery, the South and Union is explored in Robert Ernst, *Immigrant Life in New York City 1825–1863* (New York, 1949), 153; George Potter, *To The Golden Door* (Boston, 1960), 371–87; John A. Hawgood, *The Tragedy of German America* (New York, 1940), 50–51; and Cuthbert E. Allen, "The Slavery Question in Catholic Newspapers 1850–65," *Historical Records and Studies*, 26 (1936), 99–169. For the Jewish attitude, see Bertram W. Korn, *American Jewry and the Civil War* (Philadelphia, 1961), 1–56; *idem*, "Jews and Negro Slavery in the Old South," *PAJHS*, 50 (1961), 151–201; Louis Ruchames, "The Abolitionists and the Jews: Some Further Thoughts," *Marcus Festschrift*, 505–515; Morris Schappes, "The Jews and American Slavery," *Jewish Life* (May 1954), 15–19, and Maxwell Whiteman's introduction to Peter Still, *The Kidnapped and the Ransomed* (Philadelphia, 1970). For Noah's later pro-Union sentiments, see Noah and Gill, *Prospectus of the Evening Star*; *ES-Country* (April 14, 1835), 2:1; (September 1, 1835), 1:1; *T&M* (February 26, 1850), 2:2; and (March 10, 1850), 2:1.

48. Noah's pro-slavery views have been conveniently forgotten by most historians. The most blatant misrepresentations are those of Max Raisin who made Noah into an abolitionist, and Simon Wolf who claimed that Noah "advocated the abolition of slavery by laws, gradual in their effect." Wolf went on to suggest that the Civil War with all it horrors would have been averted if only Noah and "other far seeing statesmen" would have been heeded. As recently as 1973, Robert Rutland described how Noah "despised slavery while loathing abolitionists." Max Raisin, *Mordecai Manuel Noah, Zionist, Author and Statesman* (in Hebrew, Warsaw, 1905), 22; Simon Wolf, "Mordecai Manuel Noah: A Biographical Sketch," *Selected Addresses and Papers of Simon Wolf* (Cincinnati, 1926), 130; and Robert A. Rutland, *The Newsmongers: Journalism in the Life of the Nation 1690–1972* (New York, 1973), 152.

49. For some of Noah's early views on Blacks and slavery, see Noah, *Essays of Howard*, 210–214; *Nat. Adv.* (October 7, 1820), 2:3; *N.Y. Nat. Adv.* (October 3, 1825), 2:3; *Enq.-Country* (March 30, 1826), 2:1; *ES* (February 18, 1834), 2:2; *ES-Country* (September 1, 1835), 2:6; *True Sun* (August 18, 1848), 2:7; *Niles' Register*, 75 (February 14, 1849), 110; and *ES-Country* (August 11, 1838), 2:2; (January 13, 1837), 2:2; and (July 24, 1835), 3:1 which are quoted.

50.   On southern pro-slavery thought, see Eric Mckitrick (ed.) *Slavery Defended* (Englewood Cliffs, N.J., 1963); William S. Jenkins, *Pro-Slavery Thought in the Old South* (Chapel Hill, 1935); and other works cited in David Potter, *The Impending Crisis* (New York, 1976), 460–61. Noah himself denied that his upbringing was a factor in his support of slavery, see *T&M* (March 25, 1849), 2:1. See *DHJUS*, 394 for an example of a southern born Jewish opponent of slavery.

51.   Noah opposed Black enfranchisement in *Nat. Adv.* (April 19, 1819), 2:1; (June 21, 1821), 2:3; (June 29, 1821), 2:1; (September 22–October 8, 1821); and (November 5, 1822), 2:2; see also William L. Shulman, "The National Advocate, 1812–1829" (Unpublished Ed.D. thesis, Yeshiva University, 1968), 89–94; and, regarding Noah's opposition to a later enfranchisement bill, *T&M* (May 25, 1845), 2:1; quote is from *Nat. Adv.* (July 14, 1821), 2:3. See also Dixon R. Fox, "The Negro Vote in Old New York," *Political Science Quarterly*, 32 (1917), 252–75.

52.   I. Garland Penn claims that Noah's anti-Black writings stimulated the initial publication of *Freedom's Journal*. The paper itself, however, lends little support to this theory. A variety of anti-Black journalists were rebutted in its pages, Noah among them. I. Garland Penn, *The Afro-American Press and Its Editors* (New York, 1969 (1891)), 26–28; Martin E. Dann, *The Black Press, 1827–1890: The Quest for National Identity* (New York, 1971), 15–17; and Bella Gross, "Freedom's Journal and the Rights of All," *Journal of Negro History*, 17 (July 1832), 243, Gross's footnote on Noah is full of inaccuracies. Regarding other anti-Black journalists, see Crouthamel, *Webb*, 24, 55–57, 99–101, 125–6; and Oliver Carlson, *The Man Who Made News: James Gordon Bennett* (New York, 1942), 55, 231, 242–4, 256.

53.   The Charleston "plot" is discussed in Richard Wade, *Slavery in the Cities* (New York, 1972), 228–42; and Herbert Aptheker, *American Negro Slave Revolts* (New York 1943), 268–76. For Noah's reaction see *Nat. Adv.* (July 8, 1822), 2:2; (July 31, 1822), 2:2; and (August 28, 1822), 2:1. Noah admitted his fear of revenge in *ES* (October 18, 1830), 2:1. Quotes are from *Nat. Adv.* (July 31, 1822), 2:2; (July 9, 1822), 2:2; *Truth Teller*, 3 (August 11, 1827), 254; *ES-Country* (May 19, 1835); and *Nat. Adv.* (May 16, 1823), 2:3. See *Freedom's Journal* (April 20, 1827), 23; (August 17, 1827), 90; and (August 24, 1827), 95; as well as Noah's praise for the *Ram's Horn* in *T&M* (May 28, 1848), 2:5. Relevant secondary studies include: Leon F. Litwack, *North of Slavery* (Chicago, 1961); Leo Hirsch, "The Negro and New York 1783–1865," *Journal of Negro History*, 16 (1931), 415–73 and Rhoda G. Freeman, "The Free Negro in New York City in the Era Before the Civil War," (Unpublished Ph.D. thesis, Columbia University, 1966).

54.   On the 1834 riot, see *ES* (July 9–11, 1834) from where quotes are taken, as well as Gappelberg, "Noah," 157–9. For Webb's view, see Crouthamel, *Webb*, 57. See also a contemporary description, Gustave de Beaumont, *Marie or Slavery in the United States*, translated by Barbara Chipman (Stanford, 1958), 243–52; and recent secondary accounts: Linda K. Kerber, "Abolitionists and Amalgamaters: The New York City Race Riots of 1834," *New York History*, 48 (January 1967), 28–40; Leonard L. Richards, *Gentlemen of Property and Standing: Anti-Abolition Mobs in Jacksonian America* (New York, 1970), 113–22; and Bertram Wyatt-Brown, *Lewis Tappan and the Evangelical War Against Slavery* (Cincinnati, 1969), 116–20. Wyatt-Brown accuses Noah of helping to instigate the riot. While Noah did oppose abolitionists, he cannot be grouped with Webb as an inciter of the mob.

55.   Quotes are from *ES-Country* (July 24, 1835), 3:1; and (December 25, 1835), 4:1. See also Russell B. Nye, *Fettered Freedom* (East Lansing, Mich., 1949), 117–173, esp. 141, 143.

56.   *Herald* (May 4, 1842), 2:4; *Niles' Register*, 62 (May 14, 1842), 176; William Lloyd Garrison in *The Liberator* (May 20, 1842), 1; and Wendell P. Garrison, *William Lloyd Garrison 1805–1879: The Story of his Life Told by his Children* (New York, 1969, [1889]), III, 54.

57.   For Noah's use of science in his pro-slavery argument, see *ES-Country* (September 15, 1835), 1:1; *ES* (February 11, 1835), 2:2; and *ES-Country* (May 9, 1837), 2:1 which are quoted; see also, Arthur Wrobel, "Orthodoxy and Respectability in Nineteenth Century Phrenology," *Journal of Popular Culture*, 9 (1973), 38–50. Noah's religious justification of slavery is quoted

from *True Sun* (August 16, 1848), 2:6–7. See other discussions of the Bible in *NY Nat. Adv.* (April 1, 1826), 2:3; *T&M* (June 20, 1847), 2:2; (November 21, 1847), 2:1; (February 20, 1848), 2:2 and (April 22, 1849). On the question generally, see David B. Davis, *The Problem of Slavery in the Age of Revolution*, (Ithaca, 1975) 523–66. For Rabbi Morris Raphall's later, biblically based sermon on slavery, see Korn, *American Jewry and the Civil War*, 16–20; and *DHJUS*, 405–28.

58. Quotations are from *ES-Country* (February 12, 1833), 3:2; and Noah to M. C. Mordecai (October 21, 1846) in AJA Correspondence file and *Major Noah*, 265. See also Howard C. Perkins, "The Defense of Slavery in the Northern Press on the Eve of the Civil War," *Journal of Southern History*, 9 (1943), 501–32; William R. Taylor, *Cavalier and Yankee* (New York, 1961), 225–60; and Lorman Ratner, *Powder Keg: Northern Opposition to the Anti-Slavery Movement 1831–1840* (New York, 1968).

59. References to Jews in the abolitionist literature include the quoted comments (in order): *The Liberator* (August 10, 1848), 2; (September 21, 1849), 3; *Freedom's Journal* (August 17, 1827), 90; and (August 24, 1827), 95. See also *Genius of Universal Emancipation*, 1 (January 1822), 105–6; *Colored American* (February 10, 1838), 19; *Pennsylvania Freeman*, 4 (July 12, 1838), 2; *The Liberator* (May 18, 1849), 2; Walter M. Merrill, *The Letters of William L. Garrison*, (Cambridge, 1971), vol. I, #15; Freeman, "Free Negro in New York," 259, and articles by Ruchames, Schappes and Korn, cited above note 47. Regarding Noah and Horace Greeley, see *Union* (August 5–13, 1842); (August 19, 1842), 2:2; (August 25, 1842), 2:2; *New York Tribune* (August 13, 1842), 2:1; (August 26, 1842), 2:1; and James Parton, *The Life of Horace Greeley* (Boston, 1872), 189–90 which is quoted. I know of no evidence to support Parton's claim that Noah felt Greeley's attack "acutely." The last two quotes are from *Pennsylvania Freeman*, 5 (November 22, 1838), 3 and *New York Weekly Tribune*, 7 (September 2, 1848), 3:1.

60. On Noah's children see *Major Noah*, 287–93 and chart. Noah's finances are discussed in Gappelberg, "Noah," 99.

61. *ES-Country* (June 9, 1835), 1:1; cf. Gappelberg, "Noah," 200–12; and Leo Hershkowitz, "The Land of Promise: Samuel Swartwout and the Land Speculation in Texas 1830–1838," *New York Historical Quarterly*, 48 (1964), 309–15 which cites the relevant literature.

62. Quotes are from *ES-Country* (November 6, 1835), 3:1; (August 5, 1836), 3:1; (February 5, 1836), 3:1; and *Herald* (May 3, 1838), 2:1.

63. For Noah's later support of Texas, see *New York Mirror* 20 (July 16, 1842), 226; *T&M* (May 5, 1844), 2:1; (February 7, 1847), 2:1; (March 5, 1848), 2:1; and Noah to Calhoun (September 3, 1844), Calhoun Papers, Clemson University Library, Clemson, S.C.

64. *ES* (March 3, 1837), 2:3; *ES* (April 30, 1839), 2:1 and Gappelberg, "Noah," 99.

65. Noah to Seward (June 23, 1840), Noah papers, New York Public Library; Seward to Noah (February 27, 1839), Seward Papers, University of Rochester; and Noah to Seward (March 10, 1840), Historical Society of Pennsylvania, which is quoted.

66. On Noah's support of Harrison and Tyler, see *ES* (December 9, 1839), 2:1; as well as Noah to S. D. Bloodgood (April 30, 1840) and Bloodgood to Seward (May 5, 1840) in Seward Papers, University of Rochester, both quoted. The deal by which Noah ended his paper and was appointed judge is revealed in the quoted letter of Noah to Webb (undated), the pencilled date of 1839) should almost surely read 1841) Webb Papers, Box 1a, Yale University; as well as in *Herald* (October 18, 1841), 2:1; and in *Union* (July 28, 1842), 2:1. See also Charles P. Daly, *The Settlement of the Jews in North America* (New York, 1893), 132–34.

67. Quotation is from Noah to Seward (August 28, 1840), Historical Society of Pennsylvania; *ES* (August 29, 1840) contains Noah's valedictory.

CHAPTER VII. A Jew in a World of Christians

1. Leonard I. Gappelberg, "M. M. Noah and the Evening Star: Whig Journalism 1833–

1840" (Unpublished Ed.D. thesis, Yeshiva University, 1970), 219–240 is the only detailed secondary source dealing with Noah's Judaism, and its scope is rather limited. On ethnic leadership, see particularly John Higham (ed.) *Ethnic Leadership in America* (Baltimore, 1978); and Victor Greene, "Becoming American: The Role of Ethnic Leaders—Swedes, Poles, Italians, Jews," in Peter d'A Toole and Melvin G. Holli, *The Ethnic Frontier* (Grand Rapids, Mich., 1977), 143–175.

2.   Quotations are all from *Herald* of November, 1837, the month in which Bennett's anti-Jewish campaign peaked. Other epithets are too numerous to list.

3.   The ritual murder charge was nothing more than a rehash of the Damascus blood libel of 1840, trumpeted under the title "Mysteries of the Talmud." Curiously, in 1840, Bennett had taken the Jewish position in the Damascus Affair and had dismissed a correspondent's call to investigate Jewish use of blood in New York synagogues with the single word "Bah." The *Herald*'s 1850 blood libel campaign was very brief. Six days after he printed the charge, Bennett printed two letters defending Jews (one was written by Robert Lyon, editor of the Jewish newspaper, *The Asmonean*.) He then declined to print a rejoinder, sent to him by "A Christian," who cited as "positive fact" that "the Jews of Damascus actually committed the murder." After several weeks of outraged letters and press comments, the whole question died. Five months later, on September 15, 1850—the eve of Yom Kippur (Day of Atonement)—rumors that "Jews had murdered a Gentile girl for the holiday" spawned a Brooklyn riot involving, according to a contemporary report, 500 people, most of them Irish. Not without reason did Reverend J. J. Lyons of Shearith Israel fear that the blood question could arise in America. *Herald* (April 6, 1850), 1:5; (April 12, 1850), 6:5, cf. (May 7, 1840), 2:4; (May 18, 1840), 3:1; (August 10, 1840), 3:3. The James Gordon Bennett Papers, New York Public Library contain two letters reacting to his ritual murder charge, both anonymous. See also *Asmonean* 1 (1850), 204. On the Brooklyn libel, see *Allgemeine Zeitung des Judenthums* (Leipzig, October 21, 1850), reprinted in Lee M. Friedman, *Pilgrims in a New Land* (Philadelphia, 1948), 404, and translated in Rudolf Glanz, *Studies in Judaica Americana* (New York, 1970), 75, which is reprinted in Abraham J. Karp, *Golden Door to America* (New York, 1976), 39. On J. J. Lyons's fears see *DHJUS*, 624. The general subject of blood libel is treated in 'Blood Libel," *EJ*, IV, 1120–31; Joshua Trachtenberg, *The Devil and the Jews* (New Haven, 1943) and more broadly, Florence H. Tidley, "A Tale Told Too Often," *Western Folklore*, 26 (July 1967), 15–36. The more famous, 1928 Massena, New York blood libel is described in Saul Friedman, *The Incident at Massena* (New York, 1978).

4.   Noah's rebuttals are too numerous to list. See especially, *ES* (November, 1837), (June, 1840), *Union* (October 24, 1842), 2:1–2; *T&M* (March 13, 1844), 2:5; (April 14, 1844), 2:5; and (May 15, 1845), 2:5. On Noah's early loan to Bennett, see *ES* (December 9, 1837), 2:2. Following Robert P. Noah, "Mordecai M. Noah, Interesting Reminiscences of a Famous American Jew," *The Reformer and Jewish Times*, 10 (November 15, 1878), 1, many exaggerate Noah's early aid to Bennett. A more plausible account is in Samuel Lockwood, "Major M. M. Noah," *Lippincott's Magazine*, 1 (1868), 666 (the Scottish emigrant is obviously Bennett). On the moral boycotts see *ES* and *Herlad* (November 1837; June 1840); an undated letter from Noah to Webb (c. June, 1840), Miscellaneous Papers, New York Public Library; Merle M. Hoover, *Park Benjamin: Poet and Editor* (New York, 1948), 104–8; James L. Crouthamel, *James Watson Webb: A Biography* (Middletown, Ct., 1969), 86–5; Frederic Hudson, *Journalism in the United States From 1690–1872* (New York, 1873), 456–60; and the standard but inadequate biographies of Bennett: I. C. Pray, *Memoirs of James Gordon Bennett and his Times* (New York, 1855) and Oliver Carlson, *The Man Who Made News* (New York, 1942). See also Chapter VI, n. 4. The anti-Jewish spirit of the *Herald* has been ignored by historians. The best account of the *Herald*'s later anti-Jewish policy is therefore Henry Ford's laudatory comments on Bennett in his *Dearborn Independent* (February 5, 1921) reprinted in *Jewish Activities in the United States* (Dearborn, 1921), 210–19.

5.   For the Jewish population of New York, see Hyman B. Grinstein, *The Rise of the Jewish Community of New York 1654–1860* (Philadelphia, 1945), 469. Items of Jewish interest in Noah's newspapers are numerous. See in particular, *ES* (February 28, 1834) 2:3; (February 8, 1840), 2:3; *Union* (November 19, 1842), 2:5; *New York Mirror*, 17 (February 29, 1840), 285;

Herald (June 25, 1844), 1:2; *Tribune* (November 14–17, 1845); (December 12, 1845), 1 (on which Noah likely had help); and the remarkable series of "Answers to Correspondents," reprinted weekly in *T&M*. Quotations are from *ES* (February 28, 1834), 2:3 reprinted in *DHJUS*, 192; and *Tribune* (June 22, 1847), 1:2.

6. For Noah's views on the importance of education, see above, Chapter III, n. 50; quote is from *Consecration Address*, 21. Noah frequently attacked maligners of Jews; cited examples are from *ES* (July 17, 1837), 2:2, reprinted in Gappelberg, "Noah," 139–40; *ES* (June 27, 1840), 2:1; *T&M* (February 17, 1850), 2:2; *Tribune* (June 22, 1842), 2:2; (June 27, 1842), 1:1; and (November 11–14, 1845). See also a response to a Noah attack in the *Home Journal*, #211 (February 23, 1850), 2:4. On Bush see *Dictionary of American Biography*, III (1929), 347, and on Wines, XX (1936), 385–6. The subject of Jewish communal self-defense has recently been discussed in Naomi W. Cohen, "Pioneers of American Jewish Defense," *AJA* (November 1977), 116–50.

7. On Uriah P. Levy, see Noah to George Bancroft (June 2, 1846); Bancroft to Noah (June 25, 1846), Massachusetts Historical Society; and *T&M* (March 24, 1850), 2:3; as well as Abram Kanof, "Uriah Phillips Levy: The Story of a Pugnacious Commodore," *PAJHS*, 39 (1949), 1–65. On Warder Cresson see *T&M* (November 4, 1849), 2:5 and (March 25, 1851), 2:3; as well as Frank Fox, "Quaker, Shaker, Rabbi: Warder Cresson, the Story of a Philadelphia Mystic," *Pennsylvania Magazine of History and Biography*, 95 (1971), 147–94.

8. My discussion of tunnel vision profited from David H. Fischer, *Historians' Fallacies* (New York, 1970), 144. Quote is from Noah to John C. Spencer (April 20, 1843), Historical Society of Pennsylvania.

9. For somewhat different contrasts between the Jewish position in America and Europe, see Salo W. Baron, "The Emancipation Movement and American Jewry," *Steeled by Adversity* (Philadelphia, 1971), 80–105; and Abraham Karp, "Ideology and Identity in Jewish Group Survival in America," *AJHQ*, 65 (June 1976), 310–34. Quote is from Peixotto's *Anniversary Discourse* (1830) reprinted in Daniel P. Hays, "Daniel L. M. Peixotto, M.D.," *PAJHS*, 26 (1918), 229. On John Calhoun's ethnic identity, see Margaret L. Coit, *John Calhoun: American Portrait* (Cambridge, 1950), esp. 33, 51.

10. Julius Price, "Proceedings Relating to the Expulsion of Ezekiel Hart from the House of Assembly of Lower Canada," *PAJHS*, 23 (1915), 43–53; Benjamin G. Sack, *History of the Jews in Canada* (Montreal, 1945), I, 80–95 cf. 118. Noah's quoted comments on the case, and on the rebellion are from *ES* (December 5, 1837), 2:1. See my "The Canadian Connection of an American Jew: The Case of Mordecai M. Noah," *The Journal of the Jewish Historical Society of Canada*, III (1979), 115–29.

11. Heinrich Graetz, *History of the Jews* (Philadelphia, 1895), VI, 642–72; H. H. Ben-Sasson (ed.) *A History of the Jewish People* (Cambridge, 1976), 847–849; "Damascus Affair," *EJ*, V, 1249–52 and B. Mevorah, "The Effect of the Damascus Affair Upon the Development of the Jewish Press," *Zion* (in Hebrew), 23 (1958), 46–65.

12. Joseph Jacobs erroneously dates the meeting to August 17. Actually, Jews in Virginia met on that day, and theirs may have been the first American Jewish meeting on the affair. Resolutions from the Richmond meeting were read both in New York and in Philadelphia. Joseph Jacobs, "The Damascus Affair of 1840 and the Jews of America," *PAJHS*, 10 (1902), 122; *JUSDH*, III, 951; *C&E* (August 21, 1840), 2.

13. On the American reaction to the Damascus Affair, see Jacobs, "The Damascus Affair;" Jacob Ezekiel, "Persecution of the Jews in 1840," *PAJHS*, 8 (1900), 141–44; *JUSDH*, III, 924–955; *DHJUS*, 200–215; Israel Goldstein, *A Century of Judaism in New York* (New York, 1930), 70–73; Grinstein, *New York*, 420–422; Leon Jick, *The Americanization of the Synagogue* (Waltham, 1976), 63–67. Noah's early comments on Damascus are in *ES* (June 6, 1840), 2:3; (July 31, 1840), 2:5; and (August 1, 1840), 2:3. His Damascus address, long thought lost, was reprinted in *C&E* (August 21, 1840), 2.

14. *C&E* (August 21, 1840), 2.

15. David and Tamar de Sola Pool, *An Old Faith in the New World* (New York, 1955), 380–83 presents a more sympathetic view of Shearith Israel's attitude. Quote is from *C&E* (August 21, 1840), 2.

16. On the protest against the Czar, see Grinstein, *New York*, 426. On the Swiss treaty, see Noah to Webster (January 21, 1851), RG59, Miscellaneous Letters, Department of State (M179 reel 124); Webster to Noah (January 27, 1851), Department of State, Domestic Letters, 38:362 (M40 reel 36); *Occident*, 9 (1851), 99; *DHJUS*, 651; and Sol M. Stroock, "Switzerland and American Jews," *PAJHS* (1903), 7–53.

17. The standard source on Shearith Israel is Pool, *Old Faith*, which contains numerous references to Noah. See also items in the Lyons Collection, *PAJHS*, 21 (1913), 27 (1920), and Grinstein, *New York*. Reports of Noah's Shearith Israel election defeats are found in *American* (June 27, 1826), 2:2; and *Herald* (June 17, 1841), 2:1.

18. On B'nai Jeshurun, see Goldstein, *A Century of Judaism in New York*; Pool, *Old Faith*, 436–9; Grinstein, *New York*, 42–48; *JUSDH*, II, 535–45; Edwin Wolf and Maxwell Whiteman, *The History of the Jews of Philadelphia from Colonial Times to the Age of Jackson* (2nd ed., Philadelphia, 1975), 466 n. 128; and Lyons Collection, AJHS, item 82a.

19. Quotes are from Harriet Butler to Jesse Hoyt (December 4, 1830), in W. L. Mackenzie, *Life and Times of Martin Van Buren*, 170; *Voice of Jacob* (January 19, 1844), 69b–70a; *Sunday Dispatch* (March 30, 1851), in Lyons Scrapbook, I, AJHS. See also John T. Townsend, *My Own Story* (New York, 1903), 96: "He was an Israelite who aspired to be a leader of the Israelites." On efforts to unify American Jews, see Joseph Buchler, "The Struggle for Unity, Attempts at Union in American Jewish Life: 1654–1868," *AJA* 2 (1949), 21–46.

20. On Noah's loans from Jews, see Gappelberg, "Noah," 95–97, and *Herald* (May 12, 1845), 2:2. The Nones articles were in *Enq.-Country* (August 8, 1826), 3:1. On the French crisis, see *C&E* (February 21, 1835), 2:1; *ES* (February 20, 1835), 2:1; (February 13, 1836), 2:1; *ES-Country* (February 16, 1836), 1:1; Gappelberg, "Noah," 188–200, and Robert C. Thomas, "Andrew Jackson Versus France: American Policy Toward France, 1834–1836," *Tennessee Historical Quarterly*, 35 (1976), 51–64.

21. The two books which Noah recommended are Isaac Gomez, Jr., *Selections of a Father for the Use of his Children* (New York, 1820), see *JUSDH*, II, 440; and Adolphus M. Hart, *History of the Issues of Paper Money in the American Colonies Anterior to the Revolution...* (St. Louis, 1851). Noah's letter to Richard Rush (May 1, 1848), is in the New York Historical Society. On Abrahams see Pool, *Old Faith*, 402, 404, 474. For other recommendations, see *ES* (August 10, 1837), 2:4; *ES* (December 12, 1837), 2:3; Noah to I. B. Jones (?) (November 2, 1842), Historical Society of Pennsylvania; Noah to Seward (November 7, 1842), Seward Papers, University of Rochester, and Noah to Joshua Cohen (December 23, 1849), Noah Papers, AJHS; cf. *DHJUS*, 215. Among the Jews who worked on Noah's journals were Naphtali Phillips, Levi Laurens and Isaac Phillips; see *ES* (July 26, 1837), 2:2; and *Union* (February 1, 1843), 3:1.

22. The Levy plan is discussed in Bertram W. Korn, *Eventful Years and Experiences* (Cincinnati, 1954), 152–3, 199–200. For Noah's other educational efforts, see Grinstein, *New York*, 148–9, 222; Goldstein, *A Century of Judaism*, 69–70; Pool, *Old Faith*, 364; Jacob I. Hartstein, "The Polonies Talmud Torah of New York," *PAJHS*, 34 (1932), 126, 128; *Occident*, (1845), 555. Noah is listed as an incorporator of the Society for the Education of Poor Children and Relief of Indigent Persons of the Jewish Persuasion in the City of New York (April 11, 1831) in *Laws of the State of New York 54th Session*. For the Hebrew College plan, see *Occident*, I (1843), 301–7 and n. 23 below. On early American Jewish education, see Hyman B. Grinstein, "In the Course of the Nineteenth Century," in Judah Pilch (ed.) *A History of Jewish Education in America* (New York, 1969), 25–50; Moshe Davis, *The Emergence of Conservative Judaism* (Philadelphia, 1963), 34–64; Alexander M. Dushkin, *Jewish Education in New York City* (New York, 1918); and Lloyd P. Gartner, *Jewish Education in the United States: A Documentary History* (New York, 1969), which includes a valuable introduction and bibliography. Quotation is from *Occident*, 1 (1843), 303.

23.   Noah set out his Hebrew College program in *Occident* 1 (1843), 301–307 cf. 409–414; it was commented upon in *Voice of Jacob* (December 8, 1843), 46b; and Noah mentioned its failure in *Occident*, 8 (1850), 424–6. Noah's recommendations for boarding schools may be found in Lyons Scrapbook, II, p. 36e, AJHS; see also, Morton J. Merowitz, "Max Lilienthal (1814–1882)—Jewish Educator in Nineteenth Century America," *YIVO Annual*, 15 (1974), 46–65; and *New York Times* (September 4, 1854) which reported that New York contained seven Jewish private schools which educated 857 students.

24.   Noah's adult education activities are mentioned in Lyons Scrapbook, III (1841), AJHS, 141; and Grinstein, *New York*, 253. On Wines, see *Tribune* (January 17, 1848), 2:4; and above n.5. Noah's early involvement in New York University, and information on Isaac Nordheimer are both mentioned in Joshua L. Chamberlain, *New York University* (Boston, 1901), 59–61, 69. Professor Bayrd Still has provided additional information based on university archives in a personal letter (January 2, 1979). On Nordheimer, see also David de Sola Pool, "Nordheimer, Isaac," *Dictionary of American Biography*, 13 (1934), 547–8; and H. Neill, "Reminiscences of I. Nordheimer," *New Englander and Yale Review*, 33 (July, 1874), 506–12. For Noah's recommendations of Jewish newspapers, see *Union* (November 3, 1842), 2:2; Lyons Scrapbook, I (March 1849), AJHS; *Israel's Herold* (April 20, 1849), 31:2; *T&M* (March 31, 1850), 2:2. See also *Occident*, 5, (1847), 274 where a proposed Noah-Lyon weekly newspaper was announced. That newspaper never appeared. On the *Asmonean* see H. B. Grinstein, "The Asmonean: The First Jewish Weekly in New York," *Jewish Journal of Bibliography* 1 (April 1939), 62–71; and on *Israel's Herold* see Guido Kisch, "Israel's Herold: The First Jewish Weekly in New York," *Historica Judaica*, 2 (October, 1940), 65–84.

25.   On the Hebrew Benevolent Society, see Grinstein, *New York*, esp. pp. 145–7, 185–7; Noah's donation is reported in *Occident*, 2 (1844), 404. For examples of press coverage see particularly *Herald* (November 16, 1843), 2:4; (December 15, 1843), 2:4; (November 7, 1845), 2:1; and *Tribune* (December 2, 1848), 2:2. The *Occident* and most New York newspapers covered the Benevolent Society's meetings, at least briefly, every winter.

26.   On the 1849 Benevolent Society banquet, see Korn, *Eventful Years and Experiences*, 48–50; *Tribune* (November 14, 1849), 2:4; *Asmonean*, 1 (November 16, 1849), 29–30; (December 14, 1849), 57; Noah to Webster (October 31, 1849), Webster to Noah (November 9, 1849), both reprinted in Fletcher Webster, *Private Correspondence of Daniel Webster* (Boston, 1903), 346–7; also in Max J. Kohler, "Daniel Webster and the Jews," *PAJHS*, 11 (1903), 186–7; and Noah to Seward (October 31, 1849); Seward to Noah (November 6, 1849), Seward Papers, University of Rochester. For later donations, see Noah to Hamilton Fish (December 15, 1850), container 24, Fish Papers, LC; and on the Jenny Lind donation, Noah to John Jay (December 1850) reprinted in *Home Journal* (December 21, 1850), 3; *Asmonean*, 1, (December 6, 1850), 52. The true origins of the federation movement are in Boston. See Jacob Neusner, "The Impact of Immigration and Philanthropy Upon the Boston Jewish Community, 1880–1914," *PAJHS*, 46 (1956), 82–3; and Henry L. Lurie, *A Heritage Affirmed* (Philadelphia, 1961), 3–38.

27.   For Leeser's comments, see Jacob R. Marcus, *Memoirs of American Jews* (Philadelphia, 1955), II, 64. On the growing income of the Benevolent Society, see Grinstein, *New York*, 146, and on Noah's role in the early planning for a Jewish hospital (later Mount Sinai), see *29th Anniversary Circular of the Hebrew Benevolent Society* in Lyons Scrapbook I (October 15, 1850), AJHS; *Asmonean* (March 28, 1851), 180; and Tina Levitan, *Islands of Compassion: A History of the Jewish Hospitals of New York* (1961). My discussion of philanthropy has been informed by Alfred J. Kutzick, "The Social Basis of American Jewish Philanthropy" (unpublished Ph.D., Brandeis University, 1967); Daniel Elazar, *Community and Polity* (Philadelphia, 1976), Milton Goldin, *Why They Give* (New York, 1976); and Kenneth L. Kusmer, "The Functions of Organized Charity in the Progressive Era, Chicago as a Case Study," *Journal of American History* 60 (1973), 657–78.

28.   The sociological concepts of "reference group" and "role" are generally helpful in understanding Noah's relationship with the Christian and Jewish communities. See Robert K.

Merton, *Social Theory and Social Structure* (Glencoe, Ill., 1957), and Michael Banton, *Roles* (New York, 1965).

29.   Quotations are from *Consecration Address*, 28; *Enq.-Country* (September 12, 1826), 1:3; *Nat. Adv.* (October 24, 1822), 2:2.

30.   For Noah's views on Christianity, see particularly his *Restoration Discourse* and *Temple Address.* Quotations are from *ES* (August 16, 1839), 2:3 and *Temple Address*, 11. Isaac Leeser's *Catechism for Younger Children* (Philadelphia, 1839) reinforced the view that Judaism and Christianity were at root similar. On the changing Jewish attitude toward Christianity, see Jacob Katz, *Exclusiveness and Tolerance: Jewish-Gentile Relations in Medieval and Modern Times* (New York, 1961).

31.   Quote is from Noah to John Jay (n.d. [1850]) in *Home Journal* (December 21, 1850). See also *Temple Address*, 10–13. *T&M* (July 4, 1847), 2:5; (September 10, 1848), 2:1; and (November 4, 1849), 2:5.

32.   For the Protestant view, see the annual reports of the American Society for Meliorating the Condition of Jews, as well as its two periodicals, *Israel's Advocate* and the *Jewish Chronicle.* See also Charles L. Chaney, *The Birth of Missions in America* (South Pasadena, California, 1976) and works cited above Chapter III, n. 68.

33.   Robert K. Merton, *Sociological Ambivalence and Other Essays* (New York, 1976). Alexander Altmann, *Moses Mendelssohn: A Biographical Study* (Philadelphia, 1973) deals with Mendelssohn's place in German society, see especially pp. 194–263, on the Lavater affair. Mendelssohn's letter to Lavater was printed in New York (in English) in 1821 (PAJHS, 30 [1926], #214).

34.   Personal hostility notwithstanding, Noah printed ads from Wolff in his newspaper. He also printed an ad placed in his newspaper by the American Society for Meliorating the Condition of the Jews. But he failed to collect his money in advance from this group, and the debt remained on his books unpaid. Wolff to Noah, n.d. Noah Papers, AJHS; Gappelberg, *Noah*, 231 n. 514.

35.   *Journal of the Reverend Joseph Wolff* (London, 1839), 401; *Enq.-Country* (May 4, 1827), 1:3, which is quoted; *ES* (August 25, 1837), 2:2; and (August 3, 1837), 2:2.

36.   Russell E. Richey and Donald G. Jones (eds.) *American Civil Religion* (New York, 1974); Philip E. Hammond, "The Sociology of American Civil Religion: A Bibliographic Essay," *Sociological Analysis*, 37 (1976), 169–82. Quotations are from *Nat. Adv.* (November 27, 1822), 2:2–3; (July 28, 1821), 2:2–3; (September 19, 1822), 2:1–3; and *ES* (August 23, 1839), 2:2. See also Samuel Lockwood, "Major M. M. Noah," *Lippincott's Magazine* 1 (1868), 666.

37.   The same tactic was used in 1899 by Ambassador Oscar Straus to gain Turkish help in the war against the Philippines. Like Noah, Straus referred to the English text of a 1796 United States treaty with Tripoli which specifically denied the Christian character of America. Strangely, the original Arabic text of the same treaty made no mention of America's religious character, either positively or negatively. But that was only discovered in the twentieth century. Charles A. Madison, *Eminent American Jews* (New York, 1970), 93; Naomi W. Cohen, *A Dual Heritage: The Public Career of Oscar S. Straus* (Philadelphia, 1969), 94; *Major Noah*, 118.

38.   On Noah's use of the term "Christian nation" in Tunis, see *Travels*, 379 which is quoted; *T&M* (November 18, 1849), 2:2 and *Major Noah*, 114–20. Later quotes are from (in order) *Nat. Adv.* (November 3, 1821), 2:1; *New York Mirror*, 14 (April 1, 1837), 317; and Noah to Thomas Jefferson (May 7, 1818), in *JUSDH*, I, 241. For other examples of Noah's use of the word Christian, see his official declaration of the "forcible and illegal seizure of American property" (March 4, 1815) in Despatches from the United States Consuls in Tunis 1797–1909, NA (microcopy T-303); *Nat. Adv.* (February 18, 1823), 2:4; *NY Nat. Adv.* (November 12, 1825), 2:2; and Noah to Spencer (April 20, 1843) in Historical Society of Pennsylvania. Others called Noah a Christian both during and after his life, see *American Monthly Magazine and Critical Review* 4 (April 1819), 438, and "A Jew and A Christian," *International Magazine*, 3 (May

1851), 162. For Noah's disagreement with Leeser, see *Occident*, 7 (1850), 563–7, and more generally, Maxine S. Seller, "Isaac Leeser: A Jewish-Christian Dialogue in Ante-Bellum Philadelphia," *Pennsylvania History*, 35 (July 1968), 231–42. Jacob Ezekiel also reacted against the term "Christian nation," see *PAJHS*, 9 (1901), 160, and below, Chapter VIII, n. 7. On the use of the term "Christian" to mean "moral," see Robert T. Handy, *A Christian American: Protestant Hopes and Historical Realities* (pb. ed., New York, 1974), 30–42; cf. Arthur A. Cohen, *The Myth of the Judeo-Christian Tradition* (New York, 1963).

39.   In Gotthold Ephraim Lessing's play, *Nathan the Wise* (Germany, 1779), there is a sensitive portrayal of the dual meaning of the term Christian:
Friar: O Nathan, Nathan! You're a Christian soul!
By God, a better Christian never lived!
Nathan: And well for us! For what makes me for you
A Christian, makes yourself for me a Jew!
Gotthold Ephraim Lessing, *Nathan the Wise*, translated by Bayard Q. Morgan, (New York, 1955), act IV, Scene 7.

40.   Quotes are from *T&M* (January 27, 1850), 2:5, and Noah to Seward (February 4, 1841), Historical Society of Pennsylvania (also AJA microfilm 1156).

41.   For Noah's support of Bible societies, see *Travels*, 56; and *Consecration Address*, 43. Arthur A. Chiel, "The Mysterious Book of Jasher," *Judaism*, 26 (Summer, 1977), 367–73 clarifies the history of this work and answers several old questions. See also Emanuel Deutsch, "The Book of Jasher," *Literary Remains of the Late Emanuel Deutsch* (London, 1874), 440–448; Thomas H. Horne, *An Introduction to the Critical Study and Knowledge of the Holy Scriptures*, II (London, 1834), appendix, part II. Regarding later Mormon use of *Jasher*, see Edward J. Brandt, "The History, Context and Latter Day Saint Use of the Book of Jasher" (Unpublished Ph.D. thesis, Brigham Young University, 1976). Noah first mentioned Jasher in *Enq.-Country* (February 3, 1829), 1:1 and (February 6, 1829), 2:4 where he noticed that Moses Samuel had a copy. He announced Jasher in *ES* (May 5, 1840), 2:2, and engaged in a general debate over the book throughout the month. See especially *ES* (May 8, 11, 22, 1840) and (May 29, 1840), 2:2 which is quoted; and *Herald* (May 6, 8, 12, 20, 29, 1840) and (June 5, 1840), 2:4 which is quoted. Many of Noah's articles may also be found in Lyons Scrapbook, III, items 81–83, AJHS. Noah distanced himself from Jasher in *ES* (July 15, 1840), 2:3; and (July 21, 1840), 2:2. Still, the book went through two editions (*PAJHS*, 30, #453, 454) and was popular in England (*Times and Star* [December 23, 1840], 2:1). For John Q. Adams's view of Jasher, see Adams to Noah (June 23, 1840), Adams Papers, reel 513, and for the view of Rebecca Gratz, see her letter to Miriam Cohen (July 12, 1840), *JUSDH*, II, 633, and her letter to Maria Gist Gratz (August 27, 1840) in David Philipson (ed.) *Letters of Rebecca Gratz* (Philadelphia, 1929), 280–283, reprinted in part in *Major Noah*, 245. The Book of Jasher has been reprinted several times, most recently by Hermon Press (New York, 1972) with an introduction by Samuel Gross.

42.   For Noah's views on Sunday laws, see *Nat. Adv.* (November 7, 1818), 2:1; *Enq.-Country* (May 20, 1828), 2:2; *Tribune* (August 4, 1841), 2:3; and the quoted item, *T&M* (February 13, 1848), 2:3; also reprinted in *DHJUS*, 279–81 with valuable notes; see also "The Sabbath Day," *The Literary Register*, 1 (August 11, 1828), 169. For Leeser's views see *Occident*, 6 (1848), 186–93, 302, 367–8 and Maxine Seller, "Isaac Leeser: Architect of the American Jewish Community," (Unpublished Ph.D. thesis University of Pennsylvania, 1965), 145. The whole question of Jews and Sabbath ("Blue") laws has remained controversial; see the still standard Jacob Ben Lightman, "A Study of Reported Judicial Opinions of the American Courts Regarding the Status of Jews with Respect to the Sunday Laws," (Unpublished M.A. thesis, Graduate School for Jewish Social Work, 1933) and Bernard Meislin, *Jewish Law in American Tribunals* (New York, 1976), 149–74. On various aspects of the Sabbath question in America, see Winton W. Solberg, *Redeem the Time: The Puritan Sabbath in Early America* (Cambridge, 1977); John W. Pratt, *Religion, Politics and Diversity: The Church-State Theme in New York History* (Ithaca, 1967); and Bertram Wyatt-Brown, "Prelude to Abolitionism:

Sabbatarian Politics and the Rise of the Second Party System," *Journal of American History,* 58 (1972), 316–41.

43. Modern scholars agree that the "lost ten tribes" assimilated and disappeared, like most other exiled nations. It is possible that a few Jews expelled from Spain, or several wandering marranos, found their way to the new world and exerted influence over certain Indian tribes. It is also possible, as Cyrus Gordon argues, that Semitic peoples visited the new world centuries before Columbus. Most of the purported parallels between Indians and Jews, however, do not bear close scrutiny. Often they reflect nothing more than independent parallel development. George Weiner, "America's Jewish Braves," *Mankind,* 4 (1974), 56–64; Cyrus Gordon, *Before Columbus* (New York, 1971); Ronald Sanders, "Introduction," *Midstream,* 17 (May 1971), 50.

44. The most comprehensive survey of the lost ten tribes literature is William Hart Blumenthal's "The Lost Ten Tribes," an enormous unpublished tome found in AJA, box 1789. A small section of the volume was published as *In Old America* (New York, 1930). The little noticed Lumnius work is Sabin #42675. On colonial views of the Hebraic origins of the Indians, see Jacob R. Marcus, *The Colonial American Jew* (Detroit, 1970), 40–42, which cites earlier works. See also Ronald Sanders, *Lost Tribes and Promised Lands: The Origins of American Racism* (Boston, 1978), esp. 363–76; and for an interesting parallel, the legend of the Welsh Indians discussed in Edward G. Hartmann, *Americans From Wales* (Boston, 1967), 13–24, 228–229.

45. *Nat. Adv.* (March 22, 1820), 2:2 is quoted. See also *Consecration Address,* 44, n. 15 where Noah ignored the Indians in his discussion of the tribes. Doubts about the theory had been expressed in the *Portico* 4 (1818), 245–52, and in the comprehensive article by Samuel F. Jarvis, "A Discourse on the Religion of the Indian Tribes of North America," *Collections of the New York Historical Society for the Year 1821* (New York, 1821), 183–268.

46. "Ararat Address," 249. Fawn Brodie points out that Noah's Ararat address was widely reprinted in New York State, and may have influenced Joseph Smith, the Mormon prophet, who also related the Jews, the Indians, and the lost ten tribes. (Brodie erroneously makes Noah into a "Jewish rabbi.") Other ethnic groups in America claimed founder status based on their putative roles as discoverers of the new world. Jews, I believe, are the only group which has claimed status based on ties to the Indians, the Puritans, and Columbus, as well. Interestingly, Jews in Spain and Poland similarly traced their origins to the period of those nation's founders. Fawn Brodie, *No Man Knows My Story: The Life of Joseph Smith* (2nd ed., New York, 1971, 45–49; and Thomas F. O'Dea, *The Mormons* (Chicago, 1957), 24–5. For founders' myths of immigrant groups, see the bibliographies in Wayne C. Miller, *A Comprehensive Bibliography for the Study of American Minorities* (New York, 1976). The Jewish aspects of Columbus's voyage have most recently been critically assessed by Marcus, *Colonial American Jews,* 35–40, who cites the earlier sources. For similar European myths see Yitzhak Baer, *A History of the Jews in Christian Spain* (Philadelphia, 1971), 15–16, and Bernard D. Weinryb, *The Jews of Poland* (Philadelphia, 1972), 17–19. See also Kenneth J. Moynihan, "History as a Weapon for Social Advancement: Group History as told by Jewish, Irish, and Black Americans 1892–1950," (Unpublished Ph.D., Clark University, 1973).

47. Noah made his promise in "Ararat Address," 250 which is quoted. Among his later discussions of the lost ten tribes, see *ES-Country* (May 19, 1835), 2:3; (June 9, 1835), 2:6; (July 28, 1835), 2:2 and (November 22, 1836), 2:3. The address was announced in *Herald* (December 24, 1836), 2:3; (January 3, 1837), 2:3; (February 2, 1837), 2:2; (February 14, 1837), 2:2 and was reported in *Herald* (February 15, 1837), 2:1. For other comments see *Herald* (March 8, 1837), 2:1; *New York Mirror* (March 4, 1837), 287; Joseph Wolff, *Travels and Adventures of the Reverend Joseph Wolff* (London, 1864), 518; Frederick Marryat, *A Diary in America With Remarks on its Institutions* (3 vols., London, 1839), II, 188. See also Noah to Robert H. Pruya (March 20, 1837), Noah Papers, AJHS; and Blumenthal, "Lost Ten Tribes," I:II:12 and I:IV:20. The citation in I:IV:25, p. 11, is also from Noah, Blumenthal's contrary claims notwithstanding. Noah's address was printed under the title *Discourse on the Evidences of the American Indians Being the Descendants of the Lost Tribes of Israel* (New York, 1837). It was

reprinted in German translation in Altona during 1838 (*PAJHS*, 9 [1902], 172) and in Marryat's *Dairy in America*, II, 317–62. Recently, the address has been reprinted in part in *JUSDH*, III, 920–3 and in *Midstream*, 17 (May, 1971), 51–64. Quotations are from the original (in order), pp. 11, 9, 40.

48.   Quote is from *Lost Tribes Discourse*, 40; see also *Union* (December 29, 1842), 2:2. For Noah's later ideas on the Indians and Ophir, see *Baltimore Literary Monument*, 2 (September 1839), 222, and "The Ten Tribes," *The American Quarterly Register and Magazine*, 2 (March 1849), 209–11, as well as *T&M* (January 14, 1849), 2:3; (January 21, 1849), 2:3; (February 10, 1850), 2:1; and (March 3, 1850), 2:3.

49.   I know of only one occasion when Noah employed this comparison—a letter to Daniel Webster. Later generations of Jews, following the Puritans themselves, placed heavier emphasis on this alleged Hebraic character. One motivation for the extraordinary number of these uncritical comparisons, I think, was the unconscious premise that whoever rejected the Jews, rejected the Puritan Fathers who made this country great. *PAJHS* 11 (1903), 186–7; Eugene R. Fingerhut, "Were the Massachusetts Puritans Hebraic?" *New England Quarterly*, 40 (December 1967), 521–31.

50.   Quote is from *Travels*, p. v. Noah was a member of the New York Historical Society (*Travels*, title page); the American Historical Society of Military and Naval Events (Forest H. Sweet, *Autograph Letters of American Historical Materials*, list no. 157, p. 4); and the New York Museum of Natural History and Science, which he helped to found (Herman Gold Collection, AJA, Box 2089). Joshua I. Cohen claimed that at the time of his death, Noah hoped to write a history of Jewish participation in the American Revolution, see *PAJHS*, 2 (1894), 5.

51.   Quotations are from (in order) M. M. Noah, *An Address Delivered Before the General Society of Mechanics and Tradesmen...* (New York, 1822), 18; *T&M* (July 20, 1848), 2:1; (September 29, 1850), 2:1; *Nat. Adv.* (July 18, 1820), 2:3; M. M. Noah, *An Address Delivered at the Reopening of the Apprentices Library and Reading Room* (New York, 1850), 9; and *Occident* 7 (1849), 86. On the 1850 Charleston debate, see James W. Heller, *Isaac M. Wise: His Life, Work and Thought* (New York, 1955), 180–1.

52.   Quotations are from Ararat Address, *PAJHS*, 13 (1920), 250; *Restoration Discourse*, iv; and *Temple Address*, 15–16. On the 1834 address at Shearith Israel, see *PAJHS*, 21 (1913), 200, 204; *Niles' Weekly Register*, 46 (June 21, 1834), 293; David de Sola Pool, *The Crosby Street Synagogue* (New York, 1934), 27–29; and Pool, *Old Faith*, 55, 98–99. Grinstein's suggestion that Noah was influenced by Isaac Harby is unlikely. Harby had been dead for six years. For another example of Noah's support for reform, see *Tribune* (June 27, 1842), 1:2; on his earlier opposition to reform see *Consecration Address*, 32–33.

53.   On the Charleston reformers, see *JUSDH*, II, 553–65, and works cited in Lou H. Silberman, "American Impact—Judaism in the United States in the Early Nineteenth Century," B. G. Rudolph Lecture in Judaic Studies, Syracuse, 1964, reprinted in A. Leland Jamison (ed.) *Tradition and Change in Jewish Experience* (Syracuse, 1978), 89–105. For Noah's views on the reformers, see *NY Nat. Adv.* (October 18, 1825), 2:2; *Tribune* (June 27, 1842), 1:2; and *T&M* (September 29, 1850), 7:1.

54.   For Noah's view of the Talmud, see quoted items, *Enq.-Country* (June 15, 1827), 2:2; *Restoration Discourse*, iv; *Tribune* (June 27, 1842), 1:1; *Occident*, 3 (1845), 34; as well as *Tribune* (June 22, 1842), 1:1; *T&M* (February 28, 1847), 2:1; and (July 28, 1850), 2:1. On Noah's general Jewish knowledge, see Grinstein, *New York*, 220; and Robert Gordis, "Mordecai Manuel Noah: A Centenary Evaluation," *PAJHS*, 41 (1951), 25–26. Isaac Harby's views on "rabbinic interpolations" are reprinted in *JUSDH*, II, 564. See also Isaac M. Wise's description of the ignorance which he found among American Jews, *Reminiscences* (Cincinnati, 1901), 23–24. For a Christian view of the Talmud, see the influential *North American Review*, 60 (1845), 354, 357, 359, 364. A more extreme pro-Sadducean view was expressed in *Israel Vindicated* (New York, 1820), 12. Noah expressed his views on circumcision in *T&M* (September 17, 1848), 2:1; (May 13, 1849), 2:1 and (October 21, 1849), 2:3. According to Grinstein, *New York*, 346, circumcision was commonly practiced in New York. Elsewhere, the rite was more often neglected

or delayed: Rudolph Glanz, *Studies in Judaica Americana* (New York, 1970), 67; Hyman B. Grinstein, "The American Synagogue and Laxity of Religious Observance 1750–1850," (Unpublished M.A. thesis, Columbia University, 1935), 26; Alan Corre and Malcolm Stern, "The Record Book of Reverend Jacob Raphael Cohen," *AJHQ*, 59 (September 1969), 23–82. On Noah's knowledge of Hebrew, see the quoted item, *T&M* (December 23, 1849), 2:3; as well as (December 12, 1847), 1:2; *ES* (August 2, 1837), 2:2; Samuel Lockwood, "Major M. M. Noah," *Lippincott's Magazine*, 1 (1868), 669; and Grinstein, *New York*, 255. Grinstein, *New York*, 79, 219–27 presents the standard bleak view of Hebrew knowledge in early America, but see also Jonathan D. Sarna "Hebrew Poetry in Early America," *American Jewish History*, 69 (March 1980). Noah's support for the biblical Sabbath is discussed above, note 42; see *Occident*, 3 (1845), 33. Noah's view of the condition of Jewish women is in *ES-Country* (September 9, 1836), 1:4; *Tribune* (November 15, 1845), 1 and *T&M* (April 8, 1849), 2:3. See also Charleston Reformers' interest in maintaining Jewish identity, *JUSDH*, II, 559.

55.   For Noah's view of intermarriage, see *Nat. Adv.* (February 11, 1820), 2; *Occident*, 3 (1845), 34; Lyons Scrapbook II, item 33a, AJHS; *Union* (December 1, 1842), 2:2. Cf. Pool, *Old Faith*, 251; Malcolm H. Stern, "The Function of Geneology in American Jewish History," *Essays in American Jewish History* (Cincinnati, 1958), 84; Grinstein, *New York*, 372–83; *PAJHS*, 27 (1920), 115; and the interesting comments of William Wirt, in Wirt to Myers (June 12, 1818), Myers Family Papers, AJA. On children who remained Jewish, see *DHJUS*, 605 n. 1; and Wolf and Whitemen, *History of the Jews of Philadelphia*, 241, 377.

56.   Quote is from *Asmonean* (March 28, 1851), 180 cf. 181. On Jewish observance in this period, see Jeremiah I. Berman, "The Trend in Jewish Religious Observance in Mid-Nineteenth Century America," *PAJHS*, 37 (1947), 31–53; Grinstein, "American Synagogue and Laxity of Religious Observance"; Bertram W. Korn, "Judaism in the Ante-Bellum Period," *AJHQ*, 53 (June 1964), 341–51; and Jick, *Americanization of the Synagogue*, 3–113.

57.   Quote is from Noah's "Trial for Breaking Open and Publishing a Letter (1818)" reprinted in John D. Lawson (ed.) *American State Trials* (St. Louis, 1914), 676; see also *Tribune* (July 6, 1843), 2:2; and *Occident*, 3 (1845), 3.

58.   For notices of Noah's holiday observances see *Herald*, (September 22, 1836), 2:1; *Lost Tribes Discourse*, 14; *T&M* (May 19, 1850), 2:4; "The Joy of the Law," *Odd Fellows Offering for 1851* (New York, 1851), 40–43; and *T&M* (July 22, 1849), 2:4; see also Manuel M. Noah (Noah's son) "The Day of Vengeance," *Odd Fellows Offering for 1852* (New York, 1852), 294–298. For his observance of the bar mitzvah, see *Herald* (June 11, 1834), 2:1; on marriage rites, see "Incorporation Papers" (December 2, 1840), reel 6a, 271–4, AJHS; and *Herald* (June 11, 1839), 2:2; and on mourning rites, see letter quoted in *Major Noah*, 293. Quotation is from *Travels*, 116.

59.   Noah expressed his concern for kashruth in *ES* (November 24, 1830), 2:2; *Union* (December 3, 1842), 2:2; and *Occident*, I, (1843), 304, 306.

60.   *Occident*, 2 (1844), 347–9, 556 contains Noah's lard test. The formula was reprinted in *Voice of Jacob* (February 14, 1845), 120:2.

61.   "Hermippus' " article is in [Philadelphia] *Columbian Observer* (July 31, 1824), 2:4. Noah praised oysters in *ES* (July 13, 1837), 2:3 and *T&M* (August 22, 1847), 1:5; cf. *Herald* (October 28, 1847), 2:2. For other examples of Jews who enjoyed oysters, see Alex Hart to Moses Hart (October 20, 1834), Hart Papers, Three Rivers, Canada, file JFiA/1 microfilm at AJA; and Michael A. Meyer, "A Centennial History of the Hebrew Union College—Jewish Institute of Religion," in Samuel E. Karff (ed.) *Hebrew Union College—Jewish Institute of Religion at One Hundred Years* (Cincinnati, 1976), 42. On abstinence from pork, see II Maccabees, 6:18; Numbers Rabbah, S12:4; "Pig," *EJ*, XIII, 506–8; Mary Douglas, *Implicit Meanings: Essays in Anthropology* (pb. ed., Boston, 1978), 272; and the Noah quotes: *Evening Post* (August 13, 1821), 2:2; *Nantucket Inquirer* (December 27, 1824), 2:5; reprinted without the crucial words in Bayrd Still, "New York City in 1824: A Newly Discovered Description," *New York Historical Quarterly*, 46 (April 1962), 144. See also *Nat. Adv.* (October 22, 1828), 2:1; *Herald* (October 28, 1842), 2:2; (September 12, 1850), 2:1; as well as the references to pigs

in comments on Noah by Edgar Allan Poe, *Southern Literary Messenger*, 2 (1836), 604; and William Price, *Clement Falconer* (Baltimore, 1847), II, 12. Solomon Nunes Carvalho also recoiled from eating pork—even in his travels with Fremont (1854), see his *Incidents of Travel and Adventure in the Far West* (Philadelphia, 1957 [1857]), 170 cf. 189. See also the references to pork in wit and graphic humor assembled in Rudolf Glanz, *The Jew in Early American Wit and Graphic Humor* (New York, 1973), 76–80; and in his *The Jew in old American Folklore* (New York, 1963), 56–63.

62.   My understanding of Noah's Judaism has benefited from Jick, *The Americanization of the Synagogue*; Marshall Sklare and Joseph Greenblum, *Jewish Identity on the Suburban Frontier* (New York, 1967), 45–96, esp. p. 57; and Charles Liebman, *The Ambivalent American Jew* (Philadelphia, 1973), 45–49.

63.   For Noah's attitude toward Christmas, see *Union* (December 24, 1842), 2:1; and Noah to Zipporah Noah (December 24, 1848 [?]) in *Major Noah*, 293. See also Milton Matz, "The Meaning of Christmas to the American Jew," *Jewish Journal of Sociology*, 3 (1961), 129–137; and Jacob J. Petuchowski, "The Magnification of Channukah," *Commentary*, 24 (January 1961), 38–43.

CHAPTER VIII. Declining Years

1.   Quotations are from *Home Journal* (February 2, 1850), 2:2–3; and *T&M* (July 30, 1848), 2:1.

2.   Quotations are from David Lambert to William P. Mangum (May 7, 1841) and Noah to Mangum (February 6, 1841), both in Henry T. Shanks (ed.), *The Papers of Willie Person Mangum* (Raleigh, N.C., 1953), III, 153, 109. Rumors of Noah's impending appointment appeared in *Herald* (October 14, 1840), 2:1; and *Times and Evening Star* (October 15, 1840), 2. The appointment was announced in *Herald* (January 11, 1841), 2:5, and *American* (January 11, 1841), 2:1; see also, Nicholas Carroll to William A. Graham (April 7, 1841), in J. G. de Roulhac Hamilton, *The Papers of William A. Graham* (Raleigh, N.C., 1959), 183–4. On the Court of Sessions, see Henry W. Scott, *The Courts of the State of New York* (New York, 1909), 73, 103, 347. *American* (March 1, 1841), 2:1, falsely reported that Noah had been reappointed surveyor.

3.   On the battle over Noah's nomination, see Noah to Webb (n.d.—pencil date of 1839 is doubtless an error) in Webb papers, box 1a, Yale University; Noah to Seward (February 6, 1841) Historical Society of Pennsylvania, also on AJA microfilm 1156; Noah to Verplanck (February 26, 1841) and Noah to Seward (February 26, 1841) both in Verplanck Papers, New York Historical Society; *Niles' Weekly Register* (January 30, 1841), 336; (May 15, 1841), 176; miscellaneous articles in Lyons Scrapbook, III, AJHS; *Herald* (August 11, 1841), 2:1; cf. *EJ*, X, 1490–1512.

4.   Quotation is from *Commercial Advertiser* (July 3, 1841), 2:5. See also the court columns in the various New York newspapers, and *Tribune* (August 4, 1841), 2:3, which contains the text of a lengthy Noah grand jury charge.

5.   *Herald* (October 1, 1840), 2:1; (June 15, 16, 22, 1841) quoted and (July 21–23). John Morrill's letter to Noah (February 1, 1842) appears in *Tribune* (May 16, 1842), 2:3 and Noah's quoted explanatory reply (February 3, 1842) is in the private collection of Professor Leo Hershkowitz, who kindly sent me a Xerox copy. See also Noah to David Lambert (July 18, 1841) in Shanks (ed.) *Papers of W. P. Mangum*, III, 202; Nevins, *Diary of Philip Hone*, 549, 588; Charles P. Daly, *The Settlement of the Jews in North America*, ed. Max J. Kohler (New York, 1893), 136; and Charles P. Haswell, *Reminiscences of an Octogenarian of the City of New York* (New York, 1896), 385. For Noah's subsequent praise of Attree, see *T&M* (November 25, 1849), 2:3.

6.   Ira Leonard, "New York City Politics, 1841–1844: Nativism and Reform" (unpublished Ph.D. thesis, New York University, 1965), 10, 83; *the People ex relatione James Lynch vs. The Mayor, Alderman and Commonality of the City of New York*, 25 *Wendell* 680; *Herald* (May

22, 1841), 2:1; (May 25, 1841), 2:1; and (June 17, 1841), 2:2; Shanks (ed.) *Papers of Mangum*, III, 245 and *Herald* (June 27, 1842), 2:3. On Noah's resignation from the bench, see Lyons Scrapbook, III, item 80, AJHS; and *Herald* (July 30, 1842), 2:2; as well as *Union* (July 28, 1842). For a different, unsubstantiated view, see Simon Wolf, "Mordecai Manuel Noah," *Selected Addresses and Papers of Simon Wolf* (Cincinnati, 1926), 121.

7. My understanding of this period has been based on Robert Seager II, *And Tyler Too* (New York, 1963); and Glyndon G. Van Deusen, *The Jacksonian Era* (New York, 1959), 151–169. On Tyler and the Jews, see *PAJHS*, 9 (1901), 162; 11 (1903), 158–9; 39 (1949), 2–22.

8. Advance announcements of *The Union*'s publication appeared in *Commercial Advertiser* (July 12, 1842), 2; and *Sun* (July 16, 1842), 2:3. Noah reprinted the "Address" of *The Union* during the first several weeks of its publication. It first appeared in *Union* (July 18, 1842), 1. *The New Haven Herald* was quoted in *Tribune* (July 26, 1842), 2:3. For circulation figures, see H. M. Salomon to Calhoun, (n.d. [1844]), Calhoun Papers, Clemson University, S.C.; *Herald* (August 26, 1842), 2:1; (November 4, 1842), 2:1; *Tribune* (December 17, 1842), 1:2. On the *Union*'s patronage, see *Tribune* (August 5, 1842), 2:1; *Union* (September 14, 1842), 2:1; *Herald* (October 28, 1842), 2:2; Webster to Noah (December 29, 1842), Department of State, Domestic Letters, 33:34 (M40 reel 31); and *Sunday Dispatch* (March 15, 1846), 2:2.

9. On Paul George's management, see *Sunday Dispatch* (March 15, 1846); and *Atlas* (March 30, 1851). Bennett's attacks included *Herald* (August 26, 1842), 2:1; (September 15, 1842), 2:1; and (November 10, 1842), 2:2. On Noah's subservience to the *Sun*, see *Herald* (August 27, 1842), 2:2; (September 13, 1842), 2:2; but also *Sun* (November 23, 1842), 2:2 which mildly criticized Noah. The *Union* piece most frequently reprinted in other newspapers was Noah's "My First Duel," *Union* (July 20, 1842), 2:1.

10. John Tyler's biographer, Robert Seager II, refers to these memoirs as "Noah's Reminiscences." Actually, they are a series entitled "Reminiscences and Random Recollections of the Tyler Administration," by "Horace Walpole" which appeared in the New York *Sunday Dispatch* from December 1845 through May 1846. Professor Seager advises me that in the Gardiner-Tyler Papers, these articles were found in a file entitled "Noah's Reminiscences," an identification which he had no reason to doubt. Unfortunately, this file is now missing. Were it to be found, it would still not conclusively tie Noah to these memoirs, although his authorship of the articles can certainly not be ruled out. "Horace Walpole" himself merely claimed to be an "old and valued friend of Major Noah." His version of Noah's Tylerite activities correlates well with what is known from other sources. Seager, *And Tyler Too*, 587 and personal conversation with Professor Seager. I am grateful to the Library of Congress for providing me with a microfilm of extant copies of the *Sunday Dispatch* series. I found but one reference to the reminiscences in the Gardiner-Tyler papers at Yale, Julia Tyler to Julia Gardiner (April 14, 1846), Box 3, Second Series, and it makes no mention of Noah.

11. Quotation is from *Sunday Dispatch* (January 25, 1846), 2. See *Herald* (March 30, 1843), 2:1; on Noah's advice to Tyler, and Noah Papers, AJHS, for a collection of press clippings dealing with Noah's resignation from *The Union*, in addition to Noah's own comments in *Union* (December 31, 1842), 2:1. See also *Herald* (June 29, 1842), 2:4; (September 16, 1842), 2:1; and *Tribune* (August 12, 1842), 2:1.

12. On Noah's trip to Richmond, see *Salem Register* (August 3, 1843), 2:6; and Oliver Chitwood, *John Tyler: Champion of the Old South* (New York, 1934), 373. The March 15th rally (which Seager, *And Tyler Too*, 223 misdates) was reported in *Herald* (March 16, 1843), 1:4; and remembered in *Sunday Dispatch* (March 22, 1846), 2, without noticing the anti-Jewish comments of the crowd. Noah announced the end of his party in *Tribune* (March 21, 1843), 2:1; see also *Herald* (March 29, 31, 1843). The last passing reference to Noah's support of Tyler is in J. J. Bailey to Julia Gardiner (May 13, 1843), *Tyler's Quarterly Magazine* 18 (1937), 18; cf. *Herald* (May 27, 1843), 2:2; and (June 15, 1843), 2:4.

13. *Tribune* (November 14, 1842), 2:1; *Sun* (February 1, 3, 1843); Noah to John Spencer (April 20, 1843), Historical Society of Pennsylvania; Noah to Duff Green (May 24, 1843), copy at AJA, "Noah" correspondence file (quoted); John Calhoun to State Department (June 30,

1845), RG59, Letters of Application and Recommendation During the Administration of John Polk, Zachary Taylor and Millard Fillmore (M873 reel 63), NA; *Sun* (April 24, 1843), 2:3; *Herald* (May 8, 1843), 2:1; (May 27, 1843), 2:1; (June 16, 1843), 2.3; *Atlas* (March 30, 1851); *Boston Museum*, 3 (April 26, 1851), 1; and Hyman B. Grinstein, *The Rise of the Jewish Community of New York 1654–1860* (Philadelphia, 1945), 425. On later ambassadors to Turkey, see Naomi W. Cohen, *A Dual Heritage: The Public Career of Oscar Straus* (Philadelphia, 1969), 21–38, 74–101; Yonathan Shapiro, *Leadership of the American Zionist Organization 1897–1930* (Urbana, Ill., 1971), 254; and the snide remark in Samuel Ornitz, *Haunch, Paunch and Jowl: An Autobiography* (New York, 1923), 281.

14.   Quotation is from *Sunday Dispatch* (January 25, 1846), 2. Noah's official break with Tyler was announced in his *Messenger* and quoted in *Salem Register* (July 20, 1843), 2:1 and elsewhere.

15.   Herbert Donovan, *The Barnburners* (New York, 1925), 52; *Tribune* (July 6, 1843), 2:2; (July 17, 1843), 2:3; (August 7, 1843), 2:3; (January 12, 1845), 2:1; *Herald* (July 8, 1843), 2:2; (August 1, 1843), 2:1; and *T&M* (March 30, 1851), 2. No copies of the *Messenger* are known to be extant.

16.   The history and controversy surrounding Sunday papers is discussed in Frederick Hudson, *Journalism in the United States from 1690 to 1872* (New York, 1873), 337; and in Sidney Kobre, *Development of American Journalism* (Dubuque, 1969), 154; see also, Joseph P. Thompson, *Memoir of David Hale* (Hartford, 1850), 405–6. Noah had always supported the idea of Sunday papers, see *ES* (July 16, 1837), 2:2; and (November 24, 1838), 2:3. He defended his own paper in *T&M* (April 4, 1837), 2:1; and his success at molding a family paper is noted retrospectively in *T&M* (March 28, 1852), 2:2 which is quoted. Other quotations are (in order) from: *T&M* (February 28, 1847), 1:5; (June 6, 1847), 2:1; (May 23, 1847), 2:1; (February 17, 1850), 2:1 and (March 16, 1851), 2:3. I have seen only scattered issues of *T&M* before 1847; my description is therefore based principally on later numbers which are found in the New York Historical Society. Noah's correspondence column was mentioned in *Home Journal* (November 24, 1849), 3:4 and *Occident*, 9 (1851), 99. His circulation figures appear in *T&M* (November 11, 1849), 2:1; and (March 30, 1851), 2:3.

17.   Isaac Goldberg, citing a letter from *Sun* biographer Frank M. O'Brien, claimed that "Major Noah was never on the *Sun*." Contrary evidence is overwhelming. *Major Noah*, 238; Frank M. O'Brien to Isaac Goldberg (April 16, 1931), Goldberg Papers, New York Public Library, Box 1.

18.   On newspaper proposals, see Noah to Duff Green (May 24, 1843), Noah correspondence file, AJA; *PAJHS* 27 (1920), 400; Noah to M. C. Mordecai (October 21, 1846) most conveniently reprinted in *Major Noah*, 265–8; and *Mirror* 4 (July 25, 1846), 250. The attempt to purchase Burr's letters is incidentally mentioned in Thurlow Weed, *Autobiography of Thurlow Weed* (Boston, 1883), 416. The lithographed "National Volume" letter (March 1, 1845) is listed and pictured in Jacob Blanck, *Bibliography of American Literature*, VI (New Haven, 1973), 450, 452 and is found in many collections. On Noah's connections with the *Sun*, see *Young America* (January 31, 1846), 2, and *Herald* (November 24, 1845), 2:1 which are quoted, as well as Noah to Charles B. Moss (November 21, 1844), Tyler Papers, Manuscript Division, Library of Congress, copy at AJA; *Herald* (December 28, 1843), 2:4; (January 16, 1845), 2:3; William L. Mackenzie, *The Life and Times of Martin Van Buren* (Boston, 1846), 306; *T&M* (March 30, 1851), 2; I. C. Pray, *Memoirs of James Gordon Bennett and His Times* (New York, 1855), 295; and Robert P. Noah, "Mordecai M. Noah," *The Reformer and Jewish Times* (November 15, 1878), 1.

19.   Jerome Mushkat, *Tammany* (Syracuse, 1971), 208–59; Gustavus Myers, *The History of Tammany Hall* (New York, 1917), 146; William Trimble, "Diverging Tendencies in New York's Democracy in the Period of the Locofocos," *American Historical Review*, 24 (April 1919), 396–421; Noah to Duff Green (May 24, 1843), Noah Correspondence file, AJA; H.M. Salomon to Calhoun (August 21, 1843), South Carolina Library; Salomon to Webb (December 17, 1843), Webb Papers, Yale University, Box 1 c; Noah to M. C. Mordecai (October 21, 1846)

in *Major Noah*, 265–8; *T&M* (March 4, 1844; May 25, 1845; February 6, 1848; October 28, 1849); *Barnburner Letter*; *Tribune* (June 5, 1846), 2:2; (April 17, 1850), 2:2.

20. Noah to Sol Smith (October 11, 1847) printed in Smith's *Theatrical Management in the West and South for Thirty Years* (New York, 1868), 205.

21. Alex Bein, "The Origin of the Term and Concept Zionism" *Herzl Year Book*, 2 (1959), 1–27; Bernard Weinryb, "The Foundations and History of Zionism," (in Hebrew) *Tarbitz*, 8 (1937), 69–112; Jacob Katz, "Towards the Clarification of the Concept 'Precursors of Zionism'," (in Hebrew) *Shivat Zion*, 1 (1949–50), 91–105.

22. Quotations are from *Consecration Address*, 27; *National Advocate* (November 9, 1824), 2:4; and Ararat Address, *PAJHS*, 21 (1913), 232; see also *National Advocate* (December 23, 1822), 2:2. My view of Noah's restorationist thought differs from the views presented in Louis Ruchames, "Mordecai Manuel Noah and Early American Zionism," *AJHQ*, 64 (March 1975), 195–223; Grinstein, *New York*, 459–60; and Raphael Mahler, "The Historical Background of Pre-Zionism in America and its Continuity," in *Marcus Festschrift*, 341–57.

23. Quotation is from Noah's *Lost Tribes Discourse*, 37–8. For Noah's most acerbic attack on determinism, see his "The Moors in Spain," *New York Mirror*, 14 (April 1, 1837), 317.

24. Among numerous works dealing with this period, see Nahum Sokolow, *History of Zionism 1600–1918* (New York, 1969 [1919]; Franz Kobler, *The Vision Was There: A History of the British Movement for the Restoration of the Jews* (London, 1956); A. M. Hyamson, "British Proposals for the Restoration of the Jews to Palestine," *PAJHS*, 26 (1918), 127–74; M. Vėrete, "The Idea of Restoration of the Jews in English Protestant Thought," [in Hebrew] *Zion*, 33 (1968), 145–79; *idem*, "Why Was a British Consulate Established in Jerusalem," *English Historical Review*, 85 (1970), 316–45; Isidore S. Meyer (ed.) *Early History of Zionism in America* (New York, 1958); and Moshe Davis (ed.), *With Eyes Toward Zion* (New York, 1977).

25. *ES-Country* (December 1, 1835), 2:6; *Lost Tribes Discourse*, 37–8; *ES* (April 8, 1840), 2:2; (June 13, 1840), 2:3; *Herald* (June 20, 1840), 2:2; *New Yorker* (June 20, 1840), 223; *Hartford Times* (June 20, 1840), 1:3; *Herald* (June 3, 1841), 1:5; *Tribune* (June 22, 1842), 1:1; *Herald* (June 25, 1844), 1:2; and *Restoration Discourse*, esp. 33–41, 51–52, all contain various Noah pronouncements on restoration.

26. Newspaper articles describing Noah's address include *Niles' Weekly Register*, 67 (November 16, 1844), 164–5; *National Anti-Slavery Standard*, 5 (November 21, 1844), 100; and *Herald* (September 13, 1844), 2:3; (December 3, 1844), 2:2. Quotations are from Noah's *Discourse on the Restoration*, 24, 13, 25. This discourse has been reprinted many times, most recently in Abraham J. Karp, *Beginnings: Early American Judaica* (Philadelphia, 1975) and by Arno Press (1977). A Hebrew translation by Hayyim Orlan appears in Zvulun Ravid (ed.) *Zevi Scharfstein Jubilee Volume* (Tel Aviv, 1970), replacing an earlier abbreviated translation in Max Raisin, *Mordecai Manuel Noah, Zionist, Author and Statesman* (Hebrew, Warsaw, 1905).

27. Noah, *Restoration Discourse, passim*. For the origin of the Isaiah comparison, see John McDonald, *Isaiah's Message to the American People* (Albany, 1814, Philadelphia, 1824). Cf. Conrad Cherry (ed.) *God's New Israel* (Englewood Cliffs, 1971).

28. Noah, *Restoration Discourse*, 52–3; Noah to Charles B. Moss (November 21, 1844), John Tyler Papers, VI, folio 469–70, copy in AJA correspondence file "Noah."

29. An advertisement for Noah's Discourse may be found in the Noah Papers in Houghton Library, Harvard University. Reactions to the discourse include *Herald of Freedom*, 10 (April 25, 1845), 2–3; *Albion*, 3 (November 2, 1844), 529; and *Herald* (October 30, 1844), 2:2 which are all quoted, also *Knickerbocker*, 25 (March 1845), 249 and *North American Review*, 60 (April 1845), 365. See also Louis Ruchames, "The Abolitionists and the Jews: Some Further Thoughts," in *Marcus Festschrift*, 505–15.

30. Quotes are from *Voice of Jacob* (November 29, 1844), 48; *Restoration Discourse*, 40; and *Occident*, 2 (1845), 605. See also *Voice of Jacob* (January 3, 1845), 70–71; (May 9, 1845), 154–55; (June 20, 1845), 182–3; (August 1, 1845), 2; *Occident*, 3 (1845), 29–35; *Jewish Chronicle* (April 4, 1845), 130B and Maxine S. Seller, "Isaac Leeser's Views on the Restoration

of a Jewish Palestine," *AJHQ*, 58 (September 1968), 118–35 on Jewish arguments with Noah. For two interesting British responses to the address, see "A Romance That May Become a Reality," the [London] *Spectator*, 18 (1845), 638, and George Gawler, *Observations and Practical Suggestions in Furtherance of the Establishment of Jewish Colonies in Palestine* (London, 1845), 14. The address itself was not reprinted in England until 1849 when it appeared under the title *The Jews, Judea and Christianity: A Discourse on the Restoration of the Jews* (London, 1849).

31.   *Occident* 6 (May 1848), 71–2 in Seller, "Isaac Leeser on Restoration," 123; cf. Salo Baron, "The Impact of the Revolution of 1848 on Jewish Emancipation," *Jewish Social Studies*, 14 (1950), 195–248; and Jacob Toury, *Turmoil and Confusion in the Revolutions of 1848* (Hebrew, Tel Aviv, 1968), esp. 73ff. Noah, *Address Delivered at the Hebrew Synagogue in Crosby Street, New York on Thanksgiving Day to Aid in the Erection of the Temple at Jerusalem* (Jamaica, 1849) is the text which I used; the address also appeared in *Tribune* (November 25, 1848), 1. For other Noah comments on restoration and millennium, see *T&M* (1847–1850). Examples of Noah's assistance to messengers include *PAJHS*, 27, (1920), 107 regarding Moses H. Morpugo (1822); *PAJHS* 20 (1913), 167 regarding Aaron Corcos (1823); *JUSDH*, III, 917 regarding Enoch Zundal (1833); *Herald* (September 3, 1839), 2:1 regarding Rabbi Uziel (1839); and Lyons Scrapbook, II, 15, AJHS regarding Aaron Selig Ashkenazi (1839–40). On efforts to organize Palestine collections, see *Asmonean* (December 14, 1849), 61; circular dated 8th Adar 5610 (February 20, 1850) in Lyons Collection, Box 7a, AJHS; and David and Tamar de Sola Pool, *An Old Faith in the New World* (New York, 1955), 402. More generally, see Salo and Jeannette Baron, "Palestinean Messengers in America, 1849–1879: A Record of Four Journies," *Steeled by Adversity* (Philadelphia, 1971), 158–266; and Moshe Davis, "Iggrot He Pekidim Vehaamarchalim MeAmsterdam," in Saul Lieberman and Arthur Hyman (eds.) *Salo Baron Jubilee Volume* (New York, 1975), Hebrew section, 91–109, esp. 108. Both cite earlier literature.

32.   Reactions to the address include *Weekly Argus* (December 2, 1848), 376; *New London Daily Chronicle* (November 28, 1848), 2:3; *Occident*, 6 (1849), 550—559; and *Jewish Chronicle* (January 19, 1849) 117B; (January 26, 1849), 125B–126A (which is quoted); (February 2, 1849), 139A; and (March 23, 1849), 191A. One of Noah's last surviving letters, Noah to R. Shelton Mackenzie (December 2, 1850), Historical Society of Philadelphia, also on AJA microfilm, 1156, asks for a British Parliamentary Report on the commercial statistics of Syria in 1840.

33.   On old age in America, see David H. Fischer, *Growing Old in America* (New York, 1977), esp. 113–56; see p. 118 for the quotation from Nathaniel Hawthorne's *Scarlet Letter*. Comments on Noah's old age include *Truth Teller*, 10 (May 24, 1834), 165 which is quoted, as well as innumerable barbs in *Herald*, (e.g. [April 3, 1839], 2:3). See also Noah's quoted response in *ES* (November 27, 1833), 2:1; and the analysis in Robert A. Rutland, *The Newsmongers* (New York, 1973), 13–14.

34.   Jacksonians used the word "old" in two senses. Sometimes they used it as a mark of familiarity ("Old Hickory," "Old Kinderhook," or "Old Zach"). Much like the word "little" ("Little Van") or common nicknames (Tippecanoe), "old" used in this way proved that a man (usually a politician) was an "old friend"—not a stuffy aristocrat. At other times, "old" had far more negative and contemptuous connotations, connotations related to the infirmities of old age. The context is the only guide. This linguistic ambiguity between familiarity and contempt, an ambiguity still present in twentieth century English, reflects generally on Americans' ambivalent feelings toward the elderly. It may even help to explain the ambivalence. Familiarity, after all, breeds contempt. Cf. Fisher, *Growing Old in America*, 132.

35.   *ES* (February 4, 1834), 2:2. For a discussion of the "grandfather myth" and its function in a quite different context, see Dan Miron, *A Traveler Disguised: A Study in the Rise of Modern Yiddish Fiction in the Nineteenth Century* (New York, 1973), 30–31.

36.   On Noah as a journalistic veteran, see *New York Mirror*, 4 (July 25, 1846), 250. His memoirs are also mentioned in *Tribune* (March 24, 1851), 2:1; *Literary World* 8 (April 5, 1851),

269; and *Brother Jonathan* 4 (January 21, 1843), 76. Records of Noah's tenure at the Customs House (October 6, 1848–March 22, 1851) may be found in the Bureau of Customs Records, RG36, Federal Archives and Records Center, Bayonne, New Jersey. See also the attack on the sinecure in *Herald* (July 22, 1849), 2:2; (August 30, 1849), 2:2; (January 29, 1850), 2:2 and (May 7, 1850), 2:3; and more generally B. R. Brubaker, "Spoils Appointments of American Writers," *New England Quarterly*, 48 (1975), 556–64. Noah's final writings are found in *T&M*, especially the correspondence column where his writings are most easily identified. According to the *Sunday Mercury* (March 30, 1851), Noah had not actively conducted *T&M* for some time. Quotation is from a column reprinted in the [Washington, D.C.] *National Era*, 3 (March 1849), 49.

37. *Weekly Tribune* (April 1, 1848), 5:5; Noah to Henry A. Anthony (June 12, 1850), Noah Papers, Houghton Library, Harvard University; *Asmonean* (March 28, 1851), 180.

38. *Asmonean* (March 21, 1851), 172; (March 28, 1851), 180; *T&M* (March 23, 1851), 2; and (March 30, 1851), 2. The *Tribune* reported on Noah's condition from March 18 onward, and printed an informative obit, (March 24, 1851), 4:3.

EPILOGUE

1. Obituary notices are conveniently collected in Lyons Scrapbook I, Box 7a, AJHS. See also *Asmonean* (March 28, 1851), 180–181; which is quoted; *Occident* 9 (1851), 97–103; [London] *Jewish Chronicle* (April 11, 1851), 209B. The tombstone inscription is in *Jewish Messenger* (July 23, 1875) found in Lyons Scrapbook, II, p. 275, AJHS. The oft-repeated statement that Noah was the last Jew to be buried within the confines of Manhattan is incorrect, see David de Sola Pool, *Portraits Etched in Stone: Early Jewish Settlers 1682–1831* (New York, 1952), 141.

2. Morris Raphall's address is reprinted in *Asmonean* (March 28, 1851), 181.

Bibliographical Essay

My work on Mordecai Noah has led me to hundreds of primary and secondary sources. In what follows, my aim is not to list these sources, but briefly to describe and evaluate the most important of them. Many additional references may be found in the notes.

Primary Sources

The obvious point of departure for any study of Mordecai Noah is his own large corpus of writings. Jacob Blanck and his associates have compiled the most complete bibliography in volume six of *Bibliography of American Literature* (New Haven, 1973), 447–454. Blanck ignores newspapers (see below) and has missed several of Noah's contributions to contemporary magazines. But he has found a great deal, and his list of separately published items is complete with two exceptions: he casts unnecessary doubt on the ascription to Noah of *A Letter... Examining the Claims and Qualifications of DeWitt Clinton* (Charleston, 1812), and he is unaware of Noah's *Address Delivered at the Hebrew Synagogue in Crosby Street, New York on Thanksgiving Day to Aid in the Erection of the Temple of Jerusalem* (Jamaica, 1849).

Many of Noah's published plays and pamphlets are now available on microfilm in the American Culture Series and the Early American Imprints series published by University Microfilms and the American Antiquarian Society. The play *She Would Be a Soldier* was most recently reprinted in Richard Moody, *Dramas from the American Theater 1762–1909* (New York, 1966), 115–22, and is also in Montrose J. Moses, *Representative Plays by American Dramatists 1765–1819* (New York, 1918), 643–78. The "Ararat Address" is reprinted in *PAJHS* 21 (1913), 230–52. The *Restoration Discourse* is easily located in Abraham J. Karp, *Beginnings: Early American Judaica* (Philadelphia, 1975), and in the Arno Press "America and the Holy

Land" series (1977). Noah's brief account of his ancestors, the Nunez family, is reprinted as an appendix to Richard D. Barnett, "Zipra Nunes's Story," in *Marcus Festschrift*, 59–61. Lastly, the *Book of Jasher* has been reprinted by Hermon Press (1972). Reprints of correspondence, documents, and other miscellaneous items are listed below.

Noah's articles in contemporary magazines are difficult to locate. I found most helpful Nelson F. Adkins, ed. , *Index to Early American Periodicals to 1850*, a W.P.A. study now available on microcard. I located other magazine articles in various ways including scrapbooks and guesswork. No doubt many articles—especially those published pseudonymously—remain undetected.

As discussed in the preface, Mordecai Noah's newspapers are a principal source for this study. I found good runs of daily or "for the country" (semi-weekly) editions of the *National Advocate, New York National Advocate, Enquirer, Courier and Enquirer, Evening Star, Union*, and *Times and Messenger* (after 1847) in one or more of the four libraries where I did my newspaper research: the American Antiquarian Society, Library of Congress, New-York Historical Society, and New York Public Library. Actual holdings of these libraries varied somewhat from published listings which date back many years. Numerous issues of the *Enquirer, Courier and Enquirer, Evening Star for the Country*, and *Times and Messenger* are on microfilm. Unfortunately, I found that the best available editions were not in every case used by the microfilmer, and I often had to consult the original.

I found it difficult to identify Noah's articles in the *Courier and Enquirer*. Too many other hands were also at work on this paper. His *Sun* articles are completely impossible to identify. When Noah edited newspapers on his own, however, he assumed responsibility for what went out under his name, and generally wrote key editorials. His distinctive style usually makes it easy to determine his contributions—even in the *Times and Messenger* where, as indicated in the text, he had much assistance during the final years. Jerome Mushkat has reprinted several of Noah's best *Times and Messenger* articles in "Epitaphs by Mordecai Noah," *New York Historical Quarterly*, 55 (July 1971), 253–71.

Early American newspapers commented extensively on Mordecai Noah's activities. For this study, I unsurprisingly found New York newspapers most valuable, especially the *Evening Post, Columbian, American, Herald*, and *Tribune* (microfilm editions used when available). The *Herald*'s coverage of the Jewish community in general, and Noah in particular, is extremely important, and the relationship of James Gordon Bennett to the Jews deserves a separate study. I found that the *Sun* and the *Courier and Enquirer* (after 1832) contain little material of value, though this judgment is admittedly based on the incomplete microfilm edition of both newspapers. Additional New York newspaper items may be gleaned from the frustrating but valuable De Vos index located in the New York Historical Society. *Niles' Weekly Register* (Washington, D.C.) contains much on Noah's early years. Jewish newspapers, the *Occident* and the *Asmonean*, contain material on his last years.

Happily, Isaac Fine's "Niles' Weekly Register on the Jews," *PAJHS* 50 (1960), 3–22; and the unpublished index to the *Occident* at the American Jewish Archives obviate the need to search these newspapers page by page.

The American Jewish Historical Society possesses an invaluable collection of early American newspaper articles dealing with Jewish themes. Over half of these articles deal with Mordecai Noah—a fact which in itself demonstrates his role as "symbolic Jew." The newspapers come from all over the country, and are in many cases unique copies. A partial index is available at the society. A separate American Jewish Historical Society collection, the deservedly famous Jacques Judah Lyons collection, also contains some interesting newspaper clippings, including a set of Noah obituaries. Some of this collection has been listed and printed in *PAJHS* 21 (1913), 27 (1920).

The complete letters and papers of Mordecai Noah have neither been collected nor published. A variety of published sources, however, do contain reprints of some primary documents. The previous biographer of Noah, Isaac Goldberg, had access to a large collection of family letters which are now lost. As indicated in the text, Professor Hans G. Reissner's researches led him to conclude that these letters were destroyed. Happily, Goldberg printed a portion of this collection in his "Mr. Noah, American," *The Menorah Journal*, 24 (1936), 276–93, and in his *Major Noah*. Both Morris U. Schappes, ed., *A Documentary History of the Jews in the United States 1654–1875* (3rd ed., New York, 1971); and Joseph L. Blau and Salo W. Baron, *The Jews of the United States 1790–1840: A Documentary History* (New York, 1963), contain invaluable primary materials dealing with many aspects of Noah's career. Jacob R. Marcus, in his *Memoirs of American Jews, 1775–1865* (Philadelphia, 1955), I, 117–145, creates a memoir of Noah's diplomatic and dramatic career by reprinting excerpts from Noah's *Correspondence and Documents* and *Travels* (see below), as well as the full text of his letter to William Dunlap from the latter's *History of the American Theater* (1st ed., New York, 1832).

Noah himself printed a variety of primary sources dealing with his consulship in his *Correspondence and Documents Relative to the Attempt to Negotiate for the Release of the American Captives at Algiers; including Remarks on our Relations with that Regency* (Washington City, 1816); and in his *Travels in England, France, Spain and the Barbary States in the Years 1813–14 and 15* (New York, 1819). See also the documents reprinted in an unpublished paper by Gilbert S. Rosenthal, "Mordecai M. Noah, Diplomat," found at the American Jewish Archives.

Most of the other printed sources about Noah deal with his politics. G. Herbert Cone, "New Matter Relating to Mordecai M. Noah," *PAJHS*, 11 (1903), 131–7, reprints several documents including some material dealing with Ararat. Far more valuable are printed editions of the papers of Noah's acquaintances which include letters with him and letters about him. Of great importance are *The Papers of John Calhoun*, edited by W. Edwin Hemphill (Columbia, S.C., 1959–   ); *The Papers of Henry Clay*, edited by James F.

Hopkins, (Lexington, Ky., 1959–   ); *Correspondence of Andrew Jackson*, edited by John S. Bassett (Washington, D.C., 1928–33); *The Papers of Willie Person Mangum*, edited by Henry T. Shanks (Raleigh, 1950–1956); and "The Correspondence of Jews with President Martin Van Buren," edited by Albert M. Friedenberg, *PAJHS*, 22 (1914), 71–100, which unfortunately contains embarrassing transcription errors. A large number of Noah letters may be found in William L. Mackenzie, *The Lives and Opinions of Benjamin Franklin Butler and Jesse Hoyt* (Boston, 1845) and *idem*, *The Life and Times of Martin Van Buren* (Boston, 1846). Letters dealing with Noah may also be found in *Reminiscences of James A. Hamilton* (New York, 1869), and in Charles R. King, *The Life and Correspondence of Rufus King* (New York, 1900). Among other widely scattered Noah letters in print, I found particularly important those reprinted in Moshe Davis, *With Eyes Toward Zion* ('New York, 1977), and Noah's letter to Sol Smith in the latter's *Theatrical Management in the West and South* (New York, 1868), 205. References to Noah may also be found in *The Memoirs of John Quincy Adams*, edited by Charles F. Adams (Philadelphia, 1875); *The Diary of Philip Hone*, edited by Allan Nevins (New York, 1927), and *The Diary of William Dunlap* (New York, 1930).

Unpublished Mordecai Noah letters are widely scattered. The American Jewish Archives has attempted to collect as many as possible and houses a fine collection of Xeroxed and microfilmed Noah correspondence including some of what follows. The papers of David B. Warden, found at the Maryland Historical Society and the Library of Congress, contain wonderfully informative letters regarding the Tunis consulship (part microfilmed). The papers of James Madison and James Monroe, Manuscript Division, Library of Congress (and microfilm) help to explicate the administration's view of Noah, and include Noah letters on other subjects as well. The Joseph B. Nones diary, American Jewish Historical Society, may be an unreliable source on the consulship, as it was written much later. The Peter Porter Papers at the Buffalo and Erie County Historical Society (also microfilm) contain a long and important letter regarding Ararat, and an unpublished article on the same subject. The James Watson Webb Papers, Yale University, include many enlightening Noah letters bearing on journalism and the Bank of the United States. The Nicholas Biddle Papers, Library of Congress (and microfilm) are crucial to an understanding of Noah's relations with the Bank of the United States, although actual correspondence with Noah is sparse. The Noah letters in the Gratz Collection and other collections of the Historical Society of Pennsylvania contain letters particularly important for the light they shed on political matters. Similarly valuable are the Noah letters in the Seward Papers at the University of Rochester, and the Duff Green Papers at the Library of Congress.

Other collections where I found Noah's letters, or letters dealing with Noah, include the Adams Papers, Adams Family Trust (and microfilm); Myers Family Papers, American Jewish Archives; Noah Papers, New York County

Court Papers, New York County Clerk Papers, Incorporation Papers, Grace Seixas Papers, Samuel Oppenheim Papers, all at American Jewish Historical Society; Boston Public Library Archives; Webster Collection, Brandeis University; Noah Papers, Chicago Historical Society; Special Collections and Clinton Papers, Columbia University (and microfilm); Webster Collection, Dartmouth College Archives; Noah Papers, Houghton Library, Harvard University; Frank H. Elmore Papers, James H. Hammond Papers (microfilm edition), Hamilton Fish Papers, Russell Jarvis Papers and New York Executive and Miscellaneous Papers, Manuscript Division, Library of Congress; Bancroft Papers and Jefferson Papers, Massachusetts Historical Society; Noah Papers, Morristown National Historical Park; New York Historical Society Archives; Ducyckinck, Emmet, Staufer, Flagg, Myers and Miscellaneous Collections, New York Public Library; Blair-Lee Papers, Princeton University; University of Virginia Archives; Beinecke Library manuscript collection, Metzdorf Collection and Miscellaneous Manuscripts, Yale Historical Archives, Yale University.

Five published government documents shed light on various facets of Noah's career. *Journal of the Executive Proceedings of the Senate of the United States of America* (Washington, D.C., 1928) details his confirmation as consul and surveyor. *American State Papers: Naval Affairs* (Washington, 1834) contain some documents on his consulship activities in the *Abaellino* affair. *Minutes of the Common Council of the City of New York 1784–1831* (New York, 1930) contain interesting references dealing with his multifarious activities in New York from 1817–1830. James Kent (ed.) *The Charter of the City of New York... and the Journal of the City Convention* (New York, 1836) chronicles his contributions to the charter revision convention in 1829. Lastly, United States, House of Representatives, "Report 460," *Reports of Committees of the House of Representatives at the First Session of the Twenty Second Congress Begun and Held at the City of Washington* contains the lengthy proceedings of the Clayton Committee which investigated the Bank of the United States' dealings with the *Courier and Enquirer.*

Unpublished government documents in the National Archives elucidate Noah's diplomatic career, and greatly alter the standard portrait based on Noah's *Travels.* The records which I found most valuable are the General Records of the Department of State (R.G. 59): Applications and Recommendations for Public Office Under Presidents Madison, Monroe, Jackson, Harrison, Tyler and Polk; Miscellaneous Letters of the Department of State; Domestic Letters of the Department of State; Despatches from the United States Consuls in Riga and Algiers; and most important of all, Despatches from United States Consuls in Tunis. All of these records are on microfilm. Some interesting material on Noah's Tunis consulship is also found in the legation archives of Algiers, Tripoli and Tunis (R.G. 84) found only at the National Archives itself.

Published court cases involving Noah often contain interesting information not otherwise available. I found particularly useful the trials regarding Noah's alleged breaking open and publishing of a letter, reprinted with commentary in John D. Lawson, ed., *American State Trials* (St. Louis, 1914), I, pp. 671–698; and the Miller libel case, *Report of the Trial of an Action on the Case Brought by Silvanus Miller, Esq.... Against Mordecai M. Noah, Esq. for an Alleged Libel* (New York, 1823). Also worth consulting are *Rankin et al. against Noah* (1824) in John Anthon, *The Law of Nisi Prius* (2nd ed., New York, 1883), 283–5; *Thomas Snowden v. Mordecai M. Noah, John D. Brown and Others* (1825), in Samuel M. Hopkins, *Reports of Cases Argued and Determined in the Court of Chancery of the State of New York* (Albany, 1827); and *Noah and Another vs. Webb and Others* (1833) in Charles Edwards, *Reports of Chancery Cases Decided in the First Circuit of the State of New York* (New York, 1833), I, pp. 604–16.

Secondary Literature

The large secondary literature on Mordecai Noah is actually based on a few careful studies that have been repeatedly rehashed. Robert P. Noah, "Mordecai M. Noah: Interesting Reminiscences of a Famous American Jew," *The Reformer and Jewish Times*, 10 (November 15, 1878), 1, was written by Noah's son, but nevertheless contains errors. Charles P. Daly, *The Settlement of the Jews in North America*, ed., Max J. Kohler (New York, 1893), contains in its second part a long biography of Noah, written on the basis of personal knowledge and contemporary tradition. Simon Wolf's study, "Mordecai Manuel Noah: A Biographical Sketch," written in 1897 and republished in his *Selected Addresses and Papers* (Cincinnati, 1926), contains information not found elsewhere which is a mixture of truth, apologetics and fiction, and must be treated with caution. Max Raisin's Hebrew biography, *Mordecai Manuel Noah: Zionist, Author and Statesman* (Warsaw, 1905); and A. B. Makover, *Mordecai M. Noah: His Life and Work From the Jewish Viewpoint* (New York, 1917) add nothing new to the literature, nor was anything substantially new added by anyone else until Isaac Goldberg's pathbreaking study, *Major Noah* (Philadelphia, 1938). Goldberg uncovered a host of new sources, and in his book he weaves them together into an interesting narrative which, though lamentably weak on post-Ararat developments and New York politics, is still a quantum leap beyond all previous work. Many of Goldberg's deficiencies are easy to excuse when one recalls that he worked without the benefit of Xerox or microfilm. Since Goldberg's day, only Robert Gordis, "Mordecai Manuel Noah: A Century Evaluation," *PAJHS*, 41 (1951), 1–25, has attempted a full-scale interpretation, and he brings to bear very few new sources. Gordis's discussion of Noah's Jewish knowledge, however, is new and important.

A variety of theses and articles, many of them recent, have analyzed particular parts of Mordecai Noah's career—usually without attempting in any way to relate the part studied to his life as a whole. Esther Cember's "Mordecai Manuel Noah: American Diplomat in Barbary 1813–1815: A

Reappraisal" (unpublished M.A. thesis, Columbia University, 1968), shows that Noah's account of his consulship is somewhat self-serving, and that government documents cast the incident in a new light. Gilbert S. Rosenthal's unpublished essay, "Mordecai M. Noah, Diplomat" (copy at AJA), is valuable mainly for the documents it reprints. William Louis Shulman, "The National Advocate, 1812–1829" (unpublished Ed.D. thesis, Yeshiva University, 1968) picks up Noah's career where Cember left off, and demonstrates that New York newspapers must be read by any serious Noah biographer. Unfortunately, he does not deal with Noah's non-journalistic career except in passing, since the *National Advocate* rather than its most important editor is his subject. This lacuna is partially filled by Lee M. Friedman, "Mordecai Manuel Noah as Playwright," *Pilgrims in a New Land* (Philadelphia, 1948), 221–32, which is descriptive rather than analytical, but does contain new information.

No incident in Mordecai Noah's life has been more intensively studied than his Ararat plan. Much of the literature is merely redundant; in the last twenty-five years, however, many new insights into Ararat have been developed. The basic work on the subject remains Lewis F. Allen's "Founding of the City of Ararat on Grand Island by Mordecai M. Noah," *Buffalo Historical Society Publications*, 1 (1879), 305–28; reprinted with new material, 25 (1921), 113–44; also reprinted in *PAJHS*, 8 (1900) 98–118, and in A. B. Makover's *Mordecai M. Noah* (New York, 1917). Allen reprints some of Noah's own writings on Ararat, and bases his conclusions on contemporary reports and his own memory. But he came to Grand Island almost a decade after Ararat, and some of his details do not bear close scrutiny. Lee M. Friedman, "Ararat—A City of Refuge for the Jews," *Jewish Pioneers and Patriots* (Philadelphia, 1942), 107–15, adds nothing original, nor do other popular English-language studies printed before Bernard D. Weinryb's "Noah's Ararat Jewish State in its Historical Setting," *PAJHS*, 43 (1954), 170–91. Weinryb places Ararat in a broader context of Jewish history, examines its significance for the history of Zionism, and brings forward considerable new documentation. In a sense, his is a sequel to Natan M. Gelber's account in *Zur Vorgeschichte des Zionismus* (Vienna, 1927), greatly expanded in a Hebrew article, "Mordecai Manuel Noah: His Dream of a Jewish State in America," *SURA: Israeli-American Annual*, 3 (1957–8), 377–413. Gelber sees Noah as a proto-Zionist, but his account is most valuable for its unique source material on the overall European reaction to the proposed Ararat colony. The subject of Jewish reaction to Ararat is similarly the theme of Hans G. Reissner's "Ganstown—U.S.A.: A German Jewish Dream," *AJA*, 14 (April 1962), 20–31; and is considered at greater length in the same author's *Eduard Gans: Ein Leben im Vormaerz* (Tuebingen, 1965), 83–102. Reissner treats only the reaction in Germany. The account of Ararat in Selig Adler and Thomas E. Connolly, *From Ararat to Suburbia: The History of the Jewish Community of Buffalo* (Philadelphia, 1960), is not based on any new research. For an original interpretation one must turn to S. Joshua Kohn, "Mordecai Manuel Noah's Ararat Project, and the Missionaries," *AJHQ*, 55 (December 1965), 162–98, and "New Light on Mordecai Manuel Noah's Ararat Project," *AJHQ*, 59 (December 1969), 210–14, which both relate Ararat to contemporary missionary endeavors. While several historians find Kohn unconvincing, his work does open up new and profitable avenues for investigation.

To judge from the majority of published studies, Mordecai Noah's life might as well have ended at age forty with the failure of his Ararat project. The literature on his post-Ararat days is sparse and deficient. Two studies detail his connections with the Bank of the United States: Thomas Govan, *Nicholas Biddle: Nationalist and Public Banker 1786–1844* (Chicago, 1959), and more specifically, James L. Crouthamel, "Did the Second Bank of the United States Bribe the Press?" *Journalism Quarterly*, 36 (1959), 35–44. Both of these works are more sympathetic to Noah than the treatment in Leonard I. Gappelberg's broader work, "M. M. Noah and the *Evening Star*: Whig Journalism 1833–1840" (unpublished Ed.D. thesis, Yeshiva University, 1970). Unfortunately, the debate involves semantics almost as much as it does fact and interpretation. Gappelberg's work is somewhat more wide-ranging than its title implies, and it is a valuable study of Noah's *Evening Star* years. But it devotes far too little attention to Whig politics, and it does not take sufficient advantage of the *New York Herald*. I also find it strange that Gappelberg does not deal with the *Book of Jasher* (1840). Happily, Arthur Chiel clears up many of the questions connected with this work in his "The Mysterious Book of Jasher," *Judaism* 26 (Summer 1977), 367–73.

Louis Ruchames attempts an overall interpretation of Mordecai Noah's "Zionism" in his "Mordecai Manuel Noah and Early American Zionism," *AJHQ* 64 (1975), 195–223. Building on the then untranslated work of Raphael Mahler, he finds a continuity between the "Zionism" of Gershom Seixas and the "Zionism" of Noah, and he discusses Noah's "Zionism" more in terms of development than change. Surprisingly, he makes no mention at all of Noah's Temple Speech (1848). He also evinces little interest in the American reaction to Noah's Zionism, although he himself printed some reactions to it in his "The Abolitionists and the Jews: Some Further Thoughts," *Marcus Festschrift*, 505–15.

No study of Mordecai Noah's place in Jewish historical writing has been published. Jacob Kabakoff, however, has published an article on "Noah in Hebrew Literature" (in Hebrew) *Niv* 1:6 (1937), 14–17, which is updated by Libby Kahane, "Mordecai Manuel Noah in Hebrew Periodical Literature and in Israel," *AJHQ*, 67 (1978), 260–263.

To list the complete secondary literature relevant to the study of Mordecai Noah's life would be to list a considerable portion of the historical literature dealing with the period 1785–1851. What follows are only the sources which I found particularly useful.

Frederick Hudson, *Journalism in the United States From 1690 to 1872* (New York, 1873) is an unequaled source for the history of early journalism. Isaac C. Pray, *Memoirs of James Gordon Bennett and His Times* (New York,

1855) has a considerable amount on Noah, but like Hudson and all other writers he ignores Bennett's blatant anti-Jewish prejudice. Among later secondary sources, I found Sidney Kobre, *Development of American Journalism* (Dubuque, 1969), and Robert A. Rutland, *The Newsmongers* (New York, 1973) the best of a rather disappointing lot of broad surveys. Allan Nevins, *A Century of Journalism* (New York, 1922), dealing with the *Evening Post*, and Frank O'Brien, *The Story of the Sun* (New York, 1918), help to put Noah's newspapers into perspective. James L. Crouthamel, "The Newspaper Revolution in New York, 1830–1860," *New York History* 45 (April 1964), 91–114, and Elwyn B. Robinson, "The Dynamics of American Journalism From 1787 to 1865," *Pennsylvania Magazine of History and Biography* 61 (1937), 435–45 are excellent monographic studies.

Walter J. Meserve, *An Emerging Entertainment* (Bloomington, 1977), a history of early American drama, came to hand after my work was substantially completed. It adds nothing to the study of Noah as a playwright. Arthur H. Quinn, *A History of American Drama From the Beginning to the Civil War* (New York, 1923) is a standard one volume work on this period, but it contains none of the sparkling insight found in David Grimsted, *Melodrama Unveiled: American Theater and Culture 1800–1850* (Chicago, 1968).

Jerome Mushkat's *Tammany* (Syracuse, 1971) was my guide through the labyrinth of New York politics. It contains many references to Noah, and is especially strong on his connections with Tammany Hall and Tammany Society. I also made extensive use of Robert Remini, "The Albany Regency," *New York History*, 39 (October 1958), 341–55, and his *Martin Van Buren and the Making of the Democratic Party* (pb. ed. New York, 1970). Alvin Kass, *Politics in New York State 1800–1830* (Syracuse, 1965) clarified New York State's "politics of expedience"; and Michael Wallace, "Changing Concepts of Party in the United States: New York 1815–1828," *Americna Historical Review*, 74 (1968), 453–91, shows the importance of party discipline during this period. Other studies which I found helpful include Jabez Hammond's classic *The History of Political Parties in the State of New York* (Albany, 1842); Dixon R. Fox, *The Decline of Aristocracy in the Politics of New York* (New York, 1919); Gustavus Myers, *The History of Tammany Hall* (New York, 1917); and Leo Hershkowitz, "New York City 1834–1840; A Study in Local Politics" (unpublished Ph.D. thesis, New York University, 1960).

A variety of biographical studies provided valuable background information: Dorothie Bobbè, *De Witt Clinton* (New York, 1933); Denis T. Lynch, *An Epoch and a Man: Martin Van Buren and His Times* (New York, 1929); Holmes Alexander, *The American Talleyrand: The Career and Contemporaries of Martin Van Buren* (New York, 1935); James L. Crouthamel, *James Watson Webb: A Biography* (Middletown, 1969); Oliver Carlson, *The Man Who Made News* (New York, 1942); Merle M. Hoover, *Park Benjamin Poet and Editor* (New York, 1948); Robert W. July, *The Essential New Yorker: Gulian Crommelin Verplanck* (Durham, 1951);

Glyndon G. Van Deusen, *Thurlow Weed: Wizard of the Lobby* (Boston, 1947); *idem, Horace Greeley, Nineteenth Century Crusader* (Philadelphia, 1953); *idem, William Henry Seward* (New York, 1967); Marquis James, *The Life of Andrew Jackson* (New York, 1938); Margaret Coit, *John Calhoun* (New York, 1950) and Robert Seager II, *And Tyler Too* (New York, 1963).

Other helpful studies include: Ray W. Irwin, *The Diplomatic Relations of the United States With the Barbary Powers 1776–1816* (Chapel Hill, 1931); Ronald E. Shaw, *Erie Water West: A History of the Erie Canal 1792–1854* (Lexington, Ky., 1966); and Glover Moore, *The Missouri Controversy 1819–1821* (Lexington, Ky., 1953), all of which include material on Noah; as well as John Webb Pratt, *Religion, Politics and Diversity: The Church State Theme in New York History* (Ithaca, 1967); Ray A. Billington, *The Protestant Crusade 1800–1860* (pb. ed., New York, 1964), and Leo Hershkowitz, "The Land of Promise: Samuel Swartwout and the Land Speculation in Texas 1830–1838," *New York Historical Quarterly*, 48 (1967), 309–15.

The literature on Jacksonian America is too extensive to list. I have been considerably influenced by the writings of Edward Pessen, nicely summarized in his *Jacksonian America* (Homewood, Ill.,1969) with a very extensive bibliography. Marvin Meyers, *The Jacksonian Persuasion* (New York, 1957) has shaped my understanding of Jacksonian ideology, and Glyndon G. Van Deusen, *The Jacksonian Era* (New York, 1959) has proved a ready and reliable reference. For the more important literature which I consulted on the Bank of the United States, nativism, racism, and the "lost ten tribes," see the notes to Chapters V–VII.

The early national period is a dark period in American Jewish history, falling as it does between the colonial period treated in Jacob R. Marcus, *The Colonial American Jew* (3 vols., Detroit, 1970), and the Civil War period discussed in Bertram W. Korn, *American Jewry and the Civil War* (pb. ed., Philadelphia, 1961). While the source materials in the documentary histories listed above are helpful, they have yet to be synthesized. Contemporary non-Jewish newspapers have scarcely been examined at all. Nevertheless, a variety of secondary sources do prove useful. Joseph Rosenbloom's *A Biographical Dictionary of Early American Jews* (University Ky., 1960); Malcolm Stern's *Americans of Jewish Descent* (Cincinnati, 1960); and David de Sola Pool's *Portraits Etched in Stone: Early Jewish Settlers 1682–1831* (New York, 1952) are basic tools. Samuel Rezneck, *Unrecognized Patriots: The Jews in the American Revolution* (Westport, 1975) also covers the early national period. Key monographs are reprinted in volumes two and three of Abraham J. Karp, ed., *The Jewish Experience in America* (New York, 1969); and in Jacob Marcus, ed., *Critical Studies in American Jewish History* (Cincinnati, 1971). Bertram W. Korn's collected studies of this period are found in his *Eventful Years and Experiences: Studies in Nineteenth Century American Jewish History* (Cincinnati, 1958). Other valuable studies are contained in Bertram W. Korn, ed., *A Bicentennial Festschrift for Jacob Rader Marcus* (Waltham, 1976).

Other book-length studies not previously cited that shed light on this period in American Jewish history include: E. Bennet, "An Evaluation of the Life of Isaac Leeser" (unpublished Ph.D. thesis, Yeshiva University, 1959); Moshe Davis, *The Emergence of Conservative Judaism*, (Philadelphia, 1963), which is much broader than its title implies; David and Tamar de Sola Pool, *An Old Faith in the New World* (New York, 1955), which is a history of Shearith Israel; Hyman B. Grinstein, *The Rise of the Jewish Community of New York* (Philadelphia, 1945); *idem*, "The American Synagogue and Laxity of Religious Observance, 1750–1850" (unpublished M.A. thesis, Columbia University, 1936); Louis Harap, *The Image of the Jew in American Literature: From Early Republic to Mass Immigration* (Philadelphia, 1974); Leon Jick, *The Americanization of the Synagogue* (Waltham, 1976); Edgar E. MacDonald, ed., *The Education of the Heart: The Correspondence of Rachel Mordecai Lazarus and Maria Edgeworth* (Chapel Hill, 1977); L. C. Moise, *A Biography of Isaac Harby with an Account of the Reformed Society of Charleston, S. C. 1824–33* (Charleston, 1931); David Philipson, ed., *Letters of Rebecca Gratz* (Philadelphia, 1929); Maxine Seller, "Isaac Leeser: Architect of the American Jewish Community (unpublished Ph.D. thesis, University of Pennsylvania, 1965); and Edwin Wolf II and Maxwell Whiteman, *The History of the Jews of Philadelphia from Colonial Times to the Age of Jackson* (2nd ed., Philadelphia, 1975).

Index